Spanish-Language Television in the United States

"This is an essential book for those interested in understanding the history and resounding success of Spanish-language TV in the U.S."
—*Alejandro Alvarado, Florida International University, USA*

Since its introduction in the early 1960s, Spanish-language television in the United States has grown in step with the Hispanic population. Industry and demographic projections forecast rising influence through the 21st century. This book traces U.S. Spanish-language television's development from the 1960s to 2013, illustrating how business, regulation, politics, demographics and technological change have interwoven during a half century of remarkable change for electronic media.

Spanish-language media play key social, political and economic roles in U.S. society, connecting many Hispanics to their cultures of origin, each other, and broader U.S. society. Yet despite the population's increasing impact on U.S. culture, in elections and through an estimated $1.3 trillion in spending power in 2014, this is the first comprehensive academic source dedicated to the medium and its history. The book combines information drawn from the business press and trade journals with industry reports and academic research to provide a balanced perspective on the origins, maturation and accelerated growth of a significant ethnic-oriented medium.

Kenton T. Wilkinson is Regents Professor and director of the Thomas Jay Harris Institute for Hispanic and International Communication in the College of Media & Communication at Texas Tech University, USA.

Routledge Research in Cultural and Media Studies

Spanish-Language Television in the United States

Fifty Years of Development

Kenton T. Wilkinson

Routledge
Taylor & Francis Group

NEW YORK AND LONDON

First published 2016
by Routledge
711 Third Avenue, New York, NY 10017

and by Routledge
2 Park Square, Milton Park, Abingdon, Oxon OX14 4RN

Routledge is an imprint of the Taylor & Francis Group, an informa business

Library of Congress Cataloging in Publication Data

Wilkinson, Kenton T. (Kenton Todd)
Spanish-language television in the United States : fifty years of development / by Kenton T. Wilkinson.
pages cm. — (Routledge research in cultural and media studies)
Includes bibliographical references and index.
1. Ethnic television broadcasting—United States. 2. Hispanic American television viewers. 3. Television broadcasting—Social aspects—United States 4. Television broadcasting—Political aspects—United States. I. Title.
PN1992.8.H54W55 2015
791.45'62968073—dc23   2015018799

ISBN: 978-1-138-02430-4 (hbk)
ISBN: 978-1-315-77582-1 (ebk)

Typeset in Sabon
by codeMantra

Printed and bound in the United States of America by Publishers Graphics, LLC on sustainably sourced paper.

For Carol, Davis and Shane—my world.

Contents

Acknowledgments

Many individuals and organizations have contributed to this book's completion since I began researching the topic in 1988. The original suggestion that I explore U.S. Spanish-language television came from Alex Saragoza who became my M.A. thesis advisor at the University of California at Berkeley, and has remained a close friend since. The industry's intriguing international dimensions led me to the Ph.D. program in Radio-Television-Film at the University of Texas at Austin where Emile McAnany's mentoring extended beyond media research to parenthood, ethics, professionalism and other important matters. Also influential in my studies and dissertation work at U.T. Austin were John Downing, Douglas Foley, William Glade, Charles Ramirez Berg, Doug Storey, Sharon Strover and Federico Subervi, who has continued to provide valuable guidance.

I had many supportive colleagues at the Tec de Monterrey in Monterrey, Mexico, especially Juan Gómez, Omar Hernández, José Carlos Lozano, Lucrecia Lozano, Francisco Martínez Garza, Ana Cecilia Torres and Jesús Torres. Jorge García Núñez de Cáceres, Gabriela de la Peña and Los Bon Vivants were generous friends and cultural guides for my family and me. Colleagues at other universities who have influenced my development and/ or assisted with this book include: Alan Albarran (especially), Juan Pablo Artero, Cristóbal Benavides, Germán Arango, Ali Kanso, Maria Elena Gutiérrez, Sallie Hughes, Felipe Korzenny, Doran Larson, Edward Lenert, Greg Lowe, Patrick Murphy, Alex Pardo, Francisco Pérez-Latre, Clemencia Rodríguez, Enrique Sánchez Ruiz, John Sinclair, Janette Steemers, Daya Thussu, Raúl Tovares, Juan Uson and Lucila Vargas.

A number of university administrators have provided support for the researching and completion of this book. At the University of Texas at San Antonio (UTSA), Guy Bailey, Alan Craven, Dan Gelo, Steve Levitt and Jeanne Reesman were particularly helpful. Todd Chambers, Jerry Hudson, William Marcy, Juan Muñoz, Mike Parkinson, David Perlmutter, Lawrence Schovanec, Bob Smith, Rob Stewart and Jon Whitmore have been supportive at Texas Tech University (TTU). Several faculty development grants from UTSA and a Texas Tech Research Enrichment Fund grant in 2009 facilitated data gathering for this book. The Thomas Jay Harris Regents Professorship in Hispanic and International Communication that I've held since 2006 helped advance this project in many ways. Thanks to many colleagues and students in the College of Media & Communication and across campus at TTU whose contributions make it a fine place to work. Sadly, we lost one of our dear colleagues, Robert Wernsman, in March 2015. I am grateful to Robert and his wife, Dr. Marijane Wernsman, for the editing assistance they provided this project.

The staff at multiple libraries and archives helped me locate materials that support this book. The Law Library at Stanford University generously supplied copies of several cases referenced in Chapter 4. The Nettie Lee Benson Latin American Collection at U.T. Austin provided ample material regarding international Spanish-language media. Staff in the Hispanic Reading Room at the Library of Congress, the National Archives in Suitland and College Park, Maryland, and the Trinity University and UTSA libraries helped me locate materials. The Interlibrary Loan office at TTU's University Library was particularly supportive as I filled gaps in the latter stages of this project; special thanks to Minerva Alaniz for her research assistance. Many research assistants helped collect the source material for this book over a 20-year period—my sincere thanks to them all. Among the most recent at TTU are Adeniyi Bello, Kris Boyle, Daniela Contreras, Nancy García, Dustin Hahn, Prisca Ngondo, Mehrnaz Rahimi, Nathian Rodríguez and Ikram Toumi. Clara McKenney's assistance with the appendices is greatly appreciated.

Over the years many journalists and Spanish-language television professionals have given generously of their time and expertise to inform this book and its author. Especially helpful have been Sheila Aguirre, Andrew Paxman (now an academic researcher) and Mary Sutter. At Routledge, some very patient and professional folks managed this book's publication. Many thanks to Linda Bathgate, Nancy Chen, Gandhimathi Ganesan (of codeMantra), Kathleen Laurentiev, and Felisa Salvago-Keyes for their assistance and support.

Thanks to my grandparents for stressing the value of education, and my parents David T. Wilkinson and Sharon E. Harper for modeling academic excellence for my sister Wendy and me. Finally, and most importantly, unwavering love and support from my wife Carol and sons Davis and Shane kept me motivated to complete this project long after I might have otherwise abandoned it. That's no small contribution.

Introduction

In July 2013, a news report circulated that undoubtedly stunned some Americans: the Spanish-language television network Univision achieved the highest rating in prime time for adults 18 to 49 years old among *all* U.S. networks. Any doubters who wrote the milestone off as a fluke were silenced a year later when Univision repeated its feat (De la Fuente, 2013; Fitzgerald, 2014). Sure, Hispanics[1] are a fast-growing population, and July sweeps are less competitive than other periods during the year, but the achievement was remarkable nonetheless. How was it possible? This book provides a multifaceted answer by examining the steady growth of Spanish-language television in the United States from its origins in the 1960s as a small group of far-flung stations using a broadcasting technology that mainstream stations rejected, Ultra High Frequency (UHF), to becoming a multiplatform industry encompassing networks valued in the tens of billions of dollars by the 2010s.

The book takes an integrated approach, revealing the interplay among central influences on and by the industry including business, legal/regulatory, technological, demographic, and political forces during four periods of growth. In order to faithfully represent the industry's increasing relevance and clout, key episodes are contextualized amid broader conditions in U.S. media and society. Examples include political advocacy by Hispanic organizations, the globalization aims of media corporations, and the consequential shift from analog to digital media in the 1980s, 1990s, and 2000s, respectively. This book reveals the processes by which Spanish-language television gravitated from an isolated ethnic enclave towards the U.S. broadcasting norm. It also shows how the Spanish-language sector fostered industry-wide innovation in some unexpected ways.

The half-century covered by this book witnessed remarkable change on several related fronts. Spanish-language television weaned itself from the Mexican capital and expertise it depended on (although not the programming); the industry has grown to dozens of networks reaching audiences through a variety of digital platforms and, increasingly, bilingually or in English. The 1960 census counted 3.5 million Hispanics constituting less than 4% of the U.S. population; by 2010 the number had soared to 50.5 million people, accounting for 16.7% of the populace. Hispanic consumers' buying power increased from an estimated $15 billion in 1960 to

$1.3 trillion in 2014 (see Appendix B). Whereas advertisers were skeptical of audience sizes in the early decades, by the 2000s the Hispanic sector's magnitude and profitability had motivated many entities to enter the market. The same goes for investment in the industry itself as well-heeled corporations and investment groups controled the major networks. Although scattered publications have told pieces of this compelling story, this book is the first industry-focused monograph to comprehensively report and assess major developments over a 50-year period.

As an inherently social phenomenon, media communication should be understood in the context of the people and institutions who create, disseminate and engage messages. To this end the book examines key developments surrounding the production, distribution and consumption of Spanish-language television content, endeavoring to do so within the broader political, economic and/or social trends that influence, and are influenced by, the dynamic Hispanic sector. A central goal is to join together in one volume new information and existing knowledge that has been available from disparate sources, but not always easy to locate, even in the Digital Age.

In broad, historical terms this book follows the contours of emphasis on ethnic-oriented and international communication inquiry from the 1960s through 2013, a period of accelerated change in media industries. A number of major themes from the period are covered, including socioeconomic equity issues, the connections between commerce and culture, the impacts of demographic change and technological development, media globalization and neoliberal economic reforms. A key influence linking these themes is the close relationship between the U.S. Spanish-language television industry and Latin American counterparts, especially in Mexico.[2] The reader will see an evolution from Mexican direct investment and entrepreneurial acumen to an increasingly complex two-way influence developing from the 1980s on, as Spanish-language media grows in step with the U.S. Hispanic population.

The U.S. Spanish-language sector's ability to attract advertising revenues from major corporations makes it a rare case among ethnic media worldwide according to Riggins (1992), who could have added substantial direct investment through ownership by non-Hispanic companies as another unique characteristic. This book follows operations like program distribution systems, advertising sales networks and specialized ratings services, which supported business development and helped expand the industry as the population grew. These operations, among others, allowed what began in the 1960s as small-scale enterprises largely indistinguishable from other ethnic media in the U.S.—except in audience size—to become the most dynamic sector within the world's wealthiest national media market during an economic downturn beginning in 2007.

It is also important to briefly identify what this book does not emphasize. The principal focus here is on the larger U.S. Spanish-language television broadcasters: Univision, Telemundo, Galavisión and Azteca América. Pay television channels, satellite services and independent stations are discussed but not emphasized. Nor does the book cover stations located in Mexico whose signals reach U.S. cities such as San Diego, El Paso, or McAllen/ Harlingen/Brownsville. This book does not offer sustained examination of Spanish-language television's effects on viewers/society or program content issues, although they are important topics that demand greater attention.

Some academic readers may find this book insufficiently critical; criticism is included, but is not the central aim as I endeavor to pull together and cogently engage the history of an increasingly visible and influential industry. Topics and incidents that reflect unfavorably on the industry's image are presented and considered,[3] but their in-depth explication is not a goal. Rather, my intent has been to produce an informative history of U.S. Spanish-language television that is valuable to industry professionals and the general public as well as academic researchers. In this regard, the prospect of "serving too many masters" has lurked throughout the researching and writing of this book, and I understand the consequent limitations.

Central Themes

This book aims to place the dynamic growth of a specific media industry within the broader social, political and economic environments that have shaped it and which, in turn, it has affected. To this end, the multidirectional influences among business, regulatory, technological, political and cultural forces on a specific ethnic-oriented communications medium are examined over a period of accelerated change for electronic media. The following brief sections introduce central themes that interweave throughout the book.

Language

The use of Spanish served as a defining characteristic for Hispanic identity and the principal parameter for distinguishing Hispanic-oriented media during most of the 20th century. Although industry observers occasionally noted some audience members' preference for English and the potential of bilingual media (López, Enos, Nichols, LaRosa, Mellema, & McGrew, 1973; Jarboe, 1980), sustained efforts to reach Hispanics through these idioms did not develop until the 1990s. Increased space for programming opened by the so-called "multichannel universe," and a growing emphasis on the youth market around the turn of the century were largely responsible for the change. As a result, the term "Spanish-language media" has lost precision in the 21st century, leading to a shift in both industry and academic circles toward using "Hispanic-oriented" or "Latino/a-oriented."[4]

The major demographic factor fueling the growth of Spanish-language media has been immigration, of course. Yet the 2010 U.S. census found that U.S. domestic births had surpassed immigration as the leading contributor to

Hispanic population growth, signaling that greater percentages of Hispanics would be educated and socialized in English, thereby increasing demand for English and bilingual media content. At least two caveats apply, however. Traditionally, U.S. Hispanics have been language loyal, an important reason why Spanish-language media and popular culture thrived as other non-English languages declined following immigration waves, as discussed in Chapter 1 (Cafferty, 2000). There's also been an interesting movement toward retro-acculturation among some U.S. Hispanics who are making active efforts to improve their Spanish, or perhaps learn it for the first time (Hinojosa, 2013). Certainly media play an important role in such language retention and acquisition efforts.

A final point related to language concerns the relationship between the Spanish-language television industry's structural conditions and the forms of Spanish spoken in the programs. In a study assessing the central role of Mexico's Televisa network in the flow of programming from the U.S. to Latin America, and from Mexico to the U.S., Antola and Rogers (1984) maintain that the Mexican version of broadcast Spanish came to predominate in the region, largely through ample dubbing and widely watched newscasts. Because of its central position in international Spanish-language television and its constant influence over the U.S. sector since the 1960s, Televisa is discussed throughout this book. There can be little question that Mexican-accented Spanish predominates on U.S. television—even a Televisa competitor in the U.S., Telemundo, coached on-screen talent to use it (Ahrens, 2004).[5]

Demographics

Each of the U.S. censuses from 1960 through 2010 is discussed for its quantifying the Hispanic population's growth as well as influencing investment in the Hispanic market. The various census findings should be approached with caution, however, due to consistent undercounting, shifting racial/ethnic categorization schemes, and varying data collection methods—such as in-person interviews versus self-reports via mail (Rodríguez, 2000; Cohn, 2010). As Siegel and Passel (1979) put it, "a central problem is the inability of the census data to present a clear, unambiguous and objective definition of exactly who is a member of the Hispanic population" (p. 2). When the Census Bureau releases follow-up corrections to major reports, they are typically disseminated and cited less broadly than the original. An example is the 1970 census, which overcounted people in the Central and South American category by around 1,000,000, requiring a substantial adjustment (Hutchison, 1984). The uncritical acceptance of population figures is clearly problematic, and the reader is reminded that population figures are cited here as guideposts, not definitive data. Appendix A offers an overview of census findings and demographic milestones achieved over the period covered.

Of course demographics includes more than population figures, and there is a strong contemporary trend toward associating demographic information with media preferences, spending habits, lifestyle and other data to predict consumption behavior and streamline marketing, often called "big data." Early stages of those developments are discussed in the book's final section. I should point out, however, that even the first comprehensive study of Spanish-language television in the U.S. addressed demographic issues such as social class, country identification (U.S. or Mexico), and language preference (López et al., 1973).

Technology

Since the industry's inception, most analyses of U.S. Spanish-language television have emphasized market growth, ownership and control, or programming. Surprisingly little attention has focused on how the two major networks, Telemundo and Univision, have managed technological change even though the sector matured during a period of profound transformation for television technology in distribution, direct-to-home broadcasting, convergence with other media, and industry adaptation to interactive digital technologies. This book takes an initial step toward addressing the void by situating key technological changes within the broader milieu of market growth, management strategies and regulatory environment. The period covered saw a shift in technology management from a few entrepreneurs' adroit exploitation of an underutilized resource and maverick stands against inequitable, inefficient federal regulation, to frenetic efforts by media conglomerate leadership to manage change in a volatile, fast-moving digital environment.

Technology has been a central issue from the industry's inception as the first full-time Spanish-language stations initiated a trend of broadcasting on the UHF television band which, because it had fallen from favor among English-language broadcasters, provided significantly lower cost per potential viewer compared to VHF. The next major technological advance involved program distribution by satellite. In 1976, Spanish International Network became the first U.S. network to regularly distribute its programming via satellite, extending its reach beyond major cities to smaller population centers via low-power and repeater technologies. Cable television grew the audience further still, due in part to its improved picture quality compared to over-the-air television, especially on UHF channels. Television's conversion to digital technology beginning in the late 1980s greatly affected television production, distribution and reception, as did the Internet's encompassing characteristics of a mass medium beginning in the mid-1990s. By that time, Spanish-language television had become big business and deep-pocketed corporations and investors controlled the major networks. Technology became a central strategic resource in efforts to build profitable synergies across multiple media platforms and/or brands among a corporation's holdings.

Management

The effective implementation of technology is a time-intensive, consequential concern for media management (Napoli, 2011). Spanish-language television management has followed a similar historical trajectory as other industry elements, evolving from a small group of entrepreneurs and investors scrambling to establish relationships between viewers and advertisers, to large diversified companies or divisions of such—at least so far as the large network players are concerned.[6] Cottle (2000, p. 17) identifies a dynamic that this book illustrates over the course of U.S. Spanish-language television's development: "Changing media structures and processes ... shape the production contexts and frame the operations, budgets and strategic goals of media institutions, and those are condensed within senior decision making and must be professionally (pragmatically) negotiated by media professionals and producers in their daily practices." Thus we see how management responded to shifting conditions at a given time, and subsequent impacts on the industry's overall development.

The strategic management of media firms is a useful optic because it focuses on external as well as internal factors to assess why some media companies outperform their competitors (Mierzjewska & Hollifield, 2006). Picard (2004) pinpoints two particularly influential external factors. First, market complexity refers to degrees of difficulty organizations face when pursuing their objectives. We shall see that the two principal U.S. Spanish-language television companies faced increasing market complexity from the 1980s on, especially as digitization accelerated. Second, market turbulence results from instability or unclear direction in a market, and hampers managerial efforts to reduce uncertainty (Picard, 2004; Sylvie, Wicks, Hollifield, Lacy, & Sohn, 2008). Turbulence characterized Spanish-language television during most of the 1980s as two legal processes challenged Spanish International Network (now Univision), and Telemundo's arrival introduced lasting competition in the industry. Instability also prevailed during the first half of the 1990s as financial uncertainty rocked both major networks, and also accompanied the spread of interactive and on-demand technologies the following decade. History indicates that we may expect market turbulence and complexity to return to Spanish-language television, in ebbs and flows, into the foreseeable future.

Advocacy

Another theme woven through the book is efforts by advocacy organizations to influence U.S. Spanish-language television's development. From the first chapter on we will see that influence from Mexico has motivated U.S. Hispanics to seek greater control and representation in the industry. Other concerns have included non-Hispanic ownership, the threat of "Cubanization" as Univision relocated its headquarters from California to Miami in 1991, and monopoly influence as the largest group of Spanish-language radio stations, HBC, merged with Univision in 2003. As I have argued elsewhere, the alliances behind advocacy efforts shift according to the issue and whose interests are potentially impacted by an industry development (Wilkinson, 2002).

We will encounter three general categories of Hispanic advocacy organizations: groups that are devoted exclusively to media advocacy concerns (e.g. National Hispanic Media Coalition); broad ethnic advocacy organizations that include media as one of multiple advocacy areas (e.g. League of United Latin American Citizens); and organizations whose principal work is in other areas, but which join petitions or coalitions when significant issues or causes arise (e.g., Mexican American Legal Defense and Education Fund). Industry players have also joined advocacy efforts that favor their competitive interests, such as Telemundo joining petitions to deny license renewals for Univision stations, or Univision opposing ownership changes at Telemundo. Cause-specific groups have supported petitions aligning with their objectives, such as Media Access Project joining the fight to block the Univision and -HBC merger. The principal focus here is on the Hispanic advocacy organizations and their efforts to shape the contours and conditions of the industry.

Business Press and Trade Journal Sources

Staying current with media industry developments presents a challenge for academics and others who lack insider access to such information. Articles, profiles and special reports published in the business press and industry trade journals (BPTJs) offer up-to-date information about industry developments— they are employed extensively as part of this book's effort to construct a comprehensive history of Spanish-language television in the United States. "Business press" refers to general or business news media that report on people, conditions, or developments in a media industry. These may include the business sections of national newspapers, select regional newspapers,[7] news periodicals, and specialized magazines such as *Hispanic Business*. "Trade journal" refers to a publication targeting professionals in a specific industry; *Advertising Age*, *Broadcasting & Cable*, and *Variety* are examples. BPTJs frequently rely on business news services, such as *Business Wire* or *PR Newswire*, for some of their content (Wilkinson & Merle, 2013).

Although clearly published for different audiences and purposes than academic research, BPTJs can support well-informed studies of media industries, especially in the fast-paced atmosphere of 21st century digital media. Reports that are carefully researched and written by well-connected, reputable journalists or organizations provide content that is otherwise available only from the sources themselves.[8] The Internet has facilitated the distribution of industry information, making reports from research organizations such as Arbitron, Nielsen and Pew readily available, sometimes for a fee. The volume of BPTJ reports on a particular topic can signal its perceived importance, provide wider exposure to the news-reading public and underscore ties to major developments of the day. Examples drawn from the chapters to follow include the sale of the Spanish International companies, Telemundo's emergence during the Decade of the Hispanic, Univision's expansion during the 1990s, the Latin Boom in popular culture, and a surge of new TV networks targeting bilingual and English-dominant Hispanics. Such episodes of concentrated press attention also raise questions: how do they influence investment patterns in the industry, how do they impact public perceptions of the networks and their audiences, and how do the viewers perceive them?

The use of BPTJs in academic research should not imply that their value or veracity is uniform. Some trade publications, like those mentioned above, have covered U.S. Spanish language media and marketing for decades, usually with industry-knowledgeable "beat" reporters. Other publications have followed the headlines, increasing their coverage at milestone moments such as ratings or collective purchasing power achievements, network ownership changes, or demographic milestones such as decennial census reports or Hispanics surpassing African Americans as the nation's largest minority group. The journalists submitting such one-off stories are less likely to be familiar with the population and/or industry, and more prone to influence by industry players' public relations offices than their more experienced counterparts. Furthermore, some trade journals strive harder to maintain a measure of independence from the industries they cover than do others. The point to stress is that BPTJs should not be regarded in monolithic terms (Wilkinson & Merle, 2013).

As is true with *any* type of data employed in research, using these business-oriented information sources is not without pitfalls. Deadlines impose time constraints that may yield stories that are not thoroughly investigated or thoughtfully articulated. The necessity to keep open future conduits of information may restrain journalists from being critical; Hollifield (1997) notes that trade press journalists are sometimes reluctant to report on the broader social implications of media industry actions, being careful not to bite the hand that feeds them. Thus, threats to journalistic credibility may transform into threats to research validity if BPTJ reports are not judiciously evaluated before being incorporated into academic research.[9]

I should stress that notwithstanding these problems, a blanket rejection of BPTJs would do more harm than good; thoughtful use of the BPTJs—and checking them against other knowledgeable sources, such as industry representatives, regulators and media advocates—is good practice. Researchers should also keep in mind that adjustments and corrections will be made by future scholars building on the foundations we lay—in producing this book I have corrected some erroneous information, and I expect to be challenged and corrected by my contemporaries and future generations of researchers on this topic. This is an important element of the knowledge-building process.

Organization

This book is organized in four parts clustered around industry developments during specific decades. The first part begins with a historical overview of four Spanish-language media and a discussion of Hispanic popular culture prior to television's emergence. The two chapters that follow focus on the 1960s and 70s, covering the origins of full-time Spanish-language television stations and the expansion of Spanish International Network through its executives' astute use of technology, challenges to U.S. broadcast policy and promotion of the Spanish-language market to advertisers. Chapters Two and Three provide close analyses of the Los Angeles and New York markets in their early stages of development.

Part Two examines the 1980s, a seminal decade for an industry transitioning from an ethnic enclave to an emergent competitor for English-language networks. Two legal processes that wrested control of the Spanish International stations from their Mexican founders caused an important shake-up in the industry. The arrival of national-level competition in the form of Telemundo Network attracted increased attention and investment to the industry at a time when the Hispanic population, and especially its growing economic clout and political potential, were gaining notoriety.

Part Three covers the increasing expansion of and competition between the two principal networks, Univision and Telemundo, during the 1990s. Connections with international markets are traced and evaluated during a time of accelerated regionalization and globalization of Spanish-language media, including television production in the United States, principally in Miami, which emerged as a hemispheric as well as national hub. The number of Hispanic-oriented networks available on pay television increased, some of them catering to particular genres such as news, sports or movies or specific audience niches like women, youth or English speakers. Most of the networks sought to reach audiences in multiple Spanish-speaking markets, not just the United States.

Finally, Part Four explores Spanish-language television in the context of rapid growth, technological change and increasing audience and outlet fragmentation from 2000 to 2013. The major networks became worth billions of dollars as they diversified their holdings and Hispanic purchasing power accelerated. The political, economic and especially cultural influence of Hispanics was emphasized in mainstream media during the so-called Latin Boom. Three appendices illustrate the growth of the Hispanic population and its economic power, and present a timeline for key milestones in the industry's development.

This book endeavors to achieve what two pioneers in the field, Félix Gutiérrez and Jorge Schement (1983), called for: integrating the history of U.S. Spanish-language television into "a whole fabric of knowledge, not ... a fragmented part" (p. 260). By placing the industry's development within the context of broader changes in political, economic, technological and socio-cultural life in the United States, the book contributes one section to the rich mosaic that recounts the history of Hispanics' ascendancy in U.S. society during the 20th and 21st centuries—including how a Spanish-language television network could win national ratings sweeps in 2013 and 2014.

Notes

1. This book employs the term Hispanic rather than Latino/a for largely practical purposes. When the book went to press, the author directed the Thomas Jay Harris Institute for Hispanic and International Communication at Texas Tech University and was editor of the *International Journal of Hispanic Media*. He is aware of ongoing debates over usage and the potential sensitivity of ethnic labels, particularly when used by members of social outgroups.
2. It may interest the reader to know that this intriguing relationship was what drew the author to international communication, and the doctoral program in Radio-Television-Film at the University of Texas at Austin, after discovering Mexico's many connections with U.S. Spanish-language television through researching his M.A. thesis at the University of California at Berkeley (Wilkinson, 1991, 1995).
3. Examples include, but are not limited to, the sale of Spanish International Communications Corp. in 1986 (Chapter 4); the Jacobo Zabludovsky issue (1986, Chapter 5); Telemundo's original non-Hispanic leadership (1980s, Chapter 5); the Carlos Montaner incident (1990, Chapter 6); labor protests at Univision stations (1990s, 2000s, Chapters 6, 8) ownership changes at Telemundo (Chapters 6, 8), and charges of monopoly control in the Univision-HBC merger (2003, Chapter 8).
4. Again, the author's own experience provides an example. In 2013 he assumed editorship of the *Journal of Spanish Language Media*, which had been launched by Dr. Alan Albarran of the University of North Texas five years earlier. In order to be more inclusive of bilingual and English language media directed toward Hispanics, the name was changed to the *International Journal of Hispanic Media* in 2014 (http://www.internationalhispanicmedia.org).
5. In an interesting development that may be related, Telemundo claimed in 2014 that it had become the second largest international distributor of Spanish-language television programs behind Televisa (Mendoza, 2014).
6. Univision acquired Hispanic Broadcasting Corp. (HBC), the largest Spanish-language radio group in 2003, Telemundo joined the NBC Universal group in 2001, and Azteca América is the U.S. extension of Televisión Azteca, the second largest television enterprise in Mexico.
7. National newspapers like the *New York Times*, *Wall Street Journal* and *Washington Post* have tended to provide reliable reporting. More regionally focused papers like the *Chicago Tribune* and *Miami Herald* offer occasional reports on audiences and industry developments; the *Los Angeles Times* has been particularly valuable for its long-term commitment to reporting on Spanish-language media and its proximity to a key production hub. Other regional and local newspapers offer useful reporting on populations and industry players within their coverage areas, although less regularly than the aforementioned papers.
8. *Variety's* annual Latin America/U.S. Hispanic market themed issues are an example—articles by reporters who stay current with industry developments allow readers to follow annual progress through a collection of relevant articles rather than scattered across individual issues. A former *Variety* reporter, Andrew Paxman (2004), discusses the usual lack of indexing as a challenge to media historians using trade journals as sources. Those that are indexed and/or readily available through full-text databases tend to get cited most frequently.
9. The following are select examples of specific errors or omissions noted by the author while developing this research:

- Jayson Blair wrote some articles regarding Spanish-language television for the *New York Times* in 2000. Although there's no evidence that he invented information appearing in the articles, the fact that he did for others—causing strong shocks to the journalism industry and one of its cornerstone companies—underscores the threat (Bailey, 2013).
- Reporting on the 1992 ownership change at Univision identified the government's foreign ownership cap at 5%, not 20%. Several reports also stated that Azcárraga Milmo started SIN network in early 1960s—that was his father Emilio Azcárraga Vidaurreta, Milmo did not take over until 1973.
- In a profile of the Mexican journalist Jacobo Zabludovsky, Holston (1983) does not mention the political controversy surrounding his position as anchorman for the dominant *24 Horas* newscast—a major omission given the anxious political climate in Mexico and Televisa's close ties with the ruling PRI party.
- Besas (1984) wrote in *Variety*, "… various efforts to get the FCC to investigate and indict SIN as an allegedly illegal foreign operation, controlled by Mexico's Televisa, all came to naught." In fact, an administrative law judge was conducting an inquiry at the time, and Mexican interests would soon be forced to divest of their interests in a hard-fought legal battle.

References

Ahrens, Frank. (2004, August 2). Accent on higher TV ratings: Spanish-language network Telemundo coaches actors to use Mexican dialect. *Washington Post*, A1.

Antola, Livia, & Rogers, Everett M. (1984). Television flows in Latin America. *Communication Research, 11*(2), 183–202.

Bailey, Jonathan. (2013, January 9). Comparing the Jonah Lehrer and Jayson Blair plagiarism scandals. *Plagiarism Today*. Retrieved from https://www.plagiarismtoday.com/2013/01/09/comparing-the-jonah-lehrer-and-jayson-blair-plagiarism-scandals/.

Besas, Peter. (1984, September 19). SIN gets respect & clout in booming Hispanic mkt. *Variety*, 50.

Cafferty, Pastora San Juan. (2000). The language question. In P. S. J. Cafferty & D. W. Engstrom (Eds), *Hispanics in the United States: An agenda for the twenty-first century* (pp. 69–95). New Brunswick, NJ: Transaction.

Cohn, D'Vera. (2010, March 3). Census history: Counting Hispanics. *Pew Research: Social & Demographic Trends*. Retrieved from http://www.pewsocialtrends.org/2010/03/03/census-history-counting-hispanics-2/.

Cottle, Simon. (2000). Introduction: Media research and ethnic minorities: Mapping the field. In S. Cottle (Ed.), *Ethnic minorities and the media: Changing cultural boundaries* (pp. 1–30). Philadelphia: Open University Press.

De la Fuente, Anna Marie. (2013, July 30). Univision to Big Four: We're no.1 and rising. *Variety*. Retrieved from http://variety.com/2013/tv/news/univision-to-big-four-were-no-1-and-rising-1200569566/.

Fitzgerald, Toni. (2014, August 6). Once again, Univision wins sweeps: Spanish-language network takes July for second straight year. *Media Life Magazine*. Retrieved from http://www.medialifemagazine.com/once-again-univision-wins-sweeps/.

Gutiérrez, Félix, & Schement, Jorge. (1983). A retrospective analysis of Project Casa. In B. S. Greenberg, M. Burgoon, J. K. Burgoon, & F. Korzenny, *Mexican Americans and the mass media* (pp. 250–260). Norwood, NJ: Ablex.

Hinojosa, Maria. (2013, April 28). For some young Latinos: Donkey jaws and Latino roots [Code switch: Frontiers of race, culture and ethnicity]. *National Public Radio*. Retrieved from http://www.npr.org/blogs/codeswitch/2013/04/28/179277601/for-some-young-latinos-donkey-jaws-and-latino-roots.

Hollifield, C. Ann. (1997). The specialized business press and industry-related political communication: A comparative study. *Journalism and Mass Communication Quarterly, 74*(4), 757–772.

Holston, Mark. (1983, June/July). The Walter Cronkite of Mexico. *Nuestro, 7*(5), 58–59.

Hutchison, Ray. (1984). Miscounting the Spanish origin population in the United States: Corrections to the 1970 census and their implications. *Migration Review, 22*(2), 73–89.

Jarboe, Jan. (1980, November). The special case of Spanish-language television. *Washington Journalism Review*, 21–25.

López, Ronald W., Enos, Darryl D., Nichols, Lee, LaRosa, Frank, Mellema, Joel, & McGrew, Don. (1973). *The role and functions of Spanish-language-only television in Los Angeles*. Claremont, CA: Center for Urban and Regional Studies, Claremont Graduate School.

Mendoza, Jorge. (2014, August 31). Telemundo attracts a growing number of Mexican actors. *El Universal in English*. Retrieved from: http://www.eluniversal.com.mx/in-english/2014/telemundo-mexican-actors-93723.html.

Mierzjewska, Bozena I., & Hollifield, C. Ann. (2006). Theoretical approaches in media management research. In A. B. Albarran, S. M. Chan-Olmstead, and M. O. Wirth (Eds.), *Handbook of media management and economics* (pp. 37–66). New York: Routledge.

Napoli, Philip M. (2011). *Audience evolution: New technologies and the transformation of media audiences*. New York, NY: Columbia University Press.

Paxman, Andrew. (2004, December). *An ethnic media success story: The early years of Spanish-language radio, 1924–1970*. Unpublished manuscript, Department of History, University of Texas at Austin, Austin, Texas.

Picard, Robert G. (2004). Environmental and market changes driving strategic planning in media firms. In R. G. Picard (Ed.), *Strategic responses to media market changes* (pp. 1–17). (JIBS Research Reports, No. 2004–2) Jonkoping International Business School, Sweden.

Riggins, Stephen H. (Ed.). (1992). *Ethnic minority media: An international perspective*. Newbury Park, CA: Sage.

Rodríguez, Clara. E. (2000). *Changing race: Latinos, the census, and the history of ethnicity in the United States*. New York: NYU Press.

Siegel, Jacob S., & Passel, Jeffrey S. (1979). *Coverage of the Hispanic population of the United States in the 1970 census: A methodological analysis* (No. 82). U.S. Department of Commerce, Bureau of the Census.

Sylvie, George, Wicks, Jan LeBlanc, Hollifield, C. Ann., Lacy, Stephen, & Sohn, Ardyth Broadrick. (2008). *Media management: A casebook approach*. (4th ed.). New York: Routledge.

Wilkinson, Kenton T. (2002). Collective situational ethnicity and Latino subgroups' struggle for influence in US Spanish-language television. *Communication Quarterly, 50*(3–4), 422–443.

Wilkinson, Kenton T., & Merle, Patrick F. (2013). The merits and challenges of using business press and trade journal reports in academic research on media industries. *Communication, Culture & Critique, 6*, 415–431.

Part I

Origins and Consolidation in the 1950s–1970s

1 U.S. Spanish-Language Media and Audiences as Television Emerged

This chapter offers an overview of Hispanic media and audiences in the United States prior to the advent of Spanish-language television broadcasting in 1955. More detailed accounts of the rich media histories discussed are available elsewhere—the intent here is to provide a synopsis of Hispanic popular culture expressed through theater, cinema, music and radio prior to the advent of television. Because new media draw from and contribute to established means of communication, it is important to acknowledge and understand the existence of cultural practices and media business traditions prior to the emergence of a particular medium (Jenkins, 2006).

For a number of practical and conceptual reasons, the trade press, the media industries themselves and academic research tend to segment popular culture, its production as well as audiences, by language and ethnic origin. Such segmenting, however, tends to draw our attention away from the influences across categorical boundaries when we consider the history of U.S. popular culture and media (Guins & Zaragoza Cruz, 2005). This is an important point to bear in mind as we examine the popular culture and media precursors to Spanish-language television. Spanish and Mexican theater traditions influenced the early Hispanic playwrights, directors and producers in the U.S.; there have been Latin American influences on Hollywood—and vice versa—throughout film's history; Mexican and Caribbean music influenced the development of blues, jazz and other popular music genres; and recorded music and radio have introduced remote music genres that might not otherwise be heard by audiences. Paxman (2004) emphasizes the importance of geography to the development and sustainability of Spanish-language media and Hispanic popular culture in the U.S., where proximity to the northern reaches of Latin America, including the Caribbean, have facilitated a regular two-way flow of audiences as well as media talent, creative styles and ideas.

I should stress that cross-ethnic influences and collaboration also tend to escape the typical categorization schemes employed by the press, media industries and academe. There was probably more creative awareness and inspiration across regional groupings of Hispanics than is typically recognized. A few related caveats are in order. The preponderance of research regarding the four media discussed below focuses on Mexican Americans, not other national-origin groups. Given the origins of U.S. Spanish-language television, this chapter emphasizes populations and influences from Mexico—no effort is made to achieve representational balance. Finally, the principal attention here is on industry developments, not content, artists, or genres.

Theater

Kanellos (1982) states that the first European-style dramatic performance north of the Rio Grande was staged in the environs of modern-day El Paso, Texas, in 1598 when some of the conquistador Juan de Oñate's men improvised a play based on their adventures in New Mexico. From that time forward, a variety of folk dramas such as *pastorelas*,[1] heroic dramas and farmworker skits have been performed in the Southwest. Theater has been essential to Hispanic culture, Kanellos asserts, as a form of expression, cultural preservation and entertainment. Prior to the Mexican-American War (1846–1848) theaters were established in the California ports of San Diego, Los Angeles and San Francisco, where itinerant Spanish and Mexican acting troupes performed (Kanellos, 1984). The number of theaters grew following the war, and theater companies began residing in particular cities, such as López del Castillo's company in San Francisco in the 1860s. A central function of the company was to reinforce Hispanic language and culture at a time of flux as increasing numbers of Whites settled in the area (Kanellos, 1984).

Landlocked areas developed regular theater venues later than the port cities. For example, Tucson, a stop on the stagecoach circuit that served northern Mexican cities in the mid-19th century, acquired its own company in 1878. However, the city's Hispanic theater declined within ten years as the railway brought English-language companies from the East (Kanellos, 1982). In Texas, theaters in Laredo, San Antonio and El Paso became the key destinations for Mexican troupes performing along the border during the 1890s. Around the same time an eastern circuit developed that stretched from Key West and Tampa, Florida, to New York which, Kanellos (1984) explains, did not develop a Spanish-language stage tradition until the 1920s notwithstanding its importance as a literary center. The Mexican Revolution (1910–1920) drove increased numbers of potential audience members and theater professionals to the southwestern United States, as well as Chicago and other midwestern cities. Some professionals elected to remain in the U.S. after the revolution, a number of them migrating to radio, and eventually television, broadcasting. By the 1920s rail and road transportation greatly facilitated troupes' mobility, and theaters appeared in smaller cities of the Southwest (Kanellos, 1984).

The 1920s became the heyday of Spanish-language theater, with Los Angeles (~22 theaters) and San Antonio (~12 theaters) emerging as two centers in the West. Given this background, it comes as little surprise that these two cities also hosted the first full-time Spanish-language television stations established in the early 1960s. Kanellos (1984) stresses the increasing importance of Hollywood as a magnet for acting, writing and production talent that helped the theater flourish, especially between 1910 and 1940, the peak years for Spanish-language theater in Los Angeles (Koegel, 1999). A shift in content occurred whereby the *revista* (musical review) and vaudeville gained popularity as demand for classical and traditional contemporary plays from Spain and Mexico City diminished (Gunckel, 2008). In the East, Tampa and New York ascended, staging mostly Spanish material before gravitating toward Cuban *teatro bufo*, which featured Afro-Cuban music that was gaining popularity (Kanellos, 1984). Some New York–based troupes worked their way west passing through Philadelphia, Cleveland and Chicago, eventually reaching Los Angeles, where a growing number of Spanish-language playwrights were settling to produce increasingly popular (and lucrative) plays (Kanellos, 1982). These writers were

> Serving a public that was hungry to see itself reflected on stage, an audience whose interest was piqued by plays relating to current events, politics, sensational crimes and, of course, the real-life epic of a people living under the cultural and economic domination of an English-speaking, American society on land that was once part of the Mexican patrimony.
>
> (Kanellos, 1982, pp. 11–12)

Thus the theater brought people together to reinforce cultural identity and bonds to the community during a period of rapid growth in English-speaking populations, especially in California and Texas. Common themes for the writers in California were the Depression, repatriation and discrimination (Gunckel, 2008). Interestingly, traces of the lower class *pelado* character that conveyed much of the theater's Anglo critique carried over to television and remains evident in contemporary Mexican programs (Ruggiero, 2007).

Hispanic theater was hit hard by the Great Depression (1929–1939). As employment opportunities in the U.S. evaporated, many Mexicans and some Mexican Americans were sent to Mexico[2] and many Spanish-language theaters were purchased by film industry companies and converted to movie houses. Some professionals formed cooperatives such as the Compañía de Artistas Unidos (United Artists Company) to lower costs and bargain for theater space, but to little avail. Opportunities narrowed further in the post–World War II period as fewer venues were available for staging plays, though tent theaters continued to follow migrant labor in the Southwest and Midwest through the 1950s, and Spanish-language vaudeville survived in New York through the 1960s (Kanellos, 1982). Hispanic theater would experience a revival in the 1960s, but in a distinct form.

Huerta (1982) points out that little research examined Mexican American theater prior to the rise of Chicano theater in the mid 1960s, although ample work focused on the Spanish religious folk theater of the Southwest. He notes, "Chicanos were more interesting to historians and theater chroniclers as 'folk' than as activists, and a search for records of political theater in the barrios had limited results" (p. 1). *Teatro Campesino* originated in 1965 in California's San Joaquin Valley to inform farmworkers about their plight, their rights, and the United Farmworkers' Union. The *Teatro* spawned other Chicano theatre groups and in the 1970s toured across the U.S. and Europe to critical acclaim. In accounting for the flowering of Chicano theater in the wake of *Teatro Campesino*'s success, Huerta (1982, p. 2) finds its origins in three elements: a cause—the striking farm workers; an atmosphere—the Civil Rights Movement; and a growing political consciousness—the Chicano student movement.

Cinema

The growth of commercial film—which occurred at the expense of the live theater—shifted attention away from Mexican Americans' experience in the U.S. to the broader, more assimilationist orientation of Hollywood, or the nationalistic fervor of Mexico (Gunckel, 2008). Like Chicano theater, U.S.-produced cinema by and for Hispanics would appear only in the wake of the Civil Rights and Brown Power Movements of the 1950s–70s. Noriega (1993, p. 73) bluntly states, "before the Chicano Movement, Mexican Americans had no significant role in film or television production." The same was generally true for Hispanics of other national origins as well; they played bit parts and worked on production crews, but seldom occupied leadership roles. The situation was similar for distribution, but differed for film exhibition because U.S. Hispanic entrepreneurs owned Spanish-language theaters and theater chains. Spanish-language newspapers in Los Angeles noted the scant opportunities in production, criticizing Hollywood for employing talent and consultants from Spain rather than Mexican or "Hispano-American" professionals—a complaint that would carry over to television (Gunckel, 2008). As subsequent chapters illustrate, in television competition from Spaniards has been of minimal concern to U.S. Hispanics, but being supplanted by Latin Americans has long been a sensitive issue.

Mexican films began screening in the U.S. as early as 1920 when the Million Dollar Theater in Los Angeles showed *Cuauhtémoc*, a feature-length film about the last Aztec emperor. Theaters in San Antonio and El Paso also featured Mexican productions that year (Agrasánchez, 2006). These were special engagements at mainstream theaters, however; it would be another decade before movie houses dedicated exclusively to Spanish-language films appeared, due in large part to the introduction of sound in 1927. According to Dickson (1996), the first U.S. establishment to screen Spanish-language films on a full time basis was the Teatro California in Los Angeles beginning in August 1930.

After "talkies" emerged, Hollywood studios scrambled to find the most efficient and profitable means of producing scripts in multiple languages. The innovation in sound had broad implications for export-ing films to overseas markets, of course, but carried domestic implications for Spanish-language content as well (Thompson, 1985). Gunckel (2008) chronicles the period between 1927 and the decline in Hollywood's produc-tion of Spanish-language film from 1931 on, a pivotal time when language, representation and employment were at issue. Hollywood made about 180 Spanish-language films before their production ceased in the late 1930s (Agrasánchez, 2006). As this period predated viable dubbing technology, common practices were for different groups of actors to shoot the same scenes on the same sets, or for English-speaking actors to deliver their lines phonetically. Neither approach proved feasible, either economically or with audiences, and by the mid-1930s increasing numbers of films arrived from Argentina, Spain and especially Mexico, which was gaining notoriety and market share throughout Latin America. At times during its Golden Age of Cinema (1930–1959) Mexico would account for up to 90% of film book-ings in U.S. Spanish-language theaters (Agrasánchez, 2006). Because the films tended toward nationalism, they appealed to Mexican Americans who, as we saw in the case of theater, used popular culture to define and defend their cultural boundaries (Gonzales, 2006).

Clearly Mexico enjoyed an advantageous competitive position vis-á-vis U.S. audiences, and after political stability was restored in 1929, Mexico's film industry began to flourish (Mora, 1989). *Allá en el Rancho Grande* (Out on the Big Ranch) is frequently identified as the breakthrough film, a pioneering blockbuster that established the *comedia ranchera*[3] genre in film, and created lucrative synergies with *ranchera* music on records and radio. The cross-media link was strengthened by the occasional appearance of film and recording stars in theaters to perform live in conjunction with the films, a practice that started with English-language stars, but endured longer at Spanish-language theaters (Gonzales, 2006; Gunckel, 2008).

In the lead up to World War II, Mexico's film industry benefitted from American good will as the U.S. required Mexican resources and loyalty. Shifts in film production toward war-related themes occurred not only in Hollywood, but Argentina, France, Spain and Italy as well, thereby reduc-ing competition in the Spanish-language market. Mexican cinema seized the opportunity through the mid-1950s. Maciel (1992) points out that through Mexico's first seven decades of film production, the experiences of Mexican origin people in the U.S. were a consistent, if not predominant, theme. He counts more than a hundred such films produced between 1922 and 1992, with five common characteristics: didactic themes, particularly the sorrows that await those who emigrate to the U.S.; tragic endings with the main characters returning to Mexico at film's end; top Mexican film-makers participated in their production; they covered a broad range of genres; and their production corresponded with "internal issues, cycles of Mexican emigration to the U.S., and ... the country's foreign policy" (1992, pp. 105–106). Regarding this final characteristic, Maciel stresses that the films reflected internal concerns and popular mindsets in Mexico, including strong attitudes about *pochos*[4] who are typically portrayed as assimilated, pro-American and anti-Mexican. Thus Maciel concluded,

> The Chicano or Mexican in the United States was not well served by the narrative cinema of México in the time frame studied. On the whole, these productions followed and hardened Mexican stereotypes and broad generalizations about Chicanos and *braceros* more than contributing to a more sensitive and complex understanding of "the other Mexico."[5]

Nonetheless, Mexican films were popular with audiences not only in the Southwest, but the Midwest and East as well, as indicated by their dominance of screen time in a growing number of Spanish-language theaters by midcentury. In a 1938 newspaper article, the Spanish-language theater mogul Francisco ("Frank") Fouce Sr. estimated that imported films from Mexico earned about double the money that a Spanish-language Hollywood talkie did—thus we see why Mexican films were popular among theater owners as well as audiences (Agrasánchez, 2006, p. 5). During the 1940s and '50s the number of U.S. Spanish-language movie theaters grew steadily, more than doubling between 1941 and 1945, from 145 to 300 (Agrasánchez, 2006). The largest chain in Los Angeles belonged to Fouce, who, following World War II leased the Million Dollar Theater, a downtown landmark since 1918; Fouce also owned the Roosevelt, the Liberty, the Mason and the Maya (Gonzales, 2006). As cinema attendance began to wane, Fouce would become a founding investor in the principal source of its ultimate demise, the Spanish-language television industry.

Local theater chains also operated in other regions, of course. In New York City, Jeanne Ansell opened four Spanish-language movie houses in the mid 1940s and her competitor Harry Harris opened seven. Max Cohen, the owner of eleven English-language theaters, entered the Spanish market in the late 1940s. Thus, by 1951 there were 33 Spanish-language theaters operating in New York (Agrasánchez, 2006). Like their counterparts in the West, the theaters occasionally featured live performances by film and music stars, although New York tended to present idols from a broader spectrum of Latin American nations beyond Mexico (Agrasánchez, 2006). During the latter half of the 1930s, annual Spanish-language film distribution in New York consisted of about 23 films from Mexico, six from Argentina, five U.S.-produced Spanish talkies, and three imported from Spain. This predominance of Mexican content occurred in a region where Mexican-born Hispanics comprised less than 4% of the Spanish-speaking population (Agrasánchez, 2006). Yet not all Spanish-language films appeared on screens in dedicated Spanish theaters. As migrant workers moved across the West and Midwest to harvest various crops, movies followed them as local theater owners contracted Spanish-language films to meet the temporary demand. By the early 1950s there were nearly 700 screens nationwide exhibiting Spanish-language film (Agrasánchez, 2006).

An unfortunate outcome of agricultural migrant labor and other types of informal manual labor was its negative impact on schooling. As Gonzales (2006, p. 53) explains, "lacking formal education, and thus the basic skills required to create a large reading public, Mexican audiences, both in the Old Country and in the United States, found the motion picture, with its rich visual imagery, to be irresistible." Various researchers recount how industry representatives and journalists commented on Mexicans' and Mexican Americans' affinity for attending the cinema, even when they had little money to do so[6] (Maciel, 1992; Gunckel, 2008; Gonzales, 2006; Agrasánchez, 2006). Audiences of Puerto Rican origin were also identified as avid moviegoers prior to television's arrival, and Mexican film stars of the Golden Age such as Dolores del Río, Jorge Negrete and María Félix gained celebrity among audiences of Caribbean and South American origin in New York (Agrasánchez, 2006).

Gunckel (2008) points to animated discussions in the Los Angeles newspapers *La Opinión* and *El Heraldo de México* about Spanish-language films' effects on viewers as evidence that "cinema had become a site through which multiple discourses about identity and culture were negotiated, coinciding with and registering important shifts and tensions within the Mexican American population" (p. 329). Journalists and community leaders made strident claims that exposure to English-language films corrupted values and promoted cultural and linguistic assimilation, while regular viewing of Spanish-language films maintained vital connections to the culture and language. In his study of Mexican cinema in the U.S., Saragoza (1992) underscores a dynamic surrounding film that also applies to television, and is manifest throughout this book: the U.S.-born offspring to Mexican parents who favor Spanish-language cinema were likely to prefer mainstream American film. Indeed there were few other choices given the absence of a U.S.-based Chicano cinema prior to the 1960s.

Saragoza (1992) emphasizes that as the Mexican film industry fell on hard times, its production quality diminished as did demand in the United States. The Spanish-language film distribution and exhibition industries declined along with the social cachet of viewing a Mexican film in what was likely a decaying theater. Certainly the ascendance of U.S. Spanish-language television—which regularly aired Mexican films due to industry origins and conditions discussed in the next two chapters—contributed to the decline in U.S. Spanish-language cinema. The Golden Age of Mexican Cinema's waning from the mid-1950s on occurred just half a decade prior to the U.S. Spanish-language television industry's origins.

As noted above, music made important contributions to the popularity of Spanish-language film, strengthening cultural ties not only to one's country of origin, but to Latin America (and to a lesser degree Spain) as well. Recall that the larger theaters sometimes featured musical performances by prominent recording as well as film stars, reinforcing the connection between those media.

Music Recording

Music has a deep and varied history in the Spain-Caribbean-Latin America cultural nexus. During the colonial period (16th through early 19th centuries), competition among European powers for economic and strategic footholds brought a variety of musical styles into contact in the New World, as did waves of immigration, both forced and voluntary. The slave trade was particularly influential on music in the Caribbean Basin, and had a profound impact on popular music in the United States. A key distinction of music compared to other forms of popular culture discussed here is its accessibility. Even the poorest individuals could use their voices and many could construct or acquire basic instruments. Prior to the arrival of the phonograph and radio, musical performance was common in many U.S. households, middle class and above (Koegel, 1999). The blending of musical styles from differing ethnic origins is among the country's most unique and valuable attributes, one to which Hispanic cultures have long contributed.

As with the other sections of this chapter, a rich history must be reduced to basics. The two major strands discussed here are the Mexican, which has most strongly influenced the U.S. Southwest, and the Caribbean, especially Cuban and Puerto Rican, more prevalent in the East. Pacini Hernandez (2010) notes that Mexican music, popular and pervasive in the Southwest, was not very familiar outside the region prior to the commercially inspired *mambo* boom of the late 1940s and early 1950s. Although its direct exposure to broad audiences was limited, Mexican music influenced other popular genres such as blues, country and rock and roll (Narváez, 1994; Hartman, 2008; Lewis, 1991). In addition to the *rumba* (1930s) and *mambo* (1950s), other Caribbean music genres enjoyed occasional fad status among mainstream audiences, and contributed to the development of jazz, especially in New Orleans where it became an important ingredient in the musical "gumbo" that Wynton Marsalis and others argue germinated that rich genre (Lichtenstein & Dankner, 1993). Certainly the interaction among African American jazz composers and musicians and Latin American artists was seminal for Latin jazz and related genres (Quintero Rivera & Ortega Breña, 2007).

Shortly after the turn of the 20th century, Charles Fletcher Lummis (1859–1928) recorded Mexican-origin music on wax cylinders (Koegel, 1993). More anthropological than profitable in nature, Lummis's project did not produce recordings for commercial consumption, but his work underscored music's central role in the daily lives of California Hispanics during the late 1800s and early 1900s. As we have seen with theater and cinema, music was closely tied to ethnic identity. Pacini Hernandez (2010, p. 17) traces the linkages among language, identity and music back as far as 1909 by quoting a letter from Columbia to its dealers:

> Remember that in all large cities and in most towns there are sections where people of one nationality or another congregate in 'colonies.' Most of these people keep up the habits and prefer to speak the language of the old country ... To these people records in their own language have an irresistible attraction, and they will buy them readily.

Yet it wasn't until the 1930s and '40s, when phonographs became regular household items, radio expanded, and ethnicity-based music genres such as "race records" and "hillbilly music" emerged that Mexican Americans were recorded regularly and their records distributed.[7] Pacini Hernandez (2010) describes how major record companies such as Okeh, Bluebird, Decca, Victor, and Columbia searched for talent in Mexican barrios of Los Angeles, recording local musicians in makeshift studios—often hotel rooms—paying the performers a low flat fee for each recording, as was customary at the time. Pedro J. González became Los Angeles's first Mexican-origin recording star, benefiting from the broad exposure his group, Los Madrugadores ("The Early Risers"), enjoyed from his own popular Spanish-language radio program, discussed below. In the late 1940s Imperial Records emerged as a specialist label, recording popular Los Angeles performers like Los Madrugadores and Lalo Guerrero, and artists in Texas as well (Pacini Hernandez, 2010).

Among the many Texas musicians who played traditional Mexican music as well as regional genres was Lydia Mendoza who in the mid-1930s was recorded by Ralph Peer, the legendary talent scout and producer who developed the aforementioned race record and hillbilly genres. Following World War II, a number of Mexican American–owned recording companies launched in Texas to satisfy the increasing demand for locally produced music. Entrepreneurs sought to fill the void left by major record companies that showed little interest in pursuing the market after the war, a time when the Mexican-origin population in the Southwest was swelling (Pacini Hernandez, 2010). Their commitment to recording and distributing music from Texas's diverse influences helped spawn *conjunto* and *tejano*, among other genres (Hartman, 2008). The *corrido* in particular has received extensive scholarly attention as a form of cultural resistance to Anglo domination, especially in the borderlands, which have a long history of intercultural contact, much of it violent (Paredes, 1985; Flores, 1992; Peña, 1992). The *trovador* or *cantador* tradition of Mexican-origin musicians playing in the street for money sustained the *corrido* and brought Mexican influences into Black musicians' craft, especially for blues guitar players, according to Narváez (1994).

Although they managed limited domestic operations in the Southwest, the major recording and distribution companies pursued Latin American popular music on a larger scale due to its greater potential to cross over to mainstream audiences—and earn larger royalty fees. Race was a major distinction, as music from non-White communities in the U.S. was largely shunned by mainstream audiences until the 1950s and '60s, and the most profitable renditions of Latin American music were typically performed by White or mixed-race bands covering Latin compositions (Pacini Hernandez, 2010). There were political and economic motivations behind changing cultural attitudes as President Franklin Roosevelt's Good Neighbor policy extended into the Cold War when the U.S. sought loyal allies in the Western Hemisphere, and as air travel to exotic locations was promoted to middle class consumers by an emergent tourism industry. Early efforts to record Latin American artists had consisted of U.S. talent agents travelling south in search of software (recordings) for consumers to play on their employers' hardware (phonographs), which drove the industry's economics at the time. After it became clear that recording international artists in U.S. studios was a more tenable process, the Latin music scenes began to flourish in cities like New York, Los Angeles, Chicago and later Miami, adding more spice to the musical gumbo of 20th century America (Pacini Hernandez, 2010; Lichtenstein & Dankner, 1993).

Roberts (1992) maintains that of the four principal Latin American countries influencing U.S. popular music—Argentina, Brazil, Cuba and Mexico—Cuba has had the greatest, most varied and longest-lasting impact. He further argues that although Puerto Rican musicians have had ample influence over Latin music development in the U.S., music originating from the island has been less influential than Cuba's. From its origins in New Orleans where Cuban and Mexican influences were particularly strong, Latin jazz spread to New York City where it flourished in the orchestras and big bands of the 1920s through '50s and asserted ample sway over bebop (Fernández, 2002). In the late 1940s and early '50s, dance bands played the *mambo* and other dance music of Caribbean origin in ballrooms throughout New York to enthusiastic audiences of diverse ethnic and racial origins—Blacks, Italians, Poles, and especially Jews (Pacini Hernandez, 2010). Quintero Rivera and Ortega Breña (2007) argue that the "tropical spectacle" Latin big bands of the 1950s and '60s, with their "good neighbor" orientation, were not reaching many younger Hispanics, who felt alienated from mainstream U.S. culture during the tumultuous Civil Rights Era. The response by some was closer affinity for and affiliation with Black jazz, which precipitated the emergence of salsa, then hip-hop and reggaeton. As concerned the musicians themselves, Quintero Rivera and Ortega Breña (2007) contend that collaborations among musicians of different national origin contributed to the emergence of a pan-Latino identity.

In the 1950s, the rising popularity of rhythm and blues and rock and roll drew a number of non-Hispanic investors in Spanish-language music out of the industry, especially in New York. The record labels in the Southwest remained, but received increasing competition from music production in Mexico, which, as explained above, benefited from the popularity of Mexican film during the 1940s and '50s (Pacini Hernandez, 2010). This fortified Mexican cultural industries' competitive stance just prior to television's introduction, a dominant influence that remains in place. Just as radio was central to the exposure and eventual stardom of Mexican-origin performers like Pedro J. González and Lydia Mendoza in the 1930s, a quarter century later performers like Celia Cruz, Eddie Palmieri and Tito Puente were promoted by local radio DJs and producers such as George Goldner of Tico Records (est. 1948) and later Fania Records (est. 1964) (Pacini Hernandez, 2010). Rodríguez (1999) points out that Afro-Caribbean music had very limited appeal in regions populated by Hispanics of Mexican and Central American origin, a dynamic that would change over time.

Radio

This final section examines Spanish-language radio, the medium most closely related to television in terms of professional practice, regulation and technology. Note that U.S. Spanish-language radio's most remarkable growth occurred from the 1980s on, a period not discussed here (Castañeda Paredes, 2003); our objective is to trace radio's development up to the early 1960s, when full-time Spanish-language television began as a formal industry. Not surprisingly, when Emilio Azcárraga Vidaurreta launched his first television enterprise in Mexico in 1951 he staffed it with employees from his radio, film and recording enterprises (Rodríguez, 1999). A similar process occurred in the United States as Spanish-language television expanded, although employment opportunities for U.S.-born personnel were limited, an issue that persisted when this book went to press.

Although Paxman (2004) characterized the existing literature on Spanish-language radio's origins as "remarkably thin," several studies have examined the brokerage system whereby Spanish-language segments were broadcast on primarily English or multilingual radio (Gutiérrez & Schement, 1979; Rodríguez, 1999; DeMars, 2005). As described by Gutiérrez and Schement (1979), brokers purchased airtime from English language stations wishing to increase revenues at times of low listenership. The broker arranged the programming—usually consisting of live music (later recorded music), drama, discussion and community calendar items—and sold advertising in the form of announcements read during the program. Early on, few businesses were interested in reaching the Spanish-speaking audiences and could be convinced that off-peak-hours radio was an effective means to do so. Musicians able to entertain audiences with their musical talents as well as speech launched some of the first Spanish radio programs. Two of the pioneers were intriguing men. Julio Roqué, a Puerto Rican dentist who composed, arranged and played both violin and piano hosted *Revista Roqué* over New York's airwaves beginning in 1924. The program featured a variety of Latin American music played by guests—some of whom allegedly received free dental work—and featured recordings of Roqué's orchestra on the Victor label, as well as advertisements for his own line of toothpaste and mouthwash (Pacini Hernandez, 2010; Gill, 2011). In 1929, Pedro J. González, a former telegraph operator for Pancho Villa's forces during the Mexican Revolution, began broadcasting his program *Los Madrugadores* ("The Early Risers," also the name of his band), which aired in Los Angeles between 4:00 and 6:00 a.m. It quickly gained a wide following in Southern California, and apparently beyond—Paxman (2004) claims that KMPC's 1,000-watt signal reached as far as Texas, when atmospheric conditions permitted. During the early 1930s González became increasingly outspoken in his opposition to the United States' repatriation of Mexicans, as well as other affronts by Whites. Not long after Anglo politicians became aware of what he was saying over the air, González was falsely accused of rape, convicted in 1934 and served six years in San Quentin prison before being released (the girl had recanted her story), and transported to Mexico (Balderrama, 2013).[8]

Another radio broker, Rodolfo Hoyos, heard in Los Angeles from 1932 to 1967, played musical instruments and sang to entertain his listeners like González, but also read poetry, aired dramas and engaged guests in discussion. Hoyos paid the station $180 per week for an hour-long daily slot, and charged advertisers $50–60 monthly for daily spots in his program (Gutiérrez & Schement, 1979). In 1928, only four years after commercial broadcasting began in San Antonio, Ignacio E. Lozano began brokering programs to air on station KONO (Paxman, 2004). Lozano had already founded two influential Spanish-language newspapers: San Antonio's *La Prensa* (1913) and *La Opinión* in Los Angeles (1926), positioning him well to thrive in radio (González & Torres, 2011). Rodríguez (1999) emphasizes the close ties existing among radio personalities and listeners during the brokerage period, noting that advertisers purchased low-cost local spots as much to create good will and engage with community as to sell products or services. Because White station owners and advertisers did not yet conceive of Spanish-speaking audiences as a consumer bloc, the Spanish programs were of little interest (Rodríguez, 1999). Spanish-language television began along similar lines, with broadcasts during specific, non-peak time segments on English stations, and advertising sold on a strictly local basis.

Of course other non-English radio programs were broadcast to ethnic communities across the United States, many of them presented through the brokering system. The multilingual station model was particularly common in multiethnic cities of the Midwest and Northeast; WSBC in Chicago began transmitting multiple languages as early as 1925 (Paxman, 2004). A 1941 survey found this breakdown of broadcast hours aired weekly in non-English languages: Italian 358, Polish 292, Spanish 256, Yiddish 138 and German 89 (Arnheim & Bayne, 1941). Another survey conducted the following year counted 58 radio stations broadcasting in Spanish, many as part of a multilingual format; Spanish followed Polish (84) and Italian

(66) (Landry, 1946).[9] The Spanish-language programs Arnheim and Bayne (1941) analyzed were dominated by music at 88% of airtime followed by news (4%), talk (3%), drama (3%) and other (2%). News broadcast in Spanish placed heavy emphasis, around 80%, on international reports. The most commonly advertised products were medicines followed by movies, food, clothing and furniture. Arnheim and Bayne also noted strong appeals to Hispanic unity and listeners' nations of origin in advertising, a persuasive tactic that was emphasized in trade journal reports from the period.

By 1955, Spanish had surpassed the other non-English languages with 176 stations broadcasting some content in the language, 14 of them transmitting only Spanish (Paxman, 2004). After this peak, broadcasting in other languages began to diminish as immigration slowed and younger generations gravitated toward English-language media. Warshauer (1966) elaborated this point in her study of foreign-language broadcasting:

> The huge indigenous, semi-indigenous and immigrant Spanish-speaking populations of the American southwest and south are much more oriented toward radio than publications or other formal means of language maintenance and cultural expression. In this respect they differ greatly from the primarily immigrant-based groups with non-English mother tongues in the Middle Atlantic states and in other regions. This difference suggests other far-reaching difference in educational level, economic mobility, and indeed the entire cultural orientation toward American industrial and urban values, as well as toward less transmuted ethnic values and behaviors. (p. 86)

Given the Hispanic population's size, rural as well as urban character, and comparatively low educational and social mobility, Warshauer argued, Hispanics faced less threat of cultural assimilation than did other groups, thereby diminishing the pressure on Spanish broadcasting for linguistic and cultural maintenance.[10] Bilingual programs began airing in the late 1940s, but remained a minor phenomenon until the 1980s (Paxman, 2004).

Warshauer (1966) also observed that Spanish was more likely than other language programming to originate from full-time, dedicated stations. Not all of such stations were located on U.S. soil. Beginning in the 1930s and '40s signals from high-wattage Mexican stations reached far into the U.S., an especially significant phenomenon in the Southwest where Mexican American populations were concentrated (Paxman, 2004). Although long controversial due to their interference with U.S.-licensed broadcasters, these stations likely helped rather than hindered the growth of the U.S. Spanish-language industry as they promoted language loyalty and introduced Mexican performers to audiences (Paxman, 2004). The border stations clearly benefited cinema and theater owners by increasing audience recognition of, and demand for, Mexican artists who would appear live in their venues.

Such exposure for Mexican talent did not always sit well with U.S.-based radio industry professionals who strove to achieve more equitable balance between domestic- and foreign-born talent and management. For reasons discussed above, a majority of Hispanic music aired in the early years of radio originated from overseas production centers and/or performers. Similarly, many of the radio business entrepreneurs and on-air performers originated from Latin America, especially Mexico, Puerto Rico and Cuba. A shift toward more U.S. participation occurred during the 1940s and early '50s when radio stations in the borderlands, especially in Texas, began playing *conjunto*, a regional music genre produced by and for working class Mexican Americans, on programs hosted by increasing numbers of U.S.-born Mexican American disk jockeys (Mayer, 2001; Paxman, 2004). A similar process occurred in New York as new genres such as *salsa* emerged from Caribbean roots (Roberts, 1992). Despite the rise of these and other indigenous art forms, employment and representation have remained as sources of tension in Spanish-language broadcasting, sparking protests and walkouts, especially when non-U.S. workers are favored for jobs or promotions, or accent or linguistic purity issues arise (Wilkinson, 2002).

When Raoul Cortez acquired KCOR in San Antonio in 1946, it became the first U.S. Spanish-language radio station owned and operated by a Hispanic. Although Spanish content had been available to San Antonio area listeners since at least 1928 through the broker system, Cortez and others who followed conquered important new terrain via direct ownership and management of stations. The struggle to increase radio station ownership and management by Hispanics, dating from the origins of commercial radio, continues into the 21st century and has grown increasingly sensitive in the wake of ownership consolidation following the Telecommunications Act of 1996, and Univision's purchase of 68 stations owned by Hispanic Broadcasting Corp. in 2003.

In the 1950s and 1960s, U.S. Spanish-language radio began to institutionalize along network, advertising and promotional lines. Many in the Spanish-language radio industry complained of advertiser indifference to their market segment, noting mainstream advertisers' ignorance about Hispanics' increasing economic mobility and purchasing power, a complaint that would carry over to television (Paxman, 2004). Station groups with holdings in multiple markets began standardizing programming to reduce costs and increase efficiency. In 1956 Raoul Cortez founded Sombrero Network, which grew to 15 stations; its principal rival, National Spanish Language Network, included 12. The trend continued through the 1960s, pulling Spanish-language radio into the broader corporate fold of format radio, and supplanting the brokerage system (Paxman, 2004). Agencies specializing in Spanish language media began offering spot sales in multiple markets and targeted larger entities commanding more substantial advertising budgets than the local, community focused businesses that had sustained Spanish language radio in the early decades. The challenge was to convince deep-pocketed corporations that solid, long-term dividends could be earned from investing in the Hispanic market, and that Spanish language radio was an effective medium to reach Hispanic consumers. There was plenty of room for expansion. As Paxman (2004, p. 17) explains, "in 1957, with Latinos deemed to number around [four] million and at least 195 part-time and 14 full-time broadcasters serving them, Spanish-language broadcasters generated a mere $5 million." Although substantial growth has ensued, selling the Hispanic market to advertisers remains a challenge in the 21st century when advertising spending on Hispanic-oriented media (whether in English, Spanish or bilingual) remains far from parity with the group's population or consumer-spending figures (see Appendices A and B). Spanish-language radio experienced a mainstreaming process in the 1970s when credible ratings became regularly available and advertising sales and promotions moved closer to the English-language standard (Paxman, 2004). By that time, Spanish-language television had established a firm foundation in the United States and was growing.

Conclusion

Two themes that connect the four media discussed in this chapter—and that resonate through the book—are the media's interconnectedness and movement between the U.S. and Latin America by media professionals and audiences alike. These themes have persisted through Spanish-language television's development, even as profound economic, organizational and technological changes have transformed media industries since the 1960s.

When sound technology shook the film industry in the late 1920s, languages and accents became a major obstacle, and none of the initial solutions satisfied audiences. One response in the Spanish-speaking sector was to produce musical variety films (*variedades*) that facilitated insertion of local content, and significantly reduced the amount of dialogue to be translated (Gunckel, 2008). *Variedades* brought singers, musicians and dancers from the stage onto the screen. In what contemporary observers might label multimedia, well-known Mexican entertainers also performed live in Spanish-language movie theaters (Gonzales, 2006). Radio sometimes covered the festivities at theaters where live performances accompanied film screenings, in some cases utilizing a radio studio adjacent to the theater, as with the Alameda in San Antonio (Agrasánchez, 2006). Such presentations for movie audiences hastened the demise of live performance, which did not revive until the 1960s and '70s with the Brown Power and Farmworkers' Rights Movements. Cinema launched or maintained the careers of *some* recording artists performing in *some* genres while undoubtedly restricting the exposure of others. (This relationship has survived profound changes in industry and technology as many of today's *telenovela* stars also pursue recording careers and celebrity vocalists appear in film and television.)

Music recording relied heavily on other media as Pacini Hernandez (2010, p. 22) notes: "Latino-owned/Latino-operated recording ventures did not take root and thrive until sufficiently substantial and economically diversified Latino communities emerged with the capacity to support a parallel infrastructure of radio, theaters, newspapers, and record stores catering to Spanish-speaking consumers." Music's tie with radio was particularly close as the early brokers for Spanish-language radio were presenters and musicians themselves. Audience demand for specific genres like *conjunto* and *salsa* opened spaces for radio programs hosted by local aficionados. Spanish-language radio's organization along more corporate commercial lines in the 1950s and '60s influenced the structure of full-time television in Spanish when it took root in the early 1960s.

The movement of performers and populations between the U.S. and Latin American lands, especially Mexico, Cuba and Puerto Rico, is another key feature of Spanish-language media during the first half of the 20th century that remains significant early in the 21st. Mexicans have been alternatively welcomed and shunned according to labor needs and political winds in the U.S. Repatriation of Mexicans during the Depression had considerable impact on the growth of Spanish-language theater, music and electronic media as around half a million people returned or emigrated to Mexico. The Mexican community in Los Angeles shrank an estimated 30% between 1930 and 1935 (Sánchez, 1993). The massive migration of Puerto Ricans to New York between 1949 and 1954 significantly increased the audience for music, radio and, eventually, television while carrying with it the talent, or perhaps parents of the talent, who would enrich all these forms of media (Quintero Rivera & Ortega Breña, 2007). A similar dynamic followed in Florida after the Cuban Revolution (1952–1959) drove waves of immigrants to the U.S. The appeal and importance of Latin American theater, film, music and radio to recent immigrants, as well as long-established populations of Hispanics, is encapsulated in the concept of ethnic media introduced in the next chapter and reverberating throughout this book.

Notes

1. Shepherds' plays performed during the Christmas season.
2. U.S. Citizenship and Immigration Services estimates the number between 400,000 and one million, emphasizing that a relatively small number of people were formally expelled, but multiple means were employed to encourage Mexicans to leave (http://www.uscis.gov/history-and-genealogy/our-history/historians-mailbox/ins-records-1930s-mexican-repatriations).
3. In basic terms, singing cowboys and cowgirls living on *haciendas* where men were honorable and women virtuous.
4. A derogatory term for Mexicans who emigrated to the United States, assimilated and lost touch with their culture and language of origin.
5. One exception Maciel cites is the 1954 film *Espaldas mojadas* (Wetbacks) by Alejandro Galindo which he considers "by far the single best Mexican commercial production on the subject of Mexican emigration" (1992, p. 114).

6. We see this interest in Hispanics' levels of disposable income and heavy spending on entertainment relative to other groups throughout the development of U.S. Spanish-language television.
7. Narváez (1994) points out that genre categories for recorded music and the tendency to focus on commercially successful artists created blindspots to some rich influences such as Mexican American musicians' effect on blues guitarists in the Texas-Mexico borderlands, or Cuban musicians' influence over Black blues players in New Orleans.
8. Pedro J. González's life in music, radio and as a political scapegoat is chronicled in the 1988 film *Break of Dawn*.
9. Paxman (2004) makes the astute observation that broadcasting in Spanish may have been undercounted in the study given that several influential trade journals were located in New York and Chicago which, in the 1940s, had modest numbers of Hispanics compared to Italian and Polish speakers.
10. Faber et al. (1986, p. 356) offered this perspective on a study of Mexican American radio users in San Antonio:

> The findings of this study can be interpreted as lending some support to the belief that use of ethnic media is, in general, associated with lower levels of acculturation. However, this interpretation would fail to recognize the full complexity of ethnic media use. While part of ethnic media preference may be explained by general language ability and level of acculturation, ethnic radio, at least, also serves other functions for some people. These functions may include habit, keeping up with names, places or music from their past, maintaining contact with heritage and tradition, and providing common experiences to talk about with other ethnic group members. Further research which focuses on the different functions ethnic media use can play for different audiences is clearly needed.

References

Agrasánchez, Rogelio, Jr. (2006). *Mexican movies in the United States: A history of the films, theaters and audiences, 1920–1960.* Jefferson, NC: MacFarland.

Arnheim, Rudolf, & Bayne, Martha Collins. (1941). Foreign language broadcasts over local American stations: A study of a special interest program. In P. F. Lazarsfeld & F. N. Stanton (Eds.), *Radio research, 1941* (pp. 3–64). New York: Duell, Sloan and Pearce.

Balderrama, Francisco E. (2013). Revolutionary Mexican nationalism and the Mexican immigrant community in Los Angeles during the Great Depression: Memory, identity and survival. In D. W. Richmond & S. W. Haynes (Eds.), *The Mexican revolution: Conflict and consolidation, 1910–1940* (pp. 117–134). College Station, TX: Texas A&M University Press.

Castañeda Paredes, Mari. (2003). The transformation of Spanish-language radio in the U.S. *Journal of Radio Studies, 10*(1), 5–16.

DeMars, Tony R. (2005). Buying time to start Spanish-language radio in San Antonio: Manuel Davila and the beginning of Tejano programming. *Journal of Radio Studies, 12*(1), 74–84.

Dickson, Robert G. (1996). Los orígenes y desarrollo del cine hispano. In I. Durán, I. Trujillo, & M. Verea (Eds), *México, Estados Unidos: encuentros y desencuentros en el cine.* Mexico City, Mexico: Universidad Nacional Autónoma de México.

Faber, Ronald J., O'Guinn, Thomas C., & Meyer, Timothy P. (1986). Diversity in the ethnic media audience: A study of Spanish language broadcast preference in the U.S. *International Journal of Intercultural Relations, 10*(3), 347–359.

Fernández, Raúl. (2002). *Latin jazz: The perfect combination/La combinación perfecta*. San Francisco, CA: Chronicle Books.

Flores, Richard R. (1992, spring). The corridor and the emergence of Texas-Mexican social identity. *Journal of American Folklore, 105*(416), 166–182.

Gill, Jonathan. (2011). *Harlem: The four hundred year history from Dutch village to capital of Black America*. New York, NY: Grove Press.

Gonzales, Manuel G. (2006). Arturo Tirado and the Teatro Azteca: Mexican popular culture in the Central San Joaquin Valley. *California History, 84*(3), 46–63.

González, Juan, & Torres, Joseph. (2011). *News for all the people: The epic story of race and the American media*. Brooklyn, NY: Verso Books.

Guins, Raiford, & Zaragoza Cruz, Omayra (Eds.) (2005). *Popular culture: A reader*. Thousand Oaks, CA: Sage.

Gunckel, Colin. (2008). The war of the accents: Spanish language Hollywood films in Mexican Los Angeles. *Film History: An International Journal, 20*(3), 325–343.

Gutiérrez, Félix, & Schement, Jorge Reina. (1979). *Spanish-language radio in the Southwestern United States*. Mexican American Monograph Series No. 5. Center for Mexican American Studies, University of Texas at Austin.

Hartman, Gary. (2008). *The history of Texas music*. College Station, TX: Texas A&M Press.

Huerta, Jorge A. (1982). *Chicano theater: Themes and forms*. Ypsilanti, MI: Biligual Press/Editorial Bilingüe.

Jenkins, Henry. (2006). *Convergence culture: Where old and new media collide*. New York, NY: New York University Press.

Kanellos, Nicolás. (1982). *Two centuries of Hispanic theater in the Southwest* [Multimedia show program]. Houston, TX: Arte Público Press.

Kanellos, Nicolás. (1984). An overview of Hispanic theater in the United States. In N. Kanellos (Ed), *Hispanic theater in the United States* (pp. 7–14). Houston, TX: Arte Público Press.

Koegel, John. (1993). Mexican-American music in nineteenth-century California: The Lummis wax cylinder collection at the Southwest Museum, Los Angeles. *Revista de Musicología, 16*(4), 2080–2095.

Koegel, John. (1999, fall). "Canciones del país": Mexican musical life in California after the Gold Rush. *California History, 78*, 160–187.

Landry, Robert John. (1946). *This fascinating radio business*. Indianapolis, IN: Bobbs-Merrill Co.

Lewis, George. H. (1991). Ghosts, ragged but beautiful: Influences of Mexican music on American country-western & rock 'n' roll. *Popular Music & Society, 15*(4), 85–103.

Lichtenstein, Grace, & Dankner, Laura. (1993). *Musical gumbo: The music of New Orleans*. New York, NY: W.W. Norton.

Maciel, David R. (1992). Pochos and other extremes in Mexican cinema: Or el cine mexicano se va de bracero, 1922–1963. In C. A. Noriega (Ed.), *Chicanos and film: Essays on Chicano representation and resistance* (pp. 105–126). New York, NY: Garland.

Mayer, Vicki. (2001). From segmented to fragmented: Latino media in San Antonio, Texas. *Journalism & Mass Communication Quarterly, 78*(2), 291–306.

Mora, Carlos. J. (1989). *Mexican cinema: Reflections of a society*. Berkeley, CA: University of California Press.

Narváez, Peter. (1994). The influences of Hispanic music cultures on African-American blues musicians. *Black Music Research Journal, 14*(2), 203–224.

Noriega, Chan A. (1993). *Cine chicano: Between a weapon and a formula: Chicano cinema and its contexts*. In C. A. Noriega (Ed.), *Chicanos and film: representation and resistance* (pp. 141–167). Minneapolis, MN: University of Minnesota Press.

Pacini Hernandez, Deborah. (2010). *Oye como va!: Hybridity and identity in Latino popular music*. Philadelphia, PA: Temple University Press.

Paredes, Américo. (1958). *"With his pistol in his hand": A border ballad and its hero*. Austin, TX: University of Texas Press.

Paxman, Andrew (2004, December). *An ethnic media success story: The early years of Spanish-language radio, 1924–1970*. Unpublished manuscript, Department of History, University of Texas at Austin, Austin, Texas.

Peña, Manuel. (1992). Musica fronteriza/Border music. *Aztlán: A Journal of Chicano Studies, 21*(1), 191–225.

Quintero Rivera, Ángel G., & Ortega Breña, Mariana. (2007). Migration, ethnicity, and interactions between the United States and Hispanic Caribbean popular culture. *Latin American Perspectives, 34*(1), 83–93.

Roberts, John Storm. (1992). The roots. In V. W. Boggs, *Salsiology: Afro-Cuban music and the evolution of salsa in New York City* (pp. 7–22). Westport, CT: Greenwood.

Rodríguez, América. (1999). Creating an audience and remapping a nation: A brief history of US Spanish language broadcasting 1930–1980. *Quarterly Review of Film & Video, 16*(3–4), 357–374.

Ruggiero, Thomas E. (2007). Televisa's Brozo: The jester as subversive humorist. *Journal of Latino-Latin American Studies 2*(3), 1–15.

Sánchez, George J. (1993). *Becoming Mexican American: Ethnicity, culture and identity in Chicano Los Angeles, 1900–1945*. New York, NY: Oxford.

Saragoza, Alex M. (1992). Cinematic orphans: Mexican immigrants in the United States since the 1950s. In C. A. Noriega (Ed.), *Chicanos and film: Essays on Chicano representation and resistance* (pp. 127–141). New York, NY: Garland.

Thompson, Kristin. (1985). *Exporting entertainment: America in the world film market, 1907–1934*. London, England: British Film Institute.

Warshauer, Mary Ellen. (1966). Foreign language broadcasting. In J. A. Fishman (Ed.), *Language loyalty in the United States* (pp. 75–91). London: Mouton & Co.

Wilkinson, Kenton T. (2002, summer/fall). Collective situational ethnicity and Latino sub-groups' struggle for influence in U.S. Spanish-language television. *Communication Quarterly, 50* (3/4), 422–443.

2 Establishing Spanish International Network and the Growth of Ethnic Media

This chapter begins in Mexico, providing background essential to understanding U.S. Spanish-language television's origins. Emilio Azcárraga Vidaurreta (1895–1972), a pioneer in Mexican radio, film and television, began exporting programs to other Spanish-speaking countries in the 1950s. He proposed a TV network that would serve the information and entertainment needs of Hispanics across the United States, dispatching an employee, Reynold ("Rene") V. Anselmo (1926–1995), to investigate prospects. The middle portion of this chapter describes Azcárraga's expansion into the U.S. with a binational investor group that purchased/built its first two stations in San Antonio, Texas (KWEX), and Los Angeles, California (KMEX), and launched the Spanish International companies, a network and a station group. On the strategic and technology fronts, the group initiated relationships with advertisers and audience research companies, promoted set-top UHF converters that TVs required to receive signals, and began laying the groundwork for a satellite distribution system.

The various "rights" movements of the 1960s and '70s focused increased attention on ethnic-oriented media that could meet the information and entertainment needs of specific population subgroups more effectively than mainstream media. Although the profit potential for such commercially oriented media was recognized slowly, academic research was underway on related topics such as cultural identity and acculturation, education, civic participation and various obstacles to greater participation by ethnic and racial minority populations in political processes, communication industries and other social institutions. The closing sections of the chapter examine ethnic media, and focus on the specific case of Spanish-language television in Los Angeles.

Origins of Television in Mexico

As Latin American nations began adopting television during the middle years of the 20th century, they looked to two existing models: the commercial system exemplified by the United States, and the public service model of Great Britain and other European nations. In 1947, the Mexican president Miguel Alemán Valdés dispatched a committee to the U.S. and Europe to gather information on each system and submit a recommendation. To little surprise, the commercial model prevailed, although the government expressed its intention to develop public television as well. Still, the entrepreneurs advocating commercial television took the threat of government intervention seriously, and allied with colleagues within Latin America and in the U.S. to achieve strength in numbers. The Asociación Interamericana de Radiodifusión (AIR-Inter American Broadcasting Association) emerged in 1946 through the efforts of Goar Mestre of Cuba (and later Argentina, Peru and Venezuela) and Mexico's Emilio Azcárraga Vidaurreta.

At the first AIR Congress in 1946, Azcárraga Vidaurreta proposed creating a separate Latin American association focused on the specific goal of developing television as a commercial medium in Latin America. The following year, Televisión Asociada launched with Azcárraga serving as president. Its protectionist objectives were similar to AIR's, but the organization would also acquire the broadcast rights to musical, literary and artistic works, patents and programs "for commercial and cultural use on facsimile and television."[1] As Mejía Barquera (1989) points out, their common interests in collectively promoting and protecting commercial television did not prevent Latin America's early broadcasting entrepreneurs from competing among themselves for market share. In 1955, the same year he consolidated his operations within Mexico, Azcárraga established a program exporting operation and began eyeing opportunities north of the Rio Grande.

Sinclair (1986) has argued that broadcasting in Mexico is best understood by examining its three legs of support: an industrial elite, the state and foreign investors. The entrepreneurs who emerged at the forefront of Mexican radio in the 1920s and '30s were best positioned to initiate television after World War II. Two themes were very clear in the applications for concessions: television should be a commercial medium and Mexico should become a regional leader in the industry. The first concession went to Televisión de México S.A., a group headed by the auto sales titan Rómulo O'Farrill Sr., which included the American William Jenkins (Paxman, 2008). XHTV began broadcasting on Channel 4 in Mexico City on July 26, 1950. The group purchased broadcast equipment from RCA, and programming and experienced personnel also arrived from the U.S. (Portales, 1987). The only surprising aspect of Emilio Azcárraga Vidaurreta's receiving a concession was that he received the second one, not first. His XEW, Channel 2, initiated experimental broadcasts in October 1950 and regular ones in May 1951. A third concession was granted to the television engineer Guillermo González Camarena whose XHGC, Channel 5, began airing in Mexico City in August 1952.

Contending for small audiences and limited advertising sales led to aggressive competition among the three Mexico City stations. Thus, in 1955 Channels 2, 4 and 5 joined to form Telesistema Mexicano (TSM), with Azcárraga serving as president. By eliminating competition in the country's principal urban television market, TSM could focus resources on extending its reach to Mexico's interior via repeater stations and local affiliates, and consider international markets as well. The merger also united the business acumen of O'Farrill and Azcárraga with the technical prowess of González Camarena, a key figure in the development of color television technology (Mejía Barquera, 1989). All three, of course, had close contacts with government, a key aspect of what Sinclair (1986) terms "the Mexican formula" for interaction between the Mexican state and private broadcasting interests. Telesistema's—later to become Televisa's—programming formula also emerged: the three channels catered to diverse segments of the Mexican viewing public by specializing in different program genres (Sinclair, 1986; De Noriega & Leach, 1979). In 1955, stations appeared in Mexico's second and third largest cities, Monterrey and Guadalajara, and in 1956 TSM installed a 60,000 watt repeater antenna capable of reaching the heavily populated states of San Luis Potosí, Guanajuato, Querétato, Michoacán and Jalisco.

Telesistema Mexicano became the first Latin American television enterprise to make a sustained effort to export programs when an international sales company named Teleprogramas de México launched in 1955. Certainly Azcárraga's leadership positions in the regional industry groups AIR and Televisión Asociada bolstered Teleprogramas de México's image and influence. The first videotape machine arrived in Mexico in 1958, providing another important boost not only to TSM's growth within Mexico, but to its export enterprise as well (Mejía Barquera, 1989). Videotape technology allowed programs to be recorded prior to airing, and eventually facilitated both editing and distribution. TSM created another company, Teleprogramas Acapulco in 1966 to produce *telenovelas* and "explore new potentials of the format" (De Noriega & Leach, 1979, p. 22).[2] The U.S. network ABC held 25% interest in the company.

TSM faced no serious competitive threat until 1968 when Televisión Independiente de México arrived, backed by the financially and politically powerful Grupo Monterrey. Channel 8's presence in Mexico City stimulated fierce and expensive competition with TSM on several fronts such as contracting local talent, domestic program production, and acquiring rights to imported programs. The competition led to another merger in 1973, which united four channels in Mexico City and 70 throughout the country under the single administration of Televisión Vía Satélite, or Televisa, a company that would become the largest Spanish-language media conglomerate in the world, and one that has wielded strong influence over the development of Spanish-language television in the United States. With the creation of Televisa, competition was all but eliminated from Mexican television until Televisión Azteca appeared in 1993, as discussed in Chapter Seven. Just as his father led Telesistema Mexicana following the merger in 1955, Emilio Azcárraga Milmo (1930–1997) held controlling interest in Televisa and became its leader only a year after his father died in 1972 (Fernández & Paxman, 2000). These developments underscore the three constants in Mexican television history that Portales (1987) identifies: state assistance for and association with private television, the permanent weakness of state television, and the existence of a leading group: Azcárraga and associates.

Establishing a Foothold in the United States

Given the entrepreneurial vision and motivation Emilio Azcárraga Vidaurreta exhibited in Mexico, it's not surprising that he recognized the profit potential of television in the towns and barrios of the U.S. Southwest in the early 1960s. Rodríguez (1999a) points out that his strong position in the Mexican market through TSM (and later Televisa) afforded Azcárraga sufficient security to gamble in the U.S. Although television set ownership by Hispanics was limited due to sets' high cost and scant availability of Spanish-language programming, Azcárraga knew from experience that television sets would become more affordable and audiences would tune in if engaging content became available (Valenzuela, 1985; Fernández & Paxman, 2000). Azcárraga's first endeavor in U.S. television was to send an American producer working at Teleprogramas de México, Rene Anselmo, north to convince English-language networks and stations to air Mexican programming. Anselmo later recalled that the few stations that bought programming did so from a sense of obligation to comply with Federal Communications Commission (FCC) rules, and that the programs typically aired at off-peak hours such as weekend mornings (Balkan, 1986).

Not someone to be easily deterred, Azcárraga turned to the more expensive option of station ownership. There were strong economic incentives for him to do so. Telesistema Mexicana was importing various types of U.S. programming to dub into Spanish and broadcast in Mexico, meaning that U.S. dollars were spent on unfavorable exchange terms.[3] What better way to rectify the imbalance than establishing an aftermarket for Mexican programming in the U.S.? Programs produced at relatively low cost spending Mexican pesos could be distributed in the U.S. where advertising revenues would be earned in dollars. Not only would the cash flow problem be ameliorated, but market demand for Mexican programming would develop and grow in stride with the Spanish-speaking population. Because he was aware of Section 310(b) of the Communication Acts of 1934, which limits foreign ownership or control of a broadcasting entity to 20%, Azcárraga began circulating his idea among business associates holding American citizenship (Rieman, 1985). This was a reversal of the typical dynamic in Mexico-U.S. business relations whereby American investors would cobble together Mexican *prestanombres* (front men) in order to comply, at least on paper, with Mexican laws requiring domestic ownership (Paxman, 2008).

Most prominent among those who invested was Frank Fouce Sr., the president of Fouce Amusement Enterprises, which, as described in the previous chapter, owned and operated Spanish-language theaters and movie houses in California. Fouce was a long-time business associate of Azcárraga who had been involved in the Mexican film industry since the 1930s, had built

Mexico City's famed Churubusco Studios in partnership with RKO Studios in 1945 (Ryan, 1983), and who, we may assume, distributed Mexican films to Fouce's U.S. theaters. Balkan (1986) credits Fouce Sr. with having developed the U.S. television idea together with Azcárraga. An associate of both men, Julian Kaufman, had served as general manager of Bay City Television,[4] the U.S. representative for station XETV in Tijuana, México, which reached audiences in Southern California (*In re Spanish International Communications Corporation*, 1986, para. 14). Rene Anselmo, who hawked Mexican programs to U.S. stations, was also invited to invest. A second-generation Italian American who had worked for Teleprogramas de México since 1954, Anselmo would run the Spanish International operations for 25 years before advancing the global satellite market through the PanAmSat company. As Anselmo recalled, "… being an American citizen, one day I got a call to come on up, and [was] asked if I wanted to become an investor. I said 'yes,' and through a series of defaults, I sort of took on the executive role of making this thing work" (Balkan, 1986, p.19).[5]

Fouce Sr. became the largest stockholder in the station group, and Anselmo the simultaneous president of both the station group (Spanish International Communications Corp., SICC) and the network that provided programming, promotions and advertising sales (Spanish International Network, SIN). A rift, which in the mid-1970s estranged Anselmo from Fouce's son, Frank Fouce Jr., would alter the course of the U.S. Spanish-language television industry. In the early going, however, expenditures heavily outweighed profits, formidable obstacles to growth endured, Don Emilio Azcárraga Vidaurreta was in charge, and the investors and management were unified.

Station Acquisition

In September 1961, through a company named Spanish International Broadcasting Corporation, the investors purchased station KCOR-TV, Channel 41 in San Antonio for $200,000, and changed the call letters briefly to KUAL, then permanently to KWEX. KCOR-TV had been owned and operated by Raoul A. Cortez (1905–1971), a key figure in U.S. Spanish-language broadcasting. After working as a journalist, theater owner and promoter, Cortez moved into radio, launching station KCOR-AM in San Antonio in 1946 and the Sombrero radio network thereafter (Gutiérrez & Schement, 1979; Paxman, 2004). In 1955 he established the United States' first full-time Spanish-language television station, which was also among the first UHF stations in the country (Raoul A. Cortez, n.d.). As discussed in greater detail below, the UHF band was a novelty at the time, suffering from poor signal quality, limited and expensive converter boxes (until 1962 when the FCC mandated their inclusion in new sets), and indifference from many advertisers and viewers (Cooley, 1955; Darkened channels, 1962). By 1960, Cortez was ready to divest of his television station and approached Emilio Azcárraga about acquiring the station. After the sale, Cortez's son-in-law,

Emilio Nicolás Sr., became a vice president and general manager—he and his son Emilio Nicolás Jr. would be important players in the industry for decades to follow.[6] The Spanish-speaking population within KWEX's reach was estimated at more than half-a-million people when Spanish International acquired the station (Spanish-voiced TV, 1966). According to programming schedules reproduced by Valenzuela (1985, pp. 188–190), KWEX only broadcast from 5:00 to 11:00 p.m. when acquired; by 1978 it was on the air from 9:00 a.m. until midnight.

A separate company including the same principal investors in the San Antonio station received license approval for KMEX, Channel 34 in Los Angeles on November 1, 1961, and the newly constructed station went on the air September 30, 1962[7] (*In re Spanish International Communications Corporation*, 1986, para. 15). The station's prospects were good as its potential audience encompassed about 1.5 million people living in 400,000 households—not all of them owning television sets or the required converters, of course (Spanish-voiced TV, 1966). Given this large potential viewer base and its proximity to both Hollywood and Mexico, KMEX became Spanish International's operational hub from the inception of satellite distribution in 1976 until the network's move to Miami in 1989 (after being renamed Univision). KMEX and the Los Angeles Spanish-language market are discussed in greater detail below.

Valenzuela (1985, p. 122), citing *Variety* magazine, provides figures regarding the expense of acquiring these first two stations: KWEX (San Antonio) cost $200,000 and lost $225,000 in its first year; KMEX[8] (Los Angeles) was acquired "for under $600,000" and lost $200,000 in its first *three months* of operation. Altogether, within three years the capital outlay for acquisition, start up and operating expenses at the two stations was over $2.2 million (Valenzuela, 1985, p. 147). Naturally, some revenue generated was folded back into the stations for expenses, such as the conversion to color broadcasting in 1967. Valenzuela (1985, p. 115) identified the top ten national advertisers in Spanish in 1964: "five … beer companies, two … milk companies, and one cigarette manufacturing company, one food company and one automobile manufacturer;" the list for 1966 looked similar with R.J. Reynolds Tobacco Company moving from 10th place to first, and both Pepsi-Cola and Coca-Cola joining the middle of the list. Investors in the stations and network, principal among them Emilio Azcárraga Vidaurreta, patiently covered losses and continued to expand the network, holding out for a profitable future as the medium and its audience matured.

The losses did not deter the station group's expansion into New York, the country's largest Hispanic market at the time, through a new station, WXTV, located in Paterson, New Jersey. Although competition for permission to construct the station began as early as 1963, broadcasting did not start until August 1968, just two months before the Mexico City Olympic Games. WXTV and Spanish-language television's development in New York are examined in the next chapter.

In January 1971, Spanish International Communications Corp. acquired Miami station WAJA, Channel 23, which as an independent station had aired some popular Spanish-language programs since 1967.[9] The station began broadcasting under the call letters WLTV in 1971, and by the mid-1970s had phased out its remaining English-language programming. WLTV raised its advertising rates 40% in 1973[10] and benefited from being Miami's only full-time Spanish-language television broadcaster until 1985 when Telemundo appeared on Channel 51 (WSCV). WLTV's station manager, Joaquin Blaya, gained recognition for his dexterous management of the station, especially in local news.

Also in 1971, Spanish International received a construction permit for KFTV, Channel 21 in Hanford/Fresno, California, which launched in mid-1972, first repeating content from KMEX in Los Angeles, and some locally produced content shortly thereafter. Two other stations in key Spanish-speaking markets were incorporated separately from Spanish International, but included many of the same shareholders. Bahia de San Francisco Television Co.[11] purchased station, KDTV in San Francisco and went on the air in August 1975. In 1979 KDTV negotiated a transmitter and channel assignment swap with KCSM, a San Mateo based PBS affiliate station and moved from channel 60 to channel 14 (KDTV-DT, n.d.). Seven Hills Television Co. obtained a permit to build Phoenix station KTVW, Channel 33 in 1977, and the station began broadcasting in 1979.[12] KTVW was the sole full power Phoenix station broadcasting in Spanish until Telemundo affiliate station KPHZ (KTAZ since 2006) entered the market in 2001 (Habla Español?, 1968; KTVW-DT, n.d.).

The Spanish International Companies

In 1972, the Spanish International Communications Corporation (SICC) formed by merging three separate companies that previously held licenses for stations KFTV in Hanford/Fresno, KMEX in Los Angeles, KWEX in San Antonio, WLTV in Miami and WXTV in New York. Thus, the broadcasting licenses for all five stations were consolidated into one corporation whose principal shareholders were the same men who had initiated the enterprise 11 years earlier, plus a few station managers and other employees who joined along the way (Valenzuela, 1985; *In re Spanish International Communications Corporation*, 1986, para. 20). Recall that Section 310(b) of the U.S. Communications Act of 1934 limits foreign ownership or control of a broadcasting entity to 20%; thus Mexican ownership in SICC did not exceed that amount, just as it had not for any of the stations discussed in the preceding section.[13] The ownership structure of the corporation remained quite static; when Frank Fouce Sr. died in 1962 and Emilio Azcárraga Vidaurreta in 1972, their assets transferred to their sons Frank Fouce Jr. and Emilio Azcárraga Milmo.[14] Fouce Jr. was elected board chairman and treasurer of SICC in January 1972, posts he would hold for four years, until a corrosive dispute erupted. Rene Anselmo assumed the presidency of SICC upon its creation.

Although legally separate from SICC, the companies holding the licenses for KDTV in San Francisco, Bahia de San Francisco Television, and KTVW in Phoenix, Seven Hills Television, had many of the same principals as SICC stations. As translator and low-power stations were built, most came under SICC ownership.

The Spanish International Network (SIN) was created in 1961 to sell national spot advertising and distribute programs to the fledgling Spanish International stations, border stations owned by Telesistema Mexicano (TSM),[15] and non-affiliated stations as well. SIN also syndicated some TSM programming for English-language television, bullfights being an example (Habla Español?, 1968). Thus, SIN served as the U.S. complement to the Mexican production and program sales operations discussed above, even as it became "the first national network aimed at a specialized minority audience" (De Uriarte, 1980, p. 5). Because U.S. law does not prohibit for-eign ownership of programming networks, the ownership structure for SIN differed significantly from that of the stations. At SIN's inception in 1961 TSM held 100% of SIN; in 1971 25% ownership was transferred to Rene Anselmo, under prior arrangement (Valenzuela, 1985). When TSM became Televisa in 1973, the SIN shares transferred to the new company. Although many news reports identify Emilio Azcárraga, both Sr. and Jr., as SIN own-ers, technically the companies they controlled through majority ownership held the stock.[16]

In early 1963 Rene Anselmo relocated to New York to organize and manage the SIN sales office; shortly after SICC was created, the two com-panies began sharing office space as well as the same corporate president: Anselmo (*In re Spanish International Communications Corporation*, 1986; Crister, 1987). This close relationship between the two companies conserved resources and facilitated management, but it also created an environment in which one entity, usually the network, could readily be favored at the expense of the other, the station group. In fact, Frank Fouce Jr. accused Anselmo of siphoning SICC revenues off to SIN, and the exact nature of the two companies' relationship became a central focus of an FCC in the mid-1980s. Yet such proximity between the companies also worked in the stations' favor for many years, as they were not expected to pay their programming debts when advertising sales returned insufficient earnings.

Regarding business growth, Valenzuela (1985) mentions the 1968 Olympic Games in Mexico City not only for improving television in Mexico, but boosting the SIN network as well. Upgrades of production facilities at Telesistema Mexicano and the Mexican government's improvement of dis-tribution facilities throughout the country benefited entities that imported Mexican programs (De Noriega & Leach, 1979). The Spanish International station group turned its first profit in 1968, due in part to broadcasts of the games (Valenzuela, 1985, p. 105). SIN began distributing color programs in 1967, prompting the SICC stations to initiate conversions to color broadcasting, an expensive but essential investment.

Two more Anselmo-inspired, SIN-related projects emerged in the 1970s. In 1974, Magnaverde Corporation debuted as a promotions and distribution service for premium sports programming and special events to Spanish-language stations and other venues employing closed-circuit technology (Valenzuela, 1985, p. 107; De Uriarte, 1980, p. 6). The company would later become a contested asset when Frank Fouce Jr. claimed that Magnaverde used SICC employees and production facilities in promoting some of its events without compensation, and when Anselmo proposed to address SICC's debt by selling company shares to Magnaverde. Galavisión, a premium cable service that debuted in 1979, is discussed in the next chapter. Like SIN, Galavisión was owned 75% by Televisa and 25% by Anselmo, although it was less closely integrated with SIN and SICC than Magnaverde.

The Ultra-High Frequency (UHF) Band

All of the stations that Emilio Azcárraga Vidaurreta and his fellow investors acquired or built operated on the ultra-high frequency band, which the FCC opened for commercial use in 1952 to address the post–World War II rush on television licenses. UHF, which spanned the channel range from 14 to 83, was originally heralded as a local medium that could counter, or at least complement, the very high frequency (VHF) channels that had wider reach and were less prone to interference. Because of these characteristics, the major broadcast networks and deep-pocketed investors in independent television coveted and controlled VHF stations (Comstock, 1989). By 1959 many UHF stations had languished, and a number were available for acquisition just as Azcárraga and his partners sought access to key Spanish-speaking markets. Rather than reach just two or three markets on the VHF band, with UHF stations the investors could enter five markets for about the same level of investment. Thus Spanish International became the first U.S. company to form a national UHF network.

A drawback that had limited UHF television's mainstream market growth confronted the Spanish-language sector as well: in order to decode UHF signals, viewers had to purchase a converter costing between 40 and 70 dollars, according to Valenzuela (1985, p. 114). Most sets were not equipped with built-in UHF reception technology until required to do so by All-Channel Receiver Act of 1962. Because set manufactures had until the end of 1964 to include the UHF tuners, and because new sets were beyond the financial means of many Hispanic families, the Act had minimal impact on Spanish-language television until later in the 1960s. Not only did Spanish International Network and the stations have to convince viewers that their programs would merit purchasing a converter, or perhaps a new television set, they also had to persuade advertisers that an audience existed and would purchase the goods and services advertised.

Rene Anselmo recounted that when KMEX launched, some advertisers in Los Angeles argued that Spanish speakers already watched television in English—and had for 15 years—why would they invest in a UHF converter? He said,

> It was hard to convince them. Instead of using ratings, we used to run around with converter shipment data from the manufacturers to prove how many converters were being sold in Los Angeles. We'd say, "Look, they've sold out every single converter and UHF antenna in Los Angeles. The distributors are flying back East to see where they can buy them because they're running out." (quoted in Balkan, 1986, p. 25)

Of course Spanish-speaking consumers' willingness to purchase the converters also signaled their interest in tuning-in Spanish broadcasts over the long term, a selling point to advertisers. The Spanish-language market was a hard sell nonetheless, and SIN grumbled about minimal help from the television ratings services. In 1966 the network filed complaints with the Broadcast Ratings Council and Federal Trade Commission charging A.C. Nielsen Co. and American Research Bureau with "false and deceptive rating practices" in Los Angeles and San Antonio (Spanish stations protest, 1966). SIN claimed that several years of correspondence and conferences with the ratings services had yielded no improvement in their ability to measure Spanish-speaking television audiences. The complaints marked a legal strategy of aggressively challenging policies and institutions that the Spanish International companies, and later Rene Anselmo independently, would pursue for decades to follow. Anselmo recalled that in the mid-1960s an advertiser said to him, "You know, Rene, the only people who speak Spanish around here are the old folks and grandfathers, grandmothers and second and third generations who speak Spanish." Anselmo's stock response was, "I don't know who speaks Spanish, all I know is people who watch the stations, are watching in large numbers" (Balkan, 1986, p. 78).

The 1960 U.S. Census

As noted in the Introduction, the census findings discussed here and in five similar sections in subsequent chapters should be approached with caution due to differences in measuring and reporting techniques across the decennial censuses (Cohn, 2010). The 1960 census's design yielded a blurry picture of the Hispanic population because it did not include a variable directly identifying persons of Hispanic origin (Passel & Cohn, 2008). Instead, census interviewers were instructed to record "Puerto Ricans, Mexicans or other person of Latin American descent as white unless they were definitely of Negro, Indian or other nonwhite race" (Swarns, 2004). Using Spanish surname as its categorization criterion, the 1960 census counted 3.5 million Hispanic residents constituting between 3.6%

and 3.9% of the total population (Rodriguez, 1999b, p. 36). However, Gratton and Gutmann (2000) conducted post-hoc analysis of the 1960 data, counting 5,814,784 Hispanics characterized by this distribution of origins: Mexican 70.3%, Puerto Rican 17.7 %, Spanish, 3.5%, Cuban 2.8%, other 4.7%, and undetermined 1.0% (p. 143). According to Passel & Cohn (2008, p. 15), 14% of the Hispanic population in 1960 was first generation (born in another country), 23% was second generation (U.S.-born with at least one immigrant parent) and 63% was third generation (born in the U.S. to U.S.-born parents). During the period covered by this book, the percentage of foreign-born Hispanics would steadily rise to 40% in 2000, and then stabilize thereafter.

Other challenges included a lack of Spanish-language census forms, no provision for self-report (official census takers could not interview every Spanish-speaking household), limited data gathering about language use— language preference was only asked of foreign-born persons—and a "uniquely restrictive data suppression strategy" which led to incomplete data reporting (Gratton & Gutmann, 2000). Besides limiting the national origins that respondents could identify, the 1960 census, Mora (2014, p. 3) points out, "did not include a question or category that offered persons of Latin American descent the opportunity to identify as a national panethnic community." Thus, Davis, Haub, and Willette (1983, p. 5) conclude, "prior to the 1970 census, the concept of Hispanics as a group barely existed." Due to other problems with the 1970 census, not until 1980 could Hispanic census respondents self-identify in categories that adequately reflected their backgrounds.

Ethnic-Oriented Media

Ethnic-oriented media have a long and rich history in the United States, a nation with deep immigrant roots. As immigrants have arrived to the country, many have been hungry for news and entertainment from their countries/cultures of origin; to learn the practices, values, expectations, etc. of their host society;[17] and to maintain connections with other community members and institutions (like churches or civic organizations) in their city or region. Ethnic media have sated that hunger for centuries, and will continue doing so as long as people move across national boundaries in large numbers. Subervi-Vélez (1986) refers to the first two functions—staying connected with societies of origin and learning about the host country—as the "dual role" of ethnic media. The definition used here is borrowed from a textbook on the topic: "media that are produced *by* and *for* (a) immigrants, (b) ethnic, racial, and linguistic minorities, as well as (c) indigenous populations living across different countries" (Matsaganis, Katz, & Ball-Rokeach, 2011, p. 7, emphasis in the original). For Spanish-language media in the U.S., groups (a) and (b) are most apropos. We should keep in mind that the industry's heavy commercial orientation has created a stark class distinction between those who provide and those who consume Spanish-language television content (Dávila, 2001).

Historically, ethnic media have played key roles in immigrants' acculturation to U.S. society, and have been used alongside mainstream, English-language media that offer insights into the host culture (Viswanath & Arora, 2000). Substantial amounts of academic and journalistic ink have probed the processes of cultural adaptation, often pitting *assimilation*, the notion that immigrants relinquish traditional cultural, linguistic and value orientations in favor of those predominating in the host culture, against *acculturation*, the idea that immigrants gain new skills and perceptions, but not necessarily at the expense of existing ones (Hutnik, 1991; Subervi-Vélez, 1986). This assimilation/pluralism dynamic occupied the attention of much ethnic media scholarship during the second half of the 20th century (Johnson, 2010). López, Enos, Nichols, LaRosa, Mellema and McGrew (1973) asserted,

> It is now possible to observe, with considerable accuracy, the function of mass media in the preservation of the difference and separateness of non-majority cultural units and to analyze the relationship between changes in the patterns of use of the mass media and changes in the relationships between minority and majority cultures. (pp. 40–41)

This point reinforces Johnson's (2000) observation that research on ethnic media during this period tended to stress their function as "buffers from the assimilation forces of the dominant culture" (p. 232).

In a study of the U.S. ethnic press, principally newspapers, Miller (1987) identifies four stages of growth. The first period, lasting from colonial times through the late 19th century, was characterized by small, impermanent presses that tended to appear and disappear quickly. A second phase occurred from 1900 to 1930 when the foreign-language press enjoyed its heyday prior to increased restrictions on immigration. From the 1930s to 1980s a third stage featured a decline, then expansion, in non-English newspapers and periodicals. Miller suggested that the uptick from 1960, when there were 698 such publications, to 1975, when there were 960, could indicate a fourth stage (1987, p. xviii). It is significant to note that this growth spurt coincided with the establishment and early growth of Spanish-language television, and encompasses the period when Black Power, Brown Power, Women's Liberation and other social movements gained broad attention and endeavored to disseminate their messages through a variety of media. Indeed, one observer characterized ethnic media's success in the early 1970s like this, "it's not black power or brown power, it's green power" (Glenn, 1973, p. 3).

Not everyone recognized the growth, however. As Spanish-language television gained a foothold in the U.S., some observers doubted its long-term viability, based on the assumption of sweeping immigrant assimilation to mainstream U.S. culture. As one report reasoned, "since the closing of the gates to the floodtide of European immigration after the First World War, most of the nation's ethnic media began a long decline, as the children of immigrants abandoned the parental tongue and the old readers died off" (Habla Español?, 1968). The report goes on to explain that Puerto Rican and Mexican immigrants tend to retain their Spanish, sometimes through the fifth and sixth generations in the latter case. Similar questions were raised during subsequent phases of Spanish-language television's growth. The chapters to follow show that language preference and generational status within Hispanic households has been consistent (Jarboe, 1980), and that in the complex communication environment of the 21st century, bilingual and English-dominant Hispanics engage Spanish-language media for multiple reasons, including retro-acculturation[18] (Rojas & Piñón, 2014).

Connecting ethnic media's basic features back to the first decade of Spanish-language television, although Spanish accounted for two-thirds of all non-English broadcasting in the U.S. in the mid-1960s (Warshauer, 1966), and seven U.S. TV stations broadcasted 20 or more hours weekly in Spanish, López et al. (1973) concluded, "very little is known about this media and its viewers" (p. 42).[19] It's not as though television was alone in being present but largely unfamiliar. As noted above, the number of ethnic-oriented newspapers and periodicals increased during the 1960s and '70s, *Broadcasting Yearbook* identified 250 U.S. radio stations offering Spanish-language programs on their schedules, and the company Spanish Advertising & Marketing Services expected to bill $5.8 million for its services in 1973, up from $1.8 million in 1968 (Glenn, 1973, p. 3). It would take larger audiences and more money changing hands for Spanish-language media to command the recognition from the trade press and academic researchers that it received when this book went to press.

As the Introduction points out, the U.S. Hispanic sector represents a rare case among the world's ethnic media due to its persistent growth, under a commercial model, which has attracted major corporations not only to advertise regularly, but also to invest in direct ownership of networks. Such investment has produced relatively complex structures to support business operations and expand the two major networks along with the steady population growth (Riggins 1992, p. 14). The roots of this uniqueness were established by the entrepreneurs discussed in this chapter, and the next, who patiently waited for returns and folded many of the scant revenues from Spanish International operations back into the stations and network. Audiences' loyalty to ethnic media also contributed to the industry's success of course, and derives in large part from two definitional characteristics: maintaining a connection to the country of origin, its language and traditions, and keeping audiences informed about developments in their cultural community (Glenn 1973; Stoloff, 1982).

Spanish-Language Television in Los Angeles

Focusing on the nascent industry and audience in Los Angeles helps elucidate several key aspects of ethnic media, and complements the discussion of New York in the next chapter. It makes sense that Los Angeles was among the first markets that Spanish International entered, given its prominence in theater, film and recording, as well as an estimated Spanish-speaking population of between 1.3 and 1.5 million living in the metropolitan area in the late 1960s/early 1970s (López & Enos, 1974; Habla Español?, 1968). Between 1950 and 1980 Hispanics grew from 6.9% to 28.8% of LA's population, making it, by 1980, the second largest urban Hispanic population in the world, trailing only Mexico City (De Uriarte, 1980). Certainly such geodemographic concentration made Spanish-speakers more efficient to reach through broadcasting than some other minority populations, such as Blacks (Glenn, 1973, p. 3). Despite many advertisers' continued skepticism about the market, a 1972 study found that 92% of Spanish-speaking households in Los Angeles County had TV sets equipped to receive UHF broadcasts (López et al., 1973, p. 51).

KMEX had been broadcasting for five years when KLXA Channel 40 launched in January 1967 as an independent Spanish-language station owned by International Panorama TV. Like KMEX, the station began modestly, broadcasting several hours daily before expanding to around 12 hours daily within several months. In early 1974 KLXA began airing religious programs for the Trinity Broadcasting Network for two hours daily, and later the same year was sold and converted to a fulltime religious format—the call letters changed to KTBN in 1977 (KTBN-TV, n.d.). Before turning our attention to a research study offering a detailed portrait of LA's Spanish-language television audience in the early 1970s, I recount a tragic news event involving KMEX. On August 29, 1970, the Chicano investigative journalist and columnist Ruben Salazar was shot in a bar shortly after covering the National Chicano Moratorium March,[20] which had culminated in a clash between protesters and police. A police officer fired a 10-inch tear gas projectile that struck Salazar in the head, killing him instantly (Chávez, 2002). Salazar, a well-known columnist at the *Los Angeles Times* who focused on Hispanic communities, especially East LA, had become KMEX's news director just four months before his death. Together with a newsroom colleague, William Restrepo, he had been investigating accusations that some police and sheriff's deputies planted evidence when making arrests, leading to speculation that Salazar had been targeted (Rodriguez, 2014). A 2011 investigation into the killing conducted by the Los Angeles County Office of Independent Review found no evidence that Salazar had been under surveillance, but also emphasized that the original investigation by police detectives had been flawed, probably in order to protect the policeman who fired the canister (López, 2011).

SLO-TV in LA

A study of Spanish-language-only television (SLO-TV) in Los Angeles County sponsored by the John and Mary Markle Foundation and conducted by researchers at the Claremont Colleges provides insight into the industry and audience in the early 1970s (López, et al., 1973; López & Enos, 1974).

At the time, had Spanish-speaking viewers in Los Angeles County been counted as a discrete metropolitan market, SLO-TV's potential audience in LA, around 1.3 million people, would have ranked as the country's 30th television market, situated between Providence, Rhode Island, and Denver, Colorado (López & Enos, 1974, p. 311). Yet despite such a substantial presence, this "large, oppressed population ha[d] been practically 'invisible' … in th[e] sense that Chicanos and others of Spanish-speaking heritage ha[d] not been considered part of the 'American' saga" (p. 308). The researchers faced a substantial challenge in sampling the large population in their study. They selected 750 households for in-home interviews, employing a multistage modified probability sample that only included areas with a minimum 30% Spanish surnamed population. This method, while comparatively costly and time consuming, circumvented problems associated with identifying and interviewing Spanish-speaking respondents at the time. Although the study includes many interesting variables, the discussion here is truncated to those most directly related to our topic.

The researchers spoke with very few viewers who said they themselves or household members watched SLO-TV exclusively; a strong majority watched both English and Spanish stations (López, et al., 1973, p. 65). Among Spanish-speaking households that received UHF broadcasts, 34.5% identified KMEX as their preferred station; the next most popular station identified was the ABC network affiliate, KABC (25.0%). Only 1.5% of respondents cited the independent Spanish-language station KLXA as their favorite (López, et al., 1973, p. 59). Having been born in Mexico was almost perfectly correlated with preference for KMEX (+.94), and the inverse held as most U.S.-born viewers reported lower preference for either Spanish-language station, and greater affinity for English stations. The researchers made the key observation that because KMEX did not normally begin broadcasting until mid-afternoon, audiences often watched English stations earlier in the day (López, et al., 1973, p. 62). The researchers point out that restricted content availability reduced SLO-TV's popularity among children because ample kids' programming was available on English-language stations in those earlier dayparts. (This was prior to the advent of pay television channels dedicated solely to airing cartoons and other children's formats.) Additionally, the content broadcast later in the day appealed almost exclusively to post-adolescent viewers. The authors identify the approximately 50 hours per week that SLO-TV stations were "dark" as missed chances to provide educational and other prosocial programming for children and adolescents, including lost opportunities for enhancing children's linguistic development in Spanish (López et al., 1973, p. 74). They also advocated devoting some of the dark time to airing informational programs related to issues impacting the Hispanics population—like health, employment, housing, education—as well as content highlighting Chicanos' prosocial actions and achievements. The suggestion included a rather acerbic recognition that such a change would require stations to rely less on imported content from Mexico (López & Enos, 1974).

In parallel with the ethnic media functions discussed above, López and Enos (1974) acknowledge that recent immigrants need information to help them adapt to U.S. society, and that such content could be included between programs or at commercial breaks. (Such content is familiar to contemporary viewers located in smaller markets, where it appears in slots not occupied by local advertising.) López and Enos rightly emphasize financing too. Had the State of California and/or federal government seized this opportunity to subsidize programming during dark periods, the medium may have developed a more educational, prosocial orientation. However, as we saw at the beginning of this chapter, commercial media entrepreneurs have steadfastly protected their interests from government intervention and, as we will see in subsequent chapters, the Federal Communications Commission has taken only occasional interest in the medium, usually when prompted by formal complaints or political tensions—the agency's customary orientation has been laissez faire.

Demographic data about respondents in the study offer a profile of regular Spanish-language television viewers in Los Angeles County in the early 1970s:

- 75.5% were born in Mexico; only 18.4% were born in the U.S. (The remainder were born in another Spanish-speaking country.) (1973, p. 73)
- 88.3% had high school level education or less (1974, p. 309)
- 89.3% expected to earn incomes lower than $10,000 in 1974 (1974, p. 309)
- 75.2% were 30 years or older; although 18- to 21-year-olds comprised 16.5% of the sample population, they represented only 5.7% of SLO-TV viewers (1974, p. 309)

The data led López and Enos (1974, p. 301) to conclude, "thus older respondents, with little schooling, and lower incomes, are among the most frequent watchers of Spanish language television. These people also believe that Spanish language television is more truthful and accurate [than English language television]." As we saw with language preference for TV viewing, the inverse held true: younger, more educated viewers not only preferred English-language television, but also found it more credible. These findings concerning age, education and income were corroborated by a similar, simultaneous study of viewers (and Spanish-language radio listeners) in Texas (Valenzuela, 1973).[21]

Through their research, López et al. (1973) verified empirically what some industry observers had already assumed:

> The programs ... do not appeal to the "Chicano," but rather to those "Mexicans" with lower socio-economic status. It might well be that some mixed language broadcasting would increase and broaden the appeal of SLO-TV since it would more closely correspond to the experiences of the Chicano who is often bilingual. (p. 77)

The authors concluded that Spanish-language television is primarily a class phenomenon, but one with powerful ethnic aspects; knowledge of Spanish was a precondition for regular exposure, but the content tended to satisfy class-linked interests. Notwithstanding these divisions within the potential and actual viewership of Spanish-language television in Los Angeles, the researchers emphasized the broader implications, calling Spanish-speaking communities in the U.S. "the most dramatic example of the role of mass media, both in the preservation of culture, and in its impact on the potential for and nature of assimilation into the majority culture" (1974, p. 284). The Spanish sector's predominance as the country's foremost ethnic media would continue for four decades and showed no signs of abating as this book went to press.

Competition Increases into the 1980s

Our discussion of the Los Angeles market merits extension as competition increased later in the 1970s and into the early 1980s when stations KWHY, KBSC and KSCI appeared. KWHY, Channel 22, changed formats and call letters several times before being acquired by the Thomas Bunn family in 1966 (KWHY-TV, n.d.). From 1972 to 1978 the station provided stock market information and business news, switching to non-English programming after the U.S. exchanges closed. KWHY transmitted up to 40 hours per week during the first few years before scaling back beginning in 1975 (Stoloff, 1982). Although the station gained an avid following among some LA Chicanos while it broadcast *The Huggy Boy Show*, its management claimed that Spanish International's lock on programs from Mexico forced a scaling back of its Spanish schedule (Stoloff, 1982). In 1978 the station became a subscription service, which pushed most of its ethnic programming off the air. Interestingly, KWHY was an affiliate of both Emilio Azcárraga Milmo's Galavisión broadcast network and the Telemundo network before becoming a MundoFox affiliate in 2012 (KWHY-TV, n.d.).

Oak Industries acquired KBSC, Channel 52, in 1976. The television producer and agent A. Jerrold Perenchio held a 50% interest at the same time he was vice president of WNJU in New York, as described in the next chapter (Stoloff, 1982). In December 1980 KBSC was broadcasting around 64 hours a week, and distributed this programming mix during a sample week: Venezuelan origin 17.5 hours, dubbed films from various origins 17 hours, Mexican origin 11 hours, Puerto Rican origin 9.5 hours, Spanish origin 4.5 hours, locally produced 3.5 hours (Stoloff, 1982, p. 71). These programs aired during the day—the station switched to subscription service during prime time hours. Due to its limited access to Mexican programs, KBSC sought to attract non-Mexican-origin viewers, and emphasized the growing diversity among LA's Hispanic population in its promotional announcements and station identification (Stoloff, 1982).

KSCI, Channel 18, went on the air in December 1977 under the ownership of Global Television, which promoted the teachings of Maharishi Mahesh Yogi and Transcendental Meditation. It broadcast in languages other than Spanish, including Hebrew. The number of hours broadcast weekly in Spanish more than doubled from 24.5 in March 1980 to 53.5 a year later (Stoloff, 1982, p. 73). In keeping with its philosophy, the station sought to offer family-oriented programming, more uplifting news and less violent entertainment programs than KMEX and KBSC.[22] KSCI would later broadcast as many as 14 different languages, and dropped Spanish during the latter part of the 1980s before resuming in the 1990s (Holly, 1986; Valle, 1986).

By 1980, the Spanish-language television market in Los Angeles had matured considerably. Industry sources estimated the Hispanic population in Los Angeles' metropolitan area at 4 million in 1979, representing 35% of the population (Stoloff, 1982, p. 44). Recognizing Spanish-speaking residents' buying power, three of the four stations that broadcast ethnic television in LA increased their Spanish language programming in mid-1980.[23] KMEX became the first station in Southern California to broadcast Spanish-language programs 24 hours a day. As noted, KSCI more than doubled its broadcast time in Spanish, and KBSC offered 63.5 hours of Spanish language programming a week (Stoloff, 1982, p. 44). A study commissioned by KMEX in 1980 counted 19,000 adult viewers at 8:30 a.m. and 404,000 at 8:00 p.m. Station manager Daniel Villanueva claimed that the prime time audience exceeded that of the three major network affiliates combined among Spanish speaking viewers over 18 years old (Stoloff, 1982, p. 46).

Before concluding this section it should be noted that increased availability of Spanish-language television did not obscure the fact that many Hispanic Los Angelinos preferred their TV in English, or would be open to bilingual options (López et al., 1973). Acting on this pent-up demand, Moctesuma Esparza[24] launched Buena Vista Cable TV in 1980. He had previously received a cable franchise for East Los Angeles in 1977, and bid for the Boyle Heights franchise along with a partner based in Rhode Island (Bilingual cable TV, 1980). Esparza's goal was to offer 54 channels, at least two of which would be dedicated to local and regional English-language productions targeting Hispanic audiences (Bilingual cable TV, 1980).

Conclusion

This chapter has traced the early development of U.S. Spanish-language television beginning with a Mexican entrepreneur's vision to create demand for his product in an underserved region with strong growth potential. Emilio Azcárraga Vidaurreta and his fellow investors established stations in two key markets as well as a network to provide them with content and advertising sales. Clearly the acquisition and sustenance of stations required considerable capital outlay over time, yet one must look beyond the financial issues to understand how an industry develops. The Spanish International companies' use of new (or previously underdeveloped) technologies gives insight not only to Azcárraga's and Rene Anselmo's entrepreneurism, but also network expansion techniques that reduced the potential for competition. Lessons learned in Mexico were applied in the United States. Also illustrated here is the SIN leadership's disposition to employ the legal system, as seen in its challenging the two major television ratings services to pay closer attention to Spanish-speaking audiences. These are early examples of the Spanish International companies' adroit use of investment, technology and legal tactics to grow an industry and, in so doing, advance their own interests.

The Spanish International entities conformed to the ethnic media concept in some ways and diverged in others. The stations offered news and entertainment from the homeland—especially for viewers of Mexican origin—as well as information about U.S. society, its culture, and how to navigate it. However, unlike some other ethnic media in the U.S. that thrived in the wake of immigration waves then became less relevant as audiences acculturated to mainstream society, Spanish-language television, in areas like South Texas and Southern California, encompassed large and diverse populations in length of residence as well as language ability and preference. Consequently, many potential viewers possessed the language skills and desire to consume English-language media, while others were limited to Spanish.[25] (This dynamic persists in the 21st century, when the means of defining, understanding and reaching audience subgroups are more refined.) As regards ethnic media's informing audiences about developments in the community, during the period examined here tension built over locals' lack of access to stations that aired mostly imported content and produced little, if any, of their own. This was not simply a structural issue as management appeared reticent to provide access to more liberal or progressive voices whose ideas and appeals might offend the sensibilities of conservative viewers (Noriega, 2000).

This dynamic brings to mind the internal colonialism argument, which equated the treatment and living conditions of ethnic and racial minorities in the U.S. with the subjugation and economic exploitation of colonized peoples in the Third World (Blauner, 1969; Almaguer, 1974; Gutiérrez, 1976; Aguirre & Bustamante, 1993). The industry's strict commercial ethos combined with stations' operational losses made it difficult for community advocacy organizations, independent producers, educational institutions and similar groups to secure airtime for programs. In this sense, Spanish-language television did not fit the common attribute of ethnic media being "part of larger framework of social movements" (Riggins, 1992, p. 12); the profit motive trumped community development, especially at SIN where the costs of expansion and technology acquisition were high. Such an orientation influenced the character and public image of Spanish-language television, making it appear detached to many viewers (Antola & Rogers, 1984; Aguirre & Bustamante, 1993). A related perception existed among some Anglo-controlled businesses that were reticent to advertise on ethnic-oriented media due to concerns about how mainstream consumers might react to their brand image (Warshauer, 1966; Glenn, 1973). This potential stigma began eroding in the 1980s when mainstream press coverage of the Hispanic population and market increased, but remained a significant factor during the 1960s and '70s when TV was still widely regarded as a *broad*casting medium and audiences were defined more generally than in the demographically driven, niche-oriented environment from the late 1970s on (Turow, 2007).

In closing, I should note that while Spanish International was certainly the most organized and best-funded television operation, it was not alone. An article published in 1968 identified 15 other stations that aired Spanish-language programs on an occasional basis (Habla Español?, 1968), and another report five years later mentioned 60 outlets offering some type of programming in Spanish, although only a dozen on a full-time basis (Glenn, 1973). Among the stations specifically identified in 1966 was CBS affiliate WTVJ in Miami, which broadcast news in Spanish twice daily, Spanish-language voiceovers of stories and events likely to interest Hispanic viewers, and emergency broadcasting in Spanish. Also in Miami, independent station WCIX began airing a Spanish newscast in 1969 and, due to the growing Cuban-American population, quickly turned a profit (see Delgado & Veraldi [2003] for an informative discussion). WOR in New York and KCOP in Los Angeles aired hour-long shows in Spanish on weekends (Spanish-voiced TV, 1966). Valenzuela (1985, p. 127) identifies other non-SIN Spanish-language stations that emerged in the mid-1960s such as Channel 22 in Phoenix and WNJU in New York, which is discussed in the next chapter.

Notes

1. *Boletín Radiofónico* No. 3, 21 de marzo de 1948.
2. Telenovelas are Spanish-language soap operas, or serial melodramas. Teleprogramas Acapulco's president was Miguel Alemán Velasco, son of the Mexican president who introduced television. The son would be an influential player in Televisa, off and on, for decades. Rene Anselmo, who would lead many of TSM/Televisa's U.S. expansion efforts from 1960 to 1986 was a producer and manager at Teleprogramas de México.
3. As Antola and Rogers (1984) explain, this problem was rectified by Mexico becoming the favored dubbing location for American program distributors. Through a classic barter arrangement, a Televisa subsidiary dubbed programs from English to Spanish free of charge in exchange for rights to air the dubbed content in Mexico. The distributor sold the dubbed version in other Spanish-language markets for a profit.
4. Bay City was owned by the Azcárraga family and Frank Fouce Sr. served as its president (In re SICC, 1986, para. 14).
5. Other minor investors included Edward J. Noble, an advertising executive working in Mexico City, and Joseph S. Rank, an account executive at John Blair Co., the company that became the original foundation for the Telemundo network (see Chapter Five) and later a KMEX station manager (Cox, 1969).

6. According to Cox (1969, p. 10) citing the *Television Factbook*, this was the ownership distribution for Spanish International Broadcasting Corporation, which acquired the license for KWEX:

   Rene Anselmo 35% (vice president)
   Frank Fouce 20% (president)
   Edward J. Noble 20%
   Emilio Azcárraga Vidaurreta 20%
   Julian Kaufman 5% (vice president)

7. Valenzuela (1985, p. 154) points out that it was a common practice for the investor group to form separate companies for different stations. The distribution of ownership for KMEX was as follows (Cox, 1969, p. 10):

   Fouce Amusement Corp. 35% (Frank Fouce Sr., president)
   Emilio Azcárraga Vidaurreta 20%
   Rene Anselmo 15% (executive vice president)
   Edward J. Noble 15%
   Julian Kaufman 10% (vice president)
   Joseph Rank 5% (vice president and general manager)

8. In 1966 KMEX employed 35 people full time, three-quarters of whom were of Hispanic origin (Lane, 1966 as cited in Stoloff, 1982, p. 62).

9. The popular programs included a Spanish-language version of *Bozo the Clown* and a *Soul Train* style music show featuring local performers called *Solo para Bailadores*, "For Dancers Only" (WLTV-DT, n.d.). The five largest shareholders in the company owning WLTV were (*In re SICC*, 1986, para. 19):

   Fouce Amusement Enterprises 28%
   Rene Anselmo 21%
   Emilio Azcárraga Vidaurreta 20%
   Metropolitan Theaters Corp. 12%
   Daniel D. Villanueva 7%

10. Based on rate cards for June 1972 (No. 3) and April 1973 (No. 6) submitted to the FCC as documentation for license renewal (Accession No. 173–93–58, Box 45).

11. The principal owners of KDTV through the Bahia de San Francisco company were (FCC 87R-58, para. 13):

    Rene Anselmo 42% (president)
    Joaquin Blaya 12%
    Daniel D. Villanueva 12%
    Emilio Nicolás, Sr. 6%
    William D. Stiles 5%

12. The principal owners of KTVW through Seven Hills Television Co. were (FCC 87R-58, para. 15):

    Rene Anselmo 55% (president)
    Emilio Nicolás, Sr 15%
    Daniel D. Villanueva 15%
    William D. Stiles 6%
    Joaquin Blaya 4%

13. Although there were 28 corporate and individual shareholders in SICC, 91% the stock was held by six shareholders (*In re SICC,* para. 7):

    Fouce Amusement Enterprises 25.5%
    Rene Anselmo 23.9%
    Laura Investment Co. 20% (an Azcárraga family firm)
    Estate of James M. Jacobson 9.1%
    Emilio Nicolás, Sr 6.7%
    Daniel D. Villanueva 6.0%

14. Technically, Emilio Azcárraga Vidaurreta's shares were transferred first to his widow, then upon her death to the Laura Investment Company held by Emilio Azcárraga Milmo and his two sisters. The assets were managed by Azcárraga Milmo (*In re SICC,* 1986, para. 22).
15. The Telesistema stations on the Mexican side of the border that reached U.S. cities were: XEWT Tijuana/San Diego, XHBC Mexicali/Calexico, XEJ Ciudad Juárez/El Paso, and XEFE Nuevo Laredo/Laredo (Habla Español?, 1968).
16. In 1986 Televisa was owned 58% by Azcárraga Milmo (president) and other family members, 22% by Rómulo O'Farrill (chairman of the board) and 20% by the Alemán family (Miguel Alemán Velasco was executive vice president) (*In re SICC,* 1986, para. 32).
17. An example specific to Spanish-language television is López et al. (1973) suggesting that "information about how to deal with the Anglo culture" could be offered through "brief spots, short programs and features with information on health, education, housing, employment information and advice for dealing with public agencies" (p. 78).
18. Along these lines, Riggins (1992) states, "far from being an unproblematic primordial given, ethnicity can be 'rediscovered' or 'reclaimed'" (p. 2).
19. This lack would persist for other ethnic-oriented media as well; two decades later Riggins (1992, p. 3) characterized ethnic minority media as "not well understood because the topic has been relatively neglected" and Cottle (2000, p. 23) concluded, "studies of ethnic minority audiences, remarkably, remain a rarity."
20. This was one of at least ten such marches in August 1970 to protest the Vietnam War and especially the perceived overrepresentation of Hispanics being drafted and killed. On August 29, an estimated 25,000 people marched from Belvedere Park to Laguna Park in East Los Angeles. (Laguna Park was renamed Ruben F. Salazar Park in September 1970.)
21. Faber et al. (1986, pp. 348–349) also cite a national telephone survey conducted by Gallup (1979), which also found that age, income and educational level were related to Hispanic adults' Spanish-language radio use. Majorities across three adult age groups said they regularly listened to Spanish-language radio on weekdays. Only teenagers from 12 to 17 years old preferred Anglo and Black radio formats to Spanish. As with the television studies, the Gallup survey found that preference for Spanish-language radio was inversely related to income and education.
22. Interestingly, in the SLO-TV study, violent television content was only identified as a concern among middle class Hispanic viewers—those in the upper and lower class strata expressed little or no apprehension (López et al., 1973, p. 75).
23. Stoloff (1982, pp. 44–45) summarizes the local advertisers who bought time on ethnic TV in Los Angeles: "small grocery stores that stock traditional foods from the homeland and restaurants serving special dishes. Local realtors, lawyers, car

salespeople, and dentists try to attract the newcomer to the United States to their bilingual services. Sponsors of these programs also advertise records, books, and other cultural items that are specific to linguistic groups."

24. Esparza had been indicted in 1968 on conspiracy charges for participating as one of "La Thirteen" who organized school walkouts among East Los Angeles high school students (Noriega, 1993).

25. As López et al., 1973 put it, "Thus, we can theorize that when the content pertains to the 'Anglo' or majority sections of our society, English language media is used. When it pertains to the Mexican American society, or Latin America, Spanish language media is used" (p. 54).

References

Aguirre, Adalberto Jr., & Bustamante, Diana A. (1993, January). Critical notes regarding the dislocation of Chicanos by the Spanish-language television industry in the United States. *Ethnic and Racial Studies, 16*(1), 121–132.

Almaguer, Tomás. (1974). Historical notes on Chicano oppression: The dialectics of racial and class domination in North America. *Aztlán, 5*(1), 27–56.

Antola, Livia, & Rogers, Everett M. (1984). Television flows in Latin America. *Communication Research, 11*(2), 183–202.

Balkan, D. Carlos. (1986, December). "Unorthodox and energetic": An interview with Rene Anselmo. *Hispanic Business,* 17–78.

Bilingual cable TV due in East L.A. [Calendar section] (1980, December 14). *Los Angeles Times,* 6.

Blauner, Robert. (1969, spring). Internal colonialism and ghetto revolt. *Social Problems, 16*(4), 393–408.

Chávez, Ernesto. (2002). *Mi raza primero! (My people first!): Nationalism, identity, and insurgency in the Chicano Movement in Los Angeles, 1966–1978.* Berkeley, CA: University of California Press.

Cohn, D'Vera. (2010, March 3). Census history: Counting Hispanics. *Pew Research Social & Demographic Trends.* Retrieved from http://www.pewsocialtrends. org/2010/03/03/census-history-counting-hispanics-2/.

Comstock, George. (1989). *The evolution of American television.* Newbury Park, CA: Sage.

Cooley, Hazel. (1955). Monopoly in TV: Stifling the UHF bands. *Nation, 180*(8), 159–161.

Cottle, Simon. (2000). Introduction: Media research and ethnic minorities: Mapping the field. In S. Cottle (Ed.), *Ethnic minorities and the media: Changing cultural boundaries* (pp. 1–30). Philadelphia: Open University Press.

Cox, Dorrit Sue. (1969). *Spanish-language television in the United States: Its audience and its potential* (Master's thesis). University of Illinois, Urbana, IL.

Crister, Greg. (1987, January). The feud that toppled a TV empire. *Channels: The Business of Communications,* 24–31.

Darkened channels: UHF television and the FCC. (1962, June). *Harvard Law Review, 75,* 1578–1607.

Dávila, Arlene. (2001). *Latinos, Inc.: The marketing and making of a people.* Berkeley, CA: University of California Press.

Davis, Cary, Haub, Carl, & Willette, JoAnne. (1983, June). U.S. Hispanics: Changing the face of America. *Population Bulletin, 38*(3), 1–43.

De Noriega, Luis Antonio, & Leach, Francis. (1979) *Broadcasting in Mexico*. Boston, MA: Routledge & Kegan.

De Uriarte, Mercedes. (1980, December 14). Battle for the ear of the Latino. *Los Angeles Times* (Calendar section), 1–7.

Delgado, Humberto, & Veraldi, Lorna. (2003, Fall). Spanish-language television: From bold experiment to American mainstream. *Television Quarterly, 34*(1), 30–34.

Faber, Ronald J., O'Guinn, Thomas C., & Meyer, Timothy P. (1986). Diversity in the ethnic media audience: A study of Spanish language broadcast preference in the U.S. *International Journal of Intercultural Relations, 10*(3), 347–359.

Fernández, Claudia, & Paxman, Andrew. (2000). *Emilio Azcarraga Milmo y su imperio Televisa*. México D.F.: Grijalbo.

Glenn, Armon. (1973, September 3). Minorities market: Ethnic broadcasters make an effective pitch. *Barron's, 53*(36), 3, 8.

Gratton, Brian, & Gutmann, Myron P. (2000, summer). Hispanics in the United States, 1850–1990. *Historical Methods, 33*(3), 137–153.

Gutiérrez, Félix F. (1976). *Spanish-language radio and Chicano internal colonialism* (Doctoral dissertation). Stanford University, Palo Alto, CA.

Gutiérrez, Félix, & Schement, Jorge Reina. (1979). *Spanish-language radio in the Southwestern United States*. Mexican American Monograph Series No. 5. Center for Mexican American Studies, University of Texas at Austin.

Habla Español? (1968, January 15). *Television Age, 24*, 62.

Holly, Davis. (1986, June 15). Eclectic TV: KSCI's programming in 14 languages offers news, entertainment, comfort to ethnic communities. *Los Angeles Times*. Retrieved from http://articles.latimes.com/1986–06–15/local/me-11321_1_community-news.

Hutnik, Nimmi. (1991). *Ethnic minority identity: A social psychological perspective*. New York, NY: Clarendon Press/Oxford University Press.

In re Spanish International Communications Corporation. (1986, January 3). Federal Communications Commission (Release No. 86D-1). slip op.

Jarboe, Jan. (1980, November). The special case of Spanish-language television. *Washington Journalism Review*, 21–25.

Johnson, Melissa A. (2000). How ethnic are U.S. ethnic media: The case of Latina magazines. *Mass Communication & Society, 3*(2–3), 229–248.

Johnson, Melissa A. (2010). Incorporating self-categorization concepts into ethnic media research. *Communication Theory, 20*(1), 106–125.

KDTV-DT. (n.d.). In *Wikipedia*. Retrieved from http://en.wikipedia.org/wiki/KDTV-DT.

KTBN-TV. (n.d.). In *Wikipedia*. Retrieved from http://en.wikipedia.org/wiki/KTBN-TV.

KTVW-DT. (n.d.). In *Wikipedia*. Retrieved from http://en.wikipedia.org/wiki/KTVW-DT.

KWHY-TV (n.d.) In *Wikipedia*. Retrieved from http://en.wikipedia.org/wiki/KWHY-TV.

Lane, James Alfred. (1966). *A descriptive study of Spanish-language television station KMEX and the Spanish-speaking audience of Los Angeles* (Master's thesis). University of California Los Angeles, Los Angeles, CA.

López, Robert J. (2011, February 19). No evidence Ruben Salazar was targeted in killing, report says. *Los Angeles Times*. Retrieved from http://articles.latimes.com/2011/feb/19/local/la-me-ruben-salazar-20110220.

López, Ronald W., Enos, Darryl D., Nichols, Lee, LaRosa, Frank, Mellema, Joel, & McGrew, Don. (1973). *The role and functions of Spanish-language-only television in Los Angeles*. Claremont, CA: Center for Urban and Regional Studies, Claremont Graduate School.

López, Ronald W., & Enos, Darryl D. (1974). Spanish-language-only television in Los Angeles County. *Aztlán, 4*(2), 283–313.

Matsaganis, Matthew D., Katz, Vikki S., & Ball-Rokeach, Sandra J. (2011). *Understanding ethnic media.* Thousand Oaks, CA: Sage.

Mejía Barquera, Fernando. (1989). *La industria de la radio y la televisión y la política del estado mexicano: Volumen I (1920–1960).* México D.F.: Fundación Manuel Buendía.

Miller, Sally M. (1987). Introduction. In S. M. Miller (Ed.), *The ethnic press in the United States: A historical analysis and handbook* (pp. xi–xxii). Westport, CT: Greenwood.

Mora, G. Cristina. (2014). *Making Hispanics: How activists, bureaucrats and media constructed a new American.* Chicago, IL: University of Chicago Press.

Noriega, Chan A. (1993). *Cine Chicano: Between a weapon and a formula: Chicano cinema and its contexts.* In C. A. Noriega (Ed.), *Chicanos and film: representation and resistance* (pp. 141–167). Minneapolis: University of Minnesota Press.

Noriega, Chon A. (2000). *Shot in America: Television, the state, and the rise of Chicano cinema.* Minneapolis, MN: University of Minnesota Press.

Passel, Jeffrey S., & Cohn, D'Vera. (2008, February 11). *U.S. population projections 2005–2050.* Retrieved from: http://www.pewhispanic.org/files/reports/85.pdf.

Paxman, Andrew (2004, December). *An ethnic media success story: The early years of Spanish-language radio, 1924–1970.* Unpublished manuscript, Department of History, University of Texas at Austin, Austin, Texas.

Paxman, Andrew. (2008). *William Jenkins, business elites, and the evolution of the Mexican state: 1910–1960* (Doctoral dissertation). University of Texas at Austin, Austin, TX.

Portales, Diego. (1987). *La dificultad de innovar: Un estudio sobre las empresas de televisión en América Latina.* Santiago, Chile: ILET.

Raoul A. Cortez. (n.d.). Retrieved from Spanish International Network Television website: http://sintv.org/sintv/biography3.html.

Rieman, Arthur M. (1985). Foreign ownership and control of U.S. broadcast entities: In Re Spanish International Communications Corp. *UCLA Pacific Basin Law Journal 4*(1–2), 244–252.

Riggins, Stephen H. (Ed.). (1992). *Ethnic minority media: An international perspective.* Newbury Park, CA: Sage.

Rodríguez, América. (1999a). Creating an audience and remapping a nation: A brief history of US Spanish language broadcasting 1930–1980. *Quarterly Review of Film & Video, 16*(3–4), 357–374.

Rodríguez, América. (1999b). *Making Latino news: Race, language, class.* Thousand Oaks, CA: Sage.

Rodríguez, Marc Simon. (2014). *Rethinking the Chicano Movement.* New York: Routledge.

Rojas, Viviana, & Piñón, Juan. (2014). Spanish, English or Spanglish? Media strategies and corporate struggles to reach the second and later generations of Latinos. *International Journal of Hispanic Media, 7.* Retrieved from http://www.internationalhispanicmedia.org.

Ryan, Susan. (1983). Film across the border: The interaction of the Mexican and American motion picture industries. *Critical Arts, 2*(4), 55–65.

Sinclair, John. (1986). Dependent development and broadcasting: 'The Mexican formula.' *Media, Culture and Society, 8*(1), 81–101.

Spanish stations protest ratings. (1966, March 5). *Los Angeles Times*, B3.

Spanish-voiced TV gains status. (1966, October 17). *Sponsor*, 43.

Stoloff, David L. (1982). *Ethnic television in Los Angeles* (Doctoral dissertation). University of California Los Angeles, Los Angeles, CA.

Subervi-Vélez, Federico A. (1986). The mass media and ethnic assimilation and pluralism: A review and research proposal with special focus on Hispanics. *Communication Research, 13*(1), 71–96.

Swarns, Rachel L. (2004, October 24). Hispanics resist racial grouping by census. *New York Times*. Retrieved from http://www.nytimes.com/2004/10/24/national/24census.html.

Turow, Joseph. (2007). *Breaking up America: Advertisers and the new media world.* Chicago: University of Chicago Press.

Valenzuela, Nicolas. (1973). *Media habits and attitudes of Mexican Americans: Surveys in Austin and San Antonio.* Center for Communication Research, School of Communication, University of Texas at Austin.

Valenzuela, Nicolas A. (1985). *Organizational evolution of a Spanish-language television network: An environmental approach* (Doctoral dissertation). Stanford University, Palo Alto, CA.

Valle, Victor (1986, October 29). KSCI to cancel its Spanish programming. *Los Angeles Times*, 1.

Viswanath, K., & Arora, Pamela. (2000). Ethnic media in the United States: An essay on their role in integration, assimilation and social control. *Mass Communication & Society, 3*(1), 39–56.

Warshauer, Mary Ellen. (1966). Foreign language broadcasting. In J. A. Fishman (Ed.), *Language loyalty in the United States* (pp. 75–91). London: Mouton & Co.

WLTV-DT. (n.d.). In Wikipedia. Retrieved from http://en.wikipedia.org/wiki/WLTV-DT.

3 Technology, Broadcast Policy and Consolidation in the Satellite Age

The 1970s was an important decade of maturation for the fledgling Spanish-language television industry in the United States. Spanish International Communications Corp. (SICC) acquired additional conventional broadcast stations and, importantly, began reaching new audiences through low power and satellite repeater stations. During the '70s many SICC stations became self-supporting; although most of the profits were invested back in the company (Besas, 1984), some were sent to Mexico to pay down debts. Spanish International Network (SIN) expanded its program distribution and advertising sales capacity, while enjoying more success at convincing advertisers of the Hispanic market's viability. Local markets and independent stations also matured during the decade. This chapter offers profiles of two stations serving New York during the 1970s to illustrate challenges they faced in becoming profitable enterprises with greater standing among Spanish-speaking communities, as well as the television market at large.

The 1970 U.S. Census

The 1970 census counted 9.6 million Hispanics in the U.S., accounting for 4.7% of the total population. The figure was later scaled back to 9.1 million (Davis, Haub, & Willette, 1983). It was the first census to employ a mail-out, mail-back data collection system; enumerators were only used to collect information from households that did not respond by mail (U.S. Census Bureau, n.d.). Rodríguez (2000, p. 85) identifies a significant shift in how this census ascertained race:

> By 1970, the census appears to have begun departing from what it admitted was a very unscientific, contextually dependent and opinion-based approach and shifted to a self-classification of race. Although the census forms as a whole were still administered by census takers, the 1970 census noted that information on race was "obtained primarily through self-enumeration" and that respondents self-classified themselves "according to the race with which they identify themselves."[1]

Thus, unlike its predecessors, the 1970 census relied on respondents to self-identify their ethnic affiliation (Siegel & Passel, 1979). It was also the first census to tally Hispanics as a unified group and to include a separate question regarding national origin or descent.

The decision to include a question about origin/descent was made late in the census planning process, which likely contributed to problems with the data. The question, only distributed to a 5% sample of the population, inquired about household members' origin or descent among these options: Mexican, Puerto Rican, Cuban, Central or South American, Other Spanish, and None of These. Analysts detected a severe overcount in the Central or Southern American category, which reported 1,508,886 persons compared to only 556,000 identified in a Current Population Report published in 1969 (Hutchison, 1984). The Census Bureau explained that some respondents, including non-Hispanics, interpreted the question as referring to someone born in southern and central states in the U.S. rather than countries of origin located in those regions of Latin America. In follow-up checks of "Spanish origin" data, the Bureau determined that less than 75% of the Central or Southern American data was accurate, whereas more than 90% of responses regarding specific nations of origin—Mexican, Puerto Rican and Cuban—*was* accurate (Hutchison, 1984). Not surprisingly, Hispanic political organizations contested the 1970 census findings, arguing in a class-action suit that mailed questionnaires should be replaced with face-to-face interviews conducted by Spanish-speaking Hispanic interviewers. The case was never heard in court, but prompted changes to the 1980 census that listed options for Not Spanish/Hispanic, Mexican/Mexican-American/Chicano, Puerto Rican, Cuban and Other Spanish/Hispanic (Rodríguez, 2000); Central or Southern American origin was eliminated as a category. One example of the changes' impact was that the 1970 census classified 93.3% of Hispanics as White—the figure dropped to 57.7% in 1980 (Rodríguez, 2000, p. 135).

Problems with the 1970 census and the categorization shift not only challenged comparisons with 1980 data, but with figures from prior and subsequent censuses as well. Rodríguez (2000, p. 102) explains how changing classification categories aggravated the problem during the mid-20th century, "... between 1940 and 1970, Hispanics were counted according to three different cultural criteria, linguistic (1940), surname (1950 and 1960) and origin (1970)." For their part, Siegel and Passel (1979, p. 1) emphasize how "the lack of a consistent and definitive identifier for the Hispanic population" threatened the Census Bureau's credibility. The authors also point out that 1970 was first year the bureau attempted to account for undocumented immigration—it has been a thorny methodological, economic and political challenge ever since.

Of course immigration, whether documented or otherwise, has an important influence over non-English media in the United States. A 1975 study conducted by the Census Bureau found that 4.3 million U.S. residents identified Spanish as a second language, while 4 million people reported Spanish as their primary language. Between one and one-and-a-half million house-holds indicated Spanish as the primary language spoken, encompassing about 4.8 million people age four and over; many of these households spoke English as well (U.S. Bureau of the Census, 1976). As the number of Spanish speakers increased during the 1970s, so did Spanish International Network's reach through the company's adroit management of communication sat-ellites and lower-cost distribution technologies. The leadership sometimes counteracted industry trends and assumptions, or used technology in uncon-ventional ways, to expand SIN's reach among U.S. Hispanic households.

Distribution by Satellite

Spanish International Network asserted its entrepreneurial spirit in 1976 by initiating nationwide satellite distribution of its programming, the first commercial network to do so regularly (SIN television, 1984). The network's leadership demonstrated its perseverance—and the centrality of satellite communications to its future success—through persistent efforts to change U.S. telecommunications policy to its favor. SIN's first direct broad-cast via satellite transmitted the popular Mexican variety show, *Siempre en Domingo*,[2] coast to coast on July 4, 1976 (Lenti, 1984). (What better way to celebrate the bicentennial of U.S. independence?) A receiving-and-transmitting ground station in San Antonio[3] became the central node in the original network, and, the network claimed, the first such equipment to be owned and operated by a commercial TV network (SIN television, 1984). This was the U.S. segment of a broader initiative by Mexico's Televisa to link the Spanish-speaking world by satellite—the venture was called Univision, the name that would be assigned to the Spanish International companies in 1986 (Televisa's Univision, 1977). In December 1976, SIN signed a six-year contract with RCA to carry 3,000 hours of content annually on its Satcom II satellite; within three years the network was exceeding that amount, averag-ing 64 hours per week (Besas, 1984).

   In addition to enabling simulcasts of live shows and sporting events from Mexico and other areas, the new technology fostered development of the first domestically produced national Spanish-language newscast in the U.S., *Noticiero SIN*, and facilitated programming distribution among affiliate stations. By late 1978, stations in ten U.S. cities were linked by satellite, sharing both recorded content and live connections (SIN television, 1984); by 1980 the number of interconnected stations had grown to 56 (Anselmo, 1980). The economic benefits of satellite communication were clear, and they increased over time. SIN's president, Rene Anselmo (1980) explained, "[with] the price that used to get us no more than 175 miles of hookup over land lines, we can get an hour of nationwide satellite time, including cover-age in Puerto Rico and Alaska."

   This capability not only helped consolidate the Spanish International Network, but also reinforced its already dominant position in the industry, buttressing the challenge to potential competitors, be they independent stations or rival networks. The context in which SIN distinguished itself as a pioneering television network is significant: the U.S. was the world's largest satellite market, with television content comprising nearly half of all traffic. Because the U.S. enjoyed competitive advantages in satellites, computing and other communications infrastructure, benefits accrued during the information revolution from the 1980s on (Locksley, 1983). As we will see below and in subsequent chapters, satellite initiatives started by SIN in the 1970s influenced the development and launch of the world's first privately owned global satellite system, PanAmSat, as well as direct-to-home broadcasting, an important distribution medium in the Spanish-speaking world.

Legal Initiatives: Carrier-of-the-Week

Spanish International Communications Corp. was among the petitioners who, in 1978, successfully challenged the established "carrier-of-the-week" system whereby television programs were transmitted between the U.S. and other nations. Under the system, four heavyweights in the communications industry—Western Union International, RCA Global Communications, ITT Worldcom and AT&T—had taken turns carrying TV signals transmitted from overseas by the Communications Satellite Corporation (Comsat), which operated as the U.S. signatory to Intelsat, the sprawling purveyor of international satellite communications. Comsat customers such as SIN had to determine which company's turn it was for a given week, and negotiate with the designated carrier-of-the-week in order to receive their signal from a Comsat earth station. In petitioning to abolish this and other middleman services, SIN was joined by businesses and organizations having international communication interests, including the three major English-language TV networks and the U.S. Departments of Justice and Defense. The rule change allowed international signal recipients to link directly with Comsat, thereby eliminating a cumbersome and costly intermediary service.

Legal Initiatives: Satellite Deregulation

Another key legal victory was not officially won until 1984, but the groundwork started in the 1970s. Emilio Azcárraga Milmo sought a proprietary satellite system for Televisa not only for television program distribution, but other telecommunication services as well.[4] At the time, communication satellites were the domain of national governments and the aforementioned intergovernmental consortium, Intelsat, which held a monopoly over international satellite communication in the non-Soviet world. Azcárraga and other like-minded entrepreneurs faced stiff resistance from entrenched interests. As regulatory winds began to shift toward deregulation, and as satellite technology advanced in the late 1970s and early '80s, Azcárraga, along with Rene Anselmo and others, began planning a regional private satellite service that would grow to become a global endeavor. The Pan American Satellite Corporation (PanAmSat) began promoting itself in 1983 and the following year formally requested permission from the Federal Communications Commission (FCC) to construct, launch and operate a privately held regional satellite system. To protect their interests, Comsat and Intelsat petitioned the FCC to deny the request—significant legal wrangling ensued. President Ronald Reagan settled the matter through Presidential Decree No. 85–2 issued on November 28, 1984, which permitted the construction and operation of three international satellite systems to serve the national interest (without causing significant financial harm to Intelsat). PanAmSat was one of the three systems.

It was unusual, if not unprecedented, for an ethnic-oriented media company to aggressively and successfully advocate macro-level regulatory changes in order to advance its expansion goals. Central credit goes to Emilio Azcárraga Milmo, who was building the foundation for a transnational Spanish-language media empire, and Rene Anselmo, who doggedly pursued his objectives for U.S. Spanish-language television and satellite communication alike. Danny Villanueva, another pioneering Spanish-language television executive, described Anselmo as a "bold innovator who embraced new technology with unbridled enthusiasm" (Balkan, 1986, p. 19).[5]

Satellite Repeaters and Translators

Communication satellites not only lowered the cost and increased the efficiency of distributing television signals to conventional broadcast stations and cable headends, but also enabled signal distribution to urban ethnic enclaves, smaller cities and less densely populated rural areas. Satellite signals were not received directly into viewers' homes at this time—they required frequency conversion, amplification and retransmission via specialized ground equipment. Recall from the prior chapter that Spanish International Communications Corp. developed its station group by acquiring or building facilities that transmitted on the Ultra High Frequency (UHF) band because such stations were in low demand by investors, and therefore relatively inexpensive. UHF signals also had a shorter reach and poorer picture quality than the more desirable, and expensive, Very High Frequency (VHF) stations. Although average signal reach for UHF was only 32 miles versus 57 miles for VHF at 100 kilowatts of effective radiated power (Lapin, 1962), two related terrestrial technologies could be deployed to extend the reach of broadcast signals.

Repeaters use the same frequency as the station providing their signal, but transmit in a different geographical area. Translators also retransmit content from a distant source, but on a different frequency, usually to avoid interference[6] (Banks & Titus, 1990). Through the 1970s, the FCC restricted translators' transmitting power to one kilowatt, limiting their reach (Guernica, 1982, p. 143). Reasons for employing these technologies included human geography, like the distribution of target populations as discussed above, and/or physical geography such as hills and valleys or mountain ranges. Translators began appearing quite early in television's history, in the 1940s, and by the mid-1950s, more than 1000 operated, mostly in rural areas (Hilliard & Keith, 1999). As the cost of satellite communication steadily decreased from the 1970s on, so too did the cost of distributing signals to translators. This technology helped Spanish International Network reach the 100 affiliate mark in June 1981 (Guernica, 1982; SIN television, 1984).

Low-Power Television

Like repeaters and translators, low-power television was created to deliver television signals to areas that were underserved or not served at all by full power television broadcasting and cable television (Banks & Titus, 1990). An important distinction among the outlets is that translators are only authorized to change the frequency and amplitude of the parent signal, whereas low-power stations may also transmit original content or offer subscription services. Low-power stations were originally authorized to operate at 10 watts or 100 watts peak output on the VHF band, and 1000 watts peak output for UHF, representing a transmission radius of approximately 15 to 25 miles (Banks & Titus, 1990). Because they are assigned to the same channels on the VHF and UHF broadcasting spectrum as their full-power counterparts, low-power broadcasters must follow strict noninterference regulations (Hilliard & Keith, 1999). Their secondary status requires low-power stations to reduce broadcasting power or even cease transmitting if interference occurs with a primary user on the same frequency or an adjacent frequency (Hilliard & Keith, 1999). Early in low-power TV's development the FCC paid it very little attention unless prompted to do so through pressure from a broadcasting trade association or lobby group such as the National Association of Broadcasters.

During the 1960s low power technology became increasingly popular, especially in areas like the southwestern United States where natural barriers such as mountains and deserts interfered with the reception and transmission of full-power signals (Banks & Titus, 1990). This geographic focus was especially pertinent to Spanish-language television given the concentration of Spanish speakers in the region. In the late 1970s and into the 1980s, the technology was applied more regularly in urban and suburban settings as advertisers recognized the value of reaching niche audiences, and could do so more cost effectively with low power outlets compared to full-power television (Hilliard & Keith, 1999).

In addition to the geographic and economic advantages of low-power television, there were political advantages as well. The social and political upheavals of the Civil Rights Movement and the racial, ethnic and gender "power" movements of the 1960s and '70s applied pressure on state and federal governments to dedicate additional resources and open more broadcasting opportunities for women and communities of color. The FCC considered low-power television an opportune means of encouraging greater minority ownership and participation in television (Biel, 1985). Thus, federal guidelines for allocating low-power licenses were guided by these objectives: "1) to bring local origination in the form of news and community broadcasting to underserved areas of the community; 2) to extend minority ownership and operation within broadcasting; and 3) to provide greater ownership and access for local community groups" (Atkin, 1987, p. 361).

As we will see in greater detail in the next chapter, some independent broadcasters sought to challenge Spanish International Network's virtual monopoly of Spanish-language television, offering alternatives to the preponderant imported programming, especially from Mexico. Low-power television might have offered a substantial foothold under two conditions: had Spanish International's leadership been *less* keenly aware of advantages offered by low-cost technologies like low-power television, and had the FCC been *more* keenly aware of Spanish International's virtual monopoly control before the mid-1980s. In 1979 the FCC granted Spanish International Communications Corp. licenses to operate 1000-watt UHF translator stations in Hartford, CN; Austin, TX; Bakersfield, CA; Philadelphia, PA; and Denver, CO.[7] Most low-power outlets transmitting SIN programming were independently owned affiliates (FCC 45 RR 2d. 1303 [1979]). This presence of SIN programming in minor markets likely discouraged small independents from entering Spanish-language television on the local level: although an independent broadcaster might be able to undercut SIN's advertising rates, the overhead costs would be much higher than Spanish International's.

SIN was already well established in low-power TV by the early 1980s when public demand led to rapid increases in station numbers. In 1982 the FCC created a new category, LPTV, which abolished prior restrictions limiting station-produced content to 30 seconds per day (Atkin, 1987); stations were permitted to air as much original content as they wished. The heavy demand for LPTV licenses—the Commission received around 8,000 applications—led to a five-year freeze followed by assignment through a lottery system in which minority applicants were given two-to-one preference over non-minorities (Banks & Titus, 1990). By 1985, 35% of LPTV construction permit applications had been submitted by minority individuals or minority-controlled companies (Biel, 1985, p. 55). However, the results of an LPTV survey published in 1990 revealed limited progress toward the ownership diversity objective, as only 8.3% of participating stations were minority owned, although minority ownership was fairly evenly distributed among women, Black, Hispanic and Asian owners (Banks & Titus, 1990, p. 19).[8] Nearly 37% of stations participating in the survey reported serving specific demographic populations, with this basic distribution: 40% specifying audiences differentiated by age, 25% targeting Hispanic or Black populations, 25% reaching religious audiences, and 5% identifying audiences engaged in agriculture (Banks & Titus, 1990, p. 21).

In the 1990s, advertisers with particular interests in reaching ethnic audiences—airlines and long-distance telephone providers, for example—purchased ample commercial time on LPTV; AT&T claimed to advertise in 20 different languages through the technology (Cooper, 1993). A key attraction for advertisers was LPTV's efficiency in reaching niche cultural and linguistic audiences, especially in areas of high population density for a particular group. Chicago's WFTB broadcast in 14 languages, including Spanish, reaching an estimated 6.4 million viewers in a market of 8 million (Cooper, 1993). Low-power television continued to reach ethnic audiences through the end of the century, although the conversion from analog to digital broadcasting during the 2000s threatened to reduce audience sizes.

As for the fledgling Spanish-language sector, low-power television played an important role in expanding the number of households reached, and establishing a presence in local markets that would grow to support full-power television. By the mid-1980s, LPTV was delivering SIN programming to more than 500,000 Hispanic households located outside its major urban markets, and by late 1991 Univision had 15 LPTV affiliates, and previous low-power stations, like those in Austin and Denver had been upgraded to full-power (Kesler, 1986; Subervi-Vélez, Ramírez Berg, Constantakis-Valdés, Noriega, Ríos, & Wilkinson, 1994). Despite these numbers, there is a surprising dearth of discussion in key studies of low-power television about Spanish International's early role in utilizing the technology.[9] This oversight serves as a reminder of most researchers' keener interest in mainstream audiences and skirmishes among English-language players than the entrepreneurial actions of a company that astutely patched together a national-level niche industry.

A closing quote for this section underscores several interrelated technologies' importance to Spanish International's development. In response to a journalist's question about when he began to see the possibilities of building a network, Rene Anselmo replied,

> I guess what really created the impact of the network in a big way was the launching of the first domestic satellite. That of course, gave us the opportunity to interconnect on a nationwide basis, and to hook up low-power stations, translators, and do everything else that only the other networks could afford when you had to use the AT&T coaxial circuits.
>
> (Balkan, 1986, p. 20)

Cable Television

Cable television is another distribution technology that Spanish International Network used effectively. SIN developed two forms of cable: a basic service that transmitted content that was being broadcast over the air, and a premium service named Galavisión that premiered in 1979 and is most succinctly described as Home Box Office in Spanish. Rene Anselmo (1980) explained that the idea to develop cable distribution came to him as he was flying into Nogales, Arizona, which, because predominantly served by cable, had few television broadcast antennas protruding from rooftops. In such markets, paying the cable operator to carry SIN content made better business sense than spending $100,000 to install a broadcast repeater station. The tactic of paying cable operators 10 cents for each Spanish-surnamed subscriber on their roll was Anselmo's idea (Valenzuela, 1985); he was well acquainted with client skepticism from his experiences trying to sell Spanish-language programs to English-language station managers, and convincing mainstream advertisers of the Spanish market's viability. A strong perception existed among some cable system operators that "low income" Hispanics would not pay a monthly fee for television, whether basic or premium service (Beerman, 1984). Yet within three years of establishing the service, SIN programming was available on more than 200 cable systems (Valenzuela, 1985, p. 109).

Cable television grew precipitously across the U.S. during the period under scrutiny here, expanding from 1700 systems and 2.1 million households in 1967 to 5600 systems reaching 28.3 million homes in 1983 (Smith, Wright, & Ostroff, 1998, p. 125).[10] Although specific numbers of Spanish-speaking cable households are difficult to come by, Spanish International claimed that more than 100 cable systems carried its programming by the end of 1980, and the figure had doubled a year later (Valenzuela, 1985, p. 164). In 1979, before launching its initiative, SIN conducted a study of cable systems in five southwestern states, New York and Florida, finding that over half-a-million Hispanic households already subscribed to cable. At the time, a number of major cities like Boston, Philadelphia, Miami, San Antonio and Houston had low, if any, cable penetration (What is Galavisión, 1980). As a result, the reach of SIN and Galavisión would expand in step with new cable services introduced in urban, suburban and rural areas. Two technological advances propelled the growth of cable systems: a transition from vacuum tubes to solid state circuits increased the channel capacity of coaxial cables, and a single amplifier could boost a dozen channels' signals, thereby enabling broadband communications (Smith et al., 1998).

Like HBO, Galavisión offered subscribers unedited, uninterrupted films, premium sporting events and children's content; unlike HBO, it also presented the Latin American television staple, *telenovelas*. In a pattern already familiar to SIN viewers, about 90% of the 400 films Galavisión had under contract in 1980 were of Mexican origin (Mendoza, 1980). The network's feature film repeat patterns differed from HBO's and Showtime's because most contracts were for longer periods—up to five years—and not dictated by Hollywood (Beerman, 1984). Early on, Galavisión transmitted eight hours of content on weeknights (7:00 p.m. to 3:00 a.m. Eastern), 13 hours on Saturdays and 14 on Sundays (What is Galavisión, 1980; Mendoza,

1980). Subscription fees varied between seven and eleven dollars per month, in addition to basic cable fees (What is Galavisión, 1980).

Galavisión was owned 75% by Televisa and 25% by Rene Anselmo. Its corporate offices were in New York, while the satellite operations were based in Los Angeles—recall that Spanish International began satellite distribution of programs in 1976 and affiliated stations were interconnected shortly thereafter (Mendoza, 1980). In 1981 SIN created a cable television division and opened a regional office for Galavisión in Dallas (SIN expands, 1981). In August 1980, nine months after launching, Galavisión reached only 15,000 subscribers—a year later it claimed 60,000 and was operating in Puerto Rico, New York, San Antonio, El Paso, Corpus Christi and Hialeah (FL), among other cities (Mendoza, 1980; Hispanic TV, 1981; Besas, 1984). Sylvia Lyons, Galavisión's director of programming, noted the difficulty in getting some cable systems to carry the premium channel: "the stereotype still prevails that Hispanics can't afford the service," she explained (Mendoza, 1980, p. 16). We should bear in mind that Galavisión launched just prior to the so-called "Decade of the Hispanic" when increased press coverage of the Hispanic population would begin to challenge some long-held beliefs about the group. It was also a decade during which the number of affluent U.S. Hispanics grew steadily (O'Hare, 1990). Galavisión would operate as a premium cable channel until 1988 when its majority Mexican owners, having been forced to sell their holdings in the Spanish International stations, converted it to basic service as part of a new business plan, still under the GalaVision name.[11]

Spanish-Language Television in New York in the 1970s

This section focuses on two stations in the New York market, providing insight into growing pains experienced by Spanish-language television during the late 1960s and through the '70s when the industry was maturing, but not yet profitable. New York offers an instructive example because a Spanish International owned and operated station, WXTV, competed with an independent station, WNJU, to reach an audience of 2.3 million Hispanics,[12] over 56% of them of Puerto Rican origin (Strategy Research Corp., 1980). The city's importance as the nation's largest Hispanic television market and the headquarters location for many large advertising firms enhanced New York's significance. I was able to gain a close perspective on the stations' ambitions and constraints through access to select station files located in FCC archives and the National Archives in Washington, D.C.[13]

WNJU

Spanish-language television entered the New York market during an important expansion period as Puerto Ricans grew from 7.9% of New York City's population in 1960 to 12.2% in 1969, and New Jersey's Spanish-speaking population grew an estimated 33% per year (Screen Gems Broadcasting, 1969). WNJU began broadcasting on UHF Channel 47 on May 16, 1965, from Linden, New Jersey. What started as a multiethnic station catering to Spanish-speaking, Italian-speaking, Black and Jewish populations quickly evolved into a predominantly Spanish broadcaster (Cox, 1969). In a letter to the FCC in August 1967, Edwin Cooperstein, president of New Jersey Television Broadcasting Corp., WNJU's owner, explained that the station's "greatest area of service, recognition and potential advertising revenue [was] this dynamic ethnic market of over one and a half million Spanish-speaking residents" (Cooperstein, 1967). He went on to explain that the UHF station could not effectively compete for New Jersey's English-speaking audiences,[14] and thereafter would only broadcast in English on Saturday nights, and in Italian on Sunday afternoons. Documents that WNJU submitted to the FCC during a 1969 license renewal procedure confirm that in October 1968 the station broadcasted exclusively in Spanish during the week, in English for three hours on Saturday evening before switching to Spanish at 8:00, and in Italian from 3:30 until 7:00 p.m. at which time Spanish-language programming began. The broadcast day was limited, averaging 6 hours, 7 minutes on weekdays, and 7 hours, 52 minutes on Saturday and Sunday (New Jersey Television, Exhibit E, 1969). News and public affairs programs that WNJU cited to affirm its serving the "public interest, convenience and necessity"[15] discussed a 1968 school crisis in New York, drug abuse and its prevention, artists of Puerto Rican origin, veterans' affairs, improving relations with the area's Dominican community, consumer protection, and business development (New Jersey Television, Exhibit G, 1969). The station claimed to earn $2 million in revenues during 1967, but nonetheless operated at a loss, prompting Mr. Cooperstein's resignation in early 1969 (Cox, 1969, p. 32). In December 1970, when New Jersey Television Broadcasting Corp. sold WNJU to Columbia Pictures, the station was reaching approximately 250,000 Spanish-speaking homes, up from around 50,000 when it launched five years earlier (Cox, 1969).[16]

WNJU's new owners had a similar vision as SIN's proprietors, but with a different ethnic focus. Because Columbia Pictures owned WAPA, the top station in San Juan, Puerto Rico, programs created at WAPA could be rebroadcast in New York, enabling advertisers to reach both population centers as well as audience members who bounced between the two cities (Gupta, 1983). (This dynamic is reminiscent of the geographic proximity and population mobility factors stressed in Chapter One.) WNJU's Puerto Rican/Caribbean focus offered competitive advantages over WXTV, the Spanish International Network affiliate that broadcast large amounts of Mexican programming in a region where people of Mexican origin comprised less than 5% of the Hispanic population at the time (Guernica, 1982). The Cuban American population, constituting nearly 20% of the New York area's Spanish speakers, was also likely to prefer Caribbean-origin programs over Mexican ones (Screen Gems Broadcasting, 1969). Under Columbia Pictures management,

WNJU continued to offer non-Spanish programming—Italian and Greek—and continued to lose money. In a 1972 filing with the FCC, station management described upgrading its transmitter on the Empire State Building and building a translator facility to improve signal reception in New York City's Spanish-speaking neighborhoods; it also requested permission to increase advertising rates to offset the costs (Screen Gems Stations, 1972).

In a scenario that would be repeated by Hallmark Cards Corp. in the early 1990s, Columbia Pictures became disenchanted with its investment and sought a buyer for WNJU. In May 1977, Oak Broadcasting Systems negotiated an option to obtain the station for $5 million, with Columbia Pictures retaining 20% stock in the new enterprise. The option was exercised in July 1979, and following FCC approval, WNJU was transferred to Oak Broadcasting, Tandem Productions (founded by television the successful television director Bud Yorkin and writer Norman Lear), Chartwell Communications Group and A. Jerrold Perenchio in February 1980 (Gupta, 1983). The key player on the buyer side was Jerrold Perenchio, a television producer and investor who would influence the Spanish-language television industry for 25 years, first as an owner of the two independent Spanish-language stations with the largest audiences—WNJU and KBSC in Los Angeles—and later as the principal owner of Univision from 1992 to 2006 (Hispanic TV, 1981; Grover, Grow & Smith, 2004). The new owners received permission to operate WNJU as a subscription television service[17] during primetime—as KBSC also operated for a time—but apparently never acted on the plan in New York. By 1982 WNJU generated nearly $10 million in advertising revenue, resulting in a profit of over $500,000 (Gupta, 1983).

WXTV

Spanish International Television Corp. built station WXTV, which began broadcasting to the New York market on UHF Channel 41 on August 4, 1968. The project got off to a spirited start as Spanish International competed with two other applicants for the station construction permit in Paterson, New Jersey.[18] In a later interview, Rene Anselmo estimated it cost around $2 million to get the station on the air, and 14 years passed before it became profitable (Balkan, 1986, p. 20). Thus, WXTV turned lucrative at about the same time WNJU did. Like its competitor, WXTV broadcast for limited hours and in multiple languages as it sought a competitive foothold. In 1970 it converted to a Spanish-only format and became an affiliate of Spanish International Network. The station's physical location in Paterson and its transmitter location were both at issue during the 1970s.

As planning began in earnest for construction of the World Trade Center twin towers in the late 1960s, New York television stations expressed concern about how the huge structures would impact their signal distribution, as well as eagerness to transmit from atop the north tower. Rene Anselmo submitted data to the FCC indicating that the buildings interfered with

WXTV's transmitter located on the Empire State Building, then applied the same determination he displayed in his crusade to ease satellite regulation to fight the New York Port Authority over access to the World Trade Center communications tower. In 1971 the Port Authority requested an FCC hearing regarding the television transmitters—WXTV was the only station at the time formally claiming interference. Two years later, in October 1973, Anselmo threatened legal action against the Port Authority, which had questioned the need to move transmitters from the Empire State Building to the World Trade Center because signal interference was less severe than anticipated. WXTV and other stations contended that signal distribution to areas of Staten Island, Manhattan, Westchester County and Connecticut had been negatively impacted. In April 1974, the FCC approved the installation of transmitters for two UHF stations, WXTV and WNYC, on the World Trade Center.[19] WXTV's primary transmitter either never moved, or was returned to the Empire State Building (TV at the Empire, 2009). At the time of the September 11, 2001 terrorist attacks, WXTV's primary transmitter was on the Empire State Building and its backup on the World Trade Center. Consequently, it was one of two New York stations[20] whose broadcasting was not interrupted (Hudson, 2001); WXTV incorporated news reports in English to help address a television signal deficit in the region caused by the towers' collapse.

Documents from WXTV station files at the FCC recount efforts to relocate the station from Paterson, New Jersey, closer to New York City, located 17 miles away in a chronically heavy traffic zone and requiring passage through a tunnel under the Hudson River.[21] Included in license renewal documentation from 1978 were descriptions of the difficulties in conducting business between Paterson and New York City (WXTV-TV, 1978). Station personnel were clearly advocating for permission to relocate their station as they made these arguments from a business standpoint:

- Only 0.14% of the region's Spanish speakers (~21,000 people) lived in Paterson whereas 73.3% (~1,488,000) lived in New York City.
- The distance between the station and local advertisers as well as the headquarters of major advertising firms that manage national advertising accounts was problematic. (Management could not recall ever having aired advertising for a Paterson business; in 1977 accounts from New Jersey only accounted for 2.8% of the station's gross revenues.)
- "Having its production facilities so far removed from its clients causes a particular hardship for a Spanish television station like WXTV. Unlike English language television stations, WXTV must produce almost all of the commercials they run. It is not something the station does as a matter of choice. Very few advertisers have a Spanish language television commercial" (WXTV license renewal, 1978, pt. 6, p. 2).
- It was difficult to attract acting talent from New York City to the studios; talent was often reluctant to make the journey.

Arguments made from a technical standpoint included:

- An unreliable two-hop microwave link and several miles of coaxial cable existed in the connection between the New Jersey studios and the transmitter in New York (a location closer to the city could make it a one-hop connection with no coaxial transmission).
- It was difficult to transmit satellite-distributed programming from Western Union facilities in New York City to Paterson.
- It was inconvenient and inefficient for engineers to travel between the studio and transmitter locations.

Furthermore, a section titled "Paterson Working Conditions" begins thus: "It is one thing to read about the decay of the cities, the high rate of muggings, robberies, knifings and killings. It is another matter when one is personally exposed to these dangers on a day to day basis" (WXTV license renewal, 1978, pt. 7, p. 1). The document goes on to explain that during riots in Paterson shortly after the station opened, the local police claimed they were unable to secure the building, but delivered rifles for employees to protect themselves. There are also descriptions of thefts, damage to station and employee vehicles, etc.

The FCC files also include a letter on behalf of "Hispanic citizens of Paterson ... vigorously opposing" the station's plans to relocate to Secaucus, New Jersey, but without specifying the station's value to the community. The station did not relocate to Secaucus until the 1980s, and in 1998 moved again to updated, digital facilities in Teaneck, New Jersey (Brown, 1999). These documents are clearly intended to persuade the FCC to look favorably upon the station's petition to relocate, but also provide insight into potential challenges in operating a small, ethnic-oriented station having limited revenue and resources in a major market. The two stations' restricted revenues are reflected in advertising rates and net losses.

WXTV averaged annual losses of $247,310 for the years 1969 through 1977 (WXTV license renewal, 1978, pt. 8, p. 1). In 1974, a "participating" announcement airing between 6:30 and 10:00 p.m. on WXTV cost $150 for a single spot, sliding down to $110 per airing for 15 spots (WXTV, Rate Card 11B, 1974). By way of comparison, in 1973, WNJU charged $145 per participating announcement, in the same time slot, sliding to down to $90 per for 15 spots (WNJU, Rate Card 12, 1973). As an indication of how television industry growth and increased attention to the Spanish-speaking market affected the sector during the Decade of the Hispanic, by 1984 both New York stations were commanding around $800 per prime-time 30-second spot (Kirtzman, 1984).

Indeed, by the mid-1980s, both WNJU and WXTV had gained stability— both stations turned their first profit around 1982, and had differentiated themselves from one another. Although market conditions prevented the stations from producing more than 5% of the content they aired, Kirtzman

(1984) noted fundamental distinctions. Whereas WXTV, the Spanish International Network affiliate focused more on news, public affairs and community services in seeking upscale audiences, WNJU was the glitzier station emphasizing entertainment. (The differences became less pronounced after WNJU affiliated with Telemundo in 1988.) Ironically, the poor state of audience research for Spanish-language TV before the Nielsen Hispanic Television Index emerged in the 1990s worked to the stations' mutual benefit as uncertainty led advertisers to buy time on both stations (Kirtzman, 1984). At the time this book went to press, both stations remained important anchors for their respective networks.

National Spot Sale Waiver

As various distribution systems delivered Spanish International Network content to an increasing number of households, and network affiliated stations received content and interacted via satellite, SIN began to look and behave like a national television network. This higher profile raised an issue concerning its status vis-à-vis Section 73.658(i) of the FCC's rules, which prohibits broadcast networks from acting as sales representatives for their affiliated stations in national spot advertising. SIN filed for a waiver from the rule, arguing that the underdeveloped state of Spanish-language advertising and a relatively limited reach distinguished it from the major English-language television networks the rule was intended for. The waiver request argued that only a small number of advertisers regularly purchased Spanish-language television spots, and that training station managers and sales staffs at each affiliate would impose a considerable burden. Thus, compliance with the rule would impose economic hardship on the network, forcing it to reduce the quality and/or quantity of programming it provided affiliated stations, or increase its fees for program provision (*In re SICC*, 1986, para. 146). In September 1978, the FCC granted SIN a one-year waiver until a rulemaking proceeding could occur (Network representation, 1978). No further action was taken to clarify the issue until the Commission began an in-depth investigation of the relationship between the Spanish International station group and network in 1983.

   As the next chapter examines in greater detail, the Spanish International companies came under legal scrutiny during the first half of the 1980s due to allegations of illegal control by a foreign national, Emilio Azcárraga Milmo. The complaints maintained that Rene Anselmo acted as Azcárraga's agent in the U.S., and that his position as simultaneous president of both the network and station group permitted him to exploit the latter to the advantage of the former. SIN's waiver from the national spot caught the attention of Judge John H. Conlin because of the potential for network representatives to use their control over stations' programming access as leverage to dominate ad sales activity, or require stations to pay high ad sales commissions. (Although Judge Conlin did not affirm that such abuses had occurred, their potential was a cause for concern.) The owner of a competing ad sales firm, Eduardo Caballero of Caballero Spanish Media, testified during the inquiry that a single, national sales team could manipulate negotiations with an advertiser to its favor by raising national spot ad prices to make the network ad option[22] more cost effective and, thereby, more appealing (*In re SICC*, 1986, para. 154). Although Judge Conlin emphasized that no abuse had been discovered, he found that SIN's waiver impeded the emergence of competing national spot sale representatives and interfered with affiliated stations' obligation to operate independently. He asserted that the Spanish-language television advertising industry had become sufficiently robust to no longer warrant the waiver, which he recommended be rescinded.

In an interview published within a year of Judge Conlin's decision, Rene Anselmo characterized the waiver issue as a "total red herring." He claimed the rule was only meant to apply to ABC, CBS and NBC, stating,

> We filed for the request as *pro forma* protection, just in case. I think the letter that was sent said, "We don't think this applies to us, but just in case it does, here's an application for a waiver." I don't think they ever gave us a waiver. I think it just sat there in limbo. But it was nothing that we thought we'd gained any big upper hand or anything because it was irrelevant.
>
> (Balkan, 1986, p. 78, emphasis in the original)

Certainly the waiver helped foster the network's growth during a key transitional period from annual net losses due to technology investments and widespread advertiser indifference, to one of profitability and increased awareness and investment in Hispanic advertising. SIN's maturation and ability to sell national advertising raised regulators' expectations that it conform to rules designed to protect stations from potential abuses by the networks with which they are affiliated.

Conclusion

The 1970s could be described metaphorically as adolescent years for the U.S. Spanish-language television industry. Spanish International Network experienced a growth spurt, and coordination among its different component parts improved. It challenged authority and began developing a unique identity among its peers, but still depended on its parent for sustenance. Various elements were coming together for a transition to adulthood in the 1980s, the Decade of the Hispanic.

Although Hispanic population growth reported by the 1970 census did not receive the publicity that subsequent censuses would, it measured a significant uptick, and errors requiring a reassessment and correction brought attention to the complexities and challenges of counting non-mainstream populations (Hutchison, 1984). Satellite technology improved the efficiency of distributing programs among SIN-affiliated stations while translators/repeaters and low-power stations extended the reach of broadcast signals even as the expansion of cable systems delivered SIN and Galavisión programming to more homes. Yet we must keep in mind that the close relationship with Televisa provided access to entrepreneurial leadership, investment capital and technical acumen that would have been less easily (or cheaply) attained by independent owners. In this sense, the industry's development during this crucial period remained heavily reliant on resources and expertise from Mexico (Antola & Rogers, 1984).

Spanish International's success in challenging regulations that might impede its progress could be attributed to a number of factors, most prominent among them Rene Anslemo's determination and regulators' lack of attention to Spanish-language television. Anselmo's disgust with the inefficiency and favoritism of the carrier-of-the-week satellite communication system was channeled into a lawsuit that led to deregulation of that key telecommunications industry. Karim (2010, p. 401) reminds us, "ethnic media have frequently been at the leading edge of technology adoption due to the particular challenges they face in reaching their audiences." I assert that Emilio Azcárraga, Rene Anselmo and other members of Spanish International's management were particularly astute and energetic in this regard: during this period, legal dexterity became a fundamental component of the Spanish International companies' ability to maintain their virtual monopolistic control over Spanish-language television in the United States.

The FCC's lack of oversight on low-power television before heavy demand forced it to pay attention is analogous to the paucity of regulatory attention to Spanish-language television, notwithstanding its reach and revenue-generating power. Its five-year inattention to the spot sale rule waiver granted SIN is one example, another is the FCC's dismissal of Trans-Tel's charges that SIN was under illegal foreign control in 1965 when the two companies competed for the right to construct a station serving New York (Mora, 2011). Although the FCC was later prompted to action by complaints of both foreign ownership and monopoly control, the agency generally took a laissez faire attitude toward the sector.

The examination of two stations serving New York also revealed the adolescent nature of Spanish-language television in the 1970s, even in a region with an estimated 2.3 million Spanish speakers and world's greatest concentration of advertising resources. Both WNJU and WXTV started as multiethnic, multilingual stations before it became clear that a Spanish-only format was sustainable. Only a limited group of advertisers sought Spanish-speaking consumers, and inadequate audience ratings inspired little confidence in advertising buyers and sellers alike. This resulted in relatively low rates for local advertising spots, which prolonged the journey to profitability. That journey was too long for two sets of WNJU owners, and WXTV was anxious to vacate its Paterson, New Jersey, facilities for safer, more productive environs closer to New York City.

Notwithstanding the growing pains of individual stations and local markets that were playing out in areas of Hispanic population concentration nationwide, the overall picture is one of consolidation as program distribution, promotions, advertising sales and other activities became more efficient and coordinated through closer technological ties and increasingly savvy and experienced management teams. Yet there were fissures in the Spanish International leadership that would surface in the 1980s with far-reaching consequences.

Notes

1. Quotations are from U.S. Bureau of the Census (1973, p. 85).
2. This mainstay of Mexican television, a three-hour variety show hosted by Raúl Velasco, was a ratings leader for much of its tenure from 1969 to 1998.
3. Besides being home to the first Spanish International station (KWEX was acquired in 1961), San Antonio is strategically situated close to Mexico and between the two coasts where key Spanish-language markets are located.
4. See the discussion of Univisa in Chapter Five for more information on how this initiative turned out.
5. Discussion of the PanAmSat project's subsequent development appears in Chapter Seven.
6. Banks and Titus (1990, p. 16) explain, "according to the FCC, a signal booster [repeater] retransmits television signals, altering only the amplitude of the incoming signal; a translator retransmits television signals, altering the frequency, or channel, and amplitude of the original signal (47 *CFR* 74.701)."
7. In approving Spanish International's application for the licenses, the FCC emphasized that the public interest would be served: "It appears that in each of the proposed communities of license, in spite of large Hispanic populations, very little, if any Spanish language television programming is available. The Commission believes that your proposal is an efficient and desirable means of alleviating this problem and filling the gap in Spanish-language programming. Not only will your proposal bring Spanish language programming to the various communities, the proposal would also make meaningful use of what otherwise would be idle UHF frequencies" (cited in Mora, 2011, p. 250).
8. It should be noted that by another count, 46% of LPTV stations were minority owned (Waters, n.d. cited by Hilliard & Keith, 1999, p. 81).
9. Hilliard & Keith (1999) discuss the relevance of LPTV for distributing Univision and Telemundo signals in the 1990s, but not Spanish International's more entrepreneurial forays in the 1970s and '80s.
10. It is important to stress that unlike prior periods of cable television development which focused on signal enhance because over-the-air reception was poor or unavailable, the 1970s marked the beginning of differentiated content such as niche channels for sports, music or news and premium channels.
11. The capital "V" also converted to small case at some point in the transition.
12. Of these 2.3 million people, 1.6 million lived in the five boroughs of New York City, the rest resided in other areas of New York, New Jersey or Connecticut where broadcast signals reached (Strategy Research Corp., 1980).

13. The archival research was funded through a faculty development grant from the University of Texas at San Antonio and the Research Enrichment Fund at Texas Tech University.
14. Broadcast signals from New York cover most of north and central New Jersey, while Philadelphia stations cover south and central areas of the state.
15. This public interest standard, in place since the Radio Act of 1927 and Communications Act of 1934, is the basis for broadcasters' right to use the public airwaves for commercial purposes.
16. In a letter dated August 4, 1969, Jacob J. Minkowitz, a citizen of Newark, New Jersey, objected to the transfer of WNJU to Columbia Pictures citing these reasons: 90% of New Jerseyans didn't speak Spanish; the new owners were based in California; most advertising and public service programming on the station was directed to viewers in New York, not New Jersey; and the station was off the air more hours that it was on, constituting "non-service of a racially tense city" (Minkowitz, 1969). Newark experienced extensive rioting in 1967 and 1968.
17. A system by which television broadcasts are received over the air, but a decoding box is required to unscramble the signal.
18. Mora (2011) points out that the foreign ownership and control charges against Spanish International that would surface in the 1980s were raised as early as 1965 by Trans-Tel, one of the competitors for the WXTV's construction permit.
19. Information regarding the transmitter issue was gathered from abstracts of *New York Times* articles published September 30, 1971, October 3, 1973 and April 25, 1974.
20. The other was the VHF station WCBS, which had its two primary antennas at the World Trade Center, but also had a full-power backup transmitter and a weaker backup at the Empire State Building (Hudson, 2001).
21. As a document submitted in conjunction with WXTV's 1978 license renewal application put it, "not 17 miles over a West Texas Plains highway. It is a very long and difficult 17 mile journey through heavy, congested New York City and New Jersey commuter traffic" (WXTV license renewal, 1978).
22. Judge Conlin's Initial Decision (*In re SICC*, 1986, n. 27) offers these distinctions among advertising categories:

    National spot: advertising sold on an individual, market-by-market basis outside of the local area.
    Network advertising: advertising that is sold on an interconnected basis, usually with the commercials delivered together with the programming.
    Local advertising: advertising that is sold in the local market area covered by a particular station.

References

Anselmo, Rene. (1980, October). Hispanic television in the 1980s [Point of view]. *Hispanic Business*, 8.

Antola, Livia, & Rogers, Everett M. (1984) Television flows in Latin America. *Communication Research, 11*(2), 183–202.

Atkin, David. (1987). The (low) power elite: Deregulated licensing criteria for low-power television in the USA. *Telecommunications Policy, 11*(4), 357–368.

Balkan, D. Carlos. (1986, December). "Unorthodox and energetic": An interview with Rene Anselmo. *Hispanic Business*, 17–78.

Banks, Mark J., & Titus, Sara E. (1990, fall). The promise and performance of low-power television. *Journal of Media Economics, 3*(2), 15–25.

Beerman, Frank. (1984, September 19). Galavision: 5 years and ticking. *Variety*, 54.

Besas, Peter. (1984, September 19). SIN gets respect & clout in booming Hispanic mkt. *Variety*, 50.

Biel, Jacquelyn. (1985). *Low power television: Development and current status of the LPTV industry* [COM/TECH Report Series]. Washington, D.C.: National Association of Broadcasters.

Brown, Peter. (1999). Univision's East Coast hub. *Broadcasting & Cable, 129*(2), 88.

Cooper, Jim. (1993, December 13). Low-power TV speaks foreign languages. *Broadcasting & Cable,* 96.

Cooperstein, Edwin. (1967, August 31). [Letter to Federal Communications Commission]. U.S. National Archives. (FCC Accession No. 173-75-24, Box 78), College Park, MD.

Cox, Dorrit Sue. (1969). *Spanish-language television in the United States: Its audience and its potential* (Master's thesis). University of Illinois, Urbana, IL.

Davis, Cary, Haub, Carl, & Willette, JoAnne. (1983, June). U.S. Hispanics: Changing the face of America. *Population Bulletin, 38*(3), 1–43.

Grover, Ronald, Grow, Brian, & Smith, Jeri. (2004, August 9). The heavyweight on Latin airwaves: Jerry Perenchio's sprawling Univision network gives him huge Hollywood clout. *Business Week, 3895,* 62.

Guernica, Antonio. (1982). *Reaching the Hispanic market effectively: The media, the market, the methods.* New York, NY: McGraw-Hill Companies.

Gupta, Udayan. (1983, March). New York's WNJU Channel 47: Spanish TV's hottest item. *Hispanic Business,* 16–27.

Hilliard, Robert L., & Keith, Michael C. (1999). *The hidden screen: Low-power television in America.* Armonk, NY: M.E. Sharpe.

Hispanic TV is beaming in on the big time. (1981, March 23). *Business Week,* p. 122.

Hudson, Eileen, D. (2001, October 22). New York: The World Trade Center. *Mediaweek.* Retrieved from http://business.highbeam.com/137332/article-1G1-79524745/new-york-world-trade-center.

Hutchison, Ray (1984). Miscounting the Spanish origin population in the United States: Corrections to the 1970 census and their implications. *Migration Review, 22*(2), 73–89.

In re Spanish International Communications Corporation. (1986, January 3). Federal Communications Commission (Release No. 86D-1). slip op.

Karim, Karim H. (2010). Re-viewing the 'national' in 'international' communication: Through the lens of diaspora. In D. K. Thussu (Ed.), *International communication: A reader* (pp. 353–409). New York: Routledge.

Kesler, Lori. (1986, August 11). Low-power stations build up SIN's strength. *Advertising Age,* S6–S8.

Kirtzman, Andrew (1984, September 19). New York's Hispanic TV outlets carve out separate identities. *Variety,* 78, 86.

Lapin, Stanley P. (1962, November). UHF translators for expanding television coverage. *IRE Transactions on Television and Broadcast Receivers,* 78–85.

Lenti, Paul. (1984, September 19). Novelas, specs & sports power Televisa programming to SIN; Univision links Mexico & U.S. *Variety,* 63, 84.

Locksley, Gareth. (1983, September). The political economy of satellite business. *Telecommunications Policy, 7*(3), 193–205.

Mendoza, Rick. (1980, October). Programming Galavisión. *Hispanic Business*, 16–17.

Minkowitz, Jacob J. (1969, August 4). [Letter to Federal Communications Commission]. U.S. National Archives (FCC Accession No. 173-75-24, Box 78), College Park, MD.

Mora, G. Cristina. (2011). Regulating immigrant media and instituting ethnic boundaries—the FCC and Spanish-language television: 1960–1990. *Latino Studies*, 9(2/3), 242–262.

Network representation of TV stations in national spot sales; request of Spanish International Network (SIN). (1978, October 4). *Federal Register*, 43(193), 45895–45899.

New Jersey Television Broadcasting Corp. (1969). WNJU-TV license renewal documents submitted to Federal Communication Commission. U.S. National Archives (FCC Accession No. 173-75-24, Box 78). College Park, MD.

O'Hare, William. (1990, August). The rise of Hispanic affluence. *American Demographics*, 12(8), 40–43.

Rodríguez, Clara E. (2000). *Changing race: Latinos, the census and the history of ethnicity in the United States*. New York: New York University Press.

Screen Gems Broadcasting Corp. (1969, December 5). *Demographic study of the communities and areas to be served*. Exhibit P-2 of application for WNJU-TV broadcast license. U.S. National Archives (FCC Accession No. 173-75-24, Box 78). College Park, MD.

Screen Gems Stations, Inc. (1972, March 1). Additional information, Exhibit 18. U.S. National Archives (FCC Accession No. 173-82-20, Box 15) College Park, MD.

Siegel, Jacob S., & Passel, Jeffrey S. (1979). *Coverage of the Hispanic population of the United States in the 1970 census: A methodological analysis* (No. 82). U.S. Department of Commerce, Bureau of the Census.

SIN expands. (1981, November/December). *Hispanic Business*, 16.

SIN television net chronology. (1984, September 19). *Variety*, 50, 82.

Smith, F. Leslie, Wright, John W. II, & Ostroff, David H. (1998). *Perspectives on radio and television: Telecommunications in the United States* (4th ed.). Mahwah, NJ: Lawrence Erlbaum Associates.

Spanish International Network. (1974). WXTV-41 Rate Card #11B. Washington National Records Center (FCC Accession No. 173-93-18, Box 30). Suitland, MD.

Strategy Research Corp. (1980). *U.S. Hispanics—A market profile*. National Association of Spanish Broadcasters & Strategy Research Corp.

Subervi-Vélez, Federico A., Ramírez Berg, Charles, Constantakis-Valdés, Patricia, Noriega, Chon, Ríos, Diana I., & Wilkinson, Kenton T. (1994). Mass communication and Hispanics. In F. Padilla (Ed), *Handbook of Hispanic cultures in the United States: Sociology* (pp. 304–357). Houston: Arte Público.

Televisa's Univision link with SINetwork speeds shows to U.S. (1977, April 6). *Variety*.

TV at the Empire State Building. (2009, January 30). *Fybush*. Retrieved from http://www.fybush.com/sites/2009/site-090130.html.

U.S. Bureau of the Census. (1973). *Census of the population: 1970 - National origin and language*. Appendix C: Definitions and Explanations of Subject Characteristic. Subject Reports. Final Report PC(2)-1A.

U.S. Bureau of the Census (1976, July). Language usage in the United States: July 1975 [Advance Report]. Special Studies. Current Population Reports (Series P-23 No. 60). U.S. Department of Commerce, Bureau of the Census.

U.S. Census Bureau. (n.d.). 1970 (Population). Retrieved from https://www.census.gov/history/www/through_the_decades/index_of_questions/1970_population.html.

Valenzuela, Nicolas A. (1985). *Organizational evolution of a Spanish-language television network: An environmental approach*. (Doctoral dissertation). Stanford University, Palo Alto, CA.

What is Galavisión?: Pay-TV with a difference. (1980, March/April). *Hispanic Times*, 8, 26.

WNJU-TV Broadcasting Corp. (1973). WNJU-47 Rate Card #12. U.S. National Archives (FCC Accession No. 173-82-20, Box 715). College Park, MD.

WXTV-TV. (1978, January 27). License renewal application. Washington National Records Center (FCC Accession No. 173-93-18, Box 30). Suitland, MD.

Part II

Turmoil and Change in the 1980s

4 Ownership, Control and Management at Issue

The bulk of this chapter examines the legal processes whereby Spanish International Communications Corp. (SICC) lost control of its broadcast licenses for 11 television stations in 1986, the transfer of those licenses to new owners, and the ensuing legal and political fallout. Before delving into that influential development, however, we review the 1980 U.S. Census and Spanish-language television's status early in the decade. Discussion of the so-called Decade of the Hispanic and its impact on the television industry is postponed until the next chapter. In light of this organizational division, the reader should keep in mind that conceptions offered through the public and business discourses surrounding Hispanics surely influenced the developments reviewed in this chapter.

The 1980 U.S. Census

The 1980 U.S. Census initiated a pattern of animated reporting on the rapid growth and potential political, economic and cultural impacts of the Hispanic population on U.S. society.[1] By the census's count, Hispanics numbered 14.6 million, accounting for 6.4% of the population—up from approximately nine million in 1970 and four million in 1950 (Davis, Haub, & Willette, 1983).[2] Between 1970 and 1980, the Hispanic population grew at a rate 6.5 times that of the general population. In fact, 40% of the *overall* U.S. population growth during the 1970s occurred in three states—California, Texas and Florida—which ranked first, second and fourth, respectively, in Hispanic population in 1980 (Guernica, 1982). Accordingly, the number of Hispanics who joined the U.S. population during the 1980s was greater than for all other minority groups combined (Brischetto, 1993). Such statistics reported in the news media, trade journals and government reports caught the attention of advertisers, marketers and media investors. For example, Henry Silverman, the first CEO at Telemundo network, claimed his interest in the Hispanic market initiated through an article he read in an in-flight magazine (Berry, 1987).

Additional statistics derived from 1980 census data complement our view of the Hispanic population during the decade its prominence increased. As regards national origin, the population was found to be 59% Mexican, 15%

Puerto Rican, 7.4% Central and South American, 5.9% Cuban and 12.2% of other origin (Guernica, 1982, p. 52). At the time, national-origin groups were more geographically concentrated than in the 21st century, with people of Mexican origin mostly in the southwestern states, Puerto Ricans in the New York area and Chicago, Cuban-origin people most concentrated in Florida and Central and South Americans in a variety of cities, especially New York, San Francisco, Los Angeles, Chicago and Miami (Strategy Research Corp., 1980). These distributions would remain perceptible, but become less distinct, over the following three decades. In 1980, 88% of the Hispanic population lived in metropolitan areas compared to 75% of the general population, offering clear advantages for television networks targeting Hispanic viewers (Davis, Haub, & Willette, 1983).

Hispanics' median age was 23 years versus 30 for the general population, a trend that has persisted and concentrated marketing attention and resources on the youth market in the early decades of the 21st century (Davis, Haub, & Willette, 1983). Hispanic women also had a relatively high fertility rate, giving birth to an average 2.5 children compared to 1.8 for the general population. Unfortunately, Hispanic offspring had poorer economic prospects than their Anglo counterparts with Hispanic unemployment 40 to 50% higher, income 30% lower, and a poverty rate 2.7 times that for White families (Miranda & Quiroz, 1990). Although the decade saw economic gains for some, there was an overall decline in Hispanics' income, and the hope for widespread economic and political gains during the Decade of the Hispanic dissipated as the decade waned.

The Industry in the Early 1980s

A crucial advance during the first part of the decade was Spanish International's increased effort to inform viewers about the census and U.S. election system. In 1980, the network aired a series of documentaries called *Destino '80* focusing on the importance to Hispanics' future progress of voter registration, the electoral process and participation in the census. Mora (2014) points out that increased public participation in these activities benefited Spanish International Network (SIN) as the data gathered would help elucidate the number, geographic distribution and consumption habits of Hispanics, thereby supporting network efforts to increase advertising revenue. From January until Election Day in 1984, SIN implemented *Destino '84*, another campaign to increase Hispanics' awareness about the significance of participating in U.S. elections. The network spent an estimated $500,000 on public service announcements, programs produced by local affiliates, celebrity cameo appearances, and coverage of the Democratic and Republican national conventions as well as the election itself (SIN's 'Destino 84,' 1984). Univision, the renamed SIN, offered a similar campaign in 1988, when the upstart Telemundo network followed suit—on a smaller scale—and during the midterm elections as well. According to Welch and

Siegelman (1993, p. 83), exit polls in 1980 indicated that 20% of Hispanic voters identified as liberal, 32% as conservative and 48% as moderates; percentages of respondents identifying as liberal increased slightly throughout the decade.

On a different political front, SIN's news division opened a bureau in San Salvador and conducted El Salvador's first exit poll during a presidential election runoff in May 1984, obtaining anonymous responses from 2,000 voters (Goldman, 1984). Its reporting from El Salvador during the civil war raised SIN's standing among news organizations in the U.S. and Latin America alike. The network experienced a growth spurt during the early 1980s as more affiliated stations became profitable due to an expanded viewer base delivered through satellite and low-power technologies, more advertising agencies opening Spanish-language media divisions, and other factors (De Uriarte, 1980). Loftus (1984) reported that SIN:

- Had 276 affiliates, most of them cable systems.
- Earned $35,000,000 in revenues in 1983.
- Reached approximately 28,500,000 English- and Spanish-speaking households in 32 states.
- Claimed to reach 85% of U.S. Spanish-speaking population.
- Attracted top advertisers including Sears, Ford, General Foods, Miller Beer, Budweiser and Proctor & Gamble—each spending at least $1,000,000 annually.

Some SIN stations were broadcasting 24 hours a day, another indication that they were more closely resembling the English-language networks (Besas, 1984). Guernica (1982, p. 38) summarizes the content appearing on stations that were *not* broadcasting full time:

> In all, an SIN station's typical weekday from 9:00 A.M. to 1:00 A.M. the next day during 1980 consisted of [tele]*novelas*, 6 hours; movies, 4 hours; news, 2 hours; talk shows, 1½ hours; variety shows, 1 to 1½ hours; comedies, ½ to 1 hour; game shows, ½ hour; and children's programming, ½ hour.

When compared with the program schedules of stations in the 1970s discussed in the prior two chapters, this summary reflects significant expansion.

A couple of noteworthy potential competitors to SIN emerged in the early 1980s, opening the door that Telemundo would barge through later in the decade. The distribution and advertising sales company Netspan launched in January 1984 to provide content and ad sales for stations in three important Spanish-language markets: New York (WNJU), Chicago (WBBS) and Los Angeles (KSCI) (Gupta, 1984). All three stations devoted a portion of broadcasting time to other languages, and were eager to differentiate themselves from the SIN affiliates in their respective markets as well as to increase national advertising sales. The stations began airing common programming, mostly *telenovelas*, allowing them to share the costs of program acquisition (Netspan makes, 1984). This required purchasing rights to offshore programs that could compete against SIN's; therefore many programs originated from South America and the Caribbean (Gupta, 1984). Netspan's president (and WNJU station manager) Carlos Barba expressed the company's interest in producing programs for the youth market stating, "the young (Hispanic) American has a tendency to identify with Anglo programs ... as soon as we can do it financially, we'll start making shows that can appeal to [them]" (Netspan makes, 1984, p. 84). Netspan distributed some local programs produced by affiliated stations, but Barba's vision would be realized later in the decade when Telemundo acquired Netspan as its programming arm.

Another venture, TeleRed International, sought to import programs from Mexico's government-run television network, Imevisión Channel 13, selling them to U.S. stations, including SIN affiliates. Imevisión's program content was less commercial than SIN's, consisting of documentaries, serial dramas, children's programs, sports and programs about Latin American art, music and culture (Torres, 1984). The company also planned to produce videocassettes for direct purchase by consumers. In 1971 TeleRed's founder, Rene Cardenas, had launched Bilingual Children's Television, which distributed children's educational programs to as many as 265 stations before ceasing production in 1982 (Torres, 1984). Although TeleRed was unable to provide substantive competition to SIN before dissolving in 1987, the fact that a proven Hispanic television producer gained financial backing in an effort to compete with the entrenched network demonstrated a change in the industry's dynamics.

Power at Issue in International Communication and Regulation

Before jumping into the details, it bears noting that processes discussed in this chapter occurred during an important transition in international trade regimes from protectionism toward freer trade. In addition to the North American Free Trade Agreement that linked Canada, Mexico and the U.S., the Andean Pact and MERCOSUR in Latin America were efforts to shift from national markets protected by a variety of tariff and non-tariff trade barriers toward free trade based on neoliberal economic doctrine (McAnany & Wilkinson, 1996). The so-called Asian Tiger nations provided models of low-protectionism, high yield trade that other world regions sought to emulate (Gapinski, 1999). Certainly most investors who contemplated linking the U.S. Spanish-language sector with markets in Latin America viewed this as a positive movement.

A related political shift also improved the climate for international business in this period. During the 1970s and first half of the '80s, contentious discussion about establishing a New World Information and Communication

Order (NWICO) dominated meetings of the United Nations Educational, Scientific and Cultural Organization (UNESCO). The USSR, member nations of the Non-Aligned Movement, and others proposed restricting some international communication flows in order to address the deep inequities favoring a handful of Western nations, especially the United States with its powerful communication industries. Such restrictions, including a proposal to license journalists and a number of lopsided legislative defeats, led the U.S. to withdraw from UNESCO in 1984. Great Britain followed suit the next year, and the two nations took a sizable portion of the organization's budget with them (Giffard, 1989). As NWICO faded from news headlines and diplomatic agendas, a number of influential countries enacted pro-trade policy reforms and negotiations accelerated regarding trade pacts such as NAFTA, the European Union and MERCOSUR. Thus, the increased visibility of U.S. Spanish-language television came at a time when the prospects for smooth program exchange and cross-national network development looked bright.

Spanish-language television also gained standing as a consequential industry through the processes described in this chapter. The industry wielded sufficient influence to attract the attention of regulatory agencies including the Department of Justice and Federal Communications Commission (FCC), and enough money was changing hands that established competitors and potential entrants fought to gain greater shares. Thus, Spanish-language television became a conduit for Hispanics' growing political and economic power that attracted the attention, and in some cases investment, of America's elite. The next chapter covers broader elements of the Decade of the Hispanic; this one illustrates how Spanish-language television became recognized as a legitimate means to reach an increasingly desirable population.

A development that boosted Hispanics' visibility less directly was the expansion of digitization through the rapid diffusion of personal computers and workstations (Elliott & Kraemer, 1986). A trickling-down of computing resources from a specialized class of programmers, upper management and scientists to middle and eventually lower levels of organizational hierarchies facilitated the gathering, analysis and dissemination of data on audiences, consumer behavior and advertising's effectiveness.[3] The impact on Spanish-language television lagged behind English-language counterparts, but the central point is that processes described here unfolded at a time when rapid dissemination of computer technology was altering business practices as well as how the press communicated with the public.

On the regulatory front, the legal processes covered here engaged FCC rules intended to increase minority participation in broadcasting. The so-called Jefferson Radio policy forbade a licensee whose qualifications were under investigation from transferring its broadcast license(s) to another entity at full market value. The policy's intent was to make more broadcast licenses available to underrepresented groups, like ethnic/racial minorities and women, while preventing violators from profiting from their misdeeds.

A related "distress sale" policy enabled the FCC to designate licenses for acquisition at 75% of their market value. As we shall see, qualification as a distress sale beneficiary became a competitive tactic employed by competitors in the struggle to obtain the disputed Spanish International stations.

The legal challenges described below played a key role in U.S. Spanish-language television's maturation. This statement may at first seem counterintuitive, as inquiries, investigations, lawsuits and the like are usually considered detrimental to industry growth because corporate resources, attention and energy are diverted from growing the business. We will see an example of such inhibition in the book's final chapter, which describes how a lawsuit Televisa filed against Univision slowed business across the U.S. Spanish-language sector as industry participants awaited its outcome. However, I argue that during the 1980s the sector gained recognition through regular reporting on Spanish International's legal travails and the forced sale of SICC's stations. Such coverage appeared in the business press along with reports on Hispanic population growth, buying power and political clout than had been available previously. This exposure almost certainly enhanced investors' interest in the Mexican market when discussions of extending NAFTA from Canada and the U.S. to Mexico began in earnest late in the decade (discussed in Chapter Seven).

Fissures Among the Spanish International Management

The early 1970s were a difficult period for the Spanish International leadership. When Emilio Azcárraga Vidaurreta died in 1973, he left his son, Emilio Azcárraga Milmo, with complicated inheritance concerns at a time when pressures within Mexican television spurred a realignment of Telesistema Mexicana under a new name, Televisa.[4] For several years, the younger Azcárraga (Milmo) had counseled his father against further investment in the U.S. enterprises, which were not yet providing returns. The son had also clashed with Rene Anselmo, the American citizen whose legwork established Azcárraga family investments in the U.S. In 1971, when Anselmo offered Azcárraga Sr. 20% ownership in the recently acquired Miami station (WLTV), Azcárraga Milmo sensed insubordination and threatened to run Anselmo out of the family business network (Maza, 1986). Although the older Azcárraga diffused a potential explosion by accepting the offer (and having his son give Anselmo 25% ownership of SIN), tension remained in the relationship between Azcárraga Milmo and Anselmo.

Rene Anselmo's consequential quarrel with the American investor Frank Fouce Jr. began in the early 1970s, setting in motion events that would consume both Spanish International companies and, ultimately, remove Anselmo from their management ranks. Anselmo was at the center of the companies' most corrosive disagreements not only due to his simultaneous position as president of both the network (SIN) and station group (SICC); his personality was a central factor as well. The journalist Carlos Balkan's

(1986) profile of Anselmo included descriptive adjectives from fellow Spanish International executives. Among the positive descriptors: energetic, intelligent, compassionate and visionary. Less flattering were: autocratic, opinionated, stubborn, eccentric and impulsive. Anselmo was not one to back down from a challenge and fought tenaciously when negotiation seemed futile. He met a resilient opponent in Frank Fouce Jr.

Crister (1987) reported that the Anselmo/Fouce dispute originated in 1972 over an English-language business news program airing on KMEX in Los Angeles. The show's staff included both Fouce and Anselmo family members. Anselmo's firing Fouce's son angered the father, and Anselmo's subsequent efforts to cancel the program led to an angry confrontation during which each man reportedly vowed to buy out the other. The family members' involvement likely engendered deep emotional ferment on both sides, and Frank Fouce Jr. apparently never forgave Anselmo.

A document appearing in Fouce's mismanagement lawsuit references another incident that occurred after the KMEX confrontation. Fouce claimed that Magnaverde, a promotional company owned and operated by Anselmo, used SICC employees and production facilities to promote Magnaverde productions, such as 1974 World Cup Soccer games and Muhammad Ali boxing matches. The document alleges that Anselmo refused to compensate SICC in spite of Fouce's strong objections. The accusation typifies the mismanagement claims Fouce made against Anselmo and other SICC executives: the station group, SICC, served as a revenue conduit for the network, SIN, or other companies that Anselmo and/or his Mexican associates held interests in, such as Magnaverde. The discord between Fouce and Anselmo ultimately engendered two legal processes: a stockholder derivative lawsuit filed in Los Angeles, and FCC investigations and rulings centered in Washington, D.C. The pages to follow show that as the legal processes grew in amplitude and became more closely intertwined, the number of interested parties increased, as did the number of legal forums involved. Although accounts of infighting are not the preferred way for an industry to gain recognition among business, regulatory, legal and advocacy communities, the legal actions played a direct role in increasing the visibility of U.S. Spanish-language television.

Fouce Amusement Enterprises and Metropolitan Theaters Corp. v. Spanish International Communications Corp.

In November 1976, attorneys for Frank Fouce Jr. and Bruce W. Corwin, a fellow shareholder in SICC stations, served Rene Anselmo and other SICC executives with subpoenas to appear in federal court. As minority stockholders in SICC through their businesses (Fouce Amusement Enterprises and Metropolitan Theaters Corp.), the plaintiffs charged the SICC management with breach of fiduciary duty, self-dealing, and mismanagement. SICC and Televisa responded by filing a motion to dismiss the case or, failing that, to have it moved from Los Angeles to New York City, home of the Spanish International companies' corporate headquarters. The motion was unsuccessful. Anselmo also attempted to forestall the suit through a fruitless offer to purchase the plaintiffs' stock in SICC.

In 1975, Emilio Azcárraga Milmo's calling in a debt that SICC owed Televisa became a catalyst for Fouce's and Corwin's isolation from the other stockholders. Economic pressure from spiraling inflation in Mexico combined with threatening gestures toward commercial broadcasting by Mexico's left-leaning president, Luis Echeverria, sent Azcárraga Milmo in search of quick capital—SICC's nearly $2 million debt to Televisa was a ready target. Azcárraga summoned Anselmo to Mexico City, where the men had a heated meeting in December 1975 (Maza, 1986).

Anselmo returned to New York from his clash with Azcárraga to conduct equally hostile meetings of the SICC board of directors and the SICC stockholders. The most contentious item on both meetings' agendas concerned financing SICC's debt payment to Televisa; several payment strategies were considered before one was "agreed upon." A brief overview of the meetings and their resolutions offers insight into the impasse that led Frank Fouce Jr. and Bruce Corwin to file suit.

In spite of Frank Fouce Jr.'s fervent objections—he was hoping to sell his interest in SICC to finance other investments—the board approved the issuance and sale of 3 million one-dollar stocks to cover the debt to Televisa. Issuing new stock would devalue the stock Fouce was hoping to sell. Additionally, in a blatant personal attack, the board stripped Fouce of his chairmanship of the board and elected Anselmo for the position (First amended, 1977, p. 22). Anselmo offered Fouce $1 million for his 209,091 shares of SICC, the approximate equivalent of $4.79 per share. Fouce rejected the offer, later telling the court he considered the stock to be worth "no less than $20.00 per share" (Answers to first, 1977).

At a shareholders' meeting in January 1976, Anselmo proposed addressing the debt problem by merging Magnaverde Corp. and SICC. Not surprisingly, given his prior objections to Magnaverde, Fouce was cool to the plan that he considered inequitable to Spanish International. Anselmo pursued the merger nonetheless, and in a July 1976 meeting the board of directors passed a resolution to issue 404,036 shares of SICC stock to Magnaverde in order to cancel the $1.933 million debt owed to Televisa. Although the stock issue was not implemented—likely because Azcárraga also opposed it—SICC stock was again valued at $4.79 per share. Fouce later insisted in court that neither Anselmo nor any other board member attempted to ascertain the stock's actual value (First amended, 1977, p. 25).

Two incidents exemplified the corrosive environment of distrust that pervaded the last SICC board meeting that Frank Fouce Jr. attended. First, Fouce requested permission to view SICC books and records during the meeting—Anselmo and the other board members quickly passed a resolution prohibiting SICC directors from examining company records (First amended, 1977,

p. 28). Second, Fouce perturbed his fellow board members by arriving to the meeting with a court reporter so that, in his own words, "an accurate transcript of the minutes would be available" (Answers to first, 1977, p. 42). Anselmo refused entry to the court reporter, and Fouce later characterized the minutes taken by an SICC employee as slanted and distorted.

The debt issue was finally resolved in August 1976 when the SICC board voted to issue a convertible note to Televisa in the amount of $1.935 million (First amended, 1977, p. 29). The note carried an interest rate of 8% per annum and would fall due August 31, 1986. Based on the terms of the deal, Frank Fouce Jr.'s attorneys argued it was an attempt to circumvent Section 310 (b) (3) of the Communications Act of 1934, the law limiting foreign ownership of a U.S. broadcasting entity to 20% (First amended, 1977, p. 29; Rieman, 1985).

As noted, Fouce and Corwin's legal complaint filed against Rene Anselmo focused on abuse of his position as simultaneous president of SIN and SICC. FCC investigations corroborated the charge that the network, SIN (and its Mexican beneficiaries) took unfair advantage of the station group, SICC, and its stockholders.[5] Anselmo denied the accusations, countering that Fouce was using the court to artificially inflate the value of SICC stock. During the first few months of the lawsuit, Anselmo made additional unsuccessful offers to buy Fouce's and Corwin's shares of SICC.

Before the FCC began its investigations in 1980, the court case in Los Angeles was a low profile, protracted battle characterized by lengthy information requests, depositions and interrogatories. That courtroom proceedings did not begin until February 1981, almost five years after the suit was filed, indicates the high volume of attorney-generated material in the case. Not until mid-1985, when the FCC announced that forfeiture or forced sale of the stations might be warranted, did the case receive significant press attention. Thereafter coverage was steady, probably stimulated by interest in the conflict's outcome and heightened curiosity among potential investors about the fate of a strategic medium for reaching Hispanic consumers.

FCC Investigations and Decisions

Although attorneys representing SICC and SIN had occasionally argued for FCC rule changes to benefit their companies, most interactions with the regulatory agency were routine, like applying for broadcasting licenses and renewals. During one such process in 1980, a group of disgruntled potential competitors based in the U.S. objected to an SICC application. The ensuing investigation focused on the companies' ownership structure and business practices. Suggestions of possible foreign control had surfaced as early as 1965 when SICC applied for its Paterson, New Jersey license (WXTV), but the FCC dismissed the issue in part because it felt that the public interest was best served by allowing the Spanish-language network to expand (Mora, 2011).

The Spanish Radio Broadcasters Association (SRBA) was a national group of Spanish-language radio station owners and executives organized in 1970 to protect and promote their interests. In March 1980, SRBA submitted an informal objection to SICC's request for permission to construct and operate experimental television translator stations in Washington, D.C. and Denver. Although the FCC granted the applications, SRBA requested a review of the decision arguing that SICC was under illegal foreign control, misrepresented facts to the Commission, and had engaged in anti-competitive conduct in violation of Commission policies (Report to the Special, 1983, pp. 5–6). The FCC deemed information uncovered by the subsequent investigation sufficiently troubling to designate SICC's broadcasting licenses for hearing at their next renewal in 1983. The principal aim of SRBA's complaint was to loosen the Spanish International companies' tight hold on the Spanish-language television industry. Ed Gómez, SRBA's founding president, summarized the group's concerns, "the FCC is allowing a monster to be created that will ultimately stifle the development of TV programming by Hispanic Americans" (FCC probing, 1980, p. 1).

An FCC decision in 1978 to exempt Spanish International from Section 73.658(i) of the Commission's rules—the network spot sale rule discussed in the previous chapter—was not specifically cited in SRBA's complaint, but was included in the FCC investigations because of its potential to restrain Spanish-language program production in the U.S. Rule 73.658(i) prohibited television affiliates that are not network owned from being represented by a network when selling advertising time. The FCC waived the rule for one year at Spanish International's request, but then failed to follow up.

The FCC's Mass Media Bureau presented SICC with a six-point proposal in August 1982.[6] Compliance would have resolved the matter, but several of the directives—for divestiture, corporate restructuring and cancellation of the 1978 spot sale waiver—required Azcárraga Milmo and his American associates to cede control over both the network and station group. SICC's counterproposal refused to accept forfeitures or admissions of owner guilt, leading the FCC to schedule hearings for SICC license renewal applications and those of Bahia and Seven Hills, separately incorporated companies that held operating licenses for SIN-affiliated stations in San Francisco and Phoenix.

Following a thorough investigation that included interviews with at least 29 confidential informants, two of SRBA's three principal charges were dismissed. The FCC determined that SICC had not misrepresented facts regarding satellite earth stations it operated, and insufficient evidence supported the contention that SICC sought to illegally stifle competition in Spanish-language broadcasting. SRBA's third claim, that non-U.S. citizens controlled SICC, could neither be confirmed nor denied during the investigation. Therefore, the Commission ordered that the license renewal applications be designated for hearing to determine not only the foreign control issue, but also whether SICC and SIN should continue to receive the advertising sale waiver granted five years earlier.

The FCC appointed Administrative Law Judge John H. Conlin to the case. Conlin initiated a discovery process in which the burden of proof for license renewal was upon the applicants: SICC, Bahia, and Seven Hills. In August 1983, both SIN and Fouce Amusement Enterprises received permission to intervene, thereby formalizing a close relationship between the stockholder suit in federal court and the FCC license renewal hearing.[7] The FCC released Judge Conlin's initial decision on January 8, 1986. Given the large number of sensitive documents withheld during the FCC investigation and the prehearing discovery period, the initial decision offers surprisingly detailed descriptions of the two Spanish International companies' corporate structure, history, and business practices. The document offered rare access for outsiders, such as academic researchers, to closely guarded information about secretive companies.[8] The SICC stations' applications for license renewal were denied on the following grounds:

> ... alien influence and direction of the Licensee corporations greatly exceeds that permitted by Section 310 (b). This influence exists at various levels. It is reflected in the composition of the ownership and board of directors of the licensee corporations, in the stations' management, in its programming, and in the historic financial and personal ties between the Licensees and the Azcárraga family and its corporate interests. At the center of these relationships is Rene Anselmo who, realistically speaking, must be regarded as a representative of aliens within the meaning of Section 310 (b) (3) of the Act (*In re Spanish*, 1986, para. 176).

Although Azcárraga Milmo and other, minor Mexican investors complied with the 20% foreign ownership limitation in legal documents, Judge Conlin found that Azcárraga's actual *control* was greater than 20%—a violation of the law.[9] The decision regarding Rule 73.658(i), the national spot sale waiver, also went against SICC and SIN. Judge Conlin concluded that the Spanish-language market was large enough to support independent national spot sales representatives; therefore the waiver was impeding the development of competition in Spanish-language television advertising (*In re Spanish*, 1986, paras. 187–189).

Although he determined that SICC had violated federal law, Judge Conlin did not preclude the possibility that the licensees might continue to hold the licenses following a radical corporate restructuring,[10] or selling the stations at a profit (*In re Spanish*, 1986, para. 194). The group of plaintiff SICC shareholders eventually seized the opportunity to sell their stations at full market value, but only after employing the threat of a protracted appeal process as leverage to negotiate the best possible terms. SICC quickly announced its intention to challenge Judge Conlin's decision, but took no action until three months later when negotiations with the FCC regarding terms of a possible station sale became strained (Ramos, 1986; Rosenstiel & Pagano, 1986). Spanish International's subsequent appeal to the FCC Review Board claimed that Judge Conlin based his decision on two sets of invalid information: the dynamics of a long-since-changed relationship that had existed between Rene Anselmo and Emilio Azcárraga Vidaurreta some 25 years earlier, and *potential* rather than *actual* foreign control of SICC.

The FCC's Mass Media Bureau responded with a petition to the same review board claiming that Judge Conlin erred in failing to designate an "abuse of process" issue against SICC. The Bureau claimed that Spanish International personnel had harassed and intimidated members of the Spanish Radio Broadcasters Association in retaliation for SRBA's 1980 complaint (SICC and company, 1986). Although the confrontation between SICC and the Mass Media Bureau amounted to little more than thinly veiled threats, Rene Anselmo ultimately appealed Judge Conlin's decision, successfully gaining the Phoenix station (KTVW) an exemption from the order.

In May 1986 the parties in the stockholder suit reached a settlement agreement that would alter the character of both legal processes as well as the future course for Spanish-language television in the U.S. The focus shifted from Spanish International retaining control of the station group to its transfer to a new owner. Sale of the stations to unrelated buyers would resolve the FCC proceedings, while settling the stockholders' derivative lawsuit along with other litigation that was pending or in progress when Judge Conlin published his pivotal initial decision. An overview of other legal actions engendered by the stockholder suit and FCC actions shows the magnitude the entire process had achieved by the time SICC was sold. Clearly, legal processes exerted substantial influence over the industry in the mid-1980s.

Related Lawsuits

In October 1980, approximately six months after the SRBA filed its objection with the FCC, the *Los Angeles Times* reported that the U.S. Department of Justice was initiating a civil antitrust investigation into Spanish International Network (Latin network, 1980). Investigators examined the network's program distribution and advertising practices as they searched for possible violations of the Sherman Act, which prohibits conspiracies to monopolize markets or restrain trade. Apparently they found insufficient evidence of wrongdoing as the investigation was terminated without comment in 1981 (Valenzuela, 1985, p. 110). There are two likely sources of the Justice Department's investigation: the SRBA, with help from its political ally, Republican Senator Harrison Schmitt[11] of New Mexico, and the American Federation of Radio and Television Artists, which promoted more production of Spanish-language programming in the U.S., in part by stemming the flow of content from Mexico.

On multiple occasions Rene Anselmo accused the SRBA of collaborating with Frank Fouce Jr. to attack SICC and SIN. In 1984, Anselmo initiated two antitrust proceedings in federal courts. The first named members of the SRBA as well as Fouce Amusement Enterprises and Metropolitan Theaters as defendants (Antitrust litigation, 1985). The case was begun in New York but was transferred to the Northern Division of Texas to be consolidated with ten separate but similar lawsuits from across the country. In March 1984, attorneys for Fouce Amusement Enterprises and Metropolitan Theaters filed for a temporary restraining order and injunction to halt the antitrust lawsuit which they characterized as "a sham, a waste of SICC corporate assets, and an attempt to vex, annoy, and harass Fouce Amusement and Metropolitan in retaliation for their actions in commencing and prosecuting the corporate derivative litigation" (Status conference, 1984, p. 2).

The second antitrust suit was filed in Miami in mid-1984 against SRBA's attorney, Matthew L. Leibowitz, by the same plaintiffs: SICC, SIN, Bahia and Seven Hills (608 F. Supp. 178). The plaintiffs claimed that Leibowitz made "baseless and repetitive claims" against them at the FCC, acting "not solely as an attorney providing legal service, but as a person involved in the formulation of policy for the conspirators, and one of the prime implementers and actors in the conspiracy" (608 F. Supp. 178, para. 180). The judge hearing the case granted Leibowitz's motion for dismissal in January 1985, releasing an opinion strongly favoring the defendant.[12] Although ultimately unwinnable, the antitrust suits demonstrated the aggressive resolve of Spanish International's leadership, and diverted some of its challengers' attention and resources away from the FCC and stockholder derivative actions. Executives for Spanish-language television's only national network employed the resources and competitive legal tactics of a major corporation, clear signs of its continuing maturation.

Allegations of stock fraud represented another variety of legal process. Eduardo Caballero, a former SIN vice president and director of sales who in 1973 quit to launch Caballero Spanish Media (a competitor to SIN), charged Spanish International with stock fraud in federal court in New York. Caballero claimed that in 1971, while still working for SIN, he was offered an informal stock ownership plan for which he paid $15,000. Because he was a Cuban national, Caballero transferred the stock to his daughter—a 7-year-old American citizen at the time—so as to comply with federal restrictions on alien ownership and control of U.S. broadcast media. Rene Anselmo was appointed trustee of the stock. In 1973 Caballero left SICC in spite of Anselmo's attempts at persuading him to stay. Allegedly, Anselmo sold the Caballeros' stock to another Spanish International shareholder without notifying either of the Caballeros. Anselmo offered the daughter $15,000 for the stock, which her representatives refused. In a motion to dismiss, the younger Caballero claimed that Spanish International management used the stock ownership scheme to coax more work and corporate commitment out of her father while retaining full voting control of the company for themselves. The defendants moved to dismiss. The judge did indeed dismiss the case, ruling that technically no sale could actually have occurred because no trustee-beneficiary or purchaser-seller relationship existed between the plaintiff and Anselmo; securities laws were designed to prevent deception, not simple theft (1985 Fed. Sec. Law Rpts. paras. 91, 94). It was a hollow victory for Anselmo, however, as his integrity was called into question, an image that could only hurt him and the companies he represented in other legal forums.

The foregoing discussion offers insight into the turf battles fought around the fringes of the two central legal challenges to SICC. Instigators of the Justice Department's antitrust investigation likely sought a foothold in a tightly held industry. The two antitrust suits filed by Spanish International were aggressive responses to the temerity of potential competitors, and efforts to reinforce barriers to entry in a growing industry. The stock fraud case confirmed a belligerent strain of SICC business practices as it confronted Eduardo Caballero, a former employee, industry competitor and SRBA member. When considered together, these legal actions demonstrate the gravity of legal affairs surrounding the Spanish International companies by the mid-1980s. The legal actions attracted the attention of journalists, investment bankers, and potential purchasers of the SICC station group. Spanish-language television achieved standing as a fast-growth industry with strong potential for yielding high returns. Therefore it comes a little surprise that the station sale procedure—the subject to which we now turn—quickly became volatile.

Preliminary Bids for Spanish International Communications Corporation

In June 1990, the U.S. Supreme Court upheld the constitutionality of two FCC policies mandating preferred consideration of minority-owned companies that compete for broadcast licenses against non-minority companies (*Metro Broadcasting Inc. v. Federal Communications Commission*, 1990). Although the policies were later rescinded, transfer of the SICC stations and subsequent appeals illustrate how one high profile ethnicity-related license competition played out when FCC minority preference policies existed, but were implemented inconsistently.

Actions Before the District Court Sale Agreement

As we have seen, the FCC's investigation into SICC and the federal stockholder lawsuit heard in Los Angeles were closely related. Consequential judgments in the stockholder suit came within six months of FCC findings criticizing the Spanish International companies' management.[13] In April 1986, when it became clear that the companies' appeal of Judge Conlin's initial decision had dim chances, serious negotiations with the plaintiffs began. Selling the station group to an unrelated buyer was one option the parties agreed upon. If the FCC approved such a sale, it would be the surest way to "cash out" before the Commission took any further punitive action.

An initial effort toward acquiring the station group originated from within the company. William Stiles, an SICC marketing executive, attempted to orchestrate a management-leveraged buyout with assistance from several SICC station managers who feared losing their broadcast licenses.[14] The group contracted the investment banking firm L.F. Rothschild, Unterberg, Towbin, Inc., which circulated a corporate profile of SICC to potential financiers. Two recipients of the profile were E.M. Warburg, Pincus & Co., and First Capital Corporation of Chicago. Hallmark Cards Corporation joined them in March 1986, and the group began formulating bids for SICC. Although Rene Anselmo repeatedly expressed disinterest in negotiating the purchase of SICC, speculation increased about a potential takeover by outside investors.

The next month, an investor group headed by A. Jerrold Perenchio, an established Hollywood entrepreneur who held interests in WNJU (New York) and KBSC (Los Angeles), offered $300 million for SICC, and then raised the bid periodically until it reached $350 million by May 12, when litigants in the stockholder suit reached a settlement agreement. Perenchio's escalating offer diminished the likelihood of an internal-leveraged buyout by SICC employees, but did not curb other bidders' appetites. Several major communication companies, such as Lorimar Telepictures, Columbia Pictures, MCA and Paramount Pictures, expressed initial interest, but were not among the final bidders (SICC to sell, 1986). To the surprise of the Hallmark group and other observers, Rene Anselmo rejected Perenchio's $350 million offer, believing that the station group could command a higher price. Anselmo's rejection enraged Emilio Azcárraga Milmo, Televisa's powerful leader, who forced Anselmo to step down as SIN president only two weeks after resigning as president of SICC. This episode appeared to support long-standing allegations of foreign control, and marked the end of direct involvement in the Spanish International companies by Rene Anselmo, the man most directly responsible for establishing and developing the industry. (Anselmo continued to wield influence over the industry through PanAmSat, the world's first private satellite communications company with global coverage.)

Bidding After the District Court Sale Agreement

Rejection of Perenchio's offer together with approval of the SICC sale agreement stimulated a flurry of acquisition efforts and brought to the fore an owner ethnicity issue. Articles in leading U.S. newspapers and trade journals reported several Hispanic investor groups' interest in purchasing SICC to ensure the survival of Spanish-language television broadcasting in the United States. Prominent Hispanics[15] emerged as leaders of such investor groups for good reason. Hispanic buyers could apply as minority owners in order to qualify for benefits not available to non-minorities. The most appealing prospect was purchasing SICC at 75% or less of its fair market value under the FCC's "distress sale" policy (497 U.S. 547). The U.S. Supreme Court's 1990 decision upholding its constitutionality argued that the distress policy would lower station prices for minority buyers, and motivate existing licensees to seek them out (*Metro Broadcasting Inc. v. Federal Communications Commission* [1990]). Hispanic investors also underscored the threat of non-Hispanic buyers changing the stations' Spanish format. Although the sale agreement stipulated retaining Spanish for a minimum of two years, such a short time period heightened concerns among some Hispanic leaders that the licenses could be acquired by an entity more interested in gaining entry to lucrative television markets than in making a long-term commitment to Spanish-language broadcasting. Hispanic bidders played on such concerns as they jockeyed for favor with the presiding federal judge, Mariana Pfaelzer, and the committee of three SICC employees charged with choosing the winning bid.[16]

On June 23, 1986 the FCC's Mass Media Bureau filed a settlement agreement with the Commission's review board. Like its predecessor in the district court, the settlement would end the legal proceedings against SICC. The agreement's principal terms were threefold: the stations would be sold to unrelated buyers at full market value; the advertising spot-sale waiver (of Rule 73.658[i]) would be extended to the buyers for no more than six months; and SICC officers, directors, and shareholders were precluded from acquiring an equity interest in the purchasing company.[17] The settlement agreement granted SICC two months to find a buyer; the field of bidders would narrow and an intense rivalry ensued thereafter.

Bidding by the Finalists and Selection of the Winning Bid

From the bids submitted on June 30, 1986, the sale committee narrowed the field of contenders to a short list including the Hallmark/First Chicago/ Warburg Pincus group; TVL Corp., headed by Diego C. Asencio, a former U.S. Ambassador to Colombia and Brazil; Reliance Capital Corp., which subsequently formed Univision's principal competitor, Telemundo Group; the Hispanic Broadcasting Corporation, headed by Drs. M. Lee Pearce and Tirso del Junco; Forstmann Little & Co., a New York investment firm; and a group headed by television producer Norman Lear (SICC sells TVs, 1986). Two weeks later, the court narrowed the field to two competitors, the Hallmark group and TVL Corp.[18]

Diego Asencio invited Hallmark's chief executive officer, Irvine Hockaday Jr., to discuss a possible merger of his corporation with the TVL group. The plan was simple but, from Hockaday's perspective, nefarious: TVL would use its influence within Hispanic political circles to have the SICC sale designated for distress sale to minority buyers at 75% of market value. As a minority shareholder, Hallmark would enjoy future profits without the considerable expense of buying the station group at full market value. Hockaday declined the offer, saying Hallmark could not ethically abandon its investment partners by switching allegiances so late in the process. According to court documents submitted by Hallmark's attorneys, the meeting ended on a hostile note, with TVL representatives threatening to wield their political clout to block the Hallmark group from obtaining the stations (Motion of the Hallmark, 1986). Such gamesmanship echoed the contentious interactions between Frank Fouce Jr. and Rene Anselmo a decade earlier.

As the competition for SICC intensified, the two finalists employed distinct acquisition strategies. TVL sought to use ethnic identity as a wedge to disqualify their non-Hispanic opponents, while the Hallmark group sought favor by negotiating equity participation agreements with SICC management. In the words of the journalist Greg Crister, "Hallmark from this point on acquiesced to everything the general managers [of SICC stations] wanted, which turned out to be a brilliant, opportunistic move" (1987, p. 31).

The Bidding War

Hallmark/First Chicago/Warburg Pincus's initial bid of $276 million included offers of employment and stock options to William Stiles, Andrew Goldman, Joaquin Blaya, Emilio Nicolás Jr., Daniel Villanueva and Blain Decker, all of whom had expressed an interest in Stiles's failed internal buyout plan. Also included was a programming agreement with SIN whereby the network would receive 37.5% of SICC profits for two years. A key feature of the agreement stipulated that current management would be retained for a minimum of two years. It is important to note that the two Spanish International companies were renamed Univision during this upheaval in 1986; although sharing the name in common, they retained the distinction between a network and station group.[19]

For its part, TVL submitted a higher initial bid of $311 million, but did not court station management personnel. Notwithstanding its Hispanic political connections, TVL failed to reach a programming agreement with SIN before the final bids were submitted. According to one report, TVL actually alienated the same SICC general managers the Hallmark group was wooing by intimating that some might not keep their jobs once the sale was completed (Crister, 1987, p. 31). It is not hard to imagine which offer SICC and SIN management would have persuaded colleagues on the sale committee to select.

In mid-July the Hallmark group raised its offer to $290 million and dropped certain affiliation, financing and due diligence conditions in order to strengthen its bid. Meanwhile, TVL scrambled to shore up its financing, an endeavor that was hampered by the organization's short history. TVL's final offer of $320 million on July 16 still included loose ends.[20] Under pressure from the sale committee, Hallmark raised its offer to $301 million on July 15; E.M. Warburg Pincus withdrew from the group at this point, believing the price too high, the financing too inflexible, and SICC's condition and prospects "too risky" (Motion of the Hallmark, 1986, p. 17).

On the morning of July 18, Hallmark and First Chicago learned that the three-person sale committee had split, with two members favoring their bid and one favoring TVL's. The stockholders' lawsuit settlement agreement required the court to choose a buyer in the case of a sale committee deadlock. Hallmark and First Chicago strengthened their offer by adding another half-million dollars. Later that day, Judge Mariana Pfaelzer selected Hallmark and First Chicago's offer, citing strength of financial backing as the main criterion influencing her decision.

The $301.5 million sum was roughly 18 times greater than SICC's 1985 cash flow, and 14 times greater than the station group's projected cash flow for 1986 (SICC sells, 1986; Barnes, 1986). The investors were, of course, counting on more major advertisers recognizing the value of reaching Spanish-speaking consumers. Initial reports indicated that Hallmark and First Chicago would each contribute $37.5 million in cash, and finance the remaining $226.5 million. By the time the partners took control of the stations in August 1987, however, First Chicago held only 25% interest in the corporation.

Post-Sale Appeals in Federal Courts

News of the sale raised a hullabaloo in Los Angeles that echoed through the late summer and fall of 1986. The leaders of a half dozen Hispanic political organizations periodically convened press conferences to denounce the transfer of local station KMEX and other SICC stations to non-Hispanic owners. TVL appealed Judge Pfaelzer's decision, first in her courtroom and later in the Ninth Circuit Court of Appeals, and also joined Hispanic political organizations in petitioning the FCC. Elected officials were pressured to fall in line, and legislation to prevent SICC's sale to non-Hispanic buyers was introduced at the municipal, county, state and federal levels.

Five days after Judge Pfaelzer selected Hallmark and First Chicago's bid, the court received confirmation that TVL had secured financing from a commercial bank in New York. The letter both deepened TVL's despair over its missed opportunity and strengthened its conviction that the bidding process had been inequitable. TVL's attorneys applied for leave to intervene in legal proceedings to transfer the stations to Hallmark and First Chicago, arguing in its application (as well as the Los Angeles press) that the sale process had been flawed in several ways.[21] After Judge Pfaelzer denied TVL's motion to intervene on October 9, 1986, the group prepared its case for the Ninth Circuit Court of Appeals in San Francisco, which denied TVL's petition for a rehearing in August 1987.

As an appeal of last resort within the federal court system, TVL filed a petition at the U.S. Supreme Court to examine the lower courts' proceedings. The high court declined to review the case and dismissed the petition without comment in January 1988 (819 F.2d. 1145 [1988]). The legal process initiated by Frank Fouce Jr. and Bruce Corwin more than 11 years earlier had run its course through the federal courts, and brought increased public and corporate attention to the nascent industry along the way.

Attempts to Block the Sale through Legislation

U.S. Congressman Matthew G. Martinez, a Los Angeles Democrat who served as chairman of the Congressional Hispanic Caucus, became a zealous proponent of blocking the SICC stations' transfer to non-Hispanic owners. After the SICC sale agreement was announced, he asked the House Telecommunications Subcommittee to monitor the sale process, and pressured the FCC to ensure that the future licensees were Hispanic (SICC to sell, 1986). Yet even before his efforts intensified in the wake of Hallmark's selection, Martinez encountered resistance from some of his peers.[22] Thus, the political significance of Spanish-language television became recognized at the national level as politicians and political parties struggled over the ownership and control of a rapidly expanding ethnic medium.

On July 23, Martinez introduced "The Minority Ownership Improvements Act of 1986" in the U.S. House of Representatives. Despite its benign title, the bill's objective was to block transfer of SICC's licenses to Hallmark and First Chicago by forcing a "distress sale" of the stations to minority owners. Several fellow Democrats and Hispanic Caucus members opposed the bill, writing their fellow congressmen, "the bill's objective is laudatory—to promote continuation of a national Spanish-language programming service. However, we do not believe that [the bill] is a necessary or appropriate vehicle to achieve this goal" (Beale, 1986, p. 51). Opposition within his own party and caucus was sufficient to kill Martinez's bill.[23]

In early August, the Los Angeles County Board of Supervisors voted unanimously to request that the FCC only grant the license for KMEX, SICC's local station, to Hispanic buyers. The motion cited Hallmark's lack of experience in Spanish-language broadcasting, the importance of television station ownership by Hispanics, and the need to guarantee a dependable source of Spanish-language broadcasting in Los Angeles County (Valle, 1986b). Although neither the board of supervisors nor the Los Angeles City Council wielded power to act on this issue, the elected officials did not miss an opportunity to support the wishes of their Hispanic constituents—or at least the most vocal and politically active citizens among them.

Petitions and Applications to the FCC

At every major juncture of the post-sale station transfer process, the FCC responded to petitions and applications concerning the SICC licenses. Most of the petitioners were either Hispanic political groups attempting to block the transfer through legislation, or investor groups claiming to have a stake in the station sale before or after Hallmark was selected. An overview of the petitions reveals how contentious the licenses became, and illustrates the FCC's handling of specific ethnic-oriented broadcast licenses prior to the Supreme Court's ruling on the constitutionality of minority preference rules for assigning vacated licenses.

In October 1986, the FCC Review Board dismissed the Mexican American Bar Association of Los Angeles County's petition to intervene on behalf of organizations it represented. Commissioner Norman Blumenthal wrote, "the relief sought, i.e., extension of the Commission's minority 'distress sale' policy and the imposition of a condition that SICC stations be sold to a minority entity, is beyond this board's authority" (1 FCC Rcd. 92 [1986]). Another petition to reconsider the (approved) settlement agreement by the Miami-based Spanish American League Against Discrimination (SALAD), argued that the public interest would be better served if the FCC declared the SICC channels vacant or sold the stations to qualified minority buyers under the distress sale policy (1 FCC Rcd. 844–846). The petition made two basic claims. First, the SICC settlement agreement violated commission policy by allowing a licensee whose qualifications were at issue to transfer its licenses. The Commission's review board responded that the case held a strong public interest element that distinguished it from normal licensee qualifications cases—the interests of SICC's minority shareholders and the television viewing public had to be considered. SALAD's second argument asserted that the FCC had acted inconsistently with its own minority distress sale policy. In response, the commission cited a federal district court's recent remanding of a pivotal case[24] that had rendered the distress sale policy inoperative. The FCC's dismissive handling of SALAD's claims would later haunt the commission in a federal court of appeals and in the U.S. Supreme Court.

In June 1987, a year after the controversial SICC sale, the FCC released two orders regarding SICC's transfer to Hallmark and First Chicago. The first renewed SICC's broadcast licenses under the condition that they be transferred to Hallmark and First Chicago (2 FCC Rcd. 3336), and rejected competing applications filed by Hispanic Broadcasting Limited (HBL) and Hispanic Broadcasting Systems (HBS), two investor groups still hoping to obtain the licenses.[25] The second order granted SICC's and Hallmark's applications for license transfer (2 FCC Rcd. 3962). The FCC again denied petitions by organizations opposing Hallmark and First Chicago's acquisition of the station group. The unsuccessful petitioners included SALAD, HBS, HBL and The Mexican American Bar Association of Los Angeles County (and its allies) as well as several newcomers to the FCC process: TVL Corp., The Cuban American National Foundation, The Coalition for the Preservation of Hispanic Broadcasting, and The United States Hispanic Chamber of Commerce.

The petitioners' first argument concerned the public interest, arguing yet again Hallmark's lack of affiliation with the Hispanic community and the possibility that stockholder pressure could cause the stations to broadcast in English after the two-year agreement expired. The Coalition for the Preservation of Hispanic Broadcasting called for an evidentiary hearing to determine whether the public interest would be served by allowing acquisition of Spanish-language broadcasting outlets by non-Hispanic owners. SICC and Hallmark countered by emphasizing Section 310 (d) of the Communications

Act which, they argued, "directly forecloses consideration of the claim that a Hispanic-controlled licensee of these stations would serve the public interest better than Hallmark" (2 FCC Rcd. 3963). Regarding the possibility of a future format change, Hallmark maintained that Section 73.658 of the commission's rules tied its hands, prohibiting networks from entering contracts beyond two years. The company also reaffirmed its position that the marketplace, not owner ethnicity, would be the best guarantee of continued broadcasting in Spanish.

The petitioners' second concern regarded Hallmark's two-year programming agreement with SIN. It was possible, they argued, that the programming agreement would leave the station group open to the same foreign control that initially precipitated SICC's forced sale. The petitioners also questioned a settlement agreement provision allowing Hallmark to retain SICC station managers: what would prevent the same individuals who were implicated in FCC investigations from acting unlawfully again? Hallmark responded by challenging the claim of employee misconduct, and pointed out that all bidders for SICC agreed to an employee protection plan which mandated retention of certain workers after the ownership transfer. Regarding the affiliation agreement with SIN, Hallmark replied that a two-year format stipulation forced it to seek substantial quantities of Spanish-language programming, and SIN was the best source. After considering the arguments the FCC's Mass Media Bureau concluded that the petitioners had failed to raise substantial and material questions of fact, the applicants were qualified, and transferring the licenses would serve the public interest, convenience and necessity (2 FCC Rcd. 3966).

Hallmark and First Chicago took control of the former SICC stations, renamed Univision, on August 6, 1987, and KDTV in San Francisco on February 24, 1988. Several organizations that unsuccessfully attempted to block the transfer process filed applications for review of the decision to grant the license transfers, alleging that the Mass Media Bureau's prior denial contravened both federal law and the public interest; they urged the full commission to reverse or modify the bureau's finding.[26] In opposing the petitions, Hallmark again questioned the petitioners' legal standing and the adequacy of their arguments. TVL Corp. distinguished its petition from others by stressing its opposition to the sale process, not Hallmark's qualifications as a licensee. TVL sought a sale to the highest bidder in a legally sound, nondiscriminatory sale process. To this end, TVL wanted the U.S. Court of Appeals for the Ninth Circuit to remand the case to district court in Los Angeles, where the original bidding procedure could be annulled. The commission responded by asserting its inability to intervene in matters being heard in other legal fora. The FCC upheld its approved license transfers of a year earlier, yet the issue was still not settled. The petitioners took their complaints to the court charged with hearing appeals of FCC decisions: the U.S. Court of Appeals for the District of Columbia.

The District of Columbia Appeals Court Case

The case *Coalition for the Preservation of Hispanic Broadcasting v. FCC* includes a list of petitioners now familiar to the reader: Hispanic Broadcasting Systems, Hispanic Broadcasting Limited Partnership, and TVL Corp. Reversing an earlier FCC ruling, the court determined that the two "Hispanic Broadcasting" groups and TVL had standing in the case as prospective competitors. The "Coalition" received standing as a viewer. Not surprisingly, several companies whose interests could have been affected by the proceeding's outcome participated as interveners: Univision Holdings Inc. (Hallmark and First Chicago), two separately incorporated stations, Seven Hills Television Co., Bahia de San Francisco Television Co., and Fouce Amusement Enterprises (893 F.2d. 1349 [D.C. Cir. 1990]).

The case centered on the FCC's approving the sale at full market value before license renewal proceedings had run their full course. An FCC policy stipulates that a licensee whose qualifications are under investigation may not transfer a broadcast license at full market value until the commission has determined whether that licensee has already forfeited authorization to broadcast. The primary goal of this so-called Jefferson Radio policy is deterrence through the "awesome potential for economic loss that attends deprivation of license" (652 F.2d. 1026 ([D.C. Cir. 1981]). The terms of the Jefferson Radio policy, initially articulated in 1964, were challenged in 1978 when an FCC decision determined that particular circumstances warranted exceptions. The potential to profit from transferring the license(s) remained a cornerstone of the policy.

In spite of the commission's arguments that *de facto* control by foreigners and SICC's 20-year history as an incumbent licensee constituted "exceptional circumstances," the Court of Appeals found that the FCC violated its Jefferson Radio policy by approving transfer of the licenses at full market value before fully resolving the issues that had precipitated evidentiary hearings. The court remanded the case to the Commission "to complete the proceeding pending at the time the settlement agreement was approved, or to articulate a new policy that explains why 'Jefferson Radio' is no longer an appropriate precedent and to justify the transfer to Hallmark without completing the pending renewal proceeding" (893 F.2d. 1349, 1362). The FCC complied with the court, finally settling the matter.

Conclusion

This chapter describes a number of interrelated legal processes that, I argue, constitute a crucial maturation phase in the development of U.S. Spanish-language television. When Frank Fouce Jr. and Bruce Corwin filed a stockholder derivative suit in 1976, SIN and SICC were still heavily dependent on financing and content from Mexico. Ten years later much content was still imported—and remains so in the 2010s—but domestic program production was expanding, and two major mainstream corporations had invested in the industry. As we will see in the next chapter, genuine competition was on the horizon as the Telemundo network began developing in 1986.

In addition to the enhanced prospects for international trade discussed earlier in this chapter, a movement toward conglomeration in U.S. broadcasting also intensified, spurred by deregulation; both processes would gain considerable momentum in the 1990s and 2000s. These shifts toward ownership concentration and deregulation have wielded significant influence over U.S. Spanish-language television's development, as subsequent chapters will demonstrate. The essential connection here is that as broadcasting's regulatory climate relaxed some large players in U.S. media contemplated adding Spanish-language properties to their expanding portfolios (Wilkinson, 2009; Coffey, 2009). Not surprisingly, there was a parallel increase in academic research taking social scientific and political economic approaches to media industries—the trend gained momentum as media companies grew and consolidated from the 1980s on. A portion of this research concerned Spanish-language media (e.g. Greenberg, Burgoon, Burgoon, & Korzenny, 1983; Antola & Rogers, 1984; Valenzuela, 1985).

The legal processes surrounding the Spanish International companies brought Spanish-language television to the attention of corporations and political organizations that had previously paid little notice. From an ethnic-oriented medium that the FCC largely ignored—and made exceptions to accommodate—the industry transformed into a serious player with strong potential for growth. At the time it was sold, SICC was the most valuable station group ever denied license renewal by the FCC's Enforcement Bureau. The fact that an ethnic-oriented broadcasting company was at issue increased the case's visibility, and volatility, at a time when the FCC was second-guessing some of its own policies. As Zarkin and Zarkin (2006) explain, the commission enacted minority preference rules during the 1970s, in the wake of the so-called Kerner Commission[27] report that criticized news media for perpetuating racial inequalities. By the mid-1980s political winds had shifted toward deregulation and the FCC sought to dismantle rules designed to increase female and minority ownership of broadcast stations. Thus, SICC's legal processes unfolded simultaneously with legal and political struggles over minority preference rules, which heightened scrutiny of, and fervor about, the case.

Attention from major corporations and investors became a fixture of the industry, as chapters which follow will show. That interest went hand-in-hand, of course, with increased coverage of Spanish-language television by the business press and media industry trade journals. For example, the *Los Angeles Times* reported regularly on developments in the Spanish International lawsuits as well as challenges to Hallmark's acquisition of SICC, and *Variety* began publishing annual Hispanic media supplements during the 1980s. This increased exposure through press and trade journal reporting together with more general recognition of the population during the Decade of the Hispanic linked the Spanish-language television industry with a dynamic populace.

Defining and defending the interests of Hispanics had long been the main objective of advocacy groups, but their interest in media had been limited prior to the period this chapter covers. The prospect of Anglo-controlled companies having limited ties to the Hispanic community controlling a medium with the reach and influence of Univision alarmed some advocates, who were likely familiar with concepts that emerged from the critical discourses surrounding dependency, internal colonialism and the New World Information and Communication Order. The notion of media imperialism—powerful Western nations dominating developing societies culturally and ideologically through the soft power of mediated communication (Tomlinson, 1991)—was hypothesized in its reverse by Gutiérrez & Schement (1984), who argued that the U.S. Spanish-language television sector was dominated by capital, programming and managerial influence originating in Mexico. This argument, that business interests based in a developing nation were controlling a media sector in the world's richest, more powerful nation, resonated in light of the foreign ownership and control accusations affirmed by FCC investigations. The onslaught of non-Hispanic companies and investor groups that expressed interest in acquiring SICC also appeared to confirm arguments of internal colonialism—that mainstream business interests (the "core") sought access to Hispanic audiences (the "periphery") in order to extract wealth through advertising (Gutiérrez, 2004). With these and/or related concerns lurking in the background, the scale and intensity of media-related Hispanic advocacy increased during the 1980s. We will see that concerns about exploitation and equity endure, and become especially salient when a major network changes ownership or acquires new assets through a merger.

Notes

1. Chapters Six, Eight and Nine discuss the subsequent censuses that have reinforced the pattern.
2. Undercounting of the Hispanic population is a recurring criticism of the U.S. censuses. In the early 1980s estimates of the actual population sized ranged from 14 to 25 million, depending on how the population was operationally defined and the measures employed, for example whether undocumented people or residents of Puerto Rico are included. The U.S. government estimated the number of undocumented Hispanics at 7.4 million in the early 1980s (Guernica, 1982).
3. As an example, the author retrieved some of the legal documents cited in this chapter from the Lexis-Nexis database in the late 1980s, but most industry-oriented material came from bound volumes, microfilm and microfiche (Wilkinson, 1991). In the early 1990s, company profiles and trade press reports became accessible on Lexis-Nexis and similar databases. This book's final chapters, covering the 2000s, demonstrate a deepening of this trend as some industry data and analysis that would have been considered proprietary (and therefore withheld) two decades earlier are readily available from multiple electronic sources.

4. This book's final two chapters suggest a generational pattern at work, as a spate of serious challenges faced his own son, Emilio Azcárraga Jean, after Azcárraga Milmo died in 1997 (Fernández & Paxman, 2000).

5. The "First Amended and Supplemental Complaint" (1977) claims that Rene Anselmo: promoted deals with SIN, Magnaverde, and Televisa that were detrimental to SICC; charged SICC stations more for programming than SIN had originally paid Televisa; allowed transmission of a TV signal to a Sacramento/ Modesto, CA station without compensating SICC; approved services to San Francisco, Phoenix, and Corpus Christi, TX, stations without providing compensation to SICC; and failed to exercise good faith, care or skill in acting as chief executive officer, president, director and controlling shareholder of SICC.

6. The proposal called for: divestiture of Televisa ownership in SIN, divestiture of Televisa ownership in SICC, a total "disentanglement" of SICC and SIN shareholders and principals, cancellation of the spot sale waiver granted SIN in 1978, imposition of monetary forfeitures for past violations, and cancellation (repurchase) of the convertible debenture held by Televisa (Report of Special, 1983, p. 7).

7. By orders FCC 83M-2799 released 19 August 1983 (SIN), and FCC 83M-2855 released 24 August 1983 (Fouce).

8. It should be noted that the decision contains minor factual errors regarding SICC's and SIN's history and development—like the business press and trade journal reports discussed in the Introduction, legal documents also require close, critical reading and verification of key information.

9. Judge Conlin detailed several ways in which SICC stations were disadvantaged by SIN: 1) the Univision advertising sales concept required that SICC stations charge at least 50% more than Televisa charged in Mexico for the same amount of time on the same program (*In re Spanish*, 1986, paras. 54–60, 170–171); 2) SICC employees worked on Televisa, SIN and/or Magnaverde projects (such as World Cup Soccer telecasts) without compensation paid to the station group (ibid., para. 166.); 3) SICC-owned stations enjoyed less favorable local advertising agreements with SIN than did independently-owned network affiliates. Two facts illustrate the inequity. First, the SICC stations shared their local ad sale revenues with SIN (in order to avoid disputes between sales personnel at the two companies); no such arrangement was made with the non-SICC affiliates. Second, the percentage of sales charged by SIN for its programming services was not based on billings for the SICC stations, but rather on collected revenues for the independent stations. By this arrangement, any losses incurred by bad debts were absorbed solely by the SICC stations, SIN lost nothing (ibid., paras. 173–175).

10. In his report to the Los Angeles court, Special Master J. Roger Wollenberg outlined the various penalties that the FCC could have imposed on SICC. They are, in abbreviated form: 1) Loss of License—refusal to renew some or all of SICC's broadcast licenses, 2) Grant of Conditional Renewal—licenses could be renewed on condition that remedial measures be taken or that specified misconduct not occur, 3) Grant of Short-term Renewal—renewal for less than the normal five-year term (usually with conditions to be met), 4) Comparative Demerit—past illegality or demerit is considered in the granting or renewal of licenses, 5) Distress Sale—forced sale of a station or station group to a minority-controlled entity at no more than 75% of fair market value. Wollenberg considered SICC a prime candidate for distress sale. Of sale at full market value (the option which Judge Conlin ultimately pursued) Wollenberg wrote: "the circumstances in which such a sale has been permitted are highly limited, and most of the

relevant precedents are plainly inapplicable to the present case." (Report of Special, 1983, pp. 31–38, 61–65.)

11. Senator Schmitt had considerable influence at the FCC due to his co-authoring the Telecommunications Act of 1979 (FCC to look, 1980).

12. The judge identified the plaintiffs' probable motive for bringing a suit they had little hope of winning: "it is apparent that Defendant is representing a client before the FCC and that the pendency of the instant litigation offers opportunities for the opposition to claim a conflict of interest and thereby compel disqualification of Defendant Leibowitz as counsel for the SRBA. This smacks of a legal ploy which this court refused to condone" (608 F. Supp. 178, pp. 184–185).

13. District Judge Mariana Pfaelzer's preliminary ruling in favor of the plaintiffs in August of 1985 followed the FCC's "Proposed Findings of Facts and Conclusions of Law" released by Administrative Law Judge Conlin on May 15. A second major ruling by Judge Pfaelzer—approval of a settlement agreement between the opposing parties on May 12, 1986—was made possible by the Initial Decision that Judge Conlin released on January 8, 1986.

14. William Stiles approached the following SICC employees and associates as possible participants in his acquisition plan: Daniel Villanueva, general manager of KMEX in Los Angeles; Joaquin Blaya, general manager of WLTV in Miami; Blain Decker, vice president and director of sales at WLTV; José Cancela, general manager of the KTVW in Phoenix; and Emilio Nicolás Jr., vice president and general manager of KDTV in San Francisco (Motion of the Hallmark, 1986).

15. These included: Enrique "Hank" Hernandez, a former Los Angeles police lieutenant and owner of several security companies; Diego C. Ascensio a former U.S. Ambassador to Colombia and Brazil; and Dr. Tirso del Junco, a former president of the California Republican Party.

16. The sale committee was comprised of: Emilio Nicolas Sr., president and general manager of KWEX in San Antonio and acting head of SICC after Rene Anselmo's resignation; Karen Bedrosian, SICC's chief financial officer; and Irv Fuller, an SICC executive.

17. By the settlement agreement's terms, relatives of SICC principals were not prohibited from holding small percentages of stock in the corporation after it changed ownership. An FCC order released on March 8, 1989 sanctioned the transfer of 15% of Latcom (Hallmark's holding company) stock to 15 adult children of the Azcárraga, Alemán and O'Farrill families. The stock was held in tightly restricted trusts designed to prevent the possibility of influence being exerted over U.S. broadcast operations.

18. The TVL Corp. likely got its name from the initials of three of its principals: Raúl R. Tapia, a partner in the Washington D.C. law firm of Tapia & Buffington, and former deputy special assistant on Hispanic Affairs for the Carter Administration; Alfred R. Villalobos, vice chairman and president of a management company; and David C. Lizárraga, president, chairman and chief executive officer of TELACU.

19. "Univision" was first used in the mid-1970s for a venture to unite Spanish-speakers worldwide via satellite (Televisa's Univision, 1977). The potential audience was purported to encompass 270 million people living in 35 million households in 20 Spanish-speaking countries (Spanish-language TV, 1981). Televisa initiated the project, entering a joint venture with SIN and Radiotelevisión Española (RTE) to share content (Lenti, 1984). According to the project's director, Alejandro Burillo, other unifying forces behind "one vision" besides a common language

are religion and tradition (Lenti, 1984). Of course another "vision" was to amass profits through transnational, hopefully global, marketing (Spanish-language TV, 1981). This concept was very similar to the *Cadena de las Americas* project of 1992 (discussed in Chapter Seven), which coincided with the quincentennial of Christopher Columbus's arrival in the Americas, *after* the Univision name had been assigned to the U.S. enterprises formerly known as Spanish International Network and Spanish International Communications Corp.

20. TVL's offer statement included an explanatory statement that was unlikely to win confidence among sale committee members: "[TVL] has also received indications of interest from a number of prominent investment banking firms regarding its financing for this transaction and will have oral commitments for such financing this afternoon and will receive written commitment for such financing tomorrow" (*Fouce Amusement*, 1976, Vol. 17, Exhibit Q).

21. The first alleged transgression occurred shortly after Judge Conlin's initial decision, when Hallmark offered stock deals to William Stiles and other supporters of an internal SICC buyout. TVL claimed the offer violated FCC rules prohibiting more than two percent ownership by former directors of a broadcast entity once it has changed hands (Valle, 1986a). A second charge involved conflict of interest by sale committee member Emilio Nicolás Sr., and a consultant to the sale committee, William Stiles. According to TVL, Nicolás's son Emilio Jr. could gain more than $10 million if Hallmark acquired SICC. This circumstance presumably motivated the father to act with considerable self-interest when voting on the bids. TVL labeled William Stiles a biased, influential consultant during the selection process because of his close ties—financial and otherwise—with the Hallmark group (Reply memorandum, 1986). This close rapport among representatives of the Hallmark group, the sale committee, and a consultant to the sale led to other actions, which, TVL argued, prejudiced the process. When TVL raised its offer from $311 million to $320 million on July 14, word of the increase reached Hallmark and First Chicago, a fact that Hallmark's attorneys acknowledged. The problem, according to TVL, was that such knowledge motivated Hallmark's short-term offer and the judge's subsequent decision to accept it so as to prevent SICC from being left without a buyer. TVL considered Hallmark's so-called "drop dead offer" a tactic to pressure the committee into a decision before TVL's financing solidified.

22. Another Hispanic Caucus member, Henry B. González (D-Texas) wrote to Tim Wirth, Chairman of the House Telecommunication Subcommittee, "[Martinez's position] has not been taken pursuant to any consultation with the Hispanic Caucus as a whole, and is much more representative of his personal position than anything else. Certainly it does not reflect my view." González believed that the proposed legislation would be "contrary to the findings of the judge [Conlin's Initial Decision] and would negate the settlement agreement already reached in this matter" (*Broadcasting*, July 14, 1986, p. 69).

23. Henry B. González was joined by Albert Bustamante (D-Texas), Kika de la Garza (D-Texas) and Bill Richardson (D-New Mexico) in opposing the bill (Beale, 1986, p. 51).

24. *Shurberg Broadcasting of Hartford, Inc. v. FCC*, 1985.

25. HBL's most intriguing argument to have its application considered, in spite of its tardiness, claimed that the license transfer process was tainted by SICC's harassment and intimidation of the Spanish Radio Broadcasters of America. Supposedly, SRBA acquiesced to the SICC-Hallmark settlement agreement

because a slew of antitrust suits SICC filed against its members were dropped in exchange for SRBA's supporting the settlement.

26. The applications for review were submitted by Susan M. Jaramillo, The Coalition for the Preservation of Hispanic Broadcasting, Hispanic Broadcasting Limited Partnership and TVL Corp. Applications were also received from SALAD and the United States Hispanic Chamber of Commerce, but those organizations later filed motions to dismiss their pleadings (3 FCC Rcd. 4319).

27. "Kerner Commission" was the popular name for the National Advisory Commission on Civil Disorders that sought reasons behind the violent race riots of 1967.

References

Answers first set of interrogatories propounded to plaintiffs, counterdefendants and third party defendants. Interrogatory No. 37, filed May 23, 1977 in *Fouce Amusement Enterprises and Metropolitan Theaters Corp. v. Spanish International Communications Corp. et al.*, CV 76–3451 MRP (CD CA).

Antitrust litigation MDL No. 596. (1985). U.S. Court of Appeals for the Fifth District (Ft. Worth, TX) Case 85–1815.

Antola, Livia, & Rogers, Everett M. (1984). Television flows in Latin America. *Communication Research, 11*(2), 183–202.

Balkan, D. Carlos. (1986, December). 'Unorthodox and energetic': An interview with Rene Anselmo. *Hispanic Business,* 17, 78.

Barnes, Peter W. (1986, July 22). Hallmark Cards agrees to buy broadcast firm [Eastern Edition]. *Wall Street Journal,* 37.

Beale, Steve. (1986, December). Hallmark Si, Hallmark No? *Hispanic Business,* 50–51.

Besas, Peter. (1984, September 19). SIN gets respect & clout in booming Hispanic mkt. *Variety,* 50.

Berry, John F. (1987, April). The new order at Blair. *Channels,* 54–55.

Brischetto, Robert. (1993, October). Making a milestone. *Hispanic Business,* 6–10.

Coffey, Amy Jo. (2009). Growth and trends in Spanish language television in the United States. In A. B. Albarran (Ed.), *The handbook of Spanish language media.* (pp. 203–217). New York: Routledge.

Crister, Greg. (1987, January). The feud that toppled a TV empire. *Channels: The Business of Communications,* 24–31.

Davis, Cary, Haub, Carl, & Willette, JoAnne. (1983, June). U.S. Hispanics: Changing the face of America. *Population Bulletin, 38*(3), 1–43.

De Uriarte, Mercedes. (1980, December 14). Battle for the ear of the Latino. *Los Angeles Times* (Calendar section), 1–7.

Elliott, Margaret S., & Kraemer, Kenneth L. (Eds.) (2008). *Computerization movements and technology diffusion: From mainframes to ubiquitous computing.* Medford, N.J.: Information Today.

FCC probing Spanish-language TV programming service. (1980, September 5). *Los Angeles Times,* sec. 4, p. 1.

Fernández, Claudia, & Paxman, Andrew. (2000). *Emilio Azcarraga Milmo y su imperio Televisa.* México D.F.: Grijalbo.

First amended and supplemental complaint. Filed November 30, 1977 in *Fouce Amusement Enterprises and Metropolitan Theaters Corp. v. Spanish International Communications Corp. et al.*, CV 76–3451 MRP (CD CA).

Fouce Amusement Enterprises and Metropolitan Theaters Corp. v. Spanish International Communications Corp. et al., No. CV 76–3451 MRP (CD. CA, 1976).

Gapinski, James H. (1999). *Economic growth in the Asia Pacific region.* New York: St. Martin's Press.

Giffard, C. Anthony. (1989). *UNESCO and the media.* White Plains, NY: Longman.

Goldman, Kevin. (1984, September 19). SIN News wants 'credibility' in fast-growing Latino mkt.: Innovation makes up for size. *Variety,* 54.

Greenberg, Bradley S., Burgoon, Michael, Burgoon, Judee K., & Korzenny, Felipe. (1983). *Mexican Americans and the mass media.* Norwood, NJ: Ablex.

Guernica, Antonio. (1982). *Reaching the Hispanic market effectively: The media, the market, the methods.* New York, NY: McGraw-Hill Companies.

Gupta, Udayan. (1984, October). Netspan targets three leading ADI's. *Hispanic Business,* 1–19, 36.

Gutiérrez, Félix, & Schement, Jorge Reina. (1979). *Spanish-language radio in the southwestern United States.* Mexican American Monograph Series No. 5. Center for Mexican American Studies, University of Texas at Austin.

Gutiérrez, Félix, & Schement, Jorge Reina. (1984, April). Spanish International Network: The flow of television from Mexico to the United States. *Communication Research,* 11(2), 241–258.

Gutiérrez, Ramón A. (2004). Internal colonialism: An American theory of race. *Du Bois Review,* 1(2), 281–295.

In re Spanish International Communications Corporation. (1986, January 3). Federal Communications Commission Release No. 86D-1, slip op.

Latin network target of U.S. antitrust probe. (1980, October 21). *Los Angeles Times,* sec. 4, p. 1.

Lenti, Paul. (1984, September 19). Novelas, specs & sports power Televisa programming to SIN: Univision links Mexico & U.S. *Variety,* 63, 84.

Loftus, Jack. (1984, September 1984). SIN keeps rolling; govt. still lookin'. *Variety,* 49, 82.

Maza, Enrique. (1986, 14 julio). A la vista, la telaraña del poder de Azcárraga en Estados Unidos. *Proceso,* 20–25.

McAnany, Emile G., & Wilkinson, Kenton T. (Eds.) (1996). *Mass media and free trade: NAFTA and the cultural industries.* Austin, University of Texas Press.

Metro Broadcasting Inc. v. Federal Communications Commission. 110 S.Ct. 2997 (1990).

Miranda, Leticia & Quiroz, Julia Teresa. (1990, March). *The decade of the Hispanic: An economic retrospective.* Washington, D.C.: National Council of La Raza.

Mora, G. Cristina. (2011). Regulating immigrant media and instituting ethnic boundaries—the FCC and Spanish-language television: 1960–1990. *Latino Studies,* 9(2/3), 242–262.

Mora, G. Cristina. (2014). *Making Hispanics: How activists, bureaucrats and media constructed a new American.* Chicago: University of Chicago Press.

Motion of the Hallmark Group for affirmation of the July 18 order approving sale of SICC to the Hallmark Group. Filed 22 Sept. 1986 in *Fouce Amusement Enterprises and Metropolitan Theaters Corp. v. Spanish International Communications Corp. et al.* No. CV 76–3451 MRP (CD CA).

Netspan makes opening pitch as new Hispanic on the block. (1984, September 19). *Variety,* 63, 84.

Ramos, George. (1986, February 28). Owners seeking to settle Spanish TV outlets fight. *Los Angeles Times*, sec. 2, p. 3.

Report of the Special Master Roger Wollenberg to the court of the Hon. Mariana Pfaelzer. Submitted July 15,1983 to *Fouce Amusement Enterprises and Metropolitan Theaters Corp. v. Spanish International Communications Corp. et al.,* CV 76–3451 MRP (CD CA).

Rieman, Arthur M. (1985). Foreign ownership and control of U.S. broadcast entities: In Re Spanish International Communications Corp. *UCLA Pacific Basin Law Journal* 4(1–2), 244–252.

Rosenstiel, Thomas B., & Pagano, Penny. (1986, April 18). KMEX appeals to FCC in bid to keep license. *Los Angeles Times*, sec. 4, p. 2.

Shurberg Broadcasting of Hartford, Inc. v. FCC. (1985). 617 F.Supp. 825 (D.D.C. 1985).

SICC and company appeal ALJ decision. (1986, April 28). *Broadcasting*, 66–67.

SICC sells TVs for $301.5 million. (1986, July 28). *Broadcasting*, 91–92.

SICC to sell off stations. (1986, May 19). *Broadcasting*, 79–80.

SIN's 'Destino 84' urges Hispanics to vote. (1984, September 19). *Variety*, 51, 86.

Status conference statement of Fouce Amusement Enterprises, Inc. and Metropolitan Theaters Corp. (1984). Filed October 22, 1984 in *Fouce Amusement Enterprises and Metropolitan Theaters Corp. v. Spanish International Communications Corp. et al.,* No. CV 76–3451 MRP (CD. CA, 1976).

Strategy Research Corp. (1980). *U.S. Hispanics—A market profile.* National Association of Spanish Broadcasters & Strategy Research Corp.

Tomlinson, John. (1991). *Cultural imperialism: A critical introduction.* Baltimore: Johns Hopkins.

Torres, Luis. (1984, October). TeleRed preps for fall rollout. *Hispanic Business*, 20–21, 37.

Valenzuela, Nicolas A. (1985). *Organizational evolution of a Spanish-language television network: An environmental approach* (Doctoral dissertation). Stanford University, Palo Alto, CA.

Valle, Victor. (1986a, September 27). Latinos move to block transfer of TV stations. *Los Angeles Times*, sec. 5, pp. 1, 10.

Valle, Victor. (1986b, August 8). Supervisors support keeping KMEX Latino. *Los Angeles Times*, sec. 6, p. 27.

Welch, Susan, & Sigelman, Lee. (1993). The politics of Hispanic Americans: Insights from national surveys, 1980–1988. *Social Science Quarterly,* 74(1), 76–94.

Wilkinson, Kenton T. (1991). *The sale of Spanish International Communications Corporation: Milestone in the development of Spanish-language television in the United States* (M.A. thesis). University of California at Berkeley, Berkeley, CA.

Wilkinson, Kenton T. (2009). Spanish language media in the United States. In A. B. Albarran, (Ed.), *Handbook of Spanish language media* (pp. 3–16). New York: Routledge.

Zarkin, Kimberly A., & Zarkin, Michael J. (2006). *The Federal Communications Commission: Front line in the culture and regulation wars.* Westport, CT: Greenwood.

5 The Rise of Telemundo and Domestic Competition in the Decade of the Hispanic

This chapter examines an important period in U.S. Spanish-language television development between the uncertainty surrounding the legal challenges facing the Spanish International companies (renamed Univision in 1986) and the industry's increased growth and visibility in the 1990s. If legal processes and ownership struggles dominated the first six years of the 1980s, the last four revolved largely around adjusting to a new competitive environment and efforts to establish domestic program production and its international distribution. The chapter begins by discussing the 1980s' designation as the Decade of the Hispanic, which, along with the census information discussed in the prior chapter, brought new interest to the population—and by extension a key medium reaching it—by business and political interests alike.

The Decade of the Hispanic

The term Decade of the Hispanic sprung from a new presence and perceived potential for the group in the late 1970s and early '80s. The specific origins of the term are at issue, with different authors attributing it to the U.S. federal government (Miranda & Quiroz, 1990), the Coors Brewing Company (Totti, 1987; Gómez, 1992) and news magazines, such as *Time*[1] and *U.S. News and World Report*, which featured Hispanics' emergence in cover stories (del Olmo, 1989a). Whatever the origins, the general concept was shared: the population would finally emerge from the shadows to wield greater political and economic clout, in closer alignment with its numbers. As Maria Elena Toraño, the founding president of the National Hispana Leadership Institute described it, the 1960s had been the decade for Blacks, the 1970s for women, and it was Hispanics' turn in the 1980s (cited in del Olmo, 1989a).

Political Matters

As had been the case for the Civil Rights and Women's Liberation Movements, political mobilization was an important goal of the Brown Power Movement in the 1960s and 70s. Also in common with those movements, not all Hispanics felt comfortable with Brown Power's militant aspect (Lampe, 1981).

Thus, for many Hispanics and non-Hispanics alike, gaining greater influence through additional voters, political representatives and spending power was more palatable than militant resistance. Increased recognition of the ethnic, political and economic diversity encompassed by the 'Hispanic' label became a core challenge to the group's political mobilization, as emphasized in a number of news articles profiling the nascent minority group (e.g., It's your turn, 1978; Church, Goodgame, Leavitt & Lopez, 1985). A critical assessment of the Decade of the Hispanic by the Cuban American National Council claimed that diverse Hispanic groups gained a collective awareness of themselves as a unified force during the early 1980s (Cuban American National Committee [CANC], 1989). During the latter part of the decade, Hispanics pursued a national political agenda that included employment, education, equitable political representation and preserving Hispanic values and traditions as primary goals (CANC, 1989).

The number of Hispanic elected officials increased 7% between 1980 and 1988, some of them widely publicized such as Henry Cisneros's election as mayor of San Antonio in 1981 and Federico Peña becoming Denver's mayor in 1983—both men moved on to high-profile positions in the first Clinton administration in 1993.[2] President George H.W. Bush appointed the first two Hispanics to a White House cabinet: Lauro Cavazos served as Secretary of Education (1988–1990) and Manuel Lujan as Secretary of the Interior (1989–1993).[3] Yet despite these widely reported mayoral elections and federal appointments, the total number of Hispanic elected officials still represented less than 1% nationwide at a time when Hispanics comprised 8.1% of the population (CANC, 1989). Low turnouts for elections did not help in this regard. Notwithstanding the impressive efforts of regional voter registration projects, in 1988 Hispanics remained the least participatory major electoral group with only 35.5% of eligible voters registering and 28.8% voting in the presidential election. (Corresponding numbers for Blacks were 64.5% and 51.5%, and for Whites 59.1% and 67.9% [U.S. Bureau of the Census, 1989]). As noted in the prior chapter, Spanish International Network/Univision ran on-air campaigns to promote Hispanic participation in the 1980 census and to encourage viewers to register and vote in the 1980, 1984 and 1988 presidential elections— Telemundo did the same in 1988.

Economic Matters

During the Decade of the Hispanic more families enjoyed prosperity as the number of affluent Hispanic households grew from 7.2% in 1972 to 8.2% in 1980 and 10.8% in 1988[4] (O'Hare, 1990). By 1990 more than 2.6 million Hispanics resided in 638,000 affluent households, defined as those having an income of $50,000 or more (O'Hare, 1990). Unfortunately, however, almost an equal percentage of Hispanic households lived at the other extreme as 9.7% had incomes at or below 50% of the poverty line in 1988 (Miranda & Quiroz, 1990). The statistics encompassing the entire Hispanic population were equally grim. Hispanics were 23% more likely to be poor in 1988 than they had been in 1979, with 27% of the population living in poverty in 1988; 40% of Hispanic children lived in poverty in 1987 (Miranda & Quiroz, 1990; CANC, 1989). An assessment by the National Council of La Raza identified these characteristics of Hispanics' economic situation during the 1980s (Miranda & Quiroz, 1990):

- Stagnating income levels and continued high poverty
- High proportions of impoverished children
- No improvement for female-maintained households
- Deepening hardships among married couple families
- Widening income disparity
- Unequal benefits from education

Despite a recession early in the decade, the number of Hispanic-owned businesses increased 81% between 1982 and 1987, with more than 250,000 Hispanic-owned small businesses in operation (O'Hare, 1992; Miranda & Quiroz, 1990). By 1989 Hispanic buying power had reached $171 billion, fueled by a growing number of young consumers and a steady stream of immigrants (CANC, 1989). Such statistics deepened corporations' interest in Hispanics as a consumer group, some of which initiated efforts to recruit Hispanic employees (often to penetrate Hispanic communities more effectively). Many Hispanics remained in low-wage positions, however. Several studies found that employment discrimination accounted for some employment discrepancy (Miranda & Quiroz, 1990), but poor educational attainment was a major contributor as Hispanics were the least educated population in the country (CANC, 1989). In 1988 only half of Hispanics age 25 and older were high school graduates; the corresponding figures were 78% for Whites and 65% for Blacks (Miranda & Quiroz, 1990). In 1986, fewer than 30% of Hispanic high school graduates entered college, and two years later only 10% of U.S. Hispanics had four or more years of college, compared to 21% of non-Hispanics (CANC, 1989). As Miranda and Quiroz (1990, p. 22) put it, "by any standard, Hispanics lost ground economically during the 1980s."

Popular Culture

A number of observers noted an increased visibility of Hispanics in U.S. popular culture contributing to the Decade of the Hispanic. In music, Carlos Santana enjoyed a resurgence with his *Blues for Salvador* album that won a Grammy award in 1988, Linda Ronstadt celebrated her Mexican roots with her popular album *Canciones de mi padre*, and Los Lobos opened for top rock acts then became headliners themselves, offering an eclectic combination of styles ranging from hard rock to Mexican folk genres played on traditional instruments. Mejia (2104) points out that these successes in the 1980s paved the way for Hispanic artists' subsequent achievements in the Latin Boom of the late 1990s and thereafter. On English-language television, Hispanic actors played lead characters in top-rated programs such as Jimmy Smits in *L.A. Law* and Edward James Olmos in *Miami Vice* (where many of the villains were also Hispanic). Several films also brought wider public attention to Hispanic culture and challenges. *La Bamba* chronicled the short life of rock star Ritchie Valens, *Stand and Deliver* profiled Jaime Escalante's efforts to inspire students in East Los Angeles to greater achievement, and *The Milagro Beanfield War* explored equity issues and intercultural relations in the U.S. Southwest.

The *Los Angeles Times* columnist Frank del Olmo (1989a) points out that Hispanics also gained greater recognition in sports during the 1980s. The feisty light flyweight boxer Paul Gonzales became one of America's darlings during the 1984 Olympics. Fernando Valenzuela of the LA Dodgers became a household name among baseball fans (and reinforced the stereotype of Latin American baseball players speaking little or no English). The combination of coach Tom Flores and quarterback Jim Plunkett, nicknamed "The Chicano Connection," help lead the Los Angeles Raiders to a Super Bowl title in 1983.

I should note that a similar phenomenon, the so-called Latin Boom of the late 1990s and early 2000s, is discussed in Chapter Eight. Although both periods are characterized by upswings in Hispanics' visibility and influence over U.S. popular culture, there are noteworthy differences as well. We have seen that in the 1980s Hispanic leaders expressed aspirations for higher standards of living and increased political and economic influence; by contrast, the Latin Boom focused on Hispanics' influence on U.S. culture, with less attention paid to the population's wellbeing. Also, the music and film stars of the later boom[5] commanded larger audiences among the general public than did those of the Decade of the Hispanic, partly because they had wealthier, more sophisticated management and promotional operations backing them. The intervening chapters demonstrate how the Hispanic market and media came to yield greater influence and profits between these two cultural booms.

Media Matters

The Decade of the Hispanic initiated more consistent business press and trade journal coverage of the spending habits, brand loyalties and other characteristics of Hispanic consumers. Mainstream corporations like Hallmark Cards and Reliance Capital Corp. entered the Spanish-language television industry in the mid-1980s motivated to profit from a growing number of advertisers seeking access to Spanish-speaking consumers. As corporate interest in the Hispanic market intensified, the number of Spanish-language marketing campaigns increased, to the benefit of Spanish media that sold advertising space and time. Danny Villanueva, KMEX's station manager, reported in the mid-1980s that more than 30% of the Los Angeles station's advertising revenue originated from national-brand companies; he commented, "no longer is the attitude among advertisers 'Why don't you learn English?'" (Church et al., 1985). (The reader is reminded that such was the attitude that SIN's Rene Anselmo and others had faced in the 1960s and early '70s.)

Villanueva's comment reminds us that in the 1980s the Hispanic market was defined almost exclusively by Spanish language use, even though research had clearly established that many Hispanics were bilingual and many younger audience members preferred English (Valenzuela, 1973; López & Enos, 1974). A 1980 article, "The Special Case of Spanish-Language Television," identified key industry characteristics that persisted when this book went to print more than three decades later (Jarboe, 1980). These include: the aforementioned programs encouraging Hispanics to register, vote and be counted in the census; Spanish-language media consumption as a means for audiences to stay culturally connected; audience fragmentation into narrower demographic niches; the origins of political advertising on Spanish-language TV;[6] challenges in accurately counting the Spanish-speaking audience; generational differences in language and program preference; and political advocacy to increase media ownership by Hispanics (Jarboe, 1980). The article depicts a population recognizing its potential and addressing impediments to its own empowerment while being informed and entertained by a corporation, Spanish International Network, that is becoming increasingly adept at engaging and persuading both its viewers and advertising clients. This dynamic of dual recognition typified the Decade of the Hispanic: the population recognized its potential for greater influence and participation in U.S. society while economic and political interests recognized the profit and power potential of a burgeoning social group. Recognition also heightened among local, state and federal politicians and policymakers that Hispanics would grow in number and potential influence. Spanish-language media occupied a beneficial position as a principal conduit for exchange between these groups.

Assessments

This section concludes with various observers' broader assessments of the Decade of the Hispanic. The *Los Angeles Times* columnist Frank del Olmo (1989a) described the concept as "contrived and artificial" due to its designation by outsiders, rather than emergence from within the population. Along similar lines, the Cuban American National Committee (1989, p. 18) concluded, "it seems unlikely that the 1980s or any other single period will become unequivocally 'Hispanic.' Progress and regress are two contradictory but nevertheless powerful currents that are transforming the Hispanic communities." CANC identified media and political representation as areas of improvement, and education, income and limited public acceptance of cultural and linguistic plurality as areas of stagnation. Unfortunately, several forces of regress continued to limit Hispanic communities' advancement as this book went to press: underemployment and low-wage jobs, low voter participation and low educational attainment.

Returning to the prior discussion of popular culture, Richard Valencia (2002) argues that a "rediscovery" of Hispanics in the media during the late 1970s and early 1980s, especially via journalism and films, raised anticipations of educational, economic and political advances among the population. However, he states, "contrary to expected gains during the 'decade of the Hispanic,' the 1980s left many Latinos—particularly Chicanos and Puerto Ricans—worse off" (p. 52). Frank del Olmo (1989a) concurred asserting, "the most evident impact Latinos had in the '80s was in the arts," and he sardonically concluded, "on the playing field, at least, the '80s were indeed a special decade for Latinos." This perspective runs parallel with an established argument that Blacks are less threatening to dominant Anglo-American interests when they excel in popular culture and sports rather than business and politics (Hoberman, 1997).

A related issue is sheer numbers and predictions of soaring population growth well into the future. The sociologist Renato Rosaldo (1988) wrote, "official pronouncements about the 'Decade of the Hispanic' barely conceal diffuse anxieties about the impending impact of demographic projections for Latinos in the United States." This is another theme that we will pick up again, in the final chapter, which describes how pro-immigration marches in the mid-2000s followed quickly on the heels of the 2003 news that Hispanics had surpassed Blacks as the nation's largest minority group.

The concluding paragraph to the Cuban American National Committee's report (1989) provides a fitting conclusion to this discussion as well:

> The increase in political empowerment, the rise of a Hispanic market and entrepreneurship, and the emergence of a national Hispanic agenda are powerful developments that can support long-term Hispanic progress. But sustained educational decline and the perpetuation and deepening of poverty are disturbing signs of long-term Hispanic stagnation. It is the clash of these forces that most accurately defines the fate of Hispanics in the 1980s, a decade perhaps best termed "The *Elusive* Decade of Hispanics." (p. 19, emphasis added)

We now return to our discussion of Spanish-language television industry development during the tumultuous 1980s when the owners of the Spanish International Communications Corp. (SICC, renamed Univision in 1986) were forced to relinquish the stations, although permitted to turn a profit, and when competition first arrived in the form of Telemundo.

Univision After the Forced Sale

In August 1987, the FCC sanctioned SICC's sale by approving Hallmark and First Chicago's broadcast license applications. The new owners had already begun consolidating their holdings by targeting affiliated stations in Phoenix and San Francisco for acquisition. As explained in the Chapter Three, the stations were controlled by many of the same principal stockholders as SICC, but were incorporated separately. Hallmark entered a purchase agreement for the San Francisco station (KDTV) in December 1986, and bought the Phoenix station (KTVW) for $23 million in late 1988 (Landro, 1989). In the interim between those two purchases, low-power translator stations in Houston and Denver were upgraded to full power UHF. By late 1988 Univision reached roughly 85% of the approximately 5 million Spanish-speaking households in the United States (Bergsman, 1988).

The new owners' most expensive move, however, concerned programming and advertising sales, not broadcast outlets—they purchased the Univision programming and advertising sales company that had previously been named Spanish International Network (SIN). Negotiations over the network began a month after Hallmark took control of the station group and ended six months later, in February 1988. The $274.5 million deal bought Hallmark right-of-first-refusal to approximately 50% of Televisa's programming over a 10-year period, national newscast production facilities in Laguna Niguel, California, and a nationwide advertising sales infrastructure (Fitch, 1987; Bergsman, 1988). Thus Emilio Azcárraga Milmo had quietly triumphed again: he commanded a high price for the rights to programming that would be produced for other markets regardless of U.S. demand, and he profited from selling an advertising sales organization that he no longer needed. Curiously, given the ample attention to the station sale, the Univision network deal received minimal press coverage in both the U.S. and Mexico.

A new management team was assembled to run Univision. Shortly after Hallmark and First Chicago acquired the network, Irvine O. Hockaday became president and CEO of Univision Holdings, Inc., which included Univision Network and Univision Station Group. William Stiles, who had been corporate manager of the 10 stations, also became acting president of the network in February 1988. Six months later two new appointments were announced: William Grimes who previously worked at CBS and ESPN became president and CEO of the holding company, and Joaquin Blaya, an SIN employee since 1970 and a successful general manager of WLTV in Miami, became president of Univision Network (Cuff, 1988). Rosita Peru, who also had ample experience at SIN, became director of programming, and Emma Carrasco was appointed director of communications and advertising.[7] By the end of the year the two companies employed almost 800 people, 525 at the station group and 260 at the network (Bergsman, 1988).

In 1988, William Grimes identified these goals as head of the company: obtaining greater financial backing from Hallmark, convincing major advertisers to invest more heavily in the Spanish-language market, and building teamwork and solid communication among employees (Bergsman, 1988). Given its nearly $600 million investment to acquire the station group and network, persuading Hallmark to spend more on Univision's growth and sustenance was no easy task. Univision lost $64 million in 1987 and approximately $50 million in 1989 bringing the company's total debt to $555 million by decade's end (Volsky, 1990). The company subsequently defaulted on $12 million in interest payments to banks and debenture holders in early 1990, prompting Hallmark's assistance. Convincing advertisers to spend more on Spanish-language advertising is closely linked to audience research, which had been inadequate through the 1980s, but would be addressed late in the decade, as the discussion below of Nielsen Hispanic Television Index shows. At a time when all Hispanic media outlets together commanded only around $500 million annually in advertising spending—half of it directed to Spanish-language television—Grimes tasked himself with "tak[ing] the Hispanic market story to the highest level of corporate America" (Landro, 1989).

Building teamwork and communication among Univision employees was no minor task either, given years of uncertainty during the legal proceedings against the Spanish International companies and Hallmark's lack of experience in both television management and the Hispanic market. A shake-up in SIN's national newsroom, and another among station management, reflected the turmoil that roiled the industry during the latter 1980s.

The Zabludovsky Controversy

A conflict that erupted only four months after the forced sale of the Spanish International stations (before Hallmark and First Chicago took control) underscored the contentiousness of contrary professional standards and practices—or at least the strong perceptions thereof—especially when involving cross-national differences. As part of a plan to restructure Televisa's international operations, Emilio Azcárraga Milmo asked Jacobo Zabludovsky, the influential anchor of Mexico's leading newscast, *24 Horas*, to relocate in Miami and lead a transformed U.S. *noticiero*, which would evolve into an international newscast á la Cable News Network (CNN). The plan was announced in September 1986, provoking angry responses from some viewers, negative comments on Spanish-language radio and resignation threats by some SIN staff (Valle, 1986).

SIN's news director Gustavo Godoy, who had emigrated from Cuba, initially said he needed more clarity on the proposed change prior to commenting, but it soon became obvious that he opposed the change. The principal concerns were Zabludovsky's reporting style—receiving calls from reporters in the field from his desk in the studio—and especially his lack of editorial independence from the Mexican government (Nordheimer, 1986). Zabludovsky had been a controversial public figure in Mexico since he first occupied the *24 Horas* anchor chair in 1971 (and ultimately retained until 1998). The political opposition on both left and right accused him of favoring the dominant Revolutionary Institutional Party (PRI by its Spanish acronym) in reporting Mexico's news. The most recent affront had been Televisa's and Zabludovsky's—the two were often treated synonymously—light and dismissive coverage of electoral fraud accusations in Northern Mexico only after international outlets had covered them in depth (Valle, 1986).[8] Godoy received a termination notice and left SIN on October 29, as did 20 members of his staff.

Although major newspapers in the U.S. ran stories on the incident (Nordheimer, 1986; Valle, 1986), and prominent Hispanic columnists like Frank del Olmo (1986) at the *Los Angeles Times* and Guillermo Martinez at the *Miami Herald* (1986) expressed their opposition to Zabludovsky, more in-depth coverage, including an interview with Gustavo Godoy, appeared in the Mexican press (Marín, 1986; Marín, 1987). The differing emphasis is understandable given the aforementioned election controversy, which initiated a political process that would eventually end the PRI's seven-decade dynasty in 2000 as well as Zabludovsky's broad influence, which had earned him the nickname, in some quarters, "the Walter Cronkite of Mexico" (Holston, 1983).

In the U.S., news of Zabludovsky's appointment arrived when wounds from the SICC sale outcome were still tender, and objections were still in process at the FCC. Emilio Azcárraga Milmo had himself recently relocated to New York to oversee Televisa's holdings and launch the ECO project; thus most industry observers believed the company would continue to influence the U.S. Spanish-language sector despite its losing possession of the SICC stations. The activist Armando Durón, an attorney for the National Hispanic Media Coalition, summed up long-standing concerns about such a presence: "We don't want dumb programs or insulting movies or telenovelas. Hallmark's relationship with SIN represents continuation of the same foolishness. What Hispanics want are television programs that help us progress" (quoted in Marín, 1986, p. 25, my translation). Clearly that sentiment extended to news programming as well.

Gustavo Godoy became president of the new Hispanic-American Broadcasting Network shortly after leaving *Noticiero Nacional SIN*, employing many of the journalists who departed with him or shortly after. Amancio Victor Suárez, majority owner of radio station WAQI in Miami and chairman of the board at Cosmos Communications, was the principal investor in the new network, dedicating $8 million to the venture. He became chairman of its board as well (Meluza, 1986; Clary, 1987). The network headquarters were in Miami, with full-time bureaus planned for Washington D.C., New York, Los Angeles, Texas, Honduras, El Salvador, Argentina, Europe, and the Middle East (Beale, 1987). In January 1987 the network became the news provider for Telemundo network, producing the 30-minute *Noticiero Telemundo*, whose presence caused Univision to open new bureaus in Texas and California (De Cordoba, 1987). However, the newscast was replaced in June 1988 by a partnership between Telemundo and Cable News Network called *Noticiero Telemundo-CNN*. The Hispanic-American Broadcasting program was comparatively expensive,[9] and CNN was eager to expand its footprint in Latin America. In short order Zabludovsky reappeared from Mexico on ECO, a satellite-based international news service that is discussed at the end of this chapter.

Telemundo Emerges

As Chapter Four illustrates, in addition to the Hispanic-American Broadcasting Network creating news, other potential competitors to SIN, like TeleRed (production) and NetSpan (advertising), were budding from within the ranks of Spanish-language television professionals. However, it was industry outsiders who created the competitor that would deliver the most formidable, sustained challenge: Telemundo. Press reports about 1980 census data and the Decade of the Hispanic focused new attention on the burgeoning Hispanic market at a time when news of Spanish International's legal troubles circulated widely; many of the reports discussed Spanish-language television's growth potential. It was a formidable challenge nonetheless: in 1984 Spanish International Network commanded 83% of the $118 million spent on Spanish television advertising in the U.S. (Virshup, 1990).

In 1985, when station KBSC in Los Angeles was offered for sale, Reliance Capital Corp. became the majority shareholder in Estrella Communications,[10] the company that acquired the station for $38 million, changed the call letters to KVEA, and went on the air with a new identity in November (Beale, 1986). The new station quickly captured 40% of LA's Spanish-language television audience, which was growing so rapidly that KMEX, the well-established Spanish International station, experienced a simultaneous *surge* rather than decline in its viewership (Bergsman, 1987). Understandably, Reliance Capital was eager for more. Its opportunity came in 1986 when John Blair & Co. became the target of a hostile takeover bid by one of its minority (8%) shareholders, Macfadden Holdings Inc. Blair suffered two difficult years following a botched expansion effort, and in 1985 lost $29.9 million on revenues of $630 million (Berry, 1987). The company owned television stations in five markets: Salinas and San Luis Obispo California; Hollywood, Florida; Oklahoma City; and San Juan, Puerto Rico. It also held eight radio stations, an advertising brokerage firm and Advo-System, Inc., a direct-mail operation (Bid for owner, 1986). Macfadden was a publishing group that produced titles such as *True Confessions*, *Modern Romance* and *Chief Executive* (Reliance wins, 1986).

Macfadden Holdings had cause for concern when Reliance Capital intervened as a potential "white knight"[11] in June 1986 by offering to purchase 70% of Blair's 11.5 million shares for $27 a share, two dollars more per share than Macfadden's offer (Bid for owner, 1986). Reliance Capital's manager,

Saul Steinberg was a fear inspiring "greenmailer"[12] who first came to prominence on Wall Street as a financial whiz kid in the 1960s (Berry, 1987). On July 3, Reliance Capital announced its control over 10 million shares of Blair, which had sweetened the offer by agreeing to pay $1.50 each on shares that were not purchased (Reliance Capital gets, 1986). Reliance had raised its bid to $31 per share on 7 million shares; Macfadden responded by offering $32 a share—worth roughly $355 million—and filing suit in U.S. District Court in New York to block Reliance's acquisition efforts (Battle for Blair, 1986). U.S. District Judge Shirley Wohl Kram denied the request for a temporary restraining order, allowing Reliance to proceed with its acquisition, which required FCC approval[13] (Move to block, 1986). That approval was granted, and in mid-August a federal appeals court removed Macfadden's final obstacle to the takeover. In total, Reliance Capital paid approximately $325 million for John Blair & Co., $215 million of it paying off debt, and $2 million going to Macfadden for the shares it owned (Reliance wins, 1986; Berry, 1987).

Reliance immediately began selling Blair properties including the direct mail operation, and all radio[14] and television stations except for two Spanish-language TV stations, serving Miami (WSCV) and San Juan, Puerto Rico (WKAQ).[15] Station acquisitions in other key Spanish markets followed in rapid succession: WNJU serving New York City (October 1986, $75 million), KSTS in San Jose/San Francisco, California (June 1987, $13.5 million), KTMD in Galveston/Houston Texas (April 1988) and KCK/KFI in Stockton/Modesto, California (July 1991). As Telemundo's start-up capital diminished, affiliation agreements and low-power stations replaced full power station acquisition as the favored growth strategy. The network entered affiliation agreements with independently owned stations in Chicago (1987), Dallas/Ft. Worth (1988), McAllen/Brownsville (1988), El Paso (1988), Albuquerque (1989), Tucson (1989), San Antonio (1989),[16] and Tampa (1991). In similar fashion to the Spanish International Network rollout detailed in Chapter Two and Three, Telemundo used low-power television technology to reach audiences in cities such as Salinas/Monterey and Sacramento, California; Phoenix, Arizona; and Corpus Christi, Texas during the early 1990s (Key events, 1993). Cable television systems were crucial distributors as the number of multichannel television households increased rapidly during this time period. Telemundo expanded in meteoric fashion, claiming to reach 40% of the Hispanic households on its launch in January 1987, and boasting 84% reach through its various outlets five years later (Telemundo TV network, 1987; Key events, 1993).

The name Telemundo, which had long been used at the San Juan station (WKAQ) and production facilities, was adopted for the entire network when it debuted in early 1987. At the same time, Henry R. Silverman shifted jobs from chairman of John Blair & Co. to president and chief executive officer for the network (Key events, 1993). Silverman worked in investment banking before joining Reliance Capital in 1984, an occupation he returned to after leaving Telemundo in 1990. Carlos Barba, who as president of WNJU (New York) had revived the station and orchestrated its sale to Reliance Capital in October 1986, became senior vice president of programming and promotions. Donald Raider of Reliance became Telemundo's chief operating officer, and Gary McBride was appointed vice president of advertising and sales. *Business Week* magazine summarized Telemundo's senior leadership like this, "… only one of Telemundo's 18 officers and directors has worked in Hispanic programming … most have toiled at Steinberg's insurance outfits and other interests, such as motel chain Days Inn Corp., which Silverman also heads" (Barker, 1987). This dearth of experience in Spanish-language television among upper management would carry repercussions, as we will see below.

The high cost of acquiring stations and expanding the network pushed Telemundo's debt-to-equity ratio past 20:1, prompting a decision to raise capital through stock and junk bond offers (Grover & Zellner, 1989). In August 1987, Telemundo Group made an initial public stock offering of two million common shares and two series of zero coupon senior notes valued at approximately $180 million (Going public, 1987). The shares, which sold at $10.50 in mid-1987, would devalue to $6.50 two years later (Grover & Zellner, 1989). Two more stock offerings were tendered in August and September 1989 after losses of $28 million during the first half of that year produced a dangerously low supply of working capital (Grover & Zellner, 1989). Financial strains at Telemundo would persist for another decade.

The principal statistic that motivated Reliance Capital and other investors in Spanish-language media was that while Hispanics comprised 8–10% of the U.S. population, less than 1% of total advertising revenues were spent in the sector. Indeed, of the approximately $26 billion spent on all U.S. television advertising in 1989, only $240 million went to the Spanish-language networks. Had advertising expenditures strictly followed demographic data in that year, the Spanish-language networks would have shared approximately $2 billion (Bergsman, 1989). Henry Silverman faced the same challenges as William Grimes, his counterpart at Univision: convincing advertisers to dedicate more of their advertising spend to the Hispanic market—and attracting investors to Telemundo. Silverman explained the profit potential that motivated Reliance Capital to enter Spanish-language television:

> … Hallmark and Reliance have each seen this kind of potential, going from less than 1 percent of the market—even if we went to 2 percent— it is doubling in volume. And if you get to 3 percent or 4 percent, which is still only 30 percent or 40 percent of the potential, the volume has quadrupled … if in fact we got 3 percent or 4 percent of the television revenues … we'd each be making hundreds of millions of dollars a year. It would be an enormously successful venture.
>
> (Quoted in Bergsman, 1988, p. 45)

These compelling projections are what drew Hallmark, Reliance, and their investment partners into the business, but we must keep in mind that the U.S. Hispanic television market was valued at only $184.3 million in 1986 (De Cordoba, 1986). The networks' effort to bump ad spending on Spanish-language media to 4% of total met resistance from advertisers and agencies who countered that population figures, program ratings and ad dollars should not be the sole metrics determining ad buys, and that many Hispanics consumed a mix of Spanish- and English-language content (Stiven & Fitch, 1988). The available market data, combined with lingering doubts about Hispanics' income levels and spending habits, rendered increasing ad spending to even half of the group's demographic representation an unrealistic goal.

Domestic Program Production Begins

The main, and most expensive competitive front between Univision and Telemundo in the late 1980s was domestic program production. Although Univision continued to import entertainment content from Mexico through its contract with Televisa, and Telemundo continually sought low-cost off-shore supplies, both networks began producing programs intended to connect with the experiences of U.S. audiences.[17] The motivation was not only to retain existing Hispanic viewers, but also re-engage viewers who had defected to English-language television for the higher production values (Landro, 1989). Advertising revenues were the prize behind higher audience numbers, of course; Univision's Joaquin Blaya bluntly stated, "domestic product development ... more than anything, will bring the advertiser to Spanish-language television" (Bergsman, 1988, p. 46). Neil Comber, an advertising manager at Proctor & Gamble echoed Blaya's sentiment: "competition between two viable Spanish-language television networks can only stimulate the networks to improve the product" (quoted in Kilgore, 1988, p. 53). Given its status as a major advertiser, Proctor & Gamble's 1989 decision to concentrate its Spanish-language TV ad buys on domestic programs rather than imported *telenovelas* certainly encouraged the networks (Beschloss, 1990).[18] So began the relationship between imported and domestic programming that continued to characterize the industry through the mid-2010s.

The costly race for domestically produced shows was a main culprit behind the financial strains both networks experienced in the latter 1980s and early 1990s.[19] At the time, $2000, the approximate cost for acquiring the rights to a foreign-produced program, was one-tenth the cost of producing the same length show domestically (Bergsman, 1988). Nevertheless, by 1989 37% of Univision's programming originated from the U.S., costing over $40 million, compared to only 8% percent in 1986 when Spanish International executives were still in charge (Besas, 1990a; Univision, too, 1990). Telemundo's Carlos Barba claimed that his network aired 44% domestic programming in 1988; the price tag was around $20 million (Mandese, 1988).

Both Univision and Telemundo concentrated their production efforts in the Miami area. Univision transferred its production and operations unit from Laguna Niguel, California, in early 1991, expanding a 48,000 square foot studio to 115,000 square feet at a cost of $25 million (Coto, 1990). About 115 workers were transferred from California to join the 250 already working in Miami (Owens, 1990). Reasons for the move included location in the Eastern time zone, which facilitated timing for a national newscast, improved accessibility (Laguna Niguel is located 60 traffic-dense miles south of Los Angeles), and proximity to many Hispanic entertainers who were locating in South Florida. Coto (1990) also mentioned that Florida's status as a "right-to-work" state represented an appealing alternative to California's labor unions. In 1988, Telemundo spent $10 million to construct studio space adjacent to station WSCV's facilities, and expanded the studio by 40% two years later when approximately 240 people worked there (Beschloss, 1990; Owens, 1990). This expansion took place at the expense of WKAQ in San Juan, Puerto Rico, which Telemundo sought to sell; some employees and activists protested, as others had in Southern California when Univision announced its intent to relocate (Wilkinson, 2002).

A prevalent formula in the new productions was to emulate popular English-language television formats (Valle, 1998a). Telemundo's *Día a Día* and Univision's *TV Mujer* were daytime women's programs focusing on topics such as health, cooking, childcare, fashion, beauty, and travel. Importantly for the objectives discussed above, the shows offered ample opportunities for product placement and on-air discussion of commercial products and services (Mandese, 1988). Through a revenue sharing arrangement similar to the one with CNN, Telemundo teamed up with Viacom's Music Television to create *MTV Internacional,* which aired music videos, interviews with artists and concert footage for Spanish- and English-language performers. The program also propelled Daisy Fuentes from a weather reporter at WNJU in New York to an international celebrity "video jockey" (Daniels, 1988). A significant distinction from other MTV services launched during the 1980s was that *MTV Internacional* transmitted twice weekly over the air rather than appearing on a dedicated pay television channel. Univision's main music program targeting youth audiences was *Tu Música* produced by Luca Bentivoglio, who became a prolific contributor to the domestic production wave. Another popular Bentivoglio production was *Cita con el Amor*, a Spanish-language version of *The Dating Game.* For its part, Telemundo aired four game shows in 1989 (Lenti, 1989). Two other genres, and successful programs within them, merit our closer scrutiny.

Sábado Gigante *and* Cristina

Variety shows have a deep history in Latin American television. Televisa's *Siempre en Domingo,* for example, enjoyed a successful three-decade run from 1969 to 1998. Of particular relevance to U.S. Spanish-language television is *Sábado Gigante*, a three-hour-and-a-half hour variety show that first launched in Chile in 1962, transferred production to Univision's studios in Miami in 1986, and was scheduled to transmit its last show in September 2015. The show was exported throughout Latin America almost since its inception, and held the Guinness World Record for the longest running television variety show when this book went to print.[20] *Sábado Gigante* had the same host since its inauguration, the affable Chilean "Don Francisco" (born Mario Luis Kreutzberger Blumenfeld) who transitioned fluidly between contests involving audience participants, entertainment acts, recorded and live discussions with notable celebrities and leaders (including Barack and Michelle Obama), travelogues and the sponsors' favorite: on air promotion of products, sometimes with the audience singing advertising jingles (Treister, 1988). Tony Oquendo, director of operations at Univision elaborated:

> The commercial breaks run inside the program. The emcee sings his breaks. You don't need a commercial. It is a good way to tap into the market. Once you get a foot in the door, you see gigantic sales increases. The U.S.-produced programming enables a lot of people to come into the market. To the veterans it is helping them expand.
> (Quoted in Bergsman, 1988, p. 50)

Within two years of moving to Miami, *Sábado Gigante* was Univision's highest rated program, reaching two million U.S. households, sometimes garnering ratings close to 40 (Bergsman, 1988; Treister, 1988). With such a solid following, *Sábado Gigante* became the best venue for highlighting a product or launching new variations on an existing product, according to Filiberto Fernández, Hispanic marketing manager for Polaroid Corp. (Treister, 1988). A waiting list had to be established for advertisers, and local ad rates for the program doubled (Poppe, 1988). In 1990, Univision claimed that *Sábado Gigante* was the top-rated television program in 12 of 18 countries where it aired (Univision, too, 1990; Silva, 1991). The export version was edited to remove many on-air promotions and add space for local advertising. Univision's Director of International Programming, Valeria Palazio, explained that the network gauged *Sábado Gigante*'s reception by international audiences through feedback from general managers and sales representatives at their client networks and stations (personal communication, July 29, 1991). The program's success continued into the 2010s, even as Don Francisco neared retirement (Thomas, 2011; Univision gears, 2014). Telemundo aired two variety shows in the late 1980s, *Super Sábados* and *La Feria de la Alegría*, but neither came close to rivaling *Sábado Gigante*, either in the U.S. or overseas.

Telemundo beat Univision to the punch in the talk show genre by distributing *Cara a Cara* to a national audience from its KVEA station in Los Angeles beginning in November 1988. Univision's counterpunch was another knockout. *El Show de Cristina* (*ESC*), hosted by Cristina Saralegui, a former editor of the magazines *TV y Novelas* (telenovelas and celebrity gossip) and *Cosmo en Español* (fashion), began airing daily in April 1989 and by 1993 was exported to 17 countries (De la Vega, 1993). Promoted as "The Spanish Oprah Winfrey," *ESC* dedicated episodes to controversial topics such as homosexuality, fertility problems, incest, abortion and illicit drug use (V. Palazio personal communication, July 29, 1991; Miller, 1993). These provocative themes were balanced by more sober episodes focused on education, gangs, teen pregnancy and other prosocial topics as well as information intended to help recent immigrants adapt to U.S. society[21] (Rohter, 1992). The host's heavy Cuban accent and liberal use of informal language generated indignation from some older and more socially conservative viewers, and she received letters questioning how she could truly represent Hispanics having such white skin (At issue, 1998; Rigby, 1992).

El Show de Cristina stirred opposition in other Spanish-speaking countries as well, most notably in Mexico where the (female) host's overt discussion of previously broadcast-taboo subjects drew condemnation from across religious and ideological spectrums alike. Some religious conservatives opposed the explicit discussion of sexuality while left-leaning intellectuals criticized the Televisa network (still a monopoly at the time) for foisting upon the Mexican public trashy U.S. mass culture (Terrazas, 1993; Monsiváis, 1993). To answer her critics Ms. Saralegui emphasized that she brought problems occurring behind closed doors into the open for public scrutiny and discussion, and argued that viewers could always change the channel (Miller, 1993). The opposition to *ESC* was emblematic of cultural tensions being felt across the globe as television and other media of external origin penetrated more deeply into societies; sensibilities were especially delicate in countries, like Mexico, that were in the process of opening their borders, and media, to more foreign content through deregulation and free trade (McAnany & Wilkinson, 1996; Wilkinson, 2006).

In June 1992, three years after her program in Spanish debuted, Ms. Saralegui attempted to cross over to English-language television. Columbia Pictures Television slated *Cristina* for a slow market rollout during the summer before committing for the 1992–93 television season. CBS owned-and-operated stations in New York, Los Angeles and Miami were among eight stations that would "clear" the show before it was distributed more broadly. Saralegui's principal challenges in crossing the language divide were to play down her heavy Spanish accent, à la Desi Arnaz, and to "translate the feeling of the Spanish show into English" (Rohter, 1992). She claimed that focusing on ethnic diversity, embracing Blacks and Asians as well as Whites and Hispanics, would distinguish her show from the other one-name talk shows at the time—Oprah, Geraldo and Phil—which tended to focus on assimilated audiences rather than incorporating elements from viewers' cultures of origin through an acculturation approach (Rohter, 1992). However, her negatives outweighed positives among audiences, and after an 11-week run *Cristina* in English was canceled.

As for *El Show de Cristina,* it ceased daily production and became a weekly program in 2001; the final episode aired on November 1, 2010 after a more than 20-year run (Villarreal, 2010). It should be noted that over her two decades on the air Cristina Saralegui built a sub-industry consisting of *Cristina, The Magazine,* a radio program, deals with major advertisers like Procter & Gamble (Crest toothpaste) and AT&T, book publishing, and a real estate company (de la Vega, 1993). After Univision's acrimonious cancellation of her show, Cristina did not disappear from the public eye for long—during the 2012 U.S. presidential campaign she spoke at the Democratic National Convention, and also appeared in ads for President Barack Obama (Fernandez, 2010; Mason, 2012).

Two points should be emphasized before moving on. First, Telemundo saw aligning the production values of Spanish-language television more closely with English-language TV as a key goal in the domestic programming push. William Grimes, Univision's CEO asserted, "we're going to make programming that looks like what you see on the networks, only in Spanish" (Landro, 1989). Telemundo's programming partnerships with Cable News Network (CNN) and Music Television (MTV) not only sought to reduce costs, but also to emulate English-language television's production quality by joining the images created for mainstream audiences with Spanish-speaking newscasters and video jockeys. This constituted a significant acknowledgment that many viewers were also tuning in English-language channels, meaning that Univision and Telemundo were not only competing with each other, but with the major networks and pay television channels as well. Achieving an attractive and lucrative balance between the American mainstream and Hispanic cultural and linguistic elements was, and remains, a major programming challenge (Dávila, 2001; Rojas & Piñón, 2014). The next chapter illustrates problems that can arise when the balance is not maintained.

Second, developing a sustained production industry marked an important step in the United States' emergence as a major player in the international Spanish-language television market. No longer predominantly consumers of content produced elsewhere, the values, experiences, and aspirations of U.S. Hispanics began to circulate more readily through the Spanish-speaking world. I do not claim that representations were always broad or well balanced, as the *Sábado Gigante* and *Show de Cristina* examples demonstrate, but their presence clearly increased. Nor am I asserting that U.S. programs competed across the board; Telemundo's failed efforts to produce competitive *telenovelas*—like *Angélica Mi Vida*[22] in 1988 and *El Magnate* in 1990—showed that not all genres were penetrable (Stiven, 1988; Valle, 1988b). Yet the foundation was laid for future growth that would render Miami a major Hispanic and Latin American media center, prioritize the U.S. market in the rollout of Internet and mobile technologies, and establish the Hispanic sector as a relatively stable segment of U.S. media when the general market struggled.

Ethnic and Regional Controversies

As described in the previous chapter, reports that the Spanish International stations (later Univision) would be sold to Hallmark Cards and First Chicago Corp. precipitated a chorus of protests and denunciations from Hispanic groups across the country. Principal among the objections were the new owners' lack of experience in Spanish-language broadcasting, their limited understanding of Hispanic communities' needs and interests, and the possibility that the network would convert to English after a two-year programming agreement expired. The case against Spanish International was adjudicated in federal district court in Los Angeles, and Mexican American advocacy organizations in the area were particularly vocal and active in the protests and subsequent legal appeals. The groups pressured the Los Angeles City Council, the LA County Board of Supervisors, the California Legislature, and the U.S. House of Representatives to block transfer of the stations to non-Hispanic buyers.

Hallmark came under significant scrutiny as it consolidated control over Univision, as did the quickly expanding Telemundo network, also for its non-Hispanic ownership. A confluence of events in 1989 that appeared to foreshadow diminished influence by Mexican Americans at both networks was labeled "Cubanization" by the Spanish-language Los Angeles newspaper, *La Opinión* (Muñoz, 1989). Creative, managerial and editorial control over the networks, as well as jobs, were at issue in a controversy that exposed tensions between two Hispanic subgroups having distinct geographic locations, political orientations and economic statuses. The Cuban American population, concentrated in South Florida and the Middle Atlantic States, tends to be politically conservative, and had the highest average income level among Hispanic groups. In contrast, the Mexican American population was heavily concentrated in the Southwest, more politically moderate and had a substantially lower average income than Cuban Americans (see Chapter 6, footnote 3; Garcia, 2000).

The firing and early retirement of several Mexican American station managers and news directors in Los Angeles precipitated the "Cubanization" controversy. Frank Cruz, a well-known former newscaster who became vice president and general manager for Telemundo's KVEA, resigned in lieu of being fired and was replaced by Steven Levin, a non-Hispanic. Shortly thereafter, the former professional football player Danny Villanueva announced he would retire from Univision's KMEX where he had worked for 18 years, many of them as general manager. The *Los Angeles Times* reported rumors that the network's failure to promote Villanueva to station group president had prompted his departure (Valle, 1989). Univision's leadership astutely replaced Villanueva with Emilio Nicolás Jr., who was both highly experienced and Mexican American (Bergsman, 1989b). Nicolás Jr.'s appointment came against the backdrop of a petition, signed by more than 70 KMEX employees, requesting a new manager who "reflects the interests, experience and culture of the Los Angeles audience" (Mydans, 1989).[23] At around the same time, Luis Nogales lost his job as Univision's national news director during an upper-management shuffle, and when Univision's local news director, Felipe Muñoz, accepted a position in Mexico, the rumor mill suggested that his replacement would be a Cuban American. Nicolás Jr. persuaded Muñoz to stay on, but Telemundo handled an analogous situation less adroitly (Bergsman, 1989b).

While the controversial personnel changes were still fresh in the minds of Los Angelinos who followed the issue, KVEA's management team was so politically obtuse as to fire the Mexican American news director Bob Navarro and replace him with a Cuban American, Roberto Soto. Mexican American political activists picketed the KVEA studios. Telemundo's CEO, Henry Silverman, threw fuel on the fire by stating, "the problem is, there is virtually no talent pool of Hispanic television executives" (Bergsman, 1989b, p. 43), a claim that drew hostile responses from representatives of the Mexican American Legal Defense and Educational Fund, the National Hispanic Media Coalition and other organizations. In an effort to diffuse the criticism, Telemundo executives met with the Mexican American Coalition for Improvement of Mass Media, a group of local media advocates and community leaders headed by Dr. Raúl Ruiz, Chicano studies faculty at California State University, Northridge, and an organizer of protests at both KVEA and KMEX. Telemundo also organized an advisory board comprised of a half-dozen prominent Mexican Americans, but the coalition proved difficult to appease and the advisory board fell victim to the same intense political pressure that had dissolved a similar board convened by Hallmark in 1987. Ruiz argued, "… Mexican-Americans are being shoved aside and not really being taken into account in terms of opportunity" (Bergsman, 1989b, p. 42). Not surprisingly, Don Raider, executive vice president and chief operating officer at Telemundo, offered a different view, "The Mexican Coalition would like us to hire only Mexicans and disregard any consequences of reverse discrimination against other Hispanic Americans" (Professor leads, 1989, p. 36). It is significant to note that in mid-1989 neither network had a Hispanic board member or chief executive officer. At Telemundo only one of the top ten managers was Hispanic, and neither the chief executive officer or chief financial officer had even a reading knowledge of Spanish (Bergsman, 1989b). Two years earlier this situation had engendered Danny Villanueva's caustic comment to the *Wall Street Journal*, "it will be interesting to see how Mr. Silverman programs for Hispanics instead of Hispanics programming for Hispanics" (De Cordoba, 1987), but differences in the ethnic composition of the two networks' management teams diminished after Hallmark took possession of Univision. Criticisms of network hiring practices were not limited to the Mexican American versus Cuban American tension; the low percentage of Hispanics of any origin working in upper management was also at issue.

Even as Mexican American advocacy groups fought to increase their community's presence and influence in the industry through increased management-level employment, Univision announced plans to relocate its network headquarters from Southern California (Laguna Niguel) to West Miami (Coto, 1989). In addition to losing local jobs, Mexican American political activists feared that Univision's news and entertainment programming would acquire a more Cuban-American character once the network base moved to Florida (Wilkinson, 2002). In response to the ensuing kerfuffle, both networks emphasized that despite their recent investments in Miami as a production center, they were still creating content in California: approximately 60% of the domestic entertainment total in both cases (Professor leads, 1989).

Not long after the West Coast "Cubanization" issue faded from the headlines, a similar controversy brewed at Univision's New York station, WXTV. Monitoring by an advocacy group, the National Puerto Rican Foundation (NPRF) found that in 1990 WXTV employed slightly more than 100 people, 22 of who were of Puerto Rican origin, the prevalent Hispanic population in the region.[24] One of the 22 was a news director, one was an anchor, and two were reporters, with the remainder occupying lower level positions (M. Garcia, personal communication, August 6, 1992). According to Marta Garcia, director of the NPRF, most of the upper management and on-screen positions were held by Cuban Americans—a source of contention as we have seen. Shortly after the NPRF began pressuring WXTV to hire and promote more employees of Puerto Rican origin, the ethnic balance improved, Garcia noted, yet many of the new hires arrived from station WSJN in San Juan, rather than from the local talent pool. The new hires were also paid lower salaries than their local counterparts who were more familiar with U.S. industry pay scales. This brief example illustrates that economic competition can create rifts among people of common national origin, as well as across subgroups of a population. The next chapter discusses another incident in which comments by a Cuban American reporter for Univision, Carlos Alberto Montaner, led to protests and a brief advertiser boycott organized by Puerto Rican Americans in the New York area.

Returning to Los Angeles, ethnic tensions remained after Univision transferred some network resources—and jobs—to Miami. In October 1990, after only 17 months in the post, Emilio Nicolás Jr. left his position as KMEX's general manager and was replaced by Richard Ramirez, the station's sales manager of Cuban and Puerto Rican descent, who enjoyed a strong reputation as a gifted leader (Kleid, 1990). News of the change rekindled the debate about few Mexican Americans in management, offering critics another opportunity to press their case. Prof. Raúl Ruiz noted a striking imbalance between the networks' main revenue source and their hiring practices, asserting that 90% of Univision's profits derived from the Mexican-American community, while less than 40% of its station managers were Mexican American (Cantu, 1991). To critics, a glass ceiling appeared to hang above the station manager level at both networks: in 1991 one Mexican American occupied an executive position at Telemundo; none did at Univision, although seven of 17 station managers were of Mexican origin (Cantu, 1991). Esther Rentería of the National Hispanic Media Coalition cited the long-standing issue of copious imported programming saying, "we need information to improve ourselves in the American system" (Cantu, 1991, p. 64). Raúl Ruiz argued that underrepresentation in employment together with a paucity of Mexican American themes and role models in the mainstream media harmed the self-perceptions of Mexican American audience members. Whether or not one ascribes to Ruiz's causal theory, it was clear that FCC mandates requiring that the ethnic composition of station management reflect the local audience were not met by LA's Spanish-language television stations at the time of the "Cubanization" issue. If indeed the FCC was following the matter, it may have had difficulty grasping the exact injury being done to Mexican Americans.

Origins of the Nielsen Hispanic Television Index

As prior sections have noted, the networks required better audience data in their efforts to convince advertisers to dedicate larger budgets to Spanish-language television. Through the 1980s there was wide discrepancy in the data provided by services dedicated to measuring the Spanish-language television audience. In 1972 Arbitron Ratings Co. had begun providing data based on diaries and a few hundred meters (out of several thousand overall) placed in Spanish-speaking households nationwide. A.C. Nielsen began producing Spanish-American Viewing Reports based on its general ratings service in 1974, and Strategy Research Corp., launched in 1971, utilized viewer diaries and door-to-door surveys of nearly 9,000 households (Growing demand, 1989). Strategy Research's comparatively high audience figures—70% of U.S. Hispanics watching Spanish-language TV versus Nielsen's and Arbitron's 30%—were viewed with skepticism by many advertisers. The discrepancies aroused suspicion, and advertisers favored the lower figure in negotiating media buys with network representatives who could seldom offer substantial proof of higher viewership (Poppe, 1988; Bergsman, 1989c). Peter Roslow, Telemundo's director of marketing, identified a key goal in developing a new television index: "our No. 1 priority is to have a ratings service that the most cynical of media directors at advertisers or agencies can have confidence in" (Stevenson, 1989). Recall the projection that if 1989 advertising expenditures strictly followed demographic data the Spanish-language networks would have shared approximately $2 billion (Bergsman, 1989a).

Because Univision and Telemundo shared a strong common interest in acquiring more credible measurements of their reach, they agreed to pool their resources to commission a more accurate and comprehensive ratings service—which they would pay for with no assistance from local stations, advertisers or marketing firms as English-language services received (Valle, 1988c).[25] A Spanish Television Research Committee appointed by the networks solicited bids and in late 1988 narrowed the field of contenders from five to two: Nielsen's Peoplemeter and Arbitron's Scan America devices (Valle, 1988c). In July 1989, Telemundo, Univision and Nielsen Media Research entered a five-year agreement to create the first ratings service for Spanish-language television at an approximate cost of $38 million ($18 million for the first five years) to be split by the networks (Nielsen to test, 1989). In an effort to obtain more detailed data on Hispanic television viewing habits than were previously available, viewership of English-language networks was also recorded. Nielsen's Peoplemeter[26] devices were installed in 150 homes spread across five Southern California counties which together encompassed an estimated 4.3 million Hispanics, or 30.5% of the total population (Sharbutt, 1989). After analysis and adjustment in the Los Angeles market, the system would roll out to 800 sample households nationwide (Growing demand, 1989).

In the process of interviewing households for the Los Angeles sample, Nielsen discovered that a higher percentage tuned in Spanish programming than had previously been counted, according to Telemundo's Henry Silverman (Feuer, 1989). Nielsen data gathered in mid-1990 revealed other characteristics of Hispanic households in the LA area: more used television during prime time (61%) than the general market (54%); daytime viewing was also greater, 45.5% versus 31.3%; and cable subscription and video-cassette recorder (VCR) ownership was higher than previously thought at 29.6% and 71% respectively (Benson, 1990). As concerned language use, 50.8% of participant households in the Nielsen pilot study spoke only or mostly Spanish, 22.6% spoke both Spanish and English, and 24.5% spoke mostly or only English (Benson, 1990). Armed with this pilot data and Index results from other regions, the Spanish-language networks were able to press their points more convincingly, and empirically demonstrate an audience they were already delivering.

Besides the Index, the networks also cooperated on mutually beneficial projects such as delivering joint marketing presentations to potential advertisers, like the auto industry, that spent little on Spanish-language advertising at the time (Landro, 1989). Henry Silverman stressed that both Telemundo and Univision were competing against the English-language networks, and that advertisers wanting to reach the Hispanic consumer were likely to buy spots on both networks, not just one, in order to get adequate coverage.

Univisa, Galavisión and ECO

In August 1986, shortly after Hallmark and First Chicago's acquisition of the Spanish International stations was announced, Emilio Azcárraga Milmo relocated from Mexico City to New York, leaving his long-term business partner Miguel Alemán in charge of Mexican operations. Azcárraga's primary purpose was to establish a new U.S. initiative named Univisa, an umbrella company under which several U.S. operations would be organized, as well as the ECO system—the Spanish acronym for Orbital Communications Company (Beale, 1987). As it turned out, Azcárraga also got involved in building Lower Manhattan's only luxury yacht harbor at the time (he needed somewhere to moor his own vessel), and launching *The National*, a sports daily discussed in Chapter Seven (Virshup, 1990).

Univisa operated as a U.S. subsidiary for Televisa, as did its sister company, Eurovisa, established to sell television content in Europe where privatization and deregulation processes were increasing demand for commercial TV content in a number of countries (Bergsman, 1989c). Such demand was increasing in Latin America as well, accounting for why Protele, a programming distribution company, delivered around a quarter of Univisa's profits. Other entities under Univisa's control included Galavisión, the cable television service launched in 1979, Videovisa, which distributed prerecorded videocassettes, Fonovisa, a music recording and distribution enterprise and Teleseguros, an insurance company marketed primarily through television. Manufacturing facilities in Mexicali, Mexico produced blank videocassettes in large volume for Spanish-language markets, audio and video hardware was assembled for the U.S. consumer electronics market, and the world's largest video dubbing operation fed the voracious prerecorded videocassette market in North America (Bergsman, 1989c). John Sinclair (1990) called these operations "post-broadcast" because they marked a departure from the traditional model of television sets displaying content received over the air, as well as related changes in how audiences time-shift and engage content. Televisa's involuntary forfeiture of Spanish International in 1986 also supported the post-broadcast moniker, but not for long as the next chapter explains.

Univisa was also the U.S. partner in ECO, Azcárraga's gambit to create a global 24-hour news service for Spanish speakers. In a typical hour, ECO offered 20 minutes of "hard" news, and 40 minutes of lighter, more entertainment-focused content such as cooking and sports (Valle, 1988d). Televisa and Eurovisa managed the other branches, ECO Mexico and ECO Worldwide (Bergsman, 1989c). In September 1988, Univisa finished converting its cable operation, Galavisión, from a premium subscription channel to an advertising-based basic service as it prepared to distribute ECO content (Valle, 1988d). At the time, Galavisión reached about one million subscribers through 300 cable systems, representing 20–25% of Spanish-speaking television households in the U.S., compared to 85% coverage by Univision and 75% by Telemundo (Bergsman, 1989c). The ECO satellite feed[27] initiated the same month and Galavisión became a Spanish-language news channel, except on Sundays when sports and movies predominated (Bergsman, 1989c). Thus, following CNN's model with its headquarters in Atlanta, ECO linked a production center in Mexico City with news bureaus and audiences in other areas of Latin America, Europe and the U.S. ECO tried to differentiate itself from broadcast networks, like Univision and Telemundo, by appealing to three audience characteristics: younger, more affluent, opinion leaders (Bergsman, 1989c). Part of the strategy to attract this demographic and business professionals involved offering market data, teletext, and videoconferencing services following the model of Reuters and Dow Jones, companies that had diversified their information services beyond news (Sinclair, 1990). Emilio Azcárraga's intent behind sending Jacobo Zabludovsky to Miami in 1986 to run the *Noticiero Nacional SIN* was to introduce the ECO model and center the news gathering operations there. After he was rejected in Florida, Zabludovsky returned to Mexico, eventually reappearing on ECO Mexico, from where the lion's share of content originated.

In addition to the ECO news service, in March 1990 Univisa began offering a satellite-fed programming service to independent broadcast stations. The new service sought to differentiate itself from Univision and Telemundo by targeting a specific audience: U.S. Hispanics and recent immigrants of Mexican and Central American origin (Fitch, 1990; Besas, 1990b). Univisa claimed that its competitors spread themselves too thin in trying to appeal to an exceedingly diverse audience. (An interesting criticism in light of Televisa's 25-year effort to effectively knit together diverse groups of Spanish speakers into a cohesive national audience.) In order to reach its target, the new broadcast service—confusingly named Galavisión like the cable channel—concentrated on entering broadcast television markets in California, Texas, Illinois, Arizona and New Mexico—that is, areas of the heaviest Mexican and Central American population density at the time. In mid-1990, stations in the Houston (KTFH) and Los Angeles (KWHY) markets were the only affiliates, but two stations in San Antonio and Chicago expressed interest in signing on (Volsky, 1990). Expanding the network became a lesser priority once Televisa entered discussions with Jerrold Perenchio and Venevisión to partner in purchasing Univision.

Although Televisa's programming agreement with Univision gave the U.S. network initial option on 50% of Televisa's first run programming in the U.S., Televisa's volume of production was such that ample programming remained for Univisa to broadcast via Galavisión affiliates (Moncreiff Arrante, 1990). Some of the leftover programming after Univision got its pick was sold to Telemundo as well. The Galavisión broadcast service started shortly after the February 1990 expiration of a non-compete clause that prevented Emilio Azcárraga Milmo from participating in the U.S. Spanish-language television broadcasting industry (Besas, 1990b). The man whose father had launched the industry and who had himself been the principal player for 13 years was back, competing in a rapidly changing environment.

Conclusion

Two concepts undergirding the so-called Decade of the Hispanic became particularly salient in the latter part of the decade, ethnicity and market. This chapter examines several aspects of ethnicity: how it came to signify potential profit and political power when external entities attached it to a growing population group, how it influenced management of the two major networks (or at least was purported to), and how it affected perceptions of power distribution across subgroups of the Hispanic population. It is important to keep in mind that the 1980s followed two decades of ethnic, racial, gender and sexual upheaval in which various social groups challenged status quo assumptions about political, economic and social hierarchies as they advocated for their rights. These efforts continued from the 1980s on, but usually in less fervent and visible fashion. As several assessments pointed out, the Decade of the Hispanic was more focused on consumption and collective political influence (CANC, 1989; del Olmo, 1989a; Miranda & Quiroz, 1990).

The advent of mainstream corporate ownership in Spanish-language television led to an influx of upper management personnel with business experience, but not in Hispanic media. Employing a standard practice in business, Hallmark and Reliance relied on executives they knew and trusted to lead their new acquisitions, but introduced risk by appointing people (almost exclusively men) with limited knowledge of the market and language to influential positions. This raised the suspicions of community members concerned about the medium's influence and how much revenue earned from the market would be reinvested locally, an apprehension that aligned with the internal colonialism thesis referred to in prior chapters (Almaguer, 1974; Gutiérrez, 1976).

It would be a mistake to isolate network owners' and management's ethnicity as the sole source of conflict. Increased spending on domestic production heightened regional competition that was barely perceptible when programming originated almost exclusively from Mexico. The more open management styles of Hallmark and Reliance Capital compared with Spanish International also contributed. That is, before the industry became truly competitive in 1987, Televisa's close-lipped, autocratic management style and minimal U.S. production were criticized occasionally, but garnered less press attention than the conflicts this chapter discusses. The increased press attention surrounding the legal proceedings against Spanish International, derived from the Decade of the Hispanic discourse—and generated by public relations efforts of the new network owners—opened the industry to greater press and public scrutiny, including some prickly topics such as "Cubanization." Frank del Olmo (1989b), the columnist for the *Los Angeles Times* wrote in the context of the Cubanization controversy: "So I'm glad the Chicano-Cubano rivalry in Spanish-language TV is finally out in the open. It should force Latinos to admit their difference openly and honestly rather than papering them over in the interest of 'Hispanic' unity." Del Olmo's perspective critically juxtaposes the Decade of the Hispanic's constructed artificiality with the reality of competition over resources and influence among subgroups of the broader Hispanic population.

This analysis has underscored a central tension underlying the development of Spanish-language television in the United States: Spanish speakers are, for linguistic reasons, regarded by the television and advertising industries as a unified market; yet distinct cultural characteristics stemming from their diverse national origins challenges establishing a homogeneous programming market. Emilio Azcárraga referred to this tension when he criticized Univision and Telemundo for spreading themselves too thin by seeking a unified national audience.

Notes

1. *Time* ran a cover story "Hispanic Americans: Soon the largest minority" in its October 16, 1978 issue and a special issue, "Immigrants: The changing face of America" on July 8, 1985.
2. Cisneros became the nation's first Hispanic Secretary of Housing and Urban Development and Peña the first Hispanic Secretary of Transportation.
3. The *Los Angeles Times* columnist Frank del Olmo (1990a) reminded readers that the outcomes were not always positive for Hispanic politicians who rode this wave: "But the 1980s also saw setbacks for Latino politicians. Earlier this year Cisneros left office, and took a hiatus from politics, after an extramarital affair became public. Los Angeles City Councilman Richard Alatorre paid a hefty fine for violating fund-raising laws. State Sen. Art Torres (D-Los Angeles) may have had his career sidetracked by drunk-driving convictions. State Sen. Joseph B. Montoya (D-Whittier) is facing felony charges for alleged financial improprieties."
4. The corresponding figures for Black and White households in 1988 were 9.8% and 23.2% respectively (O'Hare, 1990).
5. Such as Ricky Martin, Jennifer Lopez, Cristina Aguilera, Marc Anthony and Shakira.
6. For an example see the video, "John Tower 1978 Corrido"—http://www.youtube.com/watch?v=Fxu7d56EMhA.
7. See Bergsman (1988) for information on other key management appointments at Univision.
8. Of particular concern were the Partido Acción Nacional (PAN) party's charges that its candidate, Francisco Barrio, had been robbed of Chihuahua's governorship. Barrio's 1983 election as mayor of Juárez had been the dominant PRI party's worst defeat to date (Thompson, 1986).
9. CNN had ready access to news video from around the world, including bureaus in Latin American and Spain; some English-language reports were merely voiced-over in Spanish.
10. Hallmark Cards Corp. was a minority shareholder in Estrella Communications.
11. The website *Investopedia.com* defines white knight as follows: "... an individual or company that acquires a corporation on the verge of being taken over by forces deemed undesirable by company officials (sometimes referred to as a 'black knight'). While the target company doesn't remain independent, a white knight is viewed as a preferred option to the hostile company completing their takeover. Unlike a hostile takeover, current management typically remains in place in a white knight scenario, and investors receive better compensation for their shares" (http://www.investopedia.com/terms/w/whiteknight.asp).
12. The website *Investopedia.com* defines greenmail as "An antitakeover measure that arises when a large block of stock is held by an unfriendly company that

is threatening a hostile takeover. Greenmail is a term that applies to mergers and acquisitions, and refers to the money that is paid by the target company to another company, known as a corporate raider, that has purchased a majority of the target company's stock. The greenmail payment is made in an attempt to stop the takeover bid. The target company is forced to repurchase the stock at a substantial premium (the greenmail payment) to prevent the takeover. This is also known as a 'bon voyage bonus' or a 'goodbye kiss'" (http://www.investopedia.com/terms/g/greenmail.asp).

13. The FCC had rejected Reliance Capital's initial trusteeship proposal for the Blair stations in mid-July 1986, offering Mcfadden hope that the acquisition could be annulled and the Blair stocks released (Move to block, 1986).

14. The eight radio stations were sold to Sconnix Broadcasting Co. for $152 million in July, 1987 (Telemundo Group completes, 1987).

15. The Puerto Rican station was subsequently sold for $160 million in November 1988, with the proceeds used to pay down a portion of Telemundo's substantial debt (Sale of WKAQ-TV, 1988). It had been, "the most dominant and profitable broadcast television station in Puerto Rico with the best production studio" (Subervi-Vélez, Hernández López, & Frambes Buxeda, 1990, p. 161).

16. In August 1990, Telemundo purchased 85% of Nueva Vista Productions' stock, converting KVDA-TV to an owned-and-operated station (Key events, 1993).

17. Telemundo's CEO Henry Silverman explained, "Even though we have increased national programming, this is not to say that we won't continue to buy programs produced in Latin America. Our soap operas from Venezuela and Mexico always draw high ratings, and our nightly Mexican movie is also very popular. The thing is to strike a balance between U.S. and non-U.S. material. It's the same sort of balance we maintain between movies and novelas, news and sports, etcetera" (Lenti, 1989, p. 59).

18. Proctor & Gamble's influence on some content, like Telemundo's U.S.-produced *telenovela Angélica Mi Vida*, extended to commenting on program particulars and involvement in the selection of cast members who might also appear in advertising spots (Stiven, 1988).

19. As the next chapter illustrates, Univision began to emerge from its financial doldrums in the mid-1990s while they continued at Telemundo.

20. http://www.guinnessworldrecords.com/records-3000/longest-running-tv-variety-show; retrieved November 14, 2014.

21. This is one of the central functions of ethnic-oriented media as discussed in Chapter Two.

22. Carlos Barba, Telemundo's vice president of programming and promotion summarized the plot of *Angélica Mi Vida*: "the trials, tribulations and loves of three Hispanic-American families whose origins can be traced to Mexico, Puerto Rico and Cuba. Our shooting locations have included San Antonio, Miami and New York City" (Two networks, 1989, p. A36). There was a clear effort to include a variety of U.S. Hispanic peoples and settings.

23. Nicolás Jr. later said he understood that many KMEX staff were hoping to make a positive statement, but was upset that the petition had been leaked to the press. He also expressed disgust at the idea people should be judged by their national origin, likening it to judging people according to their skin color. Referring to the protesters he concluded, "I think some of these people ought to be introduced to Martin Luther King" (Bergsman, 1989b, p. 46).

24. WXTV had experienced significant churn, with four different general managers serving from 1987 to 1989 (Bergsman, 1989c).
25. Larry McBride, senior vice president of marketing and sales at Telemundo characterized the networks' prior relationship with the research services, "without providing them some additional compensation, they've been unwilling to do a proper job. So we are now willing to pay a small fortune to get the job done properly" (Valle, 1988c).
26. Peoplemeters are electronic devices which record television viewing by all members of a household. Each viewer is identified by a number which is entered on a keypad when the television is turned on or off, or the channel is changed. Viewers are also supposed to enter their code number when they leave or enter a room in which the television is located. For more on the Peoplemeter and the controversy surrounding its use see Webster & Lichty (1991).
27. A nightly news program named *ECO* that was produced at KMEX in Los Angeles began airing nationally on Univision in January 1987, replacing *24 Horas,* the maligned newscast from Mexico. The full-time satellite news feed was a new development in 1988 (Valle, 1987).

References

Almaguer, Tomás. (1974). Historical notes on Chicano oppression: The dialectics of racial and class domination in North America. *Aztlán, 5*(1), 27–56.

At issue with Cristina. (1998, November 15). *Los Angeles Times* [Letters to the editor]. Retrieved from http://articles.latimes.com/1998/nov/15/entertainment/ca-42866.

Barker, Robert. (1987, August 10). Steinberg may have trouble making money in Spanish. *Business Week*, 29–32.

Battle for Blair goes to court. (1986, July 16). *Miami News*, 6A.

Beale, Steve. (1986, December). Turmoil and growth. *Hispanic Business*, 48, 92.

Beale, Steve. (1987, January). More changes at SIN. *Hispanic Business*, 10.

Benson, Jim. (1990, August 22). Nielsen Research confirms Hispanics watch mucho TV. *Variety*.

Bergsman, Steve. (1987, December). New blood: Fresh money. *Hispanic Business*, 30–36.

Bergsman, Steve. (1988, December). New and improved. *Hispanic Business*, 42–50.

Bergsman, Steve. (1989a, December). Item: Networks invest in Nielsen ratings. *Hispanic Business*, 38–41.

Bergsman, Steve. (1989b, September). Controversy hits L.A.'s Spanish television. *Hispanic Business*, 42–48.

Bergsman, Steve. (1989c, April). Univisa's world view. *Hispanic Business,* 22–27.

Berry, John F. (1987, April). The new order at Blair. *Channels*, 54–55.

Besas, Peter. (1990a, April 11). Mexicans ride again in Hispano TV sweeps. *Variety*, 41, 58.

Besas, Peter. (1990b, March 7). Univisa setting up Hispano web in U.S. *Variety*, 41, 56.

Beschloss, Steven. (1990, July 16). The missing pot of gold. *Channels: The Business of Communications*, 30–34.

Bid for owner of Channel 51 is authorized. (1986, June 5). *Miami News*, 12A.

Cantu, Hector. (1991, February). The gathering storm in broadcasting. *Hispanic Business*, 14, 64.

Church, George J., Goodgame, Dan, Leavitt, Russell, & Lopez, Laura. (1985, July 8). Hispanics a melding of cultures: Latins, the largest new group, are making their presence felt. *Time*, 36–41.

Clary, Mike, (1987, April). The Hispanic news wars. *Channels: The Business of Communications*, 55.

Coto, Juan Carlos. (1989, August 1). Spanish network moving base to Miami. *Miami Herald*, 4B.

Coto, Juan Carlos. (1990, April 11). Miami—New mecca for Hispano TV pilgrims. *Variety*, 55.

Cuban American National Council. (1989). *The elusive decade of Hispanics* (ERIC doc no. 320969). Miami, FL: Cuban American National Council, Inc.

Cuff, Daniel F. (1988, August 31). Univision names head of Spanish network. *New York Times*, D4.

Daniels, Robert. (1988, June 10). Telemundo slates a version of MTV for U.S. Hispanics. *Wall Street Journal*, 28.

Dávila, Arlene. (2001). *Latinos, Inc.: The marketing and making of a people.* Berkeley, CA: University of California Press.

De Cordoba, Jose. (1987, March 11). Rivalry intensifies within Spanish-language television. *Wall Street Journal*, 6.

De la Vega, Miguel. (1993, mayo 17). El imperio, la "basura", la moral y las justificaciones de Cristina Saralegui. *Proceso*, 53.

Del Olmo, Frank. (1986, September 12). Sour sweetheart deal for Spanish-language TV? *Los Angeles Times*. Retrieved from http://articles.latimes.com/print/1986–09–12/local/me-11773_1_sweetheart-deal.

Del Olmo, Frank. (1989a, December 14). Latino 'decade' moves into '90s. *Los Angeles Times*. Retrieved from http://articles.latimes.com/1989–12–14/news/ti-1_1_latino-community.

Del Olmo, Frank. (1989b, May 29). TV dispute sheds light on the 'Hispanic' myth. *Los Angeles Times*, p. 5.

Fernandez, Maria Elena. (2010, November 1). Farewell for 'El Show de Cristina.' *Los Angeles Times*. Retrieved from http://articles.latimes.com/2010/nov/01/entertainment/la-et-cristina-20101101.

Feuer, Jack. (1989, December). The meter runs for Hispanic TV. *Channels/Field Guide 1990*, 83.

Fitch, Ed. (1987, November 10). Hallmark caps Hispanic thrust. *Advertising Age*, 32.

Fitch, Ed. (1990, January 22). Univisa returns to broadcast. *Advertising Age*, 2, 54.

Garcia, John A. (2000). A topography of Latinos in the United States: Politics, policy, and political involvement. In J. D. Schultz et al. (Eds.), *Encyclopedia of minorities in American politics. Volume 2: Hispanic Americans and Native Americans* (pp. 401–411). Phoenix, AZ: Onyx.

Going public. (1987, December). *Hispanic Business*, 35.

Gómez, Laura E. (1992, autumn). The birth of the "Hispanic" generation: Attitudes of Mexican-American political elites toward the Hispanic label. *Latin American Perspectives, 19*(4), 45–58.

Grover, Ronald, & Zellner, Wendy. (1989, October 23). Hispanic TV: Great way to make a killing, right? *Business Week*, 61.

Growing demand for comprehensive Hispanic ratings. (1989, April 3). *Broadcasting*, 47–48.

Guernica, Antonio. (1982). *Reaching the Hispanic market effectively: The media, the market, the methods.* New York, NY: McGraw-Hill Companies.

Gutiérrez, Félix F. (1976). *Spanish-language radio and Chicano internal colonialism.* (Doctoral dissertation) Stanford University, Palo Alto, CA.

Hoberman, John Milton. (1997). *Darwin's athletes: How sport has damaged Black America and preserved the myth of race.* Boston, MA: Houghton Mifflin Harcourt.

Holston, Mark. (1983, June/July). The Walter Cronkite of Mexico. *Nuestro, 7*(5), 58–59.

——— It's your turn in the sun. (1978, October 16). *Time,* 48–61.

Jarboe, Jan. (1980, November). The special case of Spanish-language television. *Washington Journalism Review,* 21–25.

Key events in Telemundo's history. (1993, August). [Promotional material]. Telemundo Network.

Kilgore, Julie Kay. (1988, December). Take two. *Hispanic Business,* 52–58.

Kleid, Beth. (1990, October 11). Surprise shake-up at KMEX puts new executive at station's helm. *Los Angeles Times.* Retrieved from http://articles.latimes.com/1990–10–11/news/ti-2597_1_los-angeles.

Lampe, Philip E. (1981). "Viva La Raza:" A possible Chicano dilemma. *Social Science, 56*(3), 158–163.

Landro, Laura. (1989, January 23). Univision expansion plan is under way: Growth is fanned by Hispanic population explosion. *Wall Street Journal,* B3.

Lenti, Paul. (1989, March 22). Hispanos go loco for local TV prod. *Variety,* 59.

López Ronald W., & Enos, Darryl D. (1974). Spanish-language-only television in Los Angeles County. *Aztlán, 4*(2), 283–313.

Mandese, Joe. (1988, November). The search for El Dorado. *Marketing & Media Decisions,* 42–47.

Marín, Carlos. (1986, October 27). A Zabludovsky no se le cree por considerarlo vocero del gobierno. *Proceso* (Mexico), *521,* 20–25.

Marín, Carlos. (1987, January 17). Con ceses, Televisa engendró la caída de sus poderes en Estados Unidos. *Proceso* (Mexico), 22–25.

Martinez, Guillermo. (1986, September 25). SIN sends bad signal on Mexican 'shill.' *Miami Herald,* 25A.

Mason, Melanie. (2012, June 19). Spanish-language media star Cristina Saralegui appears in Obama ads. *Los Angeles Times.* Retrieved from http://articles.latimes.com/2012/jun/19/news/la-pn-spanishlanguage-media-star-cristina-saralegui-appears-in-obama-ads-20120619.

McAnany, Emile G., & Wilkinson, Kenton T. (Eds.). (1996). *Mass media and free trade: NAFTA and the cultural industries.* Austin, TX: University of Texas Press.

Mejia, James. (2014, July 16). Latino demographic growth does not translate to political clout. *La Voz Bilingüe.* Retrieved from http://www.lavozcolorado.com/printpage.php?id=7646.

Meluza, Lourdes. (1986, November 8). SIN ex-employees form new network. *Miami Herald,* 2B.

Miranda, Leticia, & Quiroz, Julia Teresa. (1990, March). *The decade of the Hispanic: An economic retrospective.* Washington, DC: National Council of La Raza.

Miller, Marjorie. (1993, May 25). Cristina's controversy: Imported talk show enrages conservatives and liberals alike in Mexico. *Los Angeles Times.* Retrieved from http://articles.latimes.com/1993–05–25/news/wr-39491_1_cristina-show.

Moncreiff Arrante, Anne. (1990, February 2). And Galavision makes three. *Advertising Age,* S2.

Monsiváis, Carlos. (1993, May 17). Cristina, entre el derecho a la privacidad y el rompimiento de tabúes. *Proceso* (Mexico), *863*, 46–53.

Move to block sale of Ch. 51 parent fails. (1986, July, 24). *Miami News*, p. 8A.

Muñoz, Sergio. (1989, May 10). ¿La TV en español sufre un proceso de cubanización? *La Opinión*, 1, 11.

Mydans, Seth. (1989, July 24). Charges of bias in Spanish-language television. *New York Times*, C16.

Nielsen to test Spanish-language peoplemeter. (1989, July 31). *Broadcasting*, 36.

Nordheimer, Jon. (1986, November 4). Resignations upset Hispanic TV news program. *New York Times*, C17.

O'Hare, William (1990, August). The rise of Hispanic affluence. *American Demographics, 12*(8), 40–43.

O'Hare, William (1992, January). Reaching for the dream. *American Demographics, 14*(1), 32.

Owens, Dory. (1990, March). Hollywood's cool but Miami is hot! *Hispanic Business*, 34–36.

Poppe, David. (1988, December). More for less? *Hispanic Business*, 32–39.

Professor leads boycott of Los Angeles Spanish stations. (1989, July 31). *Broadcasting*, 36.

Reliance Capital gets Blair control. (1986, July 4). *New York Times*, D3.

Reliance wins fight to buy media group. (1986, August 16). *Miami News*, 10A.

Rigby, Julie. (1992, May 31). Talk show host speaks to issues her audience understands. *Chicago Tribune*, 5.

Rohter, Larry. (1992, July 26). Aqui se habla English: A talk show twist. *New York Times*, H23.

Rojas, Viviana, & Piñón, Juan. (2014). Spanish, English or Spanglish? Media strategies and corporate struggles to reach the second and later generations of Latinos. *International Journal of Hispanic Media, 7*. Retrieved from http://www.internationalhispanicmedia.org.

Rosaldo, Renato. (1988). Ideology, place, and people without culture. *Cultural Anthropology, 3*(1), 77–87.

Sale of WKAQ-TV station in Puerto Rico is arranged. (1988, November 14). *Wall Street Journal*, B6.

Sharbutt, Jay. (1989, August 9). 2 Companies measure the Latino TV market. *Los Angeles Times*. Retrieved from http://articles.latimes.com/1989–08–09/entertainment/ca-178_1_latino-tv.

Silva, Samuel. (1991, November). The Latin superchannels. *World Press Review*, 56.

Sinclair, John. (1990). Spanish-language television in the United States: Televisa surrenders its domain. *Studies in Latin American Popular Culture, 9*, 39–64.

Stevenson, Richard W. (1989, May 4). Counting viewers of Hispanic TV. *New York Times*, D19.

Stiven, Kristine. (1988, September 26). Spanish staple now made the American way. *Advertising Age*, S18.

Stiven, Kristine, & Fitch, Ed. (1988, September 26). The 4% solution often fails to add up. *Advertising Age*, S20.

Subervi-Vélez, Federico A., Hernández López, Nitza, M., & Frambes Buxeda, Aline. (1990). Mass media in Puerto Rico. In S. H. Surlin & W. C. Soderlund (Eds.), *Mass media in the Caribbean* (pp. 149–176). New York, NY: Gordon & Breach.

Telemundo Group completes the sale of 8 radio stations. (1987, July 7). *Wall Street Journal*, 53.

Telemundo TV network to air nationally tonight. (1987, January 12). *Wall Street Journal*, 8.

Terrazas, Ana Cecilia. (1993, May 17). La porra abucheo a los impugnadores y vitoreo el monologo autocomplaciente de Cristina. *Proceso* (Mexico), *863*, 48–49.

Thomas, June. (2011, November 2). How Univision is beating English-language networks in the ratings. *Slate*. Retrieved from http://www.slate.com/articles/arts/television/2011/11/univision_is_beating_english_language_networks_in_the_ratings_wh.single.html.

Thompson, Chandler. (1986, July 3). Chihuahua State election: Key test for Mexico's ruling party. Officials worry that loss of governor's seat could sway other states. *Christian Science Monitor*. Retrieved from http://www.csmonitor.com/1986/0703/ochi.html.

Totti, Xavier F. (1987). The making of a Latino ethnic identity. *Dissent*, 537–542.

Treister, Lisa. (1988, September 26). Bigger than ever, Sabado sends out clear message. *Variety*, S1, S25–S26.

Two networks slugging it out for viewers' eyes. (1989, July 21). *Television/Radio Age*, A24–A36.

Univision gears up for big changes in 2014. (2014, February 6). *Huffington Post*. Retrieved from http://www.huffingtonpost.com/2014/02/06/univision-changes_n_4741099.html.

Univision, too, says stateside pays. (1990, April 11). *Variety*, 42, 58.

U.S. Bureau of the Census. (1989, October). *Voting and registration in the election of November 1988*. Population Characteristics, Series P-20 No. 440. Retrieved from http://www.census.gov/hhes/www/socdemo/voting/publications/p20/1988/p20–440.pdf.

Valencia, Richard R. (2002). The explosive growth of the Chicano/Latino population: Educational implications. In R.R. Valencia (Ed.), *Chicano school failure and success: Past, present, and future* (2nd ed.) (pp. 52–69). New York, NY: Routledge.

Valenzuela, Nicolas. (1973). *Media habits and attitudes of Mexican Americans: Surveys in Austin and San Antonio*. Center for Communication Research, School of Communication, University of Texas at Austin.

Valle, Victor. (1986, September 11). Mexico newsman stirs controversy. *Los Angeles Times*, 11.

Valle, Victor. (1987, January 2). New Spanish news show to bow at KMEX Jan. 19. *Los Angeles Times*, 23.

Valle, Victor. (1988a, August 18). Latino TV re-creates U.S. images. *Los Angeles Times*, 1, 9.

Valle, Victor. (1988b, September 12). Angélica with an Americano flavor. *Los Angeles Times*, 1, 10.

Valle, Victor. (1988c, December 26). Latino TV to commission own ratings. *Los Angeles Times*, 1, 11.

Valle, Victor. (1988d, September 1). 1st Spanish-language 24-hour news format. *Los Angeles Times*, 10.

Valle, Victor. (1989, March 2). Villanueva quits general manager post at KMEX channel 34. *Los Angeles Times*, 9.

Villarreal, Yvonne. (2010, August 27). Cristina Saralegui talk show to end. *Los Angeles Times*. Retrieved from http://articles.latimes.com/2010/aug/27/entertainment/la-et-cristina-20100827.

Virshup, Amy. (1990, January). The Mexican Murdoch moves into town. *Manhattan, Inc.*, 82–87.

Volsky, George. (1990, April 10). A third Hispanic network seeks viewers in U.S. *New York Times*, C15.

Webster, James G. & Lichty, Lawrence W. (1991). *Ratings analysis: Theory and practice*. Hillsdale, NJ: Lawrence Erlbaum Associates.

Wilkinson, Kenton T. (2002, summer/fall). Collective situational ethnicity and Latino sub-groups' struggle for influence in U.S. Spanish-language television. *Communication Quarterly*, *50*(3/4), 422–443.

Wilkinson, Kenton T. (2006, September). Cultural policy in a free trade environment: Mexican television in transition. *Journal of Broadcasting & Electronic Media*, *50*(3), 482–501.

Part III

Market Competition and Expansion in the 1990s

6 The Economic Foundations of Spanish-Language Television in the 1990s

This chapter extends the discussion of U.S. Spanish-language television's development under the forces of growth and competition into the 1990s, focusing on ownership changes at Univision and Telemundo, financial challenges, a new ratings system and new networks. In 1993 Univision was purchased by a partnership consisting of the U.S. producer and investor Jerrold Perenchio, Emilio Azcárraga Milmo of Televisa, and Venevisión's Gustavo Cisneros. Sony Pictures Entertainment and the cable giant Liberty Media announced their acquisition of Telemundo in 1997. These changes occurred during a period of accelerated media growth and ownership concentration prior to substantial turmoil wrought by digitization in the 2000s. Herman and Chomsky (2010) recount Ben Bagdikian's troubling findings through various editions of his classic work, *The Media Monopoly*: in 1983, 50 companies controlled the majority of U.S. media, by 1990 the number had dropped to 23 and in 2010 it was down to nine. Such was the general media environment Spanish-language television expanded within during the 1990s. Both networks focused on growing their viewership, producing and exporting content and developing profitable synergies, domestically and internationally. More network options for Hispanic audiences in the U.S. and Latin America emerged later in the decade, some of them offering bilingual content. The developments examined here are closely intertwined with those in the next chapter, which focuses on change in Latin American television, especially Mexico, also during the 1990s and under the forces of deregulation, market expansion and ownership concentration (Fox & Waisbord, 2002; Sinclair, 1999).

The 1990s was generally a business-friendly decade punctuated by the North American Free Trade Agreement (NAFTA) that expanded from Canada and the U.S. to Mexico in 1994, media deregulation through the Telecommunications Act of 1996, and the Internet generating new interest and investment in communications from mid-decade on. Some detractors challenged the wisdom and equity of these developments, expressing concerns about potential negative impacts of free trade, the concentration of media ownership in fewer hands, and commercialization of the Internet— issues that carried latent consequences for U.S. Spanish-language television (McChesney, 2008).

The 1990 U.S. Census

The 1990 U.S. Census was the first to provide subcategories allowing respondents to self-identify. It counted 22.4 million Hispanics representing 9.0% of the U.S. population. The figure was later adjusted to 23.5 million—a 61% increase over the 14.6 million counted in 1980. The non-Hispanic portion of the population grew only 7% over the same period, and more Hispanics joined the U.S. population than all other minority groups combined (Foisie, 1992; Brischetto, 1993). Respondents reported these ethnic origins: 60% Mexican, 12% Puerto Rican, 5% Cuban and 23% "other," a category that included Spain and the countries of Central and South America[1] (Brischetto, 1993). The large number of people selecting "other" reflected both a broadening of the population's ethnic origins beyond the traditional three, and the census form's new flexibility in permitting respondents to choose from more national origin options. As the final two chapters demonstrate, subsequent censuses provided even more leeway for respondents to select multiple ethnic and racial categories. These decennial changes clearly enable more accurate accounting of a rapidly diversifying U.S. population, but the category shifts also make it difficult for demographers and others to compare data across the censuses.

A study examining the Hispanic population shift between 1990 and 2000 provides a useful demographic backdrop for this chapter's emphasis on political-economic aspects of U.S. Spanish-language television. Like the prior decade, 1990–2000 saw a nearly 60% increase in the Hispanic population. Yet this growth was uneven across national origin groups as the Mexican-origin population grew 53%, the Puerto Rican population 25%, Cubans 19% and the "other Hispanic" population 97% (Guzmán & Diaz McConnell, 2002). Although the Hispanic population remained concentrated in the Southwest and a few urban areas such as Chicago, New York and South Florida, some regions that previously had very few Hispanics saw their numbers increase substantially in the 1990s. For example, the Midwest experienced an 81% increase while the southern states witnessed an average 71% growth (Guzmán & Diaz McConnell, 2002). This shift carried significant potential impact as the Hispanic population grew nearly five times faster than any other demographic group during the 1990s (Bowser, 1998).

Such ethnic diversification and geographic dispersion of the Hispanic population cut in multiple directions for the Spanish-language television networks: their possible audience size expanded and more viewers tuned in to stay connected, while it also became more challenging to deliver programs and commercial spots that would appeal to a cohesive, national audience of Hispanics.[2] Furthermore, this ethnic diversity directly affected network leadership through complaints about Anglo domination of upper management positions, limited opportunities for Mexican Americans, and the industry's apparent Cubanization as both Univision and Telemundo concentrated production resources in Miami. A controversial incident in New York underscored the challenges implicit in the effort to knit together diverse subgroups into a cohesive whole.

The Montaner Incident

On November 5, 1990, Carlos Alberto Montaner, a Cuban American commentator on Univision's news magazine program *Portada*, gave this explanation for Puerto Rican Americans' low economic standing relative to Hispanics of Cuban and Mexican origin:[3]

> There's probably more than one explanation, but the one that seems most important to me is this: There is a grave family problem in the Puerto Rican ghettos of the United States, where there are thousands of very young single mothers, who try to escape poverty through welfare or through new partners who then leave, leaving behind other children to worsen the problem.
>
> (Quoted in Navarro, 1990, p. 1)

Understandably, the National Puerto Rican Fund, other Puerto Rican political advocacy organizations, and a number of prominent community members quickly condemned this stereotype of Puerto Rican women as sexually promiscuous abusers of the welfare system. Montaner conceded that he had been "clumsy in organizing the information" but dismissed as ridiculous accusations that he was racist and sexist (Navarro, 1990). That response did little to assuage the fury of Puerto Rican advocacy organizations that pressured Univision to sack Montaner. Univision's president Joaquin Blaya said the company thought Mr. Montaner was mistaken, but supported his right to express his opinion without being censored (Fisher, 1991).

Five weeks after the offending program aired, representatives of Univision and Hallmark Cards met with leaders of 11 Puerto Rican organizations who again called for Mr. Montaner's dismissal. Blaya reiterated Univision's refusal to fire Montaner and offered to host a program focused on challenges facing the Puerto Rican community in the U.S., a response that did not placate the advocates. Carlos Piñeiro, a spokesperson for the Puerto Rican Pro-Affirmation Committee vowed, "we're going to teach Univision to respect the Puerto Rican community ... we're going to hit them where it hurts" (Nieves, 1990, my translation). The advocacy organizations began pressuring Univision's advertisers to boycott the network. They found a sympathetic reception with Goya Foods, the second largest Hispanic-owned company at the time, with 1500 employees and annual sales of more than $320 million. The company's president and one of his sons were married to Puerto Rican women (Nieves, 1990). Goya Foods suspended some advertising, but only on Univision's New York station (WXTV) and only for eight days; spots resumed airing after Mr. Montaner offered a more contrite apology on a local public affairs program (Fisher, 1991). The Coca-Cola Bottlers of New York had threatened to boycott as well, but did not pursue the matter following Mr. Montaner's second apology, which aired more than two months after his initial offending statement. This incident highlights the continuing maturation of political organizations advocating on behalf of specific Hispanic subgroups, but also illustrates the difficulty in sustaining economic threats brought to bear on commercial media.

The episode also indicated how the public relations surrounding Spanish-language television was changing in the new decade. During the height of the Montaner controversy, the Mexican media conglomerate Televisa and its U.S. affiliate Univisa purchased an advertisement in the Miami newspaper *El Nuevo Herald*, printed in bold block lettering, which read like this (my translation):

> To the Hispanic Community - We wish to respectfully clarify the following:
> 1 We have absolutely nothing to do with the management of the Univision network.
> 2 We have absolutely nothing to do with Carlos Alberto Montaner.
> 3 Our work in Spanish-language television has always been characterized by respect to all communities, particularly the Hispanics we serve, and especially its women.
> 4 We are only responsible for programming on Galavisión and its newscasts called *Eco*. Thank you for your business.

The last line suggests that the ad's intended audience was television-related businesses in the South Florida area, which, as the next chapter shows, was quickly becoming an industry focal point during the 1990s. There's also an incongruous twist in that Televisa's Emilio Azcárraga Milmo and his lawyers were actively lobbying the federal government to relax foreign ownership restrictions on U.S. broadcast stations so he could own U.S. stations again (Jessell, 1991). It wouldn't be long before Azcárraga returned to the Univision camp.[4]

The 1992 Univision Sale

The expensive competition between Univision and Telemundo together with a soft advertising market created financial strains at both networks in the early 1990s. Univision briefly faced the prospect of involuntary bankruptcy when it failed to make a $10 million interest payment in February 1990. Hallmark Cards came to the network's aid by offering to purchase $270 million worth of junk bonds at 40 cents on the dollar (Mendoza, 1992), and by seeking concessions both from a lender and its investment partner First Capital Corp. of Chicago.[5] A reporter for *The Wall Street Journal* concluded:

> … it is now clear that Hallmark and First Chicago paid too much for some of the broadcast properties and vastly underestimated the investment needed to keep the concern competitive. While the huge, relatively untapped pool of Spanish-speaking households is an attractive

market, winning advertisers and finding programming that is broadly appealing has been difficult.

(Bailey, 1990)

Hallmark communicated that it would entertain offers for the network, and on April 8, 1992 expressed its intention to sell the Univision station and network to an investment group led by A. Jerrold Perenchio, who in addition to holding stakes in Spanish-language stations WNJU (New York) and KBSC (Los Angeles), was part owner of the Loews theater chain, had partnered with Norman Lear on hit English-language shows like *All in the Family* and *The Jeffersons*, and was a successful Hollywood agent (Crook & Harris, 1981). The minor partners were Venevisión, a powerful Venezuelan broadcasting concern,[6] and Televisa (Stevenson, 1992). By the partnership terms, and to comply with Section 310 (b) of the Communications Act that limits *corporate* foreign ownership and control of broadcast outlets to 25%, Perenchio would hold 75% of the station group and Venevisión and Televisa 12.5% each.[7] The network would be owned 50% by Perenchio, and 25% each by Televisa and Venevisión; U.S. law does not limit non-nationals' ownership or control of broadcast *networks* (The secrets, 1993).

As one would expect, the news that Emilio Azcárraga Milmo would be returning to an ownership position in U.S. Spanish-language television engendered criticism and legal efforts to prevent Univision station licenses' transfer to the new ownership group. Petitions to the FCC from Hispanic advocacy organizations urged the commission to deny the license transfer, charging that the public interest would be violated, foreign control would be reinstated, and a loss of jobs, competition, and diversity in Spanish-language television would result. Three Latino advocacy organizations, the League of United Latin American Citizens (LULAC), the National Hispanic Media Coalition (NHMC) and the National Puerto Rican Forum (NPRF) joined Telemundo network in a collective petition (7 FCC Rcd [1992]). The petitioners had multiple reasons for opposing the sale, but emphasized the potential negative outcomes for the industry and Hispanic audiences if powerful foreign companies like Televisa and Venevisión were permitted to operate in the U.S. The principal arguments claimed the transfer would reduce competition in an industry where it had only recently begun; program diversity and relevance would diminish with more imported content (upsetting the 50–50 balance between imports and U.S. programs that Univision recently achieved); jobs in the U.S. industry would be lost to Latin America under the "produce in pesos, sell in dollars" strategy;[8] Televisa lacked basic qualifications as a licensee due to past legal violations; and control by foreign nationals would (again) exceed the limitations set by the Communications Act (Claudia Puig, 1992; Brennan, 1992a). Telemundo expressed additional concerns specific to its competition with Univision, including the possibility that Televisa and Venevisión would bankroll the station group while only appearing to conform with the ownership limits,[9] that the two Latin

American networks would collaborate to impede sales of Telemundo-produced programming in Latin America, that the three-network consortium could manipulate advertising sales to its advantage, and that Televisa's existing practice of blacklisting artists who appear on other networks would reduce competition (Carlos Puig, 1992).

In June 1992, the United States Hispanic Chamber of Commerce (USHCC) joined the Hispanic advocacy groups' petition, but 10 days after the filing withdrew its opposition and expressed support for the station transfer (7 FCC Rcd. 6672 [1992]). Abel Guerra, a spokesperson for USHCC, explained that the owners of 25 Univision affiliated or owned-and-operated stations were Chamber members as were 25% of the network's station managers. As to why USHCC had joined the petition in the first place, Guerra said the organization had understood that Televisa would hold 25% interest in the station group, which it perceived as a threat of renewed control from Mexico (personal communication, August 10, 1992). Apparently USHCC considered the 12.5% each held by Televisa and Venevisión more palatable. There are other likely explanations. Some chamber members' business interests may have favored the proposed station transfer, leading the organization to honor its principal goal of supporting members' interests over an ancillary goal of increasing U.S. Hispanics' control over the industry. Another possibility is that the organization was persuaded to change its position through back-channel communications.

On September 30, 1992, the FCC denied the petitions submitted by Telemundo and the Hispanic advocacy organizations in the same opinion and order with which it approved the license transfers from Hallmark to the Perenchio-Televisa-Venevisión consortium (7 FCC Rcd 6672 [1992]).[10] The document addressed the petitioners' claims one by one to support its conclusion that there was insufficient evidence to justify a hearing. Naturally Telemundo, media advocacy organizations and members of the public who followed the case were disappointed; a lawyer for the National Hispanic Media Coalition commented, "once again the FCC has been duped" (Andrews, 1992). The Coalition filed a plea in the U.S. Court of Appeals for the D.C. Circuit arguing that the FCC's decision had: rendered a public interest judgment based on insufficient information from the new owners (Brennan, 1992b); failed to articulate adequate findings on the petitioners' arguments; violated its own policies intended to promote diverse program sources for American TV viewers; and ignored the diminished diversity in Spanish-language television programming that would result (*Television Digest*, 1992). According to the Coalition, it later dropped its appeal in exchange for Univision's promise to develop educational children's programming (National Hispanic Media Coalition, n.d.).[11]

For Hallmark Cards, the 1992 sale finally stanched the financial bleeding that had begun shortly after it acquired the station group in 1986 and network in 1987. *Hispanic Business* magazine concluded, "overall, Univision has cost Hallmark at least $748 million" (Mendoza, 1992). Despite the strong financial portfolios of the investors, the Univision purchase was heavily leveraged, "a financing strategy in the style of the 1980s, complete with junk bonds and a highly-leveraged debt-to-equity ratio," also according to *Hispanic Business* (Lopes, 1993). The purchase price, at $509 million, was much lower than initially reported, but $545 million changed hands once fees and expenses were included. Perenchio contributed $50 million and Televisa and Venevisión $25 million each in cash. The remaining capital was financed by bank term loans ($210 million), bank revolving credit ($65 million), Hallmark taking back notes ($30 million), and an offering memorandum for senior subordinated notes—also known as "junk bonds"—that would mature in 2001 ($140 million) (The secrets, 1993).

Post-Sale Employment Issues

As we have seen, one concern regarding the Univision sale centered on employment—that bringing in Televisa and Venevisión would cause increased airtime dedicated to imported material and less domestic production. Critics cited as evidence a statement by Jerrold Perenchio in his application for the Univision licenses: "the programs offered to the venture by Televisa and Venevision will include at least a quantity of programs sufficient to fill a 24-hour-a-day, seven-day-a-week broadcast schedule" (cited in Claudia Puig, 1992b). Perenchio was making the case that his enterprise had access to sufficient programming to supply the stations; critics interpreted his statement as a plan to halt U.S. production at Univision. When pressed for a clarification, Bob Cahill, an attorney for Perenchio Television, responded, "it means that we have the right, but no obligation ... it's just an assurance that we have a programming source, but we don't have to take it" (Claudia Puig, 1992b). Univision president Ray Rodriguez spun the point further arguing that competition from Telemundo would keep pressure on his network to air popular programs, not just inexpensive ones, and also emphasized enhanced export opportunities for Univision-produced programs through Televisa's and Venevisión's extensive distribution networks (Brennan, 1992a). The cultural relevance of programming aired for U.S. Hispanics was at issue, as were production-related jobs.

Once the sale finalized in December 1992, the new owners began implementing changes. Although the FCC approval hurdle had been cleared, critics and the press remained vigilant. Univision's canceling three U.S.-produced shows and laying off 70 employees in February 1993 appeared to confirm predictions of a Latin American import pipeline.[12] The network defended its action as necessary cost-cutting to reduce its debt (Lopes, 1993). To justify its selection of canceled shows, Univision referred to the Nielsen Hispanic Television Index, which, opportunely, released its first national ratings for Spanish-language television in December 1992. Two of the canceled shows ranked in the top twenty, but it's important to note that the top three programs were *telenovelas*, produced by Televisa and Venevisión.

The staff reductions at Univision continued during 1993; by August at least 175 employees had been laid off nationwide, *Hispanic Business* reported (Mendoza, 1993). A number of other workers resigned, including the news director and a well-known chief correspondent, Sergio Muñoz at KMEX in Los Angeles, where turmoil followed the downsizing as a number of former employees believed the station's news declined in quality and dignity after the ownership change (Cerone, 1993; Mendoza, 1993).

Before the layoffs took place there had been realignments of executive talent at both Univision and Telemundo. The highest-profile and most controversial relocation concerned Joaquin Blaya who was acting president of Univision Holdings when Hallmark announced it would sell the network and station group. Blaya became infuriated that the sale to Perenchio and partners was presented to him as a "done deal" only hours before it was made public. He quickly tendered a management-led offer that included other Univision executives, but was turned down by Hallmark leadership. About six weeks after the sale announcement Blaya made news of his own by declaring that he had accepted the president and CEO position at Telemundo. Univision quickly indicated its intention to legally challenge Blaya's move based on the non-compete clause in his contract, arguing that his intimate knowledge of Univision's business could be used against it. The network's claim was dismissed by a state court judge in New York who ruled that the non-compete clause was too broad and, if enforced as written, would prevent Blaya from working anywhere in the U.S. Spanish-language television business (Lambert, 1992). Several other high-ranking executives also jumped ship within days after Blaya. José Cancela, who became Telemundo's station group president, was also cleared by the New York court; two others, José del Cueto (senior vice president for sales) and Filiberto Fernandez (senior vice president for marketing), were not named in Univision's suit. Luca Bentivoglio, a prolific producer of domestic programs followed the trail of executives to Telemundo in August (Claudia Puig, 1992d). Ray Rodriguez, who had been at the company for only 18 months filled the president/CEO position at Univision, while other management vacancies were filled through promotions.

The executive scramble compounded tensions surrounding the ownership change. Joaquin Blaya added fuel to the media advocates' fire by saying he'd been "alarmed" since fall 1991 when rumors circulated that Emilio Azcárraga wanted to buy back in to Univision (Carlos Puig, 1992). Blaya had long favored U.S. program production and was widely credited with achieving Univision's (self-identified) 50% domestic–50% imported programming mix prior to the sale.[13] Furthermore, he too cited Jerrold Perenchio's FCC license application in supporting the argument that domestic production would diminish and the Latin American partners' involvement would stall Univision's efforts to sell its U.S.-produced programs abroad (Claudia Puig, 1992c; Lopes, 1992). Perenchio addressed Blaya's assertion in a letter to Univision employees writing, "programming will continue to be produced on-shore as well as off, as it is today ... news will be produced in the United States ... successful shows like 'Sabado Gigante,' and 'Cristina' and others will continue to be produced in Miami" (cited in Fisher, 1992b).

The 1992 ownership change at Univision caused a less radical shake-up in U.S. Spanish-language television than had the forced sale of Spanish International Communications Corp. in 1986, but it was consequential nonetheless. Whereas the earlier change prompted a production competition between Univision and Telemundo—and export to Latin America of U.S.-produced programs to offset costs—the 1992 change further differentiated the networks. With ample, inexpensive programming readily available from two of Latin America's largest producers and distributors, Univision scaled back its U.S. production.

A Growing Market

While many were pointing out the negatives, the business magazine *Crain's* saw positive effects resulting from Univision's sale and the consequent churn: "these new developments have created more heated competition between the rivals. They are producing new and better programs faster, and are improving production values and on-air talent" (Mirabella, 1992). A substantial portion of the credit goes to Joaquin Blaya who took his domestic production emphasis to Telemundo, though the network's financial instability through much of the 1990s limited his aspirations. The next chapter describes another important contributor to stronger competition and better program quality—increased investor interest in Mexico as the North American Free Trade Agreement neared implementation in January 1994. Such interest was not focused exclusively on the Mexican market, but included the prospect of connecting Mexico with the U.S. Spanish-language sector. Thus the uptick in business press and trade journal reporting on television and other media south of the Rio Grande had an analogue to the north. Increased attention on the industry also derived from the National Hispanic Television Index releasing ratings in December 1992. The long-standing lack of credible audience data that had discouraged some advertisers from buying space in Spanish-language television was finally being addressed. Although not without its own challenges, the Nielsen data provided the industry a more stable currency for conducting business.

In 1991, U.S. television advertising spending had contracted for the first time in three decades. Univision earned an estimated $210 million in ad revenue that year, and Telemundo $134 million (Walley, 1992). However, in 1992 ad sales expanded, by 9% at Telemundo and an estimated 20% at Univision (Foisie, 1992). *Hispanic Business* reported 1992 net advertising expenditures of $176.5 million for network and national television, and $167.5 million for local television, of a total $746.6 million advertising spend on Hispanic media[14] (Acosta & Velasquez, 1992). It is important to note that such figures don't include all revenue sources like in-show promotions on *Sábado Gigante* where audience members sing advertiser jingles, a way to accommodate advertisers that don't have Spanish-language spots (Foisie, 1992).

Notwithstanding television's troubles, the *Hispanic Consumer Market Report* commissioned by Univision forecasted a bright future: Hispanic consumer spending was projected to grow from $193 billion in 1990 to $438 billion in 2000 (Brennan, 1992c; see Appendix B). *Hispanic Business* estimated Hispanic purchasing power at $195 billion in 1993, a figure more than triple the $62.5 billion in 1982 (Dow, 1993). By 1997 spending had increased 36% to $266 billion, due in part to a growing number of Hispanics moving into managerial and professional occupations (Douglas, 1997). The Univision report also cited a statistic that had nagged the industry for decades, and would persist: the low percentage of total U.S. advertising spending devoted to Hispanic consumers, estimated at less than one percent (Brennan, 1992c). The growth of Hispanic consumer spending power over the five decades covered by this book is illustrated in Appendix B.

Nielsen in the 1990s

The Nielsen Hispanic Television Index (NHTI) originated in 1989 when Univision and Telemundo pooled their resources to obtain more inclusive and accurate ratings of Spanish-language television from the A.C. Nielsen Co.[15] (Bergsman, 1989a). Together the networks anticipated investing around $40 million in NHTI in its first five years,[16] but even that sum was not expected to cover Nielsen's costs in establishing, testing and maintaining its national Hispanic sample (Lopes, 1993; Walley, 1992). The project began with a three-year pilot study in Los Angeles, expanding to the national level in September 1992. The first national report was based on the extrapolated findings from 800 Peoplemeters selected to represent an estimated 6,250,000 Hispanic television households nationwide. Beyond reporting ratings for individual programs, the index also tracked television usage within the household and all viewing sources including over-the-air networks in English as well as Spanish, cable networks, public television and independent stations (Walley, 1992). Through such broad data capture, and by including both Spanish- and English-dominant households in its sample, the NHTI provided the first comprehensive statistics regarding Hispanics' viewing habits.

Univision was the clear leader in the first two national Nielsen reports, claiming 16 of the top 20 programs in November 1992, and 18 of 20 in February 1993 (Lopes, 1993; Univision takes lead, 1993). Not surprisingly, network leadership seized the opportunity to defend its programming mix and staff reductions. The director of research Doug Darfield said the ratings "affirm ... that *novelas* continue to be the most popular format on Spanish-language television" (Foreign programs work, 1993). President Ray

Rodriguez emphasized the distinct origins of the top three programs in the February ratings: "The programming mix Univision has created between programs produced in Mexico, Venezuela and the United States has demonstrated again that we have the right strategy" (Univision takes lead, 1993). Thus the first reports from the NHTI demonstrated Univision's clear lead in audience shares, and provided a quantitative justification for show cancellations and staff cutbacks during a sensitive period of transition.

The NHTI numbers also clarified viewing patterns in local markets. In February 1993, 40% of 5 million Hispanic viewers in Los Angeles tuned in Spanish-language stations. Univision's KMEX captured a 15.1 rating for the 8:00–11:00 p.m. slot, compared to KVEA (Telemundo) with 12.4 and KWHY with 2.2 (Klein, 1993). As noted above, the NHTI measured viewing of English- as well as Spanish-language networks. In the November 1992 survey, FOX claimed four of the top five programs, with *The Simpsons* in first place. There was a notable difference across the language divide, however; *The Simpsons* averaged an 8.1 rating among 18- to 49-year-olds in *all* Hispanic households in the sample, yet only a 2.2 among Spanish-dominant ones (Moshavi, 1993). This finding raises interesting questions not only about differing acculturation levels among viewers, but also the relative appeal of TV programs in their original production language or translated (including animated ones).

The advertising agency BBDO compared NHTI data with Nielsen's general market data for 1993–94 to gauge Hispanic household viewing patterns of prime time English-language shows.[17] The study revealed that serial dramas and sitcoms, especially those having ethnic characters, were most popular among Hispanic households (McClellan, 1995). Age, a factor that would become an increasingly salient demographic marker among Hispanic audiences, also stood out as the teen and 50-years-plus groups had more viewing commonalities across languages than did age groups in between them. A central conclusion of the report—that mainstream networks and producers should create programs featuring Hispanic lifestyles, values and culture that also appeal to general audiences—has been the Holy Grail in mainstream pursuits of the Hispanic audience for a quarter century (McClellan, 1995).

In August 1994, Nielsen announced an agreement with Univision that would expand its local market analyses from two—Los Angeles and Miami—to nine more: New York, San Francisco, San Antonio, Chicago, Houston, Albuquerque, Dallas, Fresno and Phoenix, raising its local market coverage to 62% (Foisie, 1994).[18] Univision would pay an estimated $15 million over five years to support the expanded service (Fisher, 1994). Telemundo did not sign on, stating its preference that Nielsen's general market panel be enlarged, with a Hispanic breakout panel included, so that that ratings would be derived from a single "book" not two separate ones (this is essentially what happened in 2007 as explained in Chapter Nine). The challenge of using two books had been demonstrated just six weeks before the market expansion announcement when Univision's Los Angeles station KMEX complained about a 39,000 household discrepancy between Nielsen's Hispanic count (234,000) and general market count (195,000) for a World Cup soccer match; Nielsen responded that differences in sampling techniques and Peoplemeter use caused the incongruity (Cerone, 1994). Certainly Telemundo's financial situation also played a role in its decision not to support Nielsen's expansion: the network was emerging from Chapter 11 bankruptcy protection when the ratings expansion was announced (Fisher, 1994).

Before proceeding to a discussion of those financial woes, I should note the value of Nielsen's brand name. Even with its well-publicized faults, Nielsen had established an industry standard and its data functioned as the U.S. television industry's main currency. Having the name attached to the new ratings service probably encouraged some mainstream advertisers who had contemplated entering the Hispanic market, and reconfirmed the decisions of many who already had. As the advertising and marketing expert Abby Wool put it, "major advertisers had a comfort level with good old Nielsen, whereas the SRC's [Strategy Reseach Corp.'s] numbers were not perceived as quite so impartial by many in the business and advertising world" (cited in Valdéz, 2002, p. 257). Although controversy would continue to dog the organization, which would later wane in prominence as a television ratings provider, it is important to recognize the legitimacy that Nielsen Hispanic Television Index offered Spanish-language television at a crucial stage in its development.

Financial Challenges

Even as they were growing in reach, visibility and perceived legitimacy during the 1990s, both major networks faced financial strains, although of differing magnitude. Recall that Univision started the decade under the threat of involuntary bankruptcy when it missed a $10 million interest payment and was bailed out by its corporate owner, Hallmark Cards. The network subsequently assumed considerable debt with the ownership change in 1992, for which it borrowed about $480 million notwithstanding the deep pockets of its principals, Perenchio, Azcárraga Milmo and Cisneros. In April 1993, the company filed plans with the Securities & Exchange Commission to issue $140 million worth of public notes in order to buy the same amount in privately placed notes that were already outstanding (Cole, 1993).

In September 1996 Univision Communications made its initial public offering, selling 8,170,000 shares, or 19% of its common stock, at $23 per share. Thus, by 1998 Perenchio held 26.5% of the Class A common stock, while Grupo Televisa and Venevisión each held 10.3%. Because he retained full ownership of the Class P stock, however, Perenchio held 78.5% of the voting power (History of Univision, n.d.). Changes implemented by the new leadership literally paid dividends. After posting losses for 1993,

1994, and 1995, Univision reported net income of $10.4 million in 1996 and $82.6 million in 1997, which included a $19.5 million carryover from earlier losses (History of Univision, n.d.). The 1994 World Cup hosted by the United States was a boon for Univision, which gained an estimated $25 million in ad sales while paying less than $10 million for the rights to broadcast the games. This upward trend continued through the rest of the decade and became the principal reason for Univision's dominance of the industry, as we shall see at chapter's end. Conversely, Telemundo's financial woes through much of the decade prevented it from offering the sustained competition to Univision that it desperately sought.

Telemundo's expansion during the latter 1980s was rapid, expensive and had been funded largely by junk bonds. Saul Steinberg's Reliance Group Holdings owned about 80% of the company. The 1990s initiated in difficult fashion for broadcasters, especially those like Telemundo that carried large debt burdens. The network reported a net loss of $275 million for 1991 and in January 1992 failed to make payment on $250 million in debt, placing the company in default on all of its outstanding debt. Network management announced that restructuring efforts were underway. Leon Black's company Apollo Advisors acquired a majority of Telemundo's bonded debt when Executive Life Insurance Co. collapsed in 1992. Black had been a junk bond trader along with Michael Milken, but survived the market's collapse (and, unlike Milken, avoided prosecution). One debt reduction option that Black considered was to raise cash by selling stations, but doing so would clearly restrict revenue (Ozemhoya, 1993a). Among Joaquin Blaya's most appealing traits when Telemundo hired him in 1992 was his ability to raise capital, as demonstrated in his management-led effort to buy Univision (Ozemhoya, 1993a). Yet his emphasis on high quality domestic production on par with English-language television's—to create "a much younger, slimmer and aggressive company than Univision ... a FOX of Spanish TV"—would be a costly endeavor requiring nonexistent resources (Fisher, 1992c).

The restructuring talks initiated after Telemundo's loan default in 1992 dragged on for over a year. Three investors holding junior debentures in the company through Reliance became impatient with the slow proceedings and petitioned the courts to place the company in involuntary bankruptcy in June 1993 (Involuntary bankruptcy, 1993). Telemundo's debt at the time was about $300 million, including $283 in interest (Woes mount, 1993). The network emerged from Chapter 11 bankruptcy protection in August 1993 when the interested parties agreed upon a reorganization plan to reduce the company's debt from $300 million to $115 million. According to a report in *MediaWeek*, "the agreement call[ed] for the reduction of Telemundo's debt to less than one-third the current debt in exchange for cash, new senior notes, reorganization of common stock and warrant to buy more shares of the new stock" (Burgi, 1993). Two seats on the board went to Steinberg and one to the junior debt holders who initiated the bankruptcy proceedings (Burgi, 1993). Apollo Advisors swapped their bond holdings for approximately 30% equity in the company, and Apollo held a majority of seats on the board of directors. Saul Steinberg, who had put the network together by purchasing the John Blair Co. in 1986 and steadily adding stations in key markets, saw his stake fall from 78% to 3% (Mendoza, 1993). Another big change was on Telemundo's horizon.

Before discussing that change I should mention, even if briefly, the Telecommunications Act of 1996, which President Bill Clinton signed into law on February 8, 1996. Although there was no immediate impact in the Spanish-language television sector, by raising ownership caps for local markets and national audiences (to 35%) the Act stimulated a flurry of mergers and acquisitions that facilitated the incorporation of Spanish-language properties into English-language media conglomerates. The Telecommunications Act aided both NBC's acquisition of Telemundo in 2001 and Univision's incorporation of Hispanic Broadcasting Corp.'s radio stations in 2003. The Act's easing of restrictions on telecommunications and Internet media also facilitated the Spanish-language networks' incorporation of web sites and mobile phones in subsequent years.

The 1997 Telemundo Sale

Despite the high hopes under which he entered, Joaquin Blaya could not reverse Telemundo's financial difficulties or its slide in the ratings. He was replaced as president and chief executive officer by Roland A. Hernández in May 1995, yet the problems continued. In July 1997 Telemundo executives confirmed rumors that the company had retained the investment banking firm Lazard Frères & Co. to find a strategic partner to bolster programming efforts. Sony was one name circulating the rumor mill (Telemundo eyes, 1997). Speculation at the time suggested the FCC might change its station duopoly and local marketing agreement rules, which would permit one entity to own multiple UHF and VHF television stations in a single market. Therefore, Telemundo's cadre of UHF stations looked appealing to half a dozen large media players, including the major English-language broadcast networks (McClellan, 1997).

On November 24, 1997 the news broke that Sony Pictures Entertainment Co. and Liberty Media Corp., the programming unit for the cable television giant Telecommunications Inc. (TCI), and others had agreed to purchase Telemundo for $539 million. The two companies represented a significant inflow of resources and production know-how. The other partners were two venture capital companies, Apollo Management[19] and Bastion Capital Fund, whose combined ownership share increased from 35% to 50.1% with the former holding 34% and the latter 16% (Mendoza, 1998). Leon Black of Apollo Management had failed in an attempt to purchase 60% of Telemundo only days before the Sony/Liberty Media sale was announced (Group bids, 1997). Bastion Capital, the largest Hispanic-owned equity fund at the time, was headed by Daniel D. Villanueva, the former professional football player and station manager at Univision's LA station, KMEX, during the 1970s and '80s. By the partnership's terms, Sony would hold just under 25% of the company in order to conform to foreign ownership restrictions, and Liberty Media would control 5% of voting and 20% of non-voting stock in order to comply with FCC cross-ownership rules (Esparza, 1998). Following approval of the sale, a programming and marketing network would be spun off as a 50/50 joint venture between Sony Pictures Entertainment and Liberty Media (Liberty Media Corp., 1997).

Given its substantial resources and experience in programming, Sony became the managing partner of the network, which supplied Telemundo stations with content. José del Cueto of TranAmerica Media group commented on the acquisition, "it's going to inject programming and wherewithal into a group that badly needs it ... for the first time ever, Telemundo has a content component to it" (quoted in Zbar, 1997). The new partners also contributed technology to help distribute that content—shortly after the sale was made public Liberty Media announced plans to launch 10 to 12 digital channels over TCI cable systems early in 1998, and the same number again the following year.

Keeping with an established pattern for network acquisitions, the FCC received petitions to deny the license transfer. On this occasion Hispanic advocacy groups did not object, but Univision did. The charge was very familiar to the network that leveled it: Univision argued that the deal contravened Section 310 (b) of the Communications Act. Univision claimed that Liberty Media's parent company TCI had offshore influences meriting investigation, and also asserted that TCI's strong position in cable television created cross-ownership problems vis-á-vis Telemundo's 23 owned-and-operated broadcasting properties. Telemundo vigorously opposed the petition, declaring what it undoubtedly was: an effort to delay FCC approval and forestall more vigorous competition from a better-financed network (Mendoza, 1998).

Clearly, content was the principal focus of Telemundo's new management team that took shape shortly after the sale was approved on August 1, 1998. Peter Tortorici[20] a former president of CBS Entertainment became network president; Nely Galán, who had become the New York affiliate station WNJU's general manager at only 22 years old, became president of programming; former Sony Pictures Entertainment senior vice president of corporate development Alan Sokol assumed the role of chief executive officer; and Rachael Wells, also from Sony Pictures, became executive vice president of marketing. Former network president and CEO Roland Hernández became chairman of the station group (Paxman, 1998a). Programming, marketing and distribution were paramount at Telemundo under its new leadership.

The new management team faced a formidable challenge[21] as Telemundo's share of the U.S. Spanish-language television pie had diminished from a high of 40% in 1992 to 18% when it was sold (Zbar, 1997); we have seen that Univision gained significant momentum in the interim. Although the new leadership preferred to develop new U.S.-produced programs, the relatively high cost and the sale approval's timing militated against it. Instead, Sony moved quickly to create Spanish-language versions of several successful English-language shows such as *Starsky & Hutch* (*Reyes y Rey*), *The Dating Game* (*Buscando Pareja*) and *Who's the Boss* (*Una Familia con Ángel*), which debuted in September 1998 (Paxman, 1998a). These programs harkened back to the domestic programming competition of the late 1980s when both networks established roots in Miami. Yet the programs fell short of industry advocates' hopes for content that better reflected the U.S. Hispanic experience, and also fell short in the ratings—Telemundo's audience dropped more than 30% during the nine months after the ownership change, to a mere 8% of Hispanic television households (Baxter, 1998).

The dismal ratings prompted a strategy shift the following year when Telemundo placed more *telenovelas* in prime time and sought partnerships with Latin American producers, including Televisa's competitor in Mexico, Televisión Azteca, as discussed in the next chapter. The network did not cease domestic production, however; the journalist Kevin Baxter (1999a) explained:

> But the new reliance on imported programming does not mean Telemundo has completely abandoned its promise to develop domestically produced content that reflects the experience of Latinos in this country. The network is adding two new Miami-based talk shows, a series of network-branded news programs, the reality show "Donde Estara," [sic] which will reunite divided families, and the sitcom "Los Beltran."[22]

The fact that Sony held the rights to popular English-language television shows such as *The Nanny*, *The Young and the Restless*, and *Wheel of Fortune* meant little if they couldn't be adapted in ways that were compelling and meaningful for Hispanic audiences. The same was true for Liberty's content from its regional cable channels, Discovery Latin America, Discovery Kids Latin America, Travel Channel Latin America, Fox Sports America and the QVC home shopping network (Zbar, 1997).[23] Although in theory such channels could knit together vast hemispheric audiences, in the U.S. they were only as valuable as their appeal to Hispanic viewers, many of whom watched English-language television as well. This underscored the key point that although Sony and Liberty Media contributed new production talent and resources, Telemundo still lacked Univision's main competitive advantage—low-cost programs imported from Mexico and Venezuela (Paxman, 1998b).

Other Networks

An article appearing in *Forbes* early in the decade challenged a number of the foundational assumptions the U.S. Spanish-language television networks had been built on, arguing that "multiculturalists and hucksters have fostered the myth of a vast, underreached Hispanic market ... the myth is wearing thin" (Palmeri & Levine, 1991). As this book's final two chapters illustrate, industry definitions of the market have broadened, as have the programming, marketing and technological efforts to reach it (Rojas & Piñón, 2014). The roots of this redefinition are linguistic, beginning in the late 1980s and enduring through the 1990s when cable networks began specializing in content genre (such as CNN en Español and Cine Canal), audience segment (e.g., ESPN), or lifestyle (MTV Latino). This development ran in parallel with the splintering of U.S. English-language television which begun in the 1980s and accelerated during the 1990s as the multichannel environment expanded. The following is a selected, not comprehensive, list of Hispanic-oriented networks that launched, most of them in conjunction with Latin American services, for reasons detailed in the next chapter.

Cable News Network (CNN) began its 24-hour satellite Spanish-language news service in early 1989. The Turner-owned company was the first to develop a worldwide dedicated news channel launched in 1980, and also operated a nightly news production joint venture, *Noticiero Telemundo-CNN*, with the Spanish-language network from 1988 to 1993.

Telemundo-BBC-Reuters: After Telemundo's five-year news production agreement with CNN ended in May 1993, the network entered a collaborative venture with the British Broadcasting Corporation (BBC) and Reuters to provide a 24-hour international Spanish-language news service. The partnership relied on Reuters' international newsgathering resources, BBC World Service Television's extensive distribution network and Telemundo's on- and off-screen talent (BBC will be, 1993).

ESPN: The Entertainment and Sports Programming Network began distributing its content on dedicated Latin American pay television channels in 1989. By early 1993 ESPN's potential regional audience was 2.4 million television households. The service instituted Spanish-language commentary on weekends in September 1991, expanded that service to prime time in January 1992, and began 24-hour bilingual English/Spanish audio and a Portuguese audio option in early 1993 (ESPN committed, 1993). The service evolved into ESPN Deportes, which launched in 2004.

Prime Ticket La Cadena Deportiva first appeared in November 1993 as a regional sports network covering Arizona, California, Nevada and Hawaii, an area then encompassing about 30% of the nation's Hispanics. It carried Los Angeles and San Diego professional sports as well as Pacific Athletic Conference college sports (Chagollan, 1993). In 1995 the network expanded to the national level (La Cadena Deportiva Nacional) and in 1996 merged with Fox Sports Americas, which later became Fox Deportes.

Selecciones en Español was the first manifestation of HBO's interest in Spanish-speaking audiences, offering HBO and Cinemax subscribers Spanish-language audio for select programs beginning in 1989 (Valle, 1989). *HBO Olé*, also a premium pay television channel, launched in 1990 featuring Spanish-language content as well as dubbed and subtitled films and television series. By 1993, *HBO Olé* had entered programming contracts with 130 pay television operators throughout Latin America (HBO Olé is learning, 1993).

Olé-TV was a U.S. service targeting middle-class families and school systems with educational and cultural content including cartoons, documentaries, concerts and European films. The network transmitted 7 hours per day of educational material geared to children and was supported by grants and sponsorships to avoid commercialization (Ozemhoya, 1993b).

Note that this partial list does not include some Spanish-language services like Cine Canal, FOX, Marte TV, Tele-Uno and TNT Latin American which have a regional focus on Latin America, and were available on some pay-television systems in the U.S. but did not specifically target the U.S. market.

U.S. Spanish-Language Television at the Turn of the Millennium

Despite the challenges discussed in this chapter, by the turn of the millennium Spanish-language television had matured and received significant attention from the press, advertisers and potential investors. Some of this attention undoubtedly originated from the Latin Boom in popular culture, especially music, at decade's end. However, numbers are the currency for business decisions and, as we have seen, the Nielsen Hispanic Television Index, among other sources, delivered them. The central storyline was Univision's success and market dominance, and Telemundo's failed effort to reverse its downward slide through programming shifts following the 1997 ownership change.

Steady increases in viewership during the second half of the 1990s drove Univision's success. A report published in *Money* magazine in 1997 maintained that while CBS and ABC each lost two million viewers over the previous five years, Univision gained 500,000 (Espinoza, 1997). At the same time, while the WB and UPN networks battled to claim status as the country's fifth network, Univision snatched the honor by scoring higher ratings (Goldblatt, 1997). Thus Jerrold Perenchio achieved one of his goals in acquiring Univision: the network was considered as a direct competitor to English-language networks, not isolated in a separate category (Russel, 2000). This accomplishment was underscored when the Univision affiliate WLTV became the top Miami station in the May 1998 sweeps, surpassing the ABC affiliate (WPLG) with a 5.0 household rating and 12 share (Bowser, 1998). The 1998 television season was altogether strong for Univision, which experienced 25% audience growth reaching 4 million daily viewers, its largest audience on record (Baxter, 1999c). The audience for the two major networks was split approximately 80–20 in favor of Univision in 1998 (McClelland, 1998).

Univision's viewership gains translated into increased stock values and revenues even as the network paid down its considerable debt after assuming control from Hallmark in 1993. Univision stock originally offered at $21 per share in September 1996 reached $57.50 per share by November 1997, and during one five-week period in the spring of 1999 the stock's value increased 40% (Mendoza, 1998; Baxter, 1999c). It should come as little surprise that such escalating values motivated a number of Univision's top executives to exercise their stock options in 1998. One of those executives was Henry Cisneros, the former mayor of San Antonio and Housing and Urban Development Secretary who became Univision chief operating officer in January 1997 and gained $1.24 million by selling stock in 1998, and another $7.46 million in 2000 (Salary plus, 2000). Under Perenchio's leadership, Univision revenues increased from $200 million in 1992, the year before he assumed control of the network, to $693 million in 1999 (Controversy colors, 2000).

Univision's revenue flow and market dominance didn't mean it enjoyed an impeccable public image, however. *Hispanic Business* reported that during the 1995–96 election cycle Jerrold Perenchio had been the largest donor, individual or group, to California Republican governor Pete Wilson's reelection campaign, giving $276,000 (Mendoza, 1997). At issue was Wilson's 1994 support of Proposition 187, which sought to create a state-run screening system that would prevent undocumented immigrants from using health care, public education and other services. Some Hispanics concurred with concerns articulated by Alex Nogales of the National Hispanic Media Coalition: "why should the strength of the Hispanic market make Mr. Perenchio so rich that he can turn around and give it to those who are against Hispanics?" (cited in Mendoza, 1997). Of course other voices supported Perenchio and his commitment to the Hispanic community, pointing out that he had hired Henry Cisneros, a Democrat, to run Univision.

Another issue concerned Univision's apparent anticompetitive behavior. A 1999 report claimed that two celebrities and central figures in the Latin Boom, Shakira and Enrique Iglesias, cancelled scheduled visits on Telemundo's talk show *El Show de Jaime Bayly* due to retaliatory threats from Univision (Baxter, 1999b). If accurate, the situation demonstrated that Univision was a belligerent competitor, but also suggested the influence of Televisa, which has a nasty reputation for "blacklisting" performers who appear on rival networks. Controversy also surrounded Univision's refusal of advertising from dot-com companies in late 1999. As it prepared to launch its own portal, and perhaps an Internet service provider as well, the company was reluctant to support potential competitors in the Internet sector.[24]

Despite the high hopes when Sony and Liberty Media joined Telemundo in 1997, the network continued to lose ground through the remainder of the decade. The network's effort to program for a U.S. Hispanic audience failed, with significant audience losses in key markets such as Los Angeles, New York and Miami when Univision stations in those same markets prospered (Freeman, 1998). Telemundo's new owners' strategic decision to re-version English-language formats into Spanish-language shows may have been financially expedient, but audience interest didn't follow—many viewers in the desirable younger demographic watched Univision's traditional imported fare during prime time (Paxman, 1998). Consequently, Telemundo's portion of the audience fell from 43% in 1992 to only 8% in 1999 (Baxter 1999c). Spending on Spanish-language television reached nearly $1.1 billion in 1999, with 63% of it captured by Univision (Russel, 2000).

Conclusion

In a 1993 editorial, Joaquin Blaya, Telemundo's president and CEO, identified three important trends in television: the rapid expansion of broadcast entities and viewer options, the advent of niche narrowcasting, and the advancement and lower cost of new research and tracking technologies (Blaya, 1993). This chapter has shown that these developments, along with others, made U.S. Spanish-language television a more complex and vibrant industry by the end of the 1990s, one on the verge of explosive growth. New pay television channels catered to the interests of specific Hispanic audience niches that the networks also began targeting more strategically in their programming efforts. The Nielsen Hispanic Television Index provided a more stable currency for advertising sales, an important step in placing the Spanish-language sector on firmer competitive footing with the English-language mainstream. The ratings were but one component of the sector's movement toward mainstream television business practices; others included more proactive public relations to communicate with industry professionals, policymakers and potential investors, and using the legal system for strategic management.

Univision's acquisition by an ownership group that included two major Latin American television producers renewed concerns about international influence and high levels of imported programming at the network. When it canceled production on some domestic shows, however, Univision was able to justify its decisions with Nielsen ratings data. Meanwhile, Telemundo sought to differentiate itself through U.S.-produced shows, but failed to make them sufficiently appealing to domestic audiences. Telemundo's financial strains throughout the decade hindered its ability to pursue its worthy production ambitions, yet it is important to note that even when under financial strain both networks recognized the competitive importance of U.S. production. The presence of competition is the most significant difference between the pre-1986 and post-1992 circumstances of U.S. Spanish-language television. However appealing heavy program importation might look economically, it is difficult to sustain when a competing network produces programs that appeal to sufficient numbers of viewers.

The imported versus domestic programming issue has important cultural dimensions as a (non-niche) network's content offering must appeal to a variety of interests and connect with multiple cultures, whether U.S. Hispanic or otherwise. Along these same lines, this chapter has also underscored a sensitive relationship between cultural identity and economic interests. The Montaner incident demonstrated that advocacy groups can bring economic pressure to bear on television networks that offend the populations they represent, but also that punitive actions such as boycotts are difficult to sustain beyond the short term. A related process unfolded with the United States Hispanic Chamber of Commerce, which originally supported a petition to block transfer of the Univision station licenses to the Perencio-Televisa-Venevisión partnership in order to protect U.S. business interests, but later flipped positions, likely under pressure from its members—both corporate and individual—who were in some way associated with Univision. Such conflicts between economic interests and advancing an ethnic group's influence are a recurring feature of advocacy and collective cultural identity that merits greater scholarly attention.

Notes

1. The "other" category encompasses the following subcategories, the numbers in parentheses are in thousands: Other Hispanic (1,403), Salvadoran (565), Dominican (520), Spanish (519), Colombian (379), Guatemalan (269), Nicaraguan (203), Ecuadorian (191), Other South American (190), Peruvian (175), Other Central American (156), Honduran (131) and Argentine (101).
2. As a decade earlier, in early 1990 the networks frequently aired public service announcements and special presentations urging Hispanics to take part in the census. A high count of Spanish-speaking residents in markets they served would fortify the networks' position when negotiating advertising rates.
3. Data gathered by the U.S. Bureau of the Census in 1990 illustrates the low socioeconomic level of Puerto Rican Americans in comparison with the other major Latino subgroups.

Socioeconomic Indicator	Puerto Rican Origin	Mexican Origin	Cuban Origin
Median Family Income (in U.S.$)	19,933	22,245	31,262
% of Families Living Below Poverty Level	30.4	19.6	12.5
% of Families Headed by a Single Female	38.9	25.7	18.9

Adapted from: North American Congress on Latin America. (1992, September). Roots of empowerment: Latino politics and cultures in the United States. *NACLA Report on the Americas, 16* (2), table 3, p. 24.

4. The American Hispanic Owned Radio Association, representing about 110 stations, opposed relaxing of foreign ownership rules that Azcárraga was pushing (Fisher, 1992a). During a visit with President George H.W. Bush in Monterrey, and through a legal team, Azcárraga was pressuring the U.S. government to reciprocate Mexico's relaxing foreign ownership limits as part of NAFTA reforms.

5. This incident prompted First Chicago to divest of its holdings in the network.
6. As described by Foisie (1992),

   Venevision is the largest TV network in Venezuela, but unlike Televisa, is part of a diversified business conglomerate. Founded in 1929 as a materials transport firm by Diego Cisneros Bermudez, Venevision's parent company, Organización Diego Cisneros (ODC) is now involved in department stores, bottling, events promotion, banking, mining, petrochemicals and records, and holds the franchises for distribution of products by companies including Gerber and Frito-Lay. In the mid-1980's, ODC also bought Spalding sports goods and Evenflo baby products. Already a major player in Hispanic programming, Venevision redoubled its foreign syndication and production efforts under the name of Venevision Internacional in 1991.

7. Recall from Chapter Four that in 1986 Emilio Azcárraga was forced to divest of Televisa's holdings in Univision stations for violating the foreign ownership and control law.
8. Félix Gutiérrez, a U.S. Spanish-language media expert since the 1970s, summarized the petitioners' concerns:

   Clearly the way [the network] operated before 1987 was to produce in Mexico and then recycle the product up here, which made our people second-class audiences twice: first, with the Anglo media and then with our own media as well. [Univision] has done some good things with domestic production and beefing up the news. That clearly has to be threatened now by the Azcarraga [sic] reconnection. Any time you can produce for pesos and sell for dollars, you have a real moneymaking machine (quoted in Claudia Puig, 1992).

9. This claim didn't square well with reports that Perenchio was investing at least $50 million of his own money in the enterprise, and that *Forbes* magazine had estimated his net worth at $655 million (Mendoza, 1992).
10. The order also granted the new owners' request for a waiver of the advertising spot rule (Section 73.658[i] of the commission's rules (see Chapter Three).
11. Apparently Univision's commitment was limited as in 2007, when the network sold, it was required to pay a $24 million fine for violating children's programming regulations, the largest penalty that had been assessed by the FCC up to that time (see Chapter Nine).
12. The cancellations were the news magazines *Portada* and *Al Mediodia*, and the variety show *Charytín Internacional*. Two of the three shows were replaced by Mexican programs (Puig, 1993).
13. Laura Marella, vice president and media director of Casanova Pedrill Inc., an ad agency specializing in the Hispanic market, pointed out the lack of research to support Blaya's claim: "I don't think there's been any research done on the appeal of domestic versus foreign-produced programming ... I don't think there's a difference in where it's produced. It has more to do with the content of the programming itself" (Leventhal, 1993).
14. For comparative purposes, expenditure on other Hispanic media were as follows: national radio $46.7 million, local radio $175.9 million, print $109.3 million, outdoor $15.0 million, promotion $51.1 million and transit $4.6 million (Acosta & Velasquez, 1992).

15. Strategy Research Co. and Arbitron Ratings Co. had provided ratings throughout the 1980s, but their research methods and findings diverged (the former providing high counts and the latter low). The discrepancy caused conflicts during advertising rate negotiations between advertisers and network representatives (Poppe, 1988).
16. Other, minor contributors to the service were "Leo Burnett, Busch Media Group (a subsidiary of Anheuser-Busch), Spanish Communications (a subsidiary of Western International Media), and The Clorox Company" (Nielsen releases, 1993).
17. ABC scored highest with ten of the top twenty shows in Hispanic households. FOX ranked second with eight shows, followed by NBC with two and CBS with none (McClellan, 1995).
18. Only New York, Chicago and San Antonio would be wired with Peoplemeters so they could provide overnight ratings—the other markets would rely solely on diaries and data in quarterly reports (Foisie, 1994).
19. The company's name had been changed from Apollo Advisors in the interim.
20. Tortorici's prior production credits included successful shows such as *Murphy Brown, Picket Fences, Northern Exposure, Touched by an Angel* and *Chicago Hope* (Stroud, 1998).
21. The *Los Angeles Times* characterized the challenges facing Telemundo's new management team like this: "what Tortorici inherited at Telemundo was a financially troubled company with a history of internal problems, little original programming and even less direction. Telemundo has seen its audience share fall by half in five years, and despite three management changes, one reorganization and a bankruptcy filing, it was still bleeding red ink" (Baxter, 1998).
22. It merits mentioning that *Los Beltran* innovated on two fronts that would become increasingly important for Spanish-language television: dialog on the program was in English as well as Spanish, and the program, which focused on a contemporary Cuban-American family, included two gay characters. Notwithstanding these innovations, the critically acclaimed show was cancelled after two seasons because it cost too much (Calvo, 2001).
23. The expansion of pay television networks like these into Latin America is discussed in Chapter Seven.
24. Some market participants, like advertising executive Carl Kravetz, observed a double standard at work: "if Microsoft was doing it, they would be in front of a judge right now" (cited in Debate over dot-com ban, 2000).

References

Acosta, Sarah, & Velasquez, Rene. (1992, December). The Hispanic market's leading indicators. *Hispanic Business*, 30–34.

Andrews, Edmund L. (1992, October 1). F.C.C. clears Hallmark sale of Univision TV network. *New York Times*, C8.

Bailey, Jeff. (1990, February 6). Hallmark offers to buy junk bonds of Univision, seeks lender concessions. *Wall Street Journal*, A4.

Baxter, Kevin. (1998, December 20). As Telemundo turns. *Los Angeles Times*, 8.

Baxter, Kevin. (1999a, May 18). Ailing Telemundo seeks cure by adopting proven format. *Los Angeles Times*. Retrieved from http://articles.latimes.com/1999/may/18/entertainment/ca-38253.

Baxter, Kevin. (1999b, May 12). Telemundo claims rival network pressured 2 singers. *Los Angeles Times*, 2.

Baxter, Kevin. (1999c, April 13). Univision means success in any language. *Los Angeles Times*, 1.
BBC will be junior partner in Latin news channel. (1993, June 10). *Satellite TV Finance*.
Blaya, Joaquin. (1993, June 7). Don't miss out on Hispanic market. *Electronic Media*, 20.
Bowser, Andrew. (1998, November 9). Univision rules with telenovelas. *Broadcasting & Cable*, 34–35.
Brennan, Steve. (1992a, June 19). Hispanics urge FCC to prevent Univision sale. *Hollywood Reporter*. Retrieved from Baseline II database.
Brennan, Steve. (1992b, October 1). FCC approves Univision sale. *Hollywood Reporter*. Retrieved from Baseline II database.
Brennan, Steve. (1992c, June 30). Hispanic TV's growth to boom, report predicts. *Hollywood Reporter*. Retrieved from Baseline II database.
Brischetto, Robert. (1993, October). Making a milestone. *Hispanic Business*, 6–10.
Burgi, Michael. (1993, August 2). Telemundo to operate under Chapter 11. *Media Week*, 3(31), 4.
Calvo, Dana. (2001, May 10). Citing cost, Telemundo axes 'Los Beltran.' *Los Angeles Times*. Retrieved from http://articles.latimes.com/2001/may/10/entertainment/ca-61431.
Cerone, Daniel. (1993, April 3). KMEX-TV's news director resigns. *Los Angeles Times*, B8.
Cerone, Daniel. (1994, June 24). KMEX finds discrepancy in World Cup TV ratings. *Los Angeles Times*. Retrieved from http://articles.latimes.com/1994–06–24/entertainment/ca-8140_1_world-cup.
Chagollan, Steve. (1993, May 24). Prime Ticket to launch Spanish-language service. *Electronic Media*, 16.
Cole, Benjamin Mark. (1993, April, 5). Spanish language broadcaster sets $140 million issue. *Los Angeles Business Journal*, 15(14), 30.
Controversy colors network success. (2000, May). *Hispanic Business*, 30.
Crook, David, & Harris, Kathryn. (1981, December 13). Jerry Perenchio: Hollywood's consummate deal maker. *Los Angeles Times*, I1, I3, I15.
Debate over dot-com ban. (2000, May). *Hispanic Business*, 28.
Douglas, Nick. (1997, December). Strong economy buoys purchasing power. *Hispanic Business*, 58.
Dow, Gary. (1993, December). Purchasing power keeps growing. *Hispanic Business*, 46–47.
Esparza, Elia. (1998, February). The Telemundo takeover: Can a corporate coup save the embattled network? *Hispanic*. Retrieved from http://www.hisp.com/janfeb98/telemundo.html.
Espinoza, Galina. (1997, December). Five U.S. stocks with Latin heat. *Money*, 26, 140–142.
ESPN committed to play the field. (1993, March 29). *Variety*, 70.
Fisher, Christy. (1991, January 28). Univision still catching flak for host comments. *Advertising Age*, 34.
Fisher, Christy. (1992a, February 3). Azcarraga looms as return player. *Advertising Age*, 25–27.
Fisher, Christy. (1992b, June 8). Turmoil in wake of Univision sale. *Advertising Age*, 4.
Fisher, Christy. (1992c, October 5). Telemundo president hopes to emulate Fox. *Advertising Age*, 30.

Fisher, Christy. (1994, August 8). Nielsen expands Hispanic TV ratings with Univision *Advertising Age*, 27.

Foisie, Geoffrey. (1992, October 26). Hispanic TV's top two networks still growing. *Broadcasting, 122*(44), 60.

Foisie, Geoffrey. (1994, August 8). Nielsen expands Hispanic TV's ratings. *Broadcasting & Cable*, 35.

Foreign programs work fine for us, rival says. (1993, January 18). *Variety*.

Fox, Elizabeth, & Waisbord, Silvio (Eds.). (2002). *Latin politics, global media*. Austin: University of Texas Press.

Freeman, Michael. (1998, December 7). American programs failing. *Mediaweek*, 14–16.

Goldblatt, Henry. (1997, August 18). Univision: The real fifth network. *Fortune, 136*, 42.

Group bids for rest of Telemundo (1997, November 20). *Los Angeles Times*. Retrieved from http://articles.latimes.com/1997/nov/20/business/fi-55737.

Guzmán, Betsy, & Diaz McConnell, Eileen. (2002). The Hispanic population: 1990–2000 growth and change. *Population Research and Policy Review, 21*, 109–128.

HBO Olé is learning to speak Portuguese. (1993, March 29). *Variety*, 48.

Herman, Edward S., & Chomsky, Noam. (2010). *Manufacturing consent: The political economy of the mass media*. New York: Random House.

History of Univision Communications, Inc. (n.d.). Funding Universe. Retrieved from http://www.fundinguniverse.com/company-histories/univision-communications-inc-history/.

Involuntary bankruptcy sought for Telemundo. (1993, June 14). *Broadcasting & Cable*, 64.

Jessell, Harry A. (1991, December 2). Univisa wants back in TV station ownership. *Broadcasting, 121*(23), 52.

Klein, Richard. (1993, March 5). Hispanics flock to Spanish TV. *Daily Variety*, 40.

Lambert, Wade. (1992, July 30). Univision is told president can take job at chief rival. *Wall Street Journal*, 6A.

Leventhal, Larry. (1993, January 18). New focus on U.S. shows. *Variety*.

Liberty Media Corp. (1997, November 24). Apollo Management, Bastion Capital Fund, Sony Pictures Entertainment and Liberty Media make successful bid for Telemundo Group, Inc [Press release]. Retrieved from http://biz.yahoo.com/prnews/971124/ny_bastion_1.html.

Lopes, Humberto. (1992, July). Musical chairs at TV networks. *Hispanic Business*, 8–10.

Lopes, Humberto. (1993, February). Bad vibes but good business? *Hispanic Business*, 30–34.

McChesney, Robert. W. (2008). *The political economy of media: Enduring issues, emerging dilemmas*. New York: Monthly Review Press.

McClellan, Steve. (1995, January 9). Hispanic favorites differ from U.S. households. *Broadcasting & Cable*, 49.

McClellan, Steve. (1997, August 4). Majors line up for Telemundo. *Broadcasting & Cable*, 6.

McClellan, Steve. (1998, November 9). Telemundo: Time for Plan B. *Broadcasting & Cable*, 33.

Mendoza, Rick. (1992, May). Univision: Still for U.S. Hispanics? *Hispanic Business*, 24–26.

Mendoza, Rick. (1993, December). The television wars, Part II. *Hispanic Business,* 52–54.

Mendoza, Rick. (1997, November). Univision CEO speaks—sort of. *Hispanic Business,* 12.

Mendoza, Rick. (1998, June). Unwelcome competition. *Hispanic Business,* 14.

Mirabella, Alan. (1992, October 19–25). Telemundo puts focus on programs' overhaul. *Crain's.* Retrieved from Baseline II database.

Moshavi, Sharon D. (1993, March 22). Fox shows rank high in Hispanic survey. *Broadcasting & Cable, 123*(12), 41.

National Hispanic Media Coalition (n.d.). History - 1992. Retrieved from http://www.nhmc.org/about-us/history/.

Navarro, Mireya. (1990, December 31). Comments on Puerto Ricans embroil Hispanic network. *New York Times,* 1, 10.

Nielsen releases first national Hispanic report. (1993, January 15). *PR Newswire.*

Nieves, Gladys. (1990, December 28). Goya Foods retira sus anuncios de Univision. *Nuevo Herald* (Miami), 1A, 4A.

Ozemhoya, Carol U. (1993a, April 9). Telemundo's fate rests with bondholders. *South Florida Business Journal, 13*(33), 1A.

Ozemhoya, Carol U. (1993b, January 8). Olé-TV network plans to start airing in April. *South Florida Business Journal, 13*(20), 7.

Palmeri, Christopher, & Levine, Joshua. (1991, December 23). No habla español. *Forbes,* 140–142.

Paxman, Andrew. (1998a, August 17). Tortorici, Galan top Telemundo exec team. *Variety,* 29.

Paxman, Andrew. (1998b, June 8). Tube community waits to see if Sony can save Telemundo. *Variety,* 14.

Poppe, David. (1988, December). More for less? *Hispanic Business,* 32–39.

Puig, Carlos. (1992, August 10). Piden al Departamento de Justicia que no autorice la venta de Univisión a Azcárraga. *Proceso, 823,* 20–25.

Puig, Claudia. (1992a, April 27). Univision sale raises concerns. *Los Angeles Times,* F1.

Puig, Claudia. (1992b, June 19). Latino group asks FCC to block sale of Univision. *Los Angeles Times,* D2.

Puig, Claudia. (1992c, May 27). Univision president bolts to rival Telemundo. *Los Angeles Times,* D2.

Puig, Claudia. (1992d, August, 14). Another Univision exec wooed away by Telemundo. *Los Angeles Times.* Retrieved from http://articles.latimes.com/1992-08-14/entertainment/ca-5333_1_univision-network.

Puig, Claudia. (1993, January 22). Univision scraps three U.S.-made shows. *Los Angeles Times,* F4.

Rojas, Viviana, & Piñón, Juan. (2014). Spanish, English or Spanglish? Media strategies and corporate struggles to reach the second and later generations of Latinos. *International Journal of Hispanic Media, 7.* Retrieved from http://www.internationalhispanicmedia.org.

Russel, Joel. (2000, May). A broadcaster without rival. *Hispanic Business,* 26–34.

Salary plus: Public documents reveal Univision's executive compensation. (2000, May). *Hispanic Business,* 32.

The secrets behind Univision's sale. (1993, February). *Hispanic Business,* 32, 34.

Sinclair, John. (1999). *Latin American television: A global view.* New York: Oxford University Press.

Stroud, Michael. (1998, August 17). Totorici heads remade Telemundo. *Broadcasting & Cable, 128*(34), 13.

Telemundo eyes mates. (1997, July 2). *Variety*. Retrieved from http://variety. com/1997/ tv/news/telemundo-eyes-mates-1116677548.

Television Digest. (1992, October 26). Notebook. *Television Digest*, 4.

Univision takes lead position in audience approval. (1993, March 18). *PR Newswire*.

Valdéz, M. Isabel. (2002). *Marketing to American Latinos: A guide to the in-culture approach*. Ithaca, NY: Paramount Market Publishing.

Walley, Wayne. (1992, October 26). Nielsen sets Hispanic TV ratings. *Electronic Media*, 3.

Woes mount at Telemundo. (1993, June 10). *USA Today*, 2B.

Zbar, Jeffrey D. (1997, December 1). Acquisition by Sony, TCI to be boon for Telemundo. *Advertising Age, 68*, 85.

7 Connections with Latin American Television Markets

This chapter pursues a theme running throughout the book: the relationship between the U.S. industry and Spanish-language television production, distribution and consumption in Latin America. During the 1980s, accelerated development of new communication technologies coincided with significant realignment of existing communication industries even as new industry sectors emerged. Media "convergence" became a buzzword for these technological and organizational shifts (Baldwin, 1996). At the same time, neoliberal economic reforms reduced governments' support of and regulatory influence over media-related industries while encouraging greater private sector participation in the creation and dissemination of cultural products (Lewis & Miller, 2003). Although the attention here is on the 1990s, an important period of growth and change, Latin American, especially Mexican, influence has persisted throughout the U.S. industry's past, as revealed in prior chapters. That influence extended into the first two decades of the 2000s and will continue into the foreseeable future.

The adhesive holding regional media markets together are cross-national cultural and linguistic ties. The decade examined here witnessed a renewed interest in how culture and language influence the international flow of television programs, a topic that emerged in the 1970s (Pool, 1977) and received only sporadic attention during the 1980s (e.g., Antola & Rogers, 1984). The close relationship between Mexico's television industry and the U.S. Spanish-language sector has already been established—the focus here is on developments that have bound television systems closer together at the regional level. Examples include the Cadena de las Américas programming exchange, free-trade agreements, accelerated pay television growth and direct-to-home broadcasting. Seeking to account for these developments in theoretical terms became a goal of academic research on *regional* markets for cultural products, like television, that operated between and amid the national and global levels (e.g. Straubhaar, 1991; Sinclair, 1999; Wilkinson 1995, 2003).

Technology played a key role by providing multiple language tracks for TV programs through features such as Second Audio Program (SAP) and multiple language tracks accompanying a single video signal in distribution systems. Direct-to-home broadcasting brought multichannel television into hundreds of thousands of additional affluent households. Increased standardization of business practices and services across the region—the multinational ratings company Ibope is an example—also facilitated the trade in television programs and advertising. Televisa's ECO project, an initiative to provide around-the-clock news and information to Spanish-language television viewers worldwide was another exemplar. In the U.S., ECO was a division of Univisa, an umbrella company that managed Televisa-owned enterprises in various media including television distribution (Protele), music recording and distribution (Fonovisa), videocassette duplication and sales (Videovisa) and print media. An example of the latter deserves our review for the light it sheds on transnational media endeavors in the early 1990s as media globalization was gaining momentum.

The National Sports Daily

After being forced to relinquish his holdings in the Spanish International television station group, Televisa's Emilio Azcárraga Milmo sought new opportunities to conduct business in dollars during a volatile time for the Mexican peso (Virshup, 1990). He decided to pursue his long-standing dream: to create a national, English-language sports daily in the United States such as had long existed in Latin America and Europe. Azcárraga hired two experienced players in publishing (and college classmates): Peter O. Price, previously publisher of *The New York Post*, and Frank Deford, who sought a change after 27 years at *Sports Illustrated* (Virshup, 1990). In a resumption of their collegiate roles and partnership at the *Daily Princetonian*, Price served as publisher and Deford as editor of *The National Sports Daily*. Azcárraga Milmo committed $125 million to the publication for a five-year period, and paid annual salaries as high as $250,000 to lure top sports writers to the project[1] (Serrill, 1990). Following a brief start-up period during which minimal market research was conducted, the newspaper published its first edition on January 31, 1990. The paper appeared daily—except Saturday—in New York, Los Angeles and Chicago, with ambitious plans to operate in at least a dozen more cities by the end of 1991 (Donaton, 1990; Virshup, 1990). Bud Shaw (2009), a writer for *The National*, described the paper as, "terrific reading and unquestioned fun, [it] was a mini-newspaper—complete with editorial page, gossip columnist, cartoonist, crossword puzzle, columnists, game coverage, humor (Norman Chad) and investigative reporting." More than two decades after its demise, the publication continued to receive accolades for its content and impact on subsequent sports journalism, if not its business plan and management (French & Kahn, 2011).

The National Sports Daily published its last issue on June 13, 1991, after a 17-month run. Despite positive early reports that major national advertisers had signed on before the first issue appeared (Donaton, 1990), *The National* attempted to build its base during a media recession and encountered distribution as well as cost-control problems (The National strikes, 1991; Shaw, 2009). The publication's circulation never reached much beyond 200,000 copies—of a projected 1,000,000 in the first year—due largely to distribution difficulties. Computer networks were not yet facilitating the simple, rapid exchange of files they would later in the 1990s, and the scores from night games played on the West Coast were often available only after delivery trucks in the East had begun their deliveries. Some subscribers received as few as two editions per week, resulting in canceled subscriptions, while other readers stopped dropping quarters into newspaper boxes after finding only out-of-date issues inside (Fernández & Paxman, 2000; Shaw, 2009). Another strike against *The National* was entering the sports news market during a period of intense competition not only among print publications, as local newspapers fought hard to maintain loyal readers, but also when increasing numbers of sports channels and pay-per-view options were available on pay television (The National strikes, 1991). Although most news reports at the time focused on these problems and the far-fetched whim of a mysterious Mexican billionaire, more recent assessments have recognized *The National's* substantial contribution to sports journalism in the U.S.:

> … what transpired in that year and a half launched careers and developed the voices and thoughts that would go on to frame the next generation of sports media. On the outside, *The National* seems long forgotten. But on the inside, there's no doubt at all that *The National Sports Daily* completely changed the game.
>
> (French & Kahn, 2011)

In a profile of Azcárraga Milmo published just before *The National* launched, the journalist Amy Virshup (1990, p. 87) concluded, "with his latest venture, Azcarraga [sic] seems to be blossoming into a full-fledged media tycoon, a Mexican Murdoch, no longer restricted by the language barrier." Although this venture into the U.S. English market failed, Azcárraga didn't abandon his roots or quench his thirst to expand Televisa's international footprint. Simultaneously with the launch of *The National*, he planned a television network to unite the principal countries of the Spanish-speaking world.

Cadena de las Américas

In anticipation of the quincentennial of Christopher Columbus's arrival in the Americas in 1492, the Organización de Televisiones Iberoamericanas (OTI), a trade organization for television enterprises in the Americas, Spain and Portugal, created a short-term program service featuring content from 19 participant nations.[2] Given that OTI's president at the time was Guillermo Cañedo White, a member of Emilio Azcárraga's brain trust at Televisa, it comes as little surprise that the Mexican network took a lead role in programming and managing the project called Cadena de las Américas

(The Americas Channel). The project, which aired April 20 through October 12, 1992 (Columbus Day in the U.S.), was expedited by decreasing costs of satellite transmission due to the emergence of private satellite companies like PanAmSat (discussed below) in the wake of telecommunications deregulation, as well as the efficiencies afforded by digitization, especially digital compression technology which considerably increased the signal carrying capacities of satellite transponders (Pelton, 2010).

The Cadena service transmitted four hours of programming daily, although not all participating networks broadcast all four hours. Each participating network was expected to contribute 20 to 35 hours of programming representing its home country's history, culture, contemporary status and connections with other societies in the Iberoamerican world. For example, Televisión Española (TVE), Spain's national public broadcaster, contributed content focused on the Universal Exposition (World Expo '92) in Seville and the Olympic Games in Barcelona during July and August 1992 (Salvador, 1992). TVE aired Cadena de las Américas programs during the morning on its national channel in Spain, "La 2," as well as via its Latin American service available on pay television systems throughout the region (Amado Mier, 1992). In Mexico, Televisa aired four hours of Cadena content at midday on Channel 4 and one hour in late night on Channel 2 (Toussaint, 1992). Televisa also produced a children's *telenovela* for Cadena named *Carrusel de las Américas*, which resembled its popular domestic program, *Carrusel de niños*. Compared to Mexico's domestic version focusing on class differences, the international one emphasized national differences among children attending the school where the show took place, *Escuela de las Américas* (not to be confused with the notorious military training program at Fort Benning, Georgia!). As visual affirmation of the program's—and entire project's—emphasis on Iboeroamerican unity, the opening sequence featured flags of various Spanish-speaking nations prominently displayed behind a turning carousel and the show's characters. Many of the televised classroom lessons focused on the quincentennial.

Although the U.S. was not among the official participant nations, viewers north of the Rio Grande were able to view Cadena de las Américas programs via the Galavisión network, which programmed four hours daily and was available over the air in select markets as well as on pay television (Vallescar, 1992). It is unfortunate that content about the history, cultural practices and contemporary status of U.S. Hispanics was not included in the Cadena project's effort to increase mutual understanding among its transnational audience. U.S.-produced Spanish-language television programs were being distributed throughout the Spanish-speaking world in the early 1990s, but the leading programs were highly commercialized, like *Sábado Gigante*, or carried significant shock value, like *El Show de Cristina*, which some international viewers considered an affront to traditional Iberoamerican values, as discussed in Chapter Five (Miller, 1993). As a result, U.S.-produced Spanish-language programs likely underscored persistent stereotypes of U.S. society among some viewers in other countries. This not to say that Cadena de las Américas programming was not commercial or racy in nature; much of it was, according to Toussaint (1992). U.S. viewers of Cadena would have been familiar with its content due to close similarities with imported programs that domestic channels, especially Univision, were airing; some might also have felt a discomforting recognition that no experiences, environments or aspirations of U.S. Hispanics were being depicted.

Profile of Televisa as NAFTA and Domestic Competition Arrive

Before moving on to discuss other significant developments in regional television, let us consider Televisa's status in 1993 as a new Mexican television network emerged, offering the first substantial competition in 20 years, and as the North American Free Trade Agreement was about to be implemented. Dozens of corporate profiles regarding Televisa were published in the business press and industry trade journals between 1991 and 1993 due to the company's improved performance, increased investor interest in Mexico on the eve of NAFTA,[3] the company's listing on the Mexico City and then the New York stock exchanges, and its ambitious expansion efforts. The company underwent significant reorganization following the 1990 departures of major partners Rómulo O'Farrill Jr., who had been with the company since the 1950s, and Miguel Alemán Velasco, who entered government service. (Both were reportedly upset that losses from *The National Sports Daily* came out of Televisa coffers, not Emilio Azcárraga's own pocket.) Azcárraga Milmo paid an estimated $400 million to $500 million in cash and other assets to buy out his partners, leaving his sister and him with a combined 73% control of the company (Besas, 1990).

Mexico remained the home port of Televisa's business as it sought to expand its reach in the early 1990s, and television remained the anchor. The company commanded a 97% share of Mexican television via three national networks[4] and produced 80% of its own content (Paxman, 1992). Televisa enjoyed strong holdings in other media as well, including ten radio stations, the country's largest cable system, record labels, 110 magazine titles, an outdoor advertising firm, two football (soccer) teams, the Azteca stadium in Mexico City and a major museum—the Cultural Center of Contemporary Art (Fraser, 1992; Silverstein, 1992). In 1992, sales grew by 33.5% over the prior year to $1.1 billion, with this distribution among divisions of the company: broadcast TV 61%, cable TV 6%, music 5%, radio 4% and other businesses 24% (Televisa on investment, 1993). Cable television was poised to capture an increasing percentage of sales as Televisa strove to double the number of Mexico City households reached by its Cablevision system from 150,000 in 1991 to 300,000 in 1996 (Top Latin American, 1993).

Prior chapters have established that Televisa was adept at producing and distributing content; *Euromoney* magazine described it as "a vertically integrated company *par excellence*" (Televisa a dominant, 1993). In addition to ample studios and post-production facilities featuring state-of-the-art technology, the company developed proprietary acting academies and scriptwriting workshops. Favorable contracts with telecommunications providers kept distribution costs low. In order to guarantee long-term returns on its investments in television talent, Televisa invoked the carrot of access to other media platforms within the company, such as recording contracts, but also the stick of threatened blacklisting. *Business Mexico* magazine estimated that 600 artists and producers worked under exclusivity contracts with Televisa in 1994 (Russell, 1994). A similar dynamic was at play in Televisa's relations with the Mexican government, although power was less lopsided at such lofty domains. In return for favorable news coverage and other forms of support, the dominant PRI party allowed Emilio Azcárraga "an unfettered monopoly on popular culture—a concentration of power unparalleled by any media baron anywhere" (Silverstein, 1992).

Although Televisa sustained net losses from 1988 through 1990 and absorbed *The National*'s costs, Emilio Azcárraga Milmo was Mexico's richest man, worth $2.8 billion (Paxman, 1992; Fraser, 1992). Some of his estimated net worth derived from Televisa becoming a publicly traded company when it listed on the Mexico City stock exchange in December 1991, raising about $845 million (Television in Mexico, 1993). *Forbes* reported the company's valuation at $3.9 billion based on the sale of shares, a figure that was 40 times earnings and 5 times revenues (Millman, 1992). In preparation for listing on the New York Stock Exchange, Televisa split its shares three for one in fall 1993, increasing the number of shares from 309 million to 927 million (DePalma, 1993; Watling, 1993). The company officially joined the New York Stock Exchange, and several others worldwide, on December 14, 1993, offering 10 million shares at $64 each (Craig, 1994). A significant corporate shift imposed by the public listings was that the notoriously secretive company had to begin reporting its business activities to shareholders. Such disclosure is essential to attracting investors, of course, and has facilitated the tasks of market analysts and academic researchers alike.[5]

Televisa's 1991 annual report identified three areas of expansion for the following year: increase the volume and intensity of its operations in Mexico, take advantage of improved economic conditions in Mexico to bring new products to Mexican consumers, and expand the company internationally (Martínez Staines, 1992). These goals acquired a distinct public relations spin when articulated in the press statements of Fernando Diez Barroso, the vice chairman of Televisa's board: "[our] vision is to expand the global reach of our products through a distribution system using the entire range of media and technology" (Daniels, 1993); "it is one-stop shopping, we try to walk away with as much of the pie as possible for Televisa" (Top Latin American, 1993); and "we may or may not own the wires—but we will be there—it will be ours to a great extent in the Spanish-speaking world" (Televisa a dominant, 1993).

Thus, the monies acquired from stock sales were not only used to pay off debts, but also funded an ambitious expansion strategy within Mexico and the region. Despite its misadventure in the U.S. publishing market with *The National*, Televisa invested heavily in Spanish-language publishing. In 1992 it bought a 75% stake in the world's largest Spanish-language newspaper, *Ovaciones*, for $63 million, and paid $130 million for the American Publishing Group, the world's largest Spanish-language publisher with more than 80 titles[6] and 120 million copies distributed annually (Televisa on investment, 1993; Grupo Televisa acquires, 1992). These acquisitions, which supplemented existing holdings, moved publishing to second place, at $231 million, behind television ($771 million) for 1994 sales (Malkin, 1995).

Televisa produced 42,000 hours of television in 1992 and sold programming to 63 countries, accounting for about 40% of all Spanish-language television aired in Spanish Latin America and the U.S. (Russell, 1994; Fraser, 1992). So as to have a hand in the distribution of that content, in 1993 the company paid $200 million for a 50% stake in PanAmSat (discussed below). Of course Televisa was a partner in the group that purchased the Univision companies from Hallmark Cards in 1992, holding 25% of the network and 12.5% of the station group. To the south, Televisa sought partial ownership of television stations in Argentina, Chile and Peru during a period when television was deregulating and commercializing in those countries. Such investments in Latin American broadcasting systems constituted a central element of Televisa's strategy to "go global with Latin America as an anchor" (Reyes, 1994). Not surprisingly, Spain was a prized target for broadcast stations as well as pay television, but competitors and regulators alike were wary of a "reconquista" by a shrewd entrepreneur who the Spanish press had labeled the Rupert Murdoch of Mexico.

Televisa was consolidating its position in the regional television market as an onslaught of free trade- and globalization-inspired investments hit Latin America. Although the Mexican peso devaluation of 1994–95 and the prospect of direct-to-home broadcasting caused Azcárraga to scale back on his regional expansion plans, including divesting of station investments in Peru and Chile (Sinclair, 1999), he had proven his ability to adjust to market conditions that changed rapidly under the influences of globalization and technological transformation.

Emilio Azcárraga Milmo died in 1997 amid uncertainty about how Televisa would navigate Mexico's roiling political currents. His death initiated an internal struggle for control of the company that was worthy of its own *telenovela* series (Friedland & Millman, 1998; Fernández & Paxman, 2000). His son, Emilio Azcárraga Jean, who had joined the board of directors in 1991 after the ownership restructuring, was 29 years old when his father died; he had developed more experience in television production and marketing than management. Between 1997 and 2000, Azcárraga Jean moved to consolidate his control of the firm, separate himself from his father's brain trust while building his own, and chart a new course for a conglomerate

whose influence had waned for reasons discussed below. The tenacious-
ness and strategic acumen that Azcárraga Jean exhibited in consolidating
his control of Televisa would later be applied in navigating the sometimes
treacherous terrain of digital media and, as is evident in the final chapter, in
his dealings with Univision in U.S. boardrooms and courtrooms.

The North American Free Trade Agreement

The successful export-led growth strategies of four "Asian Tiger"[7] nations
caught the attention of Latin American governments, some of which were in
transition from military to democratic rule in the late 1980s and early 1990s.
Trade protectionism had largely failed as an economic paradigm in the region,
stimulating efforts toward trade policy reform. A more outward-oriented
economic approach encouraged not only trade liberalization, but also privatization of state-owned enterprises, deregulation of domestic industries, and
reductions in state spending on social welfare programs (NACLA, 1993).
Two key goals of these measures, and other efforts at controlling inflation
and balancing budgets, were repatriating capital invested abroad and attracting foreign investment. The early 1990s witnessed a considerable increase in
direct foreign investment in Latin America. Between 1990 and 1992 nearly
$100 billion was invested in the region, up from $24 billion during the previous three-year period. Furthermore, in 1991 and 1992 Latin America raised
approximately $12 billion annually in stock and bond offerings in new or
revitalized equity markets—this contrasts with less than $1 billion per year
throughout the 1980s (Nash, 1993; Welch, 1993). Easier access to capital
helped stimulate an upsurge in U.S.-Latin American trade volume from a
decade low of $56 billion in 1986 to $101 billion in 1990 (Freer, 1992).

The most visible manifestation of trade liberalization in the Western
Hemisphere was the negotiation of free trade agreements among some of its
nations. Whereas import substitution industrialization had mandated high
tariffs on imported goods to foster domestic industry development, neoliberal policies advocated minimal restrictions on trade in order to increase
efficiency and raise national income and employment. The economist Sydney Weintraub explained countries' basic motivations in entering a free
trade pact:

> The purpose of a free trade area is to increase the efficiency of pro-
> duction and to garner the welfare benefits from trade where efficien-
> cies vary between countries. Countries make the choice of a free trade
> area—that is free trade with only a few other countries—as opposed
> to worldwide free trade because they wish to retain the option of some
> protection against outsiders. (1990, pp. 120–121)

Although the North American Free Trade Agreement, widely known as
NAFTA, and Latin American trade blocs such as the Andean Pact and

Mercosur had only minor impacts on television, which already traded quite freely in the commercial sector (M. Vinay, personal communication, January 27, 1993; Galperin, 1999), their presence helped increase direct foreign investment in the region, including advertising buys, and in some cases, such as Mexico, stimulated political change that carried broad consequences (Lawson, 2002). As indicated below, pay television's ability to target consumers of means and influence was a driving force behind the increased interest from investors.

In 1988, as Canada and the United States finalized the first phase of the North American Free Trade Agreement, negotiations regarding the media sector became strained when Canada claimed an exception for cultural products, and the U.S. countered by reserving the right to limit Canadian imports in *any* trade sector if American media exports were constrained (Hoskins, Finn & McFadyen, 1996). This set an intriguing precedent for the ensuing tripartite negotiations, but Mexico, having an economy only 6% the size of the U.S.'s, was in no position to set terms. As prior chapters have shown, Televisa already had a firm foothold in the U.S. Spanish-language sector when the NAFTA negotiations began. Conversely, Telemundo would endeavor to establish a foothold in Mexico to bolster its domestic and international presence.

Despite these business connections, among others, mainstream media coverage of the United States' southern neighbor prior to NAFTA's ratification was seldom positive, as reports emphasized outsourcing U.S. jobs, environmental degradation and increased drug trafficking, along with corruption and political assassinations. Unfortunately, such negativity had a lengthy precedent in U.S. news media (Reilly, 2010; Chavez, 2001). Contrary to numerous dire prognostications, Mexico's economic reforms to accommodate NAFTA unleashed forces of political change that transformed the Mexican press and brought competition to the television sector, as we shall see below (Lawson, 2002; Wilkinson, 2006). A severe peso devaluation in 1994 and '95 tempered a flurry of interest in Mexican media by U.S., Canadian and European investors, but corporate efforts to tie the U.S. Spanish-language sector more closely with Mexico and other Spanish-language markets were already underway.

Mexico

The incorporation of Mexico into NAFTA beginning January 1, 1994, symbolically underscored the possibilities of reaching multiple Spanish-speaking markets with the same television content. To this end, program libraries were purchased and hastily translated, programming joint ventures emerged, and a variety of pay television services with a Latin American focus launched, most including the U.S. Spanish-language sector. The major population centers in Latin America had been wired with cable or were served by Multichannel Multipoint Distribution Systems (MMDS, "wireless cable") by the early 1990s, opening more channels for imported content and bypassing over-the-air broadcasting restrictions on foreign content in some countries. Taken together, these developments reflected the strong push toward globalization that characterized media businesses from the late 1980s through the 1990s. In addition to the NAFTA ties, Mexico's geographical proximity and history of U.S. investment and influence in the media sector rendered it the logical stepping-stone from North America to the broader Spanish-speaking world (Sinclair, 1986; Wilkinson, 1995). Given its wealth and expansion potential, the U.S. Spanish-language television market was a coveted piece of the strategic expansion puzzle.

Televisión Azteca Instigates Domestic Competition in Mexico

As part of the neoliberal economic reform that accompanied joining NAFTA, in 1993 the Mexican government privatized its anemic Imevisión television network, auctioning it off for $620 million and fostering the first sustained competition in Mexican broadcast television since the 1950s. The network, renamed Televisión Azteca, faced a formidable challenge as Televisa controlled about 85% of television viewing and 90% of ad revenues at the time. Other features of Mexican television suggested its profit potential in 1994:

- Mexico's annual advertising expenditure was $1.5 billion, of which $945.9 million (63%) was spent on television.
- 27% of Mexico's 92.3 million inhabitants resided in its three largest cities: Mexico City, Guadalajara and Monterrey.
- 15.3 million households owned at least one TV set and watched an average of 2.9 hours per day. (*BiB World Guide*, 1994, p. A-231).

Televisión Azteca's new owners, led by Ricardo Salinas Pliego, president of the Elektra and Salinas y Rocha department store chains, had bid $100 million more than their closest competitor, leading to speculation that they had overpaid and were perhaps involved in the illegal financial schemes of President Carlos Salinas de Gortari's notorious brother Raúl (Preston & Dillon, 2004). The amount of money at stake, the privatization's potential impact on close ties between Televisa and the ruling party—the Partido Revolucionario Institucional (PRI)—and the political opposition's strident demands to democratize Mexico's media, combined to render the sell-off, as *The New York Times* put it, "the most politically sensitive deal in President Carlos Salinas de Gortari's campaign to scale back the economic role of the state" (Golden, 1993).

Under Salinas Pliego's leadership, the new owners acted quickly to cut costs, improve efficiency and extend Televisión Azteca's reach, both over the air and via pay television systems.[8] All of these changes were essential to the upstart network's ability to compete against the mighty Televisa. Most apparent to TV viewers, of course, were shifts in content as the two networks transgressed the traditional limits on television decorum in their efforts to attract audiences. A brief overview of the notable political changes Mexico experienced in step with the NAFTA-inspired economic opening helps contextualize the content shifts, which U.S. viewers also witnessed.

Politics, News and Scandal

Several events during the 1980s stirred public opinion against the PRI, the political party that had maintained a firm grip on the Mexican government for over half a century. A destructive earthquake in 1985 revealed corruption in construction and building inspection as well as public services that were ill-prepared to respond to crises. Irregularities in a number of gubernatorial elections during the late 1980s reeked of vote rigging by the PRI, and strong suspicions of fraud surrounded the 1988 presidential election in which Carlos Salinas de Gortari defeated Cuauhtémoc Cárdenas (PRD) and Manuel Clouthier (PAN) (McCann & Domínguez, 1998). For many of the Mexicans who followed such matters, Televisa was implicated in these suspicions due to its progovernment reporting and the network's close association with the ruling party (Emilio Azcárraga Milmo once went so far as to declare himself a "foot soldier of the PRI") (Ortega Pizarro, 1993; Fernández & Paxman, 2000).[9]

Thus, Televisión Azteca had an opportunity to attract disgruntled and/or suspicious audiences by offering an alternative to Televisa's party line. There were limitations, however, as the network had been acquired from the government and the possibility of concession revocation loomed. Therefore, Ricardo Salinas Pliego dutifully professed his admiration for President Salinas de Gortari, yet sought to win over irritated Televisa viewers and distance his network from the PRI (Ortega Pizarro, 1993). The implication of several PRI leaders in the tragic murders of prominent PRI politicians Donaldo Colosio and Francisco Ruiz Massieu in 1994, together with a variety of political and economic scandals following the peso devaluation at year's end, facilitated Azteca's efforts (Preston & Dillon, 2004; Wilkinson, 2007). As the PRI continued unraveling up to the 2000 election, when a victory by the PAN's Vicente Fox ended the PRI's seven-decade hold on the presidency, Televisa was forced to renegotiate its political affiliations while it experienced a tumultuous internal power struggle as Emilio Azcárraga Jean confronted an effort to wrest the network from his control after his father died in 1997.

When political events involved the rival network, newsrooms became aggressive in reporting them, as two examples demonstrate. In mid-1996, Ricardo Salinas Pliego at first denied but then gradually admitted having received $29 million from the Swiss bank accounts of Raúl Salinas de Gortari (brother of the former president) who was convicted in 1999 of orchestrating the aforementioned murder of Francisco Ruiz Massieu, his brother-in-law, and of illicit enrichment. Salinas Pliego's admission led to immediate speculation that Raúl Salinas had influenced the selection of his group's bid, and unsuccessful investor groups claimed their bids were rejected because they had refused advances by the president's brother (Preston, 1999a). Shortly after Salinas Pliego admitted he'd received the money transfers, Raúl Salinas identified another close associate: Abraham Zabludovsky, a Televisa journalist and son of the iconic and controversial anchorman Jacobo (Sutter, 1996). Ignoring an exhortation by President Ernesto Zedillo to end (or at least stop airing) the feud, prime time accusations and innuendos continued until Emilio Azcárraga Milmo forbade Televisa employees from further comment. Although the content of this news battle was lamentable for Mexico and its international image, the intense competition causing it had been absent from television for 40 years.

Amid several high-profile shootings in Mexico City in 1999, the one garnering the most television coverage and public outrage was the June 7 assassination of the popular TV comedian Francisco "Paco" Stanley, as he left a restaurant. Mr. Stanley, after a long career as the jocular host of Televisa game shows, had recently bolted to Televisión Azteca. Both networks interrupted scheduled programs to offer incendiary coverage of the murder in a game of indignation one-upmanship. Jacobo Zabludovsky came out of retirement for Televisa, and Ricardo Salinas Pliego appeared on Azteca to condemn the shooting and especially Cuauhtémoc Cárdenas's (and the left-leaning PRD's) poor governance of crime-ridden Mexico City (Preston, 1999a; Angeles Jiménez, 1999). Journalistic objectivity was in short supply as coverage of Stanley's murder degenerated into a political feeding frenzy. Less than 24 hours after the shooting, police announced that Stanley had been a heavy cocaine user and possessed the drug when he died. Further investigation suggested that the assassins were professionals, perhaps employed by the drug lord Luis Amezcua Contreras. Two of Stanley's fellow performers[10] at Televisión Azteca were jailed for more than a year under suspicion of aiding the murder; after their release the case remained unsolved until 2011 when a cellmate's testimony implicated Luis Alberto Salazar Vega.

These brief examples underscore how closely intertwined political change, the television industry and scandal became at a key transitional point in Mexico's recent history. As a number of journalists pointed out, they were fit for a *telenovela*, our next topic.

Entertainment Content[11]

In a development that will ring familiar to readers who follow television history, the line between news and entertainment became especially murky when Televisión Azteca debuted the tabloid news program *Ciudad Desnuda* (Naked City) in August 1995. The motivation was to open another competitive front with Televisa while further differentiating the networks. Within a year, the show earned ratings in the high teens and helped Azteca's nightly news program, *Hechos*, obtain ratings comparable to those of Televisa's *24*

Horas.[12] *Ciudad Desnuda* tapped a persistent print genre, the *nota roja,* which since the 1920s offered Mexican readers lurid details of crimes and sexual perversions that were not reported in the legitimate press (Hallin, 2000; Piccato, 2014). The immediacy of these reality shows likely rang true for certain viewers, especially poor crime victims who traditional news media regularly ignored. However, the establishment pushed back. Despite their solid ratings, both *Ciudad Desnuda* and Televisa's counterpoint, *Fuera de la Ley* (Outside the Law), were cancelled in late 1997 after two influential sources pressured the networks: President Ernesto Zedillo urged a curtailing of television violence, and a group of business executives threatened an economic boycott (Hernández & McAnany, 2001).

The blurred distinction between tabloid shows and hard news had an analogue in the once strictly apolitical and fictional *telenovela* genre, which got a dose of reality and was met with a positive reception by many audiences (Hernández & McAnany, 2001). The *telenovela* had been the linchpin of Televisa's production and broadcasting monopoly in Mexico for nearly four decades, and the network became a leading exporter of the genre, including to the United States, of course. Televisión Azteca's first *telenovela, Nada Personal,* (Nothing Personal, 1996) beat Televisa's counterparts in the ratings, demonstrating that Mexican viewers were eager for deviations from the romantic formulas that Televisa *novelas* typically follow. *Nada Personal* centered on the murder of a fictitious federal attorney general and a subsequent investigation that revealed a web of violence, corruption, and drug trafficking (Robinson, 1997; Preston, 1999b). The story makes faintly disguised references to political scandals like the ones discussed above that began unraveling Mexican politics in 1994 and that vilified the PRI in many Mexicans' minds. Such a thinly veiled critique of Mexico's political elite would never have emerged from Televisa. Thus, *Nada Personal* emerged from a new environment of competitive television to demonstrate that Mexican audiences indeed *were* interested in non-formulaic, not-entirely-fictional *telenovelas.*

Televisión Azteca's second production, *Mirada de Mujer* (Woman's Gaze, 1997–98) confirmed audiences' interest in non-traditional *novelas.* The story explored in an open and respectful manner the emotional needs and anxieties of a 50-year-old wife whose husband left her for a younger woman. *Mirada de Mujer* tackled a range of sensitive subjects including abortion, AIDS, racial difference, rape and juvenile eating disorders, all without deviating from the central plot: the legitimate love between a socially prominent but betrayed middle-aged woman and a much younger divorced professional man. What Azteca's first two *telenovelas* shared in common was a novel perspective that the audience could engage with, and even enjoy clever dialogue and socially provocative themes.

Although traditional parameters on television content may have bent, they did not dissolve under the new Azteca scheme or Televisa's short-lived efforts to follow suit by experimenting with more realistic and less formulaic *telenovelas*. For example, the Azteca *novela Tentaciones* faltered under pressures from the Catholic Church and other conservative groups objecting to its plot of a priest falling in love with a beautiful woman who turns out to be his half-sister. *Mirada de Mujer* had caused discomfort, but representing the church in this way was too much for some audiences. Further research on how a domestically produced *telenovela* elicited similar negative reactions from conservative Mexican viewers as Univision's *El Show de Cristina* could yield informative findings on program genre, program origin and other elements (Miller, 1993; Dávila, 2001).

Televisión Azteca's Partnerships

Less than a year after launching, Televisión Azteca announced a partnership with NBC to provide programming, technology, and promotional assistance, including the right to incorporate NBC's logo, the colorfully plumed peacock, into Azteca publicity materials (Television Azteca forges, 1994). In return, NBC retained an option to acquire 10% of Azteca stock by the end of 1994, and to augment that investment to 20% over a three-year period (Malkin, 1994). NBC cited NAFTA as a key factor influencing its decision to enter the partnership. However, the relationship became strained following the 1994–95 peso devaluation, and in 1997 NBC announced that it would restrict its equity participation to 1%, citing breach of the two networks' licensing and management agreement (Mandel-Campbell, 2000). Azteca countered that NBC had failed to deliver on several contractual obligations and had inflated the commercial value of its logo used in Televisión Azteca programming, promotions and advertising. The International Chamber of Commerce in Paris arbitrated the dispute for three years before the companies settled privately. Televisión Azteca agreed to pay NBC $46 million, and NBC acquired a 1% stake in the Mexican network for $26 million (Druckerman, 2000). As a sign of the times, NBC was looking beyond television to a mobile phone network (Unefon) and Internet portal (*Todito.com*) that Televisión Azteca was developing. Through their settlement the entities appeared to recognize the value of affiliating, yet the rapprochement was short-lived, as the next chapter demonstrates (Donohue & Lafayette, 1999).

Because Televisa remained a major player on both sides of the border more than three decades after Emilio Azcárraga Vidaurreta and his associates established Spanish International Network, it was logical that Televisa's principal Mexican and U.S. competitors—Televisión Azteca and Telemundo—would join forces to face their common rival. As both Azteca and Telemundo needed programming, they entered a partnership in 1996 to co-produce four *telenovelas* annually. The plan was to share production costs, with each partner retaining international distribution rights to half of the co-produced *novelas*. As with the NBC deal, the Azteca-Telemundo partnership functioned less smoothly than intended. Particularly problematic was Telemundo's acquisition by Sony and Liberty Media in 1997 (Paxman, 1998a).

Early on, Televisión Azteca's leadership had expressed interest in obtaining U.S. stations and had bid to acquire Telemundo. That failing, they pushed, unsuccessfully, to reach a programming-for-equity deal that would provide a foothold north of the border. When Hispanic Television Network began building its station group in January 2000, Azteca attempted to buy in, but was stymied again. Thus, the network's participation in U.S. broadcasting was limited to signal spillover from Mexican border cities until September 2000, when it announced yet another partnership, this time with Pappas Telecasting, to launch the Azteca América network.

Beyond the competitive advantages that an Azteca-Telemundo partnership might provide each entity, a personal rivalry was at play. As investor groups had prepared bids to acquire Imevisión in 1993, Televisa's news programs reported on Telemundo's financial woes in the U.S. (Mejía Barquera, 1993). Telemundo's president at the time, Joaquin Blaya, had been Univision's CEO before Hallmark sold the network to the Perenchio-Televisa-Venevisión group in 1992. Bad blood between Blaya and Emilio Azcárraga Milmo over the circumstances of Blaya's departure may explain his aggressive courting of the Imevisión bidders. Blaya appeared to relish the possibility of Telemundo programming competing on his former boss's home turf, and he found an ally in Ricardo Salinas Pliego. Behind both companies' endeavors lurked the Televisa-Univision nexus, revived by Televisa's return as a co-owner of Univision in 1992.

Before closing this discussion of Televisión Azteca, it should be noted that prior to establishing a U.S. presence, the network expanded southward through partnerships or partial station ownership in El Salvador, Guatemala and Costa Rica. The network's synergistic[13] strategy was to expand southward alongside the Elektra retail stores owned by the Salinas Pliego family, stores that sell television sets—as well as computers and mobile phones—that consumers could use on Azteca-owned networks (Torres, 1997; Luna, 1998).

Cultural Implications of NAFTA for Mexico

Media represent only one sector of Mexican society impacted by NAFTA's implementation, yet it is an area wielding strong potential to affect a nation's cultural life. Critical communication scholars of the 1970s and '80s adapted economic dependency theory to account for perceived cultural domination of the developing nations by the West, especially the United States. Mexico was particularly ill-situated vis-à-vis cultural imperialism, given its geographic proximity and long history of U.S. intervention in its political and economic affairs. Although cultural imperialism as a *theory* had been largely discredited in scholarly circles by the time NAFTA was adopted—due to a conspiratorial slant and some questionable assumptions about collective cultural resistance and how audiences engage media content—the *concept* of cultural hegemony conveyed through the media was, and remains, a topic of concern (Tomlinson, 1991).[14] Not surprisingly, some critically oriented members of Mexico's intelligentsia raised questions about the cultural impacts of an agreement that would link it more closely with its northern neighbor.

Mexico's critical intelligentsia was certainly contemplating issues related to media, technology, identity and cultural sovereignty prior to NAFTA, but the agreement focused attention on a specific policy and helped organize their arguments (e.g. Guevara Niebla & García Canclini, 1992). One shared concern was Mexico's weak cultural policy concerning media, which allowed commercial interests to largely dictate their own terms and act with broad latitude.[15] Some observers feared that NAFTA would open the country's media to greater commercial exploitation, not only by Mexicans, but by outside investors as well. A related argument pointed out that Canadian and U.S. media received greater government support for production and international distribution, placing Mexico at a competitive disadvantage. María y Campos (1992) stressed that Mexico's market size, volume of content production and (relatively) advanced use of technologies offered competitive advantages in television over other Spanish-speaking countries, but he also noted limited opportunities for expansion to the U.S. as the Spanish-language sector represented less than 2% of the total market at the time.

The intelligentsia also questioned the neoliberal claim that free trade could "level the playing field" among the NAFTA signatory nations. Bonfil Batalla (1992, p. 177) asked, "what areas will be leveled, where will we go, and how will we get there? What does it mean to level the conditions of Mexican society with the other two in terms of lifestyle, aspirations for the future and culture?" Another anthropologist, García Canclini (1992), observed that cable television and video markets grew rapidly in the 1980s and '90s, thereby accelerating in-home cultural consumption to the detriment of film, live performance and other cultural activities requiring people to congregate in public. Other observers shared his concern about the long-term impacts of such developments on Mexicans' traditional collectivism and national identity.

The government representatives responsible for managing the cultural aspects of NAFTA brushed aside the critical intelligentsia's apprehensions, among other potential barriers, to usher the treaty through. In addressing Mexico's senate, Secretary of Industry and Commerce Jaime Serra Puche (1991) stated:

> [Our] strategy does not limit or erode sovereignty nor lead to the loss of cultural identity. … The exercise of sovereignty and the affirmation of cultural identity do not exist in hypothetical isolation. Both are realized in the daily cultural and economic exchanges among nations, groups, and individuals. (p. 659, my translation)

Over a three-month period, Serra Puche's office hosted civic forums to ascertain public views on NAFTA's potential impacts. The secretary characterized the forums as "inclusi[ve] of opinions, commentary and criticism from all political persuasions and social groups" (1991, p. 657). As one might suspect, the intelligentsia took a different view. De la Vega (1995) said the forums "lack[ed] openness and [featured] centralization of decisions within a small bureaucracy, even when public hearings are held where representatives of industrial and other distinct interest groups and experts participate" (p. 351). The celebrated writer and critic Carlos Monsiváis, who highlighted inconsistencies in Secretary Serra Puche's public statements, characterized the government's attitude toward the public as "depreciative and paternalistic" (1992, p. 206).

Indeed, the government's standard reply to questions regarding NAFTA's impact on Mexican culture was that it was irrelevant (María y Campos, 1992). In what became a commonly cited exchange, here is how Serra Puche responded when asked whether including cultural industries in the agreement would affect Mexico's national identity: "This has little relevance for Mexico. If you have time, you should see the [art] exhibit 'Mexico, Thirty Centuries of Splendor,'[16] and you will realize there is no cause for concern" (cited in García Canclini, 1996, p. 143). It was exactly such cultural patrimony that the critical intelligentsia and others were concerned to protect. The fact that Televisa was a principal organizer and sponsor of the exhibit offered little comfort for those concerned about commercial encroachment on public art (Schiller, 1991).

Thus, government representatives asserted Mexico's cultural and linguistic distinctiveness from Canada and the U.S. as a shield from northern cultural influences, and this became the standard position for Mexican government officials not wishing to discuss the cultural implications of the country's entry into NAFTA. María y Campos (1992) acknowledged that the Spanish language and Mexico's cultural idiosyncrasies offered some protection, but he stressed that as Mexicans' media consumption habits transformed under globalization, this barrier would become more permeable. This notion of cultural preservation or protection through language difference corresponds with the U.S. Hispanic market and audience being defined exclusively by the use of Spanish until the latter 1990s when bilingual media outlets surfaced, followed by more Hispanic-oriented English-language media in the 2010s.

Mercosur

As in NAFTA, the participant nations in the Mercosur (Mercado Común del Sur, Southern Common Market) also have language differences, dissimilar market sizes and largely exempted broadcasting and other cultural industries from the trade agreement (Galperin, 1999). However, the negotiations regarding the promotion and protection of culture were less strident than in the European Union and NAFTA (McAnany & Wilkinson, 1996).

The common market's origins lay in the Argentina-Brazil Integration and Economics Cooperation Program (PICE) signed between the economic rivals in 1985. Two neighboring countries with much smaller economies, Paraguay and Uruguay, joined Argentina and Brazil under the Treaty of Asunción in 1991. Chile did not join at the time, partly due to discussion of its joining NAFTA, but later became an associate member of Mercosur along with Bolivia, Colombia, Ecuador and Peru; Venezuela joined as a full member in 2012. The treaty's intent was to create a free-trade zone through the elimination of national tariffs in favor of a common tariff, coordination of macroeconomic and sector-specific policies, and harmonization of national regulatory legislation (Galperin, 1999). Such coordination and harmonization would be no minor undertaking in the television sector given the sizable differences among nations: in 1995 Argentina, Brazil and Uruguay averaged 220 televisions per 1,000 inhabitants, whereas had Paraguay only 93 sets per 1,000 (Getino, 2001). As regards audiovisual exports, Brazil earned about $40 million annually, Argentina $10 million, Chile $1–2 million and Paraguay and Uruguay only "negligible amounts" (Getino, 2001).

Although all of the Mercosur nations except Argentina exempted some of their cultural industries from the treaty,[17] the general attitude toward promotion and protection of culture generally aligned with that of Secretary Serra Puche in Mexico, discussed above: there was little concern about effects from outside influences. Cultural policy tended to focus on high culture, such as museums and art films, as well as indigenous arts expressive of the region's cultural diversity. García Canclini (2007) argues that major cultural industries like television, radio, commercial film and the press wield greater potential influence on the public than high art, but commanded little attention in academic research, or diplomatic and cultural policy circles. Thus the limited resources that Mercosur cultural offices have dedicated to audiovisual media have gone to film, ignoring television (Crusafon, 2009). Although certainly an important medium worthy of support and protection, García Canclini points out that for every 20 television programs imported to Latin America (mostly from the U.S.), only one was exported out of the region, and the majority originated from the most internationalized production centers: Argentina, Brazil and Mexico (2007).

A common refrain among Latin American scholars who have studied Mercosur's cultural dimensions is the need to include the commercial sector in policy discussions. Galperin (1999) considers this a weak point of integration efforts because state trade representatives who negotiate and implement agreements play a diminishing role in the region's media industries due to neoliberal reforms. Dumont (2010) argues that failure to engage the private media has diminished state efforts to promote and regularize the commercialization of culture beyond national borders, both within the Mercosur area and more broadly. Getino (2001) emphasizes the detrimental impact on cultural diversity of media ownership concentration and transnationalization, forces which constantly threaten small- and medium-sized commercial media. A possible explanation for this commercial blindspot is offered by Crusafon (2009), who argues that Mercosur policy regarding cultural industries has developed under stronger influence from the European Union than from NAFTA.

If U.S. Spanish-language media received limited attention in Mexico's discussions about NAFTA, the topic did not register at all in the Mercosur deliberations. Certainly differences in media industry history and geographic proximity are at play, but the U.S. market's wealth and growth potential were well publicized in the business press and industry trade journals, and at industry trade shows. Furthermore, in the 1990s satellite systems such as PanAmSat had lowered the cost of program distribution, opening new competitive spaces to smaller producers in the region. Although Univision's partial ownership by Mexican and Venezuelan partners and long-term programming agreement reduced sales opportunities at that network, Telemundo sought international content, as did a growing number of pay television networks targeting U.S. Hispanics.

PanAmSat

The success of free trade agreements like NAFTA and Mercosur depended on the rapid flow of information between nations, and the television industry required reliable, cost-effective distribution channels for its globalization push in the 1980s and 1990s. Geosynchronous communication satellites were key purveyors of such services. During the 1970s satellite services available to Latin American governments, businesses and consumers were the exclusive domain of Intelsat, at that time an international consortium of more than 120 government members (Hudson, 1990). In subsequent decades, nations joined forces or worked individually to develop their own satellite programs. Brazil and Argentina developed national systems named Brasilsat and Nahuel, respectively. The Simon Bolívar satellite started as a joint project among the governments of Colombia, Ecuador and Peru, evolved into a partnership with private telecommunication companies, and finally launched in 2008 as a Venezuelan-Chinese joint venture named Venesat-1. In another example of neoliberal influence, the Mexican government partnered with Televisa to help finance the nation's Solidaridad satellites, launched in 1994–95 which complemented and then replaced the existing Morelos satellite program (1985).

The remainder of this section examines the regional significance of PanAmSat (PAS) during a crucial period of telecommunications and television development in Latin America. An earlier period of PanAmSat's history is discussed in Chapter Three, which describes how Spanish International Network pressed to deregulate the U.S. satellite industry. Rene Anselmo invested much of the profit he made from the Spanish International companies—he held 25% of the network and 24% of the station group—in PAS. In 1988, when the company's maiden satellite, PAS-1, launched as the world's first privately held communications satellite, Anselmo had invested

$70 million of his own money in the $110 million project (Cardenas, 1993). *Hispanic Business* magazine dubbed PanAmSat "the gamble of the decade" not only because the satellite hardware was insured for a mere $40 million, but also due to stiff resistance from Intelsat, which controlled regional communication by satellite, and Comsat, its U.S. signatory (Cardenas, 1993; Stephens, 1990). Much of Intelsat's signal capacity at the time was dedicated to telephone and data services, leaving limited space for television distribution, which mostly occurred via terrestrial microwave systems or shipping physical copies of programming between stations. In contrast, in late 1993 66% of PanAmSat's business was from broadcasting, 31% from business communications and 3% from long distance telephone service; more than 25 full-time television programmers used the service (Cooper, 1994).

Anselmo had to attract more funding in order to build and launch additional satellites. In 1993, Emilio Azcárraga Milmo invested $200 million in exchange for a 50% senior equity position in PanAmSat—this was a key piece of Televisa's bold international expansion efforts discussed above. "We expect dramatic growth in satellite demand over the next decade," Azcárraga said, "our association with PanAmSat will permit Grupo Televisa to expand the domestic and international distribution of our programming to the world's 350 million Spanish-speaking people" (Hartshorn, 1993, p. 17). The most important satellites for reaching that goal were PAS-1, positioned above the equator at 45 degrees West Longitude, and PAS-3, at 43 degrees West Longitude, which launched in 1996. Two other satellites that provided PanAmSat with truly global coverage were PAS-2 over the Pacific Ocean (169 degrees East Longitude, launched 1994) and PAS-4 over the Indian Ocean (68/72 degrees East Longitude, launched 1995). With almost ubiquitous distribution capacity, PanAmSat relayed television programming all over the globe, including U.S.-produced Spanish-language programs throughout Latin America.

The critical innovation through which PanAmSat increased its signal carriage capacity and met the growing demand for its services is compression technology. In very general terms, compression is an electronic process by which an analog signal is converted to a digital format and streamlined through the elimination of redundant information. Using this technology, a full-motion analog television signal could be compressed from occupying 6 megahertz to as little as 2 megahertz of bandwidth (Compression Labs announces, 1992), thereby allowing as many as 6 broadband digital signals to share a satellite transponder previously occupied by a single analog signal (in 1992). A related technology, integrated receiver decoder devices, was used to encrypt satellite signals, reducing piracy; they also permitted multiple audio tracks, so that several different languages—English, Spanish and Portuguese, for example—could accompany the same video signal. This development significantly increased the efficiency of program distribution to large, linguistically-diverse audiences.

In sync with a common theme of media history (Schramm 1988; Standage, 2013), the widespread adoption of communication satellites during the 1980s and 1990s ushered significant change into Latin American societies. An article in the *Los Angeles Times*, "The Future Hovers over Latin America," identified some such changes (Valle, 1988). One concerned the cultural imperialism issue discussed above: as the number of routine television viewers increased, previously isolated communities would receive "the gospel of consumerism and informationism" that could "raise expectations the continent's inflation- and debt-ridden nations would be powerless to satisfy." The threat was not only from external sources like the U.S., but internal ones such as Peru's Panamericana network which, as one of PanAmSat's first customers, increased its coverage area by 35% (Valle, 1988). The adoption of commercial satellite services also threatened government-controlled telecommunication systems, which were mostly organized under the European post, telephone and telegraph model (PTT), and relied on Intelsat to carry international content. The demand for television content quickly outstripped that infrastructure's signal-carrying capacity. The satellite article concludes with an interesting reference to the U.S. Hispanic market's centrality in the regional television trade. The advertising executive Carlos Kravetz opined,

> Among all Latinos in the world, the U.S. Hispanic is the most dynamic economic force. He is interacting with the U.S., with Japanese interests. He is living closer to the future than the people ... left behind at home. I think the U.S. Latino is really the leading edge of where (the Spanish-speaking) world is heading.
>
> (Valle, 1988)

During its peak growth period in the 1990s, PanAmSat launched satellites and signed on telecommunications clients at a vigorous pace; one industry analyst speculated that the system carried so much television traffic that its mere presence stimulated business that would not have existed otherwise (Cooper, 1994). Competition over direct-to-home television in the late 1990s brought large players into the market, causing multiple ownership changes for PanAmSat. In 1996, Hughes Electronics paid nearly $3 billion for the company, which was owned 40% by Anselmo, 40% by Televisa and 20% by other investors. Eight years later, an investment group headed by Kohlberg Kravis Roberts & Co acquired PanAmSat and took it public the following year, in 2005, raising $900 million. Two years after that, PanAmSat merged with its old nemesis, Intelsat, which had itself become a privately held company in 2001.

This brief overview illustrates deep changes in satellite and television industries under the influences of digitization, deregulation and capitalization during the two decades straddling the new millennium (Pelton, 2012). A key force in the industry traced its humble origins to a small television network's desire to distribute Spanish-language programming to far-flung stations in the U.S. more cheaply and effectively. Rene Anselmo's drive and tenacity propelled telecommunications deregulation and technological innovation, first within the U.S., then across the Western Hemisphere and, finally, globally.

Pay Television Growth in Latin America

Pay-television growth in Latin America during the 1990s brought the region's viewers more U.S. television content from both the English- and Spanish-language sectors. Many of the major U.S. studios and cable networks launched Spanish (and, in some cases, Portuguese) services, seeking what one report called "multichannel El Dorado" (Horwitz, 1994). For investors, attractive features included the multichannel element— new systems could carry many specialized channels—and access to relatively affluent audiences in multiple countries who could return profits through subscription fees, advertising and promotions. Projections of prodigious increases in the number of Latin American pay-television subscribers stimulated heavy investments in this sector at a time of significant free-trade fervor in business circles. Kagan World Media (1993) found that multichannel services had penetrated only 7% of the 76 million television households in Latin America, which contrasted with 23.5% penetration in Western Europe and 59.9% in the U.S. The capital investment in pay television was also significantly lower for Latin America, at $5.6 billion, than the $38.7 billion for Western Europe and $67.3 billion in the U.S.

Investment interest in the region buoyed by improved national economies and consumer income levels, free trade initiatives, cost-effective distribution by satellite and optimistic projections such as 30 million pay television subscribers in Latin America by 2005 (30 millones, 1997) initiated programming services' scramble into the Latin American regional market. Pressure mounted on government regulatory agencies to accommodate the new business. Between 1989 and mid-1994 about 50 pay-television services began targeting Latin America, many of them launching in the U.S. Spanish-language sector simultaneously (Horwitz, 1994). Among the most notable of channels, and their launch dates were MTV International, 1988; CNN, 1989; ESPN International Network, 1989; HBO Olé, 1990; TNT Latin America, 1991; Cine Canal, 1993; Canal de Noticias NBC, 1993; FOX Latin America, 1993; Cartoon Network, 1993; and Discovery Latin America, 1994. Latin America's favorable investment conditions were heralded in many trade journal headlines such as the annual "Latin Americas" sections in *Variety* magazine, which turned from glum in the mid-1980s to gleeful in the early 1990s: "DBS and Cable Fuel Latin Showbiz Surge," "Yanks Seek TV El Dorado" and "Latins Plug into Cable" are examples. A handful of other assessments were more circumspect, such as an eight-page article in *International Cable* titled "Latin American Pay TV: Facing the Issues" (Shackleford, Perez & Baker, 1993).

Although most of the new pay television systems in Latin America used coaxial cable, some did not. Multichannel multipoint distribution service (MMDS, or "wireless cable") employed terrestrial microwave signals to circumvent the cable installation and subscriber dispersion problems associated with wired systems (Ramsey, 1993). These attributes can be particularly favorable in developing regions with hilly or mountainous topography and infrastructure challenges, as in Latin America. MMDS could also be installed relatively quickly and cheaply, often requiring fewer regulatory permissions than cable television. However, due to line-of-sight microwave characteristics and power typically limited to 50 watts or less, MMDS signals offer clear reception only within a 15- to 25-mile radius of the source antenna, necessitating multiple antennas to cover expansive or obstacle-ridden areas (Gross, 1990).[18] The larger MMDS players, including Multivisión in Mexico and Brazil's TV Abril, became important players in Latin American pay television as the costs of receiving equipment fell (Ramsey, 1993), but they had difficulty recovering from the region-wide economic downturn in 1995 that the Mexican peso devaluation precipitated—the so-called "Tequila Effect"—as well as competition from a new distribution system.

Direct-to-Home Broadcasting

Direct-to-home broadcasting (DTH) avoids terrestrial distribution infrastructure altogether by beaming programs and advertising from satellite transponders straight to consumers' homes. It demanded higher levels of capital investment, advanced technology, and programming supply than standard cable TV. The Latin American DTH market opened in 1996 accompanied by persistent trade journal and business press reports of untapped subscribers and ample profit potential. It also redrew some historic competitive alignments in the region's media, signifying a shift from family-centered empires to more shareholder-driven enterprises in the emerging Digital Age (the U.S. dot-com boom was occurring simultaneously).

Initially, Televisa joined its chief regional rival, TV Globo of Brazil, in the Sky Latin America partnership, which also included Rupert Murdoch's News Corp. as an equal (30%) partner, and Liberty Media Corp. (a co-investor in Telemundo 10%). Sky's principal competitor was DirecTV Latin America, which had been named Galaxy Latin America (GLA) until November 2000. Hughes Electronics, a subsidiary of General Motors and AT&T, was Galaxy's principal shareholder with 60%; initially, the Latin American partners included Venezuela's Cisneros Group, owners of Venevisión, the Argentine conglomerate Grupo Clarín and the two wireless cable services mentioned above: TV Abril and Multivisión. Although Televisa and Venevisión were partners in Univision, they joined opposing forces in the DTH competition. (Televisión Azteca was not included among the investors in either system.)

DTH broadcasting offered 80 or more television channels plus additional audio channels, but it was an expensive enterprise for providers and consumers alike. The two competing entities had invested a combined $2 billion in their ventures by the end of 2006, just as their services were reaching many consumers. Galaxy lost $126 million in 1998, and Sky lost $150 million in the first nine months of the same year (Satellite TV, 1999), and the red ink continued flowing thereafter—Sky reportedly lost $400 million in 2001 (Sutter, 2002). An industry analyst at Bear, Sterns & Co. estimated that Sky was spending $500 to $600 *per subscriber* in Mexico in 1999, when monthly subscription fees were about $30 (Satellite TV, 1999). Although this seems like good value to access premium content, subscribers paid substantial upfront costs. In 1996, Brazilian subscribers to Sky paid $970 for a dish, decoder box and installation; although the price dropped to $335 by 1998 when the decoders were assembled locally, this still represented a sizable investment for many families (Molinski, 1996; Dolan, 1998). Pay television subscription levels tend to fluctuate in sync with economic indicators in Latin America, as in most areas of the world; only the most affluent consumers would consistently pay such upfront costs plus a monthly fee.

Content also became an important competitive front as Sky and GLA/DirecTV sought appealing combinations of regional content, such as the channels identified above, and national content for each country. The ownership alignments facilitated access to national material, as audiences tend to prefer local news and accents. However, the variety of content options available to satellite customers diminished this local effect compared to the limited-channel broadcast model of prior decades (Dulac & Godwin, 2008). For example, GLA subscriptions outsold Sky in Brazil despite Globo's affiliation with the latter (Paxman, 1998b). There were also relative strengths in program genres that likely influenced consumers' choices when deciding between the two services: following Rupert Murdoch's mantra for pay TV success, Sky was stronger in sports, while GLA enjoyed an edge in film channels (Paxman, 1998b).

Both DTH services lost money for eight straight years until Rupert Murdoch ended the costly competition by purchasing controlling interest in GM Hughes for $6.6 billion in 2003 and then merging the two services under the DirecTV moniker the following year.[19] As this book went to press, Sky Mexico was owned 59% by Televisa and 41% by DirecTV, and also served Central America and the Dominican Republic. As for Sky Brazil, Globo owned 7% and DirecTV 93% (Baker & Lopes, 2014). In July 2015, AT&T completed its purchase of DirecTV for $48.5 billion.[20] The reasoning cited in its press release should be familiar: "Latin America has an underpenetrated pay-TV market, about 40 percent of households subscribe to pay TV, and a growing middle class, and is DirecTV's fastest-growing customer segment" (Baker & Lopes, 2014). DirecTV's capacity to offer subscribers broadband Internet access was another incentive for the telecommunications giant to pursue the network. The shifting alignments of competitors since DTH entered Latin America is evidence of the considerable impact global economics and technological change are having on the region's cultural markets. A clear stratification of television markets has emerged along class lines, a process that unfolded simultaneously with the Internet's growth as a consumer medium. Both technologies, while seen by some as challenges to national integration, connected the U.S. Spanish-language sector more closely with Latin America. South Florida had become the central connecting node, in terms of geography and business, as well as technology.

Miami: Business Center for Latin American Television

Miami's progress toward becoming a production center and business hub began before the 1990s and has continued, but it was during that decade when the essential elements came together. Chapter Five describes how in the late 1980s both Univision and Telemundo focused their production efforts in Greater Miami. The city appealed to Latin American media companies for the same reasons that attracted the U.S. networks: advanced infrastructure, especially telecommunications and air transportation; geographical proximity to Latin America; an ever-growing consortium of Latin American celebrities, production talent and executives; access to financing amid relative economic stability; and an amenable cultural and linguistic climate. Two scholars who have studied the city emphasize the interplay of economic and cultural factors in Miami's ascendancy, although with slightly different emphases. Strover (1998) underscores the city's geographic location as key to media industries' spatialization, or presence across boundaries of time, space and media product types. She argues that the factors listed above stimulated a concentration of financial, creative and technical talent supporting the growth of post-production, dubbing and satellite services in the South Florida region. Thus, Miami became a command and control center for the Latin American/U.S. Spanish-language market as well as a key node in the accelerating global media economy. Sinclair (2003) employs related models to account for Miami's position as a regional trade center for Latin American television. Deterritorialization is one theorized outcome of globalization, but in this case location very much matters for elements such as easy access to Latin American cities, favorable business conditions and placement in the Eastern time zone for news distribution within the U.S.

Language and culture are clearly attracting forces that have brought generations of Latin Americans to Miami, and also adhesive agents that encourage them to settle.[21] The city remains highly segregated along class and country-of-origin lines (Nijman, 2011), partly due to the resources, political fervor and first-mover advantages that many Cubans fleeing revolution on the island brought with them in the 1960s. Later, fallout from the so-called "lost decade" of the 1980s and neoliberal reform measures in some Latin American countries created economic and physical insecurity as well as political instability, which acted as push-factors impelling migration to the United States (Aranda, Hughes, & Sabogal, 2014). South Florida became the preferred destination for many immigrant groups from South American and Caribbean countries. Class elements of the migration that fueled Miami's growth as a Spanish-language media center demand attention: the professional class clearly assisted industry advances, but lower- and middle-income population growth increased audience sizes for Spanish-language media not only in Miami, but nationwide. This growth, along with the increasing regional demand for television content discussed in prior sections, combined to stimulate media industry development.

The class division, a central theme of Arlene Dávila's book *Latinos, Inc.* (2001), occurred in other key markets, such as New York and Los Angeles, but its effect resounded more broadly from Miami, given the agglomeration of resources there. Dávila argues that the Spanish-language television industry's effort to span the U.S. Hispanic and Latin American markets perpetuated a dynamic by which the latter was favored over the former. Just as high percentages of Mexican programs were imported to the U.S. before competition arrived in the 1980s, content production in Miami privileged a pan-Latin American orientation over a U.S. Hispanic one. Prior chapters of this book have revealed that U.S. Hispanics' limited opportunities to produce content for an industry that profits from them has endured as a point of contention between industry management and Hispanic community advocates— the concentration of command and control over Spanish-language television production and trade on U.S. soil without a concomitant rise in influence for U.S. Hispanic personnel or themes deepened the historical affront.

Conclusion

This chapter has discussed the major elements that rendered the 1990s an important transitional decade in Spanish–language television. The demands of technology, new sources of competition, and global economics fostered unprecedented market conditions requiring significant adaptation by Latin American television enterprises. Early in the decade, satellites distributed programming among broadcasters throughout Latin America and in Spain via the Cadena de las Américas project—by decade's end, those satellites' more efficient descendants beamed dozens of channels to pay television systems and directly into millions of homes throughout the region. These changes carried related management challenges that transformed the competitive landscape for transnational media corporations (Gershon, 2000), and have continued to do so since, as the chapters to follow demonstrate. Not only did traditional alignments shift among competitors based in the region, but global media conglomerates also entered the region with their own resources and agendas. Consequently, organizations had to adapt internally to address transformations in the external environment, as shown by Televisa's transition due to its 1990 restructuring, its listing on multiple stock exchanges, shifting political and competitive terrain within Mexico, and Emilio Azcárraga Milmo's death in 1997. According to a Televisa executive, the company's organizational culture changed gradually to accommodate the new market conditions, including pressures for more transparency and accountability that accompanied its becoming a publicly traded company (R. Mendiola, personal communication, August 20, 1998).

As is common, shifts in the television industry were also influenced by significant political, economic and social changes. Other observers in the region shared the Mexican critical intelligentsia's concerns about the long-term impacts of free trade on media industries and culture. Monsiváis (1996) dubbed television "the main translator of the Mexican experience in Mexico" (p. 138). At the same time the country experienced profound political and economic changes, the ways Mexican audiences made meaning of content delivered by television and other media changed as well. Certainly, more advantaged citizens' access to the Internet beginning in the mid-1990s influenced how television and other media were used, yet even among less-privileged populations the nature of television changed with the advent of competition and the rapid political change that swept Vicente Fox of the PAN, an opposition party candidate, to Mexico's presidency in 2000 (Paxman & Saragoza, 2001). Similar, although less dramatic, changes occurred in other Latin American countries.

The developments in Latin American television covered in this chapter were instrumental in moving the industry toward what Piñón (2014) identifies as its multilayered condition in the mid-2010s. Pay television growth attracted a new cadre of Western media conglomerates into the region, and direct-to-home technology coaxed nationally dominant entities like Televisa, TV Globo and Venevisión out of traditional, monolithic rivalries to new alignments and strategies. These processes were accelerated with the introduction and accommodation of subsequent digital technologies like broadband Internet and mobile devices, as the two chapters in Part Four demonstrate.

Notes

1. Besides Frank Deford, *The National* hired other distinguished writers and editors including Vince Doria, John Feinstein, David Kindred, Mike Lupica, Van McKenzie, Scott Ostlen and Bud Shaw (Shaw, 2009).
2. The participant nations/territories were Mexico, Argentina, Venezuela, Bolivia, Chile, Ecuador, Cuba, Colombia, Guatemala, Honduras, El Salvador, Costa Rica, Nicaragua, Panama, Spain, Paraguay, Uruguay, Peru, the Dominican Republic and Puerto Rico.
3. Once Televisa listed on the Mexico City stock exchange in December 1991, public information became available about the secretive company. For example, see company reports for Grupo Televisa S.A. de C.V. by L.R. Barron, S.G. Warburg and Co., published January 27, 1992, and by K.M. Goldman, Bear Stearns & Co., published June 24, 1992.

4. These were Channels 2, 4 and 5. In December 1993, Red Televisora de México Norte, a subsidiary of Grupo Televisa, was awarded the rights to operate a 62-station TV network, ceding the conglomerate a fourth national chain (Televisa subsidiary wins, 1993).

5. The author's experience is illustrative in this regard. In 1989, when conducting master's thesis research in Mexico City with funds from a Tinker Foundation grant (Wilkinson, 1991), it was impossible to obtain an interview at Televisa. By contrast, in 2000 the author was able to quickly arrange in-person interviews with executives at two different Televisa facilities.

6. Editorial América, the principal subsidiary of American Publishing Group, published popular titles such as *Vanidades Continental, TV y Novelas, Teleguía, Cosmopolitan en Español, Buenhogar, Mecánica Popular, Tu, Marie Claire, Geomundo* and *Harlequin Romance Novels* (Grupo Televisa acquires, 1992).

7. Hong Kong, Singapore, South Korea and Taiwan.

8. The network fired 160 workers in August 1993 while simultaneously investing $50 million in transmission equipment, thereby increasing the network's coverage from 50% to 97% of Mexican television households (Robinson, 1997).

9. To express their displeasure with Televisa's editorial bias, some Mexican households displayed a poster having an image of the *24 Horas* anchorman Jacobo Zabludovsy with a red slash across his face and this text printed below: "In this house we love the truth—therefore we DO NOT watch 24 Horas."

10. Mario Bezares, Stanley's comedic sidekick, and an on-camera assistant, Paola Durante.

11. The author acknowledges Omar Hernández's and Aida Cerda's contributions to material in this section through a co-authored paper, "Have Monopolies Become Part of Mexico's Past? Lessons From the Television Industry," presented at the International Communication Association conference, Acapulco, Mexico (2000).

12. According to IBOPE, in April 1994, *24 Horas* had 17.6 ratings points, while *Hechos* only 2.7. In November, 1996, after *Ciudad Desnuda* had been on the air for three months, things changed: *24 Horas* and *Hechos* tied at 10.0, while *Ciudad Desnuda* had 50% more viewers than either with a 15.0 rating (Hernández & McAnany, 2001).

13. Synergy: "the interaction of elements that when combined produce a total effect that is greater than the sum of the individual elements, contributions, etc." (dictionary.com). Media companies began emphasizing synergy as a competitive strategy in the 1980s (McAnany & Wilkinson, 1992); the concept persists in the Digital Age.

14. A vibrant discussion of cultural hegemony through international communication persists in the media globalization literature. See Tomlinson (1999) and Pieterse (2009), for examples.

15. A common term for this phenomenon is "capture theory." It has been a recurring theme in discourses surrounding media, commerce and the state in Mexico, most recently under the so-called Televisa Law that would distribute additional electromagnetic spectrum to commercial media interests (Guerrero, 2010).

16. A major exhibit of diverse Mexican art that visited museums in Los Angeles, New York and San Antonio in 1990–91.

17. Galperin (1999, p. 639) explains: "Article 2 of the Annex specifies each country's exemptions to the protocol: Brazil excluded its radio, TV and

telecommunications industries; Paraguay and Uruguay both exempted their radio, TV, publishing and telecommunications sectors; interestingly, Argentina whose government had embraced more open policy toward foreign investors, did not make exemptions in the communication sector."

18. Charlotte Leonard (personal communication, January 27, 1993), senior vice president of Turner Broadcasting Services, commented that the quantity of tall buildings and large concrete surfaces in Brazil's principal cities negatively affected MMDS services; thus, some areas were beginning to install coaxial cable systems.

19. Exceptions are the Mexican and Brazilian markets, where the Sky names were retained.

20. AT&T claimed to reach 19 million subscribers in Latin America, including Mexican customers of Sky Mexico in which DirecTV held a minority stake. (http://about.att.com/story/att_completes_acquisition_of_directv.html)

21. Hispanic language and culture have also acted as a repellant to some non-Hispanics who migrated elsewhere, including many north along the Atlantic coast or west to the Gulf coast (Booth, 1998).

References

30 millones de suscritores de cable en el 2005. (1997, April 1–15). *Producción y Distribución*, 8.

Amado Mier, Ines. (1992, April 20). La Cadena de las Américas comienza mañana sus emisiones en 20 países. *El País*. Retrieved from http://elpais.com/diario/1992/04/20/radiotv/703720802_850215.html.

Angeles Jiménez, Alejandro. (1999). Inside politics. *Business Mexico, 9*(7), 20.

Antola, Livia, & Rogers, Everett M. (1984). Television flows in Latin America. *Communication Research, 11*(2), 183–202.

Aranda, Elizabeth M., Hughes, Sallie, & Sabogal, Elena. (2014). *Making a life in multiethnic Miami: Immigration and the rise of a global city*. Boulder, CO: Lynne Rienner.

Baker, Liana B., & Lopes, Marina. (2014, May 19). Latin America could be jewel of AT&T-DirecTV deal. *Reuters*. Retrieved from http://www.reuters.com/article/2014/05/19/us-att-mergers-directtv-idUSBREA4I02320140519.

Baldwin, Thomas F. (1996). *Convergence: Integrating media, information & communication*. Thousand Oaks, CA: Sage.

Besas, Peter. (1990, December 24). Dynastic quarrels undo Mex media mix. *Variety*, 1, 60.

BiB world guide to television and film 1994. (1994). Philadelphia, PA: North American.

Bonfil Batalla, Guillermo. (1992). Dimensiones culturales del tratado de libre comercio [Cultural dimensions of the free trade agreement]. In G. Guevara Niebla & N. García Canclini (Eds.), *La educación y la cultura ante el tratado de libre comercio* (pp. 157–178). Mexico City, Mexico: Nueva Imagen.

Booth, William. (1998, November 11). A white migration north from Miami. *Washington Post*, A1.

Cardenas, Francisco. (1993, December). The gamble of the decade. *Hispanic Business*, 54.

Chavez, Leo R. (2001). *Covering immigration: Popular images and the politics of the nation*. Berkeley, CA: University of California Press.

Compression Labs announces SpectrumSaver PAL. (1992, November 9). *Business Wire.*

Cooper, Jim. (1994, February 7). PanAmSat closes in on global goal. *Broadcasting & Cable,* 38.

Craig, David. (1994, February 14). Best new stocks: From high-tech to hairdos. *USA Today,* 3B.

Crusafon, Carmina. (2009). La política audiovisual del MERCOSUR y la influencia del modelo europeo. *Cuadernos de Información, 25,* 93–104.

Daniels, Jeffrey. (1993, April 27). QVC links with Grupo Televisa for Latin net. *Hollywood Reporter.*

Dávila, Arlene. (2001). *Latinos, Inc.: The marketing and making of a people.* Berkeley, CA: University of California Press.

DePalma, Anthony. (1993, September 15). Televisa plans stock split before listing on big board. *New York Times,* C19.

Dolan, Kerry A. (1998, October 5). Gustavo vs. Rupert. *Forbes,* 68–69.

Donaton, Scott. (1990, January 22). 'National' scores big. *Advertising Age,* 3, 52.

Donohue, Steve, & Lafayette, Jon. (1999, April 26). Azteca-Telemundo LINK? *Electronic Media, 18*(17), 8.

Druckerman, Pamela. (2000, May 3). NBC and TV Azteca end feud with a friendly pact. *Wall Street Journal,* A21.

Dulac, Stephen P., & Godwin, John P. (2008) Television via satellite. In D. Gerbarg (Ed.), *Television goes digital* (pp. 79–97). New York, NY: Springer.

Dumont, Juliette. (2010, April 11). Culture in the world of MERCOSUR. *INA Global.* Retrieved from http://www.inaglobal.fr/en/ideas/article/culture-world-mercosur.

Fernández, Claudia, & Paxman, Andrew. (2000). *Emilio Azcárraga Milmo y su imperio Televisa.* Mexico, D.F.: Grijalbo.

Fraser, Damian. (1992, August 4). If it's in Spanish on the box, it must be Televisa. *Financial Times,* 3.

Freer, Jim. (1992, February). Latin trade finance attractive once more. *United States Banker, 102*(2), 46–50.

French, Alex, & Kahn, Howie. (2011, June 13). The greatest paper that ever died. *Grantland.* Retrieved from http://grantland.com/features/the-greatest-paper-ever-died/.

Friedland, Jonathan, & Millman, Joel. (1998, July 10). Fresh lineup: Led by a young heir, Mexico's Televisa puts new stress on profits. *Wall Street Journal,* A1, A4.

Galperin, Hernan. (1999). Cultural industries policy in regional trade agreements: The cases of NAFTA, the European Union, and MERCOSUR. *Media, Culture, and Society, 21,* 627–648.

García Canclini, Néstor. (1992). Prehistoria económica y cultural del tratado de libre comercio [Economic and cultural antecedents of the free trade agreement]. In G. Guevara Niebla & N. García Canclini (Eds.), *La educación y la cultura ante el tratado de libre comercio* (pp. 3–14). Mexico City, Mexico: Nueva Imagen.

García Canclini, Néstor. (1996). North Americans or Latin Americans? The redefinition of Mexican identity and the free trade agreements. In E. G. McAnany & K. T. Wilkinson (Eds.), *Mass media and free trade: NAFTA and the cultural industries* (pp. 142–156). Austin, TX: University of Texas Press.

García Canclini, Néstor. (2007). *Cooperación, Diálogo: ¿Son las palabras más apropiadas?* V Campus Euroamericano de Cooperacão Cultural. Almada, Portugal. Retreieved from http://redculturalmercosur.org.

208 *Market Competition and Expansion in the 1990s*

Gershon, Richard A. (2000). The transnational media corporation: Environmental scanning and strategy formulation. *The Journal of Media Economics*, *13*(2), 81–101.

Getino, Octavio. (2001, mayo). *Aproximación a un estudio de las industrias culturales en el Mercosur (Incidencia económica, social y cultural para la integración regional)*. Organizacion de Estudios Iberoamericanos: Seminario Internacional "Importancia y Proyección del Mercosur Cultural con miras a la Integración." Santiago, Chile. Retrieved from http://www.oei.es/cultura2/getino.htm.

Golden, Tim. (1993, June 7). In sale of TV networks, Mexico seeks to create a rival to mighty Televisa. *New York Times*, D6.

Gross, Lynne S. (1990). *The new television technologies*. Dubuque, IA: William C. Brown.

Grupo Televisa acquires Grupo America, the largest Spanish magazine publishing group and network of distribution companies in the Americas. (1992, July 29). *PR Newswire*.

Guevara Niebla, Gilberto, & García Canclini, Nestor (Eds.). (1992). *La educación y la cultura ante el tratado de libre comercio. (Education and culture in the face of the free trade agreement)* Mexico City, Mexico: Nueva Imagen.

Guerrero, Manuel Alejandro. (2010). Broadcasting and democracy in Mexico: From corporatist subordination to State capture. *Policy and Society*, *29*(1), 23–35.

Hallin, Daniel C. (2000). *La nota roja*: Popular journalism and the transition to democracy in Mexico. In C. Sparks and J. Tulloch (Eds.), *Tabloid tales: Global debates over media standards* (pp. 267–284). Latham, MD: Rowman & Littlefield.

Hartshorn, David. (1993, February). Grupo Televisa: PanAmSat's missing link? *Satellite Communications*, 17.

Hernández, Omar, & McAnany, Emile. (2001). Cultural industries in the Free Trade Age: A look at Mexican television. In G. Joseph, A. Rubinstein, and E. Zolov (Eds.), *Fragments of a golden age: The politics of culture in Mexico since 1940* (pp. 389–414). Durham, NC: Duke University Press.

Horwitz, Carolyn. (1994, June). A forecast for Latin American pay TV. *Satellite Communications*, 25–31.

Hoskins, Colin, Finn, Adam, & McFadyen, Stuart. (1996). Television and film in a freer international trade environment: U.S. dominance and Canadian responses. In E.G. McAnany & K.T. Wilkinson (Eds.), *Mass media and free trade: NAFTA and the cultural Industries* (pp. 64–91). Austin, TX: University of Texas Press.

Hudson, Heather E. (1990). *Communication satellites: Their development and impact*. New York, NY: Free Press.

Latin America: Is it safe to get back in the water? (2004, June 1). *Via Satellite*. Retrieved from http://www.satellitetoday.com/telecom/2004/06/01/latin-america-is-it-safe-to-get-back-in-the-water/.

Lawson, Chappell H. (2002). *Building the Fourth Estate: Democratization and the rise of a free press in Mexico*. Berkeley, CA: University of California Press.

Lewis, Justin, & Miller, Toby (Eds.). (2003). *Critical cultural policy studies: A reader*. Oxford, UK: Blackwell.

Malkin, Elisabeth. (1994, May 30). Will a *Yanqui* partner make TV Azteca a player? *Business Week*, 56.

Malkin, Elisabeth. (1995, December 11). The Rupert Murdoch of Mexico? *Business Week*, 61.

Mandel-Campbell, Andrea. (2000, May 3). NBC takes stake in TV Azteca broadcasting: US TV network to invest dollars 26m in Mexican company following settlement of dispute. *Financial Times*, 34.

María y Campos, Mauricio de. (1992). Las industrias culturales de entretenimiento en el marco de las negociaciones del tratado de libre comercio [The entertainment cultural industries in the framework of negotiations over the free trade agreement]. In G. Guevara Niebla & N. García Canclini (Eds.), *La educación y la cultura ante el tratado de libre comercio* (pp. 235–298). Mexico City, Mexico: Nueva Imagen.

Martínez Staines, Javier. (1992, 14 octubre). Grupo Televisa: Quien rie al ultimo, ¿rie mejor? *Expansión*, 72–73.

McAnany, Emile G., & Wilkinson, Kenton T. (1992). From cultural imperialists to takeover victims: Questions on Hollywood's buyouts from the critical tradition. *Communication Research, 19*(6), 724–728.

McCann, James A., & Domínguez, Jorge I. (1998). Mexicans react to electoral fraud and political corruption: An assessment of public opinion and voting behavior. *Electoral Studies, 17*(4), 483–503.

Mejía Barquera, Fernando. (1993, 15 de junio). Telemundo y Univisión: La lucha se intensifica. *El Nacional*, 8E.

Miller, Marjorie. (1993, May 25). Cristina's controversy: Imported talk show enrages conservatives and liberals alike in Mexico. *Los Angeles Times*. Retrieved from http://articles.latimes.com/1993-05-25/news/wr-39491_1_cristina-show.

Millman, Joel. (1992, January 6). El Tigre pounces again. *Forbes*, 44.

Molinski, Michael. (1996, October 30). Sky Entertainment starts Brazil satellite TV. *Bloomberg Business News*. Retrieved from Lexis-Nexis database.

Monsiváis, Carlos. (1992). De la cultura mexicana en vísperas del tratado de libre comercio [On Mexican culture on the eve of the free trade agreement]. In G. Guevara Niebla & N. García Canclini (Eds.), *La educación y la cultura ante el tratado de libre comercio* (pp. 179–209). Mexico City, Mexico: Nueva Imagen.

Monsiváis, Carlos. (1996). Will nationalism be bilingual? In E.G. McAnany and K.T. Wilkinson (Eds.), *Mass media and free trade: NAFTA and the cultural industries* (pp. 131–141). Austin, TX: University of Texas Press.

NACLA-North American Congress on Latin America. (1993, February). A market solution for the Americas? *Report on the Americas, 26*(4), 16–17.

Nash, Nathaniel C. (1993, April 11). A new rush into Latin America. *New York Times*, 1.

The National strikes out. (1991, August). *Hispanic Business*, 48.

Nijman, Jan. (2011). *Miami: Mistress of the Americas*. Philadelphia, PA: University of Pennsylvania Press.

Ortega Pizarro, Fernando. (1993, 26 de julio). Los nuevos dueños de canal 13 y canal 7 en su primer autorretrato. *Proceso*, 6–13.

Paxman, Andrew. (1992, August 10). Mexico's media giant meets few obstacles to expansion. *Christian Science Monitor*, 7.

Paxman, Andrew. (1998a, August 10). FCC approves Telemundo takeover. *Variety*, 22.

Paxman, Andrew. (1998b, June 8). Rising Sky sets in on Galaxy in satcaster wars. *Variety, 371*(5), M15.

Paxman, Andrew & Saragoza, Alex M. (2001). Globalization and Latin media powers: The case of Mexico's Televisa. In V. Mosco & D. Schiller (Eds.), *Continental order? Integrating North America for cybercapitalism* (pp. 64–85). Lanham, MD: Rowman & Littlefield.

Pelton, Joseph N. (2010). Satellites as worldwide change agents. In D.K. Thussu (Ed.), *International communication: A reader* (pp. 13–35). New York: Routledge.

Pelton, Joseph N. (2012). *Satellite communications.* New York, NY: Springer.

Piccato, Pablo. (2014). Murders of *nota roja*: Truth and justice in Mexican crime news. *Past and Present, 223*(1), 195–231.

Pieterse, Jan Nederveen. (2009). *Globalization and culture: Global mélange.* Lanham, MD: Rowman & Littlefield Publishers.

Piñón, Juan. (2014). A multilayered transnational broadcasting television industry: The case of Latin America. *International Communication Gazette, 76*(3), 211–236.

Pool, Ithiel de Sola. (1977). The changing flow of television. *Journal of Communication, 27*(2), 139–179.

Preston, Julia. (1999a, June 10). As Mexico mourns TV figure, cocaine clouds the picture. *New York Times*, 3.

Preston, Julia. (1999b, August 29). Indictments unveil the dark side of a Mexican TV comedian. *New York Times*, 8.

Preston, Julia, & Dillon, Sam. (2004). *Opening Mexico: The making of a democracy.* New York, NY: Farrar, Straus & Giroux.

Ramsey, John. (1993, August). MMDS: The advent of Latin American pay TV. *Satellite Communications*, 17.

Reilly, Tom. (2010). *War with Mexico!: America's reporters cover the battlefront.* Lawrence, KS: University Press of Kansas.

Robinson, Edward A. (1997, 10 de noviembre). TV Azteca: Nace una estrella. *Fortune Americas* (*El Norte* newspaper, Monterrey, Mexico), 12–13.

Russell, Joel. (1994, January). The sky's not the limit! [Special edition]. *Business Mexico, 4*(1/2), 68–69.

Salvador, Isabel. (1992, March 13). La OTI crea la Cadena de las Américas para emitir la Expo. *El País.* Retrieved from http://elpais.com/diario/1992/03/13/radiotv/ 700441203_850215.html.

Satellite TV comes down to Earth (1999, April 12). *Businessweek Online.* Retrieved from http://www.businessweek.com/stories/1999–04–11/satellite-tv-comes-down-to-earth-intl-edition.

Schiller, Herbert I. (1991). *Culture, Inc.: The corporate takeover of public expression.* New York, NY: Oxford University Press.

Serra Puche, Jaime. (1991, July). Principios para negociar el tratado de libre comercio de América del Norte [Principles for negotiating the North American Free Trade Agreement]. *Comercio Exterior, 41*, 653–660.

Serrill, Michael S. (1990, February 5). Mexico's mystery mogul. *Time*, 33.

Shackleford, John, Perez, Alberto, & Baker, Jonathan. (1993, December). Latin American pay TV: Facing the issues. *International Cable*, 21–30.

Shaw, Bud. (2009, December 2). The rise and fall of The National sports daily. *Mental Floss.* Retrieved from http://mentalfloss.com/article/23401/rise-fall-national-sports-daily.

Schramm, Wilbur L. (1988). *The story of human communication: Cave painting to microchip.* New York, NY: Harper & Row.

Silverstein, Jeffrey. (1992, December 28). Mexico's telecommunications mogul expanding his empire. *San Francisco Chronicle*, B1.

Sinclair, John. (1986, January). Dependent development and broadcasting: "The Mexican formula." *Media, Culture & Society*, 8, 81–101.

Sinclair, John. (1999). *Latin American television: A global view.* New York: Oxford University Press.

Sinclair, John. (2003, August). The Hollywood of Latin America: Miami as regional center in television trade. *Television & New Media, 4*(3), 211–229.

Standage, Tom. (2013). *Writing on the wall: Social media, the first two thousand years.* New York, NY: Bloomsbury.

Stephens, Guy M. (1990, November). PamAmSat: Fighting the good fight. *Satellite Communications, 14*(10), 19.

Straubhaar, Joseph D. (1991). Beyond media imperialism: Asymmetrical interdependence and cultural proximity. *Critical Studies in Mass Communication Research,* 8, 39–59.

Strover, Sharon. (1998, November). Spatialization and international communication industries: The case of Miami. *Javnost-The Public, 4*(3), 35–45.

Sutter, Mary. (1996, August 1). TV battle turns personal. *Business Mexico,* 6(8), 15.

Sutter, Mary. (2002, April 1–7). Border crossing. *Variety, 386*(7), A11.

Televisa: A dominant force. (1993, May). *Euromoney*, 133–134.

Televisa subsidiary wins government concession for new television network. (1993, December 15). *SourceMex Economic News & Analysis on Mexico.*

Television Azteca forges partnership with U.S. television network NBC. (1994, May 25). *SourceMex.*

Television in Mexico: Changing channels. (1993, May 1). *The Economist, 327,* 76.

Tomlinson, John. (1991). *Cultural imperialism: A critical introduction.* Baltimore, MD: Johns Hopkins University Press.

Tomlinson, John. (1999). *Globalization and culture.* Chicago, IL: University of Chicago Press.

Top Latin American companies – Televisa. (1993, May). *Euromoney*. Retrieved from Reuter Textline database.

Torres, Craig. (1997, September 30). Mexican rivals heed Elektra's expansion—Central America move highlights retail saturation at home. *Wall Street Journal*, A19.

Toussaint, Florence. (1992, May). Cadena de las Américas. *Proceso, 810,* 60.

Valle, Victor (1988, November 27). The future hovers over Latin America: New satellite will have major sociopolitical impact--and will open new markets for U.S. TV programming [Calendar section]. *Los Angeles Times.* Retrieved from http://articles.latimes.com/1988-11-27/entertainment/ca-702_1_latin-america/4.

Vallescar, Eva. (1992, April 20). Hoy inicia enlace televisivo de la 'Cadena de las Americas' de Televisa. *La Opinión, 66* (218), 5D.

Virshup, Amy. (1990, January). The Mexican Murdoch moves into town. *Manhattan, Inc.,* 82–87.

Watling, John. (1993, November). Holding steady. *Business Mexico*, 52.

Weintraub, Sydney. (1990, autumn). The North American free trade debate. *Washington Quarterly,* 119–130.

Welch, John H. (1993). The new face of Latin America: Financial flows, markets and institutions in the 1990s. *Journal of Latin American Studies, 25*(1), 1–24.

Wilkinson, Kenton T. (1991*). The sale of Spanish International Communications Corporation: Milestone in the development of Spanish-language television in the United States* (M.A. thesis). University of California at Berkeley.

Wilkinson, Kenton T. (1995*). Where language, culture and communication converge: The Latin American cultural-linguistic television market* (Doctoral dissertation). University of Texas at Austin, Texas.

Wilkinson, Kenton T. (2003, spring). Language difference in the telenovela trade. *Global Media Journal*, 2(2). Retrieved from: http://lass.purduecal.edu/cca/gmj/sp03/gmj-sp03-wilkinson.htm.

Wilkinson, Kenton T. (2006, September). Cultural policy in a free trade environment: Mexican television in transition. *Journal of Broadcasting and Electronic Media*, 50(3), 482–501.

Wilkinson, Kenton T. (2007). Democracy sponsored by NAFTA? Mexican television in the free trade era. In I. A. Blankson & P. D. Murphy (Eds.), *Negotiating democracy: Media transformations in emerging democracies* (pp. 199–218). Albany, NY: State University of New York Press.

Part IV

Growth, Digitization and Fragmentation in the 2000s

8 The "Latin Booms" in Population, Popular Culture and Industry Profile

Hispanic culture experienced a boom in visibility and popularity in the United States at the outset of the new millennium. Population growth, with its attendant profit potential was again a main driver, but not the sole one. Innovations in online and mobile communication technology also attracted attention and capital, leading to an unsustainable overvaluation of start-up companies and some established players in the digital field as well. The Spanish-language networks kept close tabs on emerging digital media and strove to keep pace with change in an environment of media convergence. This chapter recounts those efforts and other key developments, covering the years 2000 to 2006.

The early years of the new century also witnessed significant changes in the disposition of U.S. Spanish-language television. NBC purchased the Telemundo network, providing needed stability. Televisión Azteca, the privatized Mexican network that began competing with Televisa in 1993, launched a U.S. network named Azteca América, and an array of smaller networks also vied for audiences as the distribution capacity of pay television increased. Univision extended its domain in Spanish-language media by acquiring Hispanic Broadcasting Corp., a collection of 68 radio stations. Yet these changes did not all unfold smoothly. As in earlier periods, financial, regulatory and management challenges confronted the major industry players, with technology and demographics becoming salient factors that intertwined with the others.

Demographics

The 2000 U.S. Census

The 2000 U.S. census counted 35.3 million Hispanics, comprising 12.5% of the population (Ennis, Ríos-Vargas, & Albert, 2011). The Census Bureau yet again employed a new approach for asking Hispanics to report their ethnicity and race, this time to comply with changes established by the Office of Management and Budget in 1997. The OMB instructed federal agencies that collect data on race and ethnicity to allow respondents to choose more than one race to self-identify, thereby broadening the options beyond a few mutually exclusive categories (National Research Council, 2004). The ethnicity question appeared first, asking respondents whether they considered themselves Spanish, Hispanic or Latino; this permitted the federal government to report data in two categories: "Hispanic or Latino" and "Not Hispanic or Latino" (Grieco & Cassidy, 2001). Unlike the 1990 census questionnaire, a race question immediately followed the ethnicity question, asking respondents to identify themselves in one or more of these categories: White, Black or African American, American Indian and Alaska Native, Asian, Native Hawaiian and Other Pacific Islander, or some other race. As in the 1990 census, nearly 97% of respondents selecting "some other race" were Hispanic (National Research Council, 2004). The distribution by national or regional origin in 2000 was Mexican 58.5%, Puerto Rican 9.6%, Central American 4.8%, South American 3.8%, Cuban 3.5%, Dominican 2.2% and other 17.6% (Ennis et al., 2011).

As with prior censuses, findings from the 2000 count stimulated discussion in industry circles, as three representative examples that appeared in the press illustrate.

- "The Census 2000 results were a wakeup call, says Mary Molina, manager of Hispanic corporate relations at P&G [Proctor & Gamble]. Census data shows that during the past 10 years, the Hispanic population in the US has increased by 58% and now represents 13% of the overall population of 284.8 million." (Heim, 2003)
- "... the 'single largest contributor' to the growth of the Hispanic market ... it validated [the numbers] for corporate America." (Ana María Fernández Haar cited in Case & Freeman, 2003)
- "Classification by race has become an increasingly complex enterprise as the composition of the U.S. population has changed and the notions of race and ethnicity have shifted in meaning." (National Research Council, 2004, p. 303)

Even if the nation's complexion and conceptions of ethnicity had begun to change, its general social categorization schemes, and their influence, had not.

Hispanic Population Surpasses Blacks

On January 21, 2003, the U.S. Census Bureau confirmed a significant population shift that demographers had been anticipating for more than a decade: Hispanics outnumbered Blacks. Many news outlets reported that the Hispanic population had grown to 37 million people, compared to 36.2 million Blacks. The bureau did not issue its own analytical report, but rather released raw data for news organizations to interpret and report. Given this announcement procedure, and in light of respondents' freedom to select multiple races and ethnicities in the 2000 census, it's not surprising that news reports varied—or that controversy arose—regarding this demographic milestone.

A key dispute centered around associating figures for an ethnic group, Hispanics, who can be of any race, with those of a group defined by race, Blacks. As a critical article published in the *Columbia Journalism Review* put it, "it's like comparing organic apples with red apples" (Scherer, 2003). A group of approximately 1.7 million people who self-identified in the census as both Hispanic and Black could be counted in either category. Many news reports counted those respondents exclusively as Hispanic, following the lead of intermedia agenda setters such as the Associated Press or the *New York Times* (Clemetson, 2003; Scherer, 2003). A handful of news organizations, including *USA Today*, delayed reporting the story until several months later when new figures released by the Census Bureau indicated a clear Hispanic majority, regardless of Black Hispanics' categorization (El Nasser, 2003). The news media's handling of this story raises two issues that are germane to this book. As discussed in the Introduction, some academic researchers rely on news and trade journal reports for information about media industries—when these sorts of variations in reporting arise they pose threats to research validity through the secondary sources (Wilkinson & Merle, 2013). Second, when an organization such as the Census Bureau releases data without providing in-house analysis or clear guidelines for its evaluation, it becomes fodder for "advocacy groups, policy people and politicians [who] pick the interpretation ... that works best for them" (William H. Frey cited in Clemetson, 2003). Such interpretations are clearly warranted as free speech, but may fan the flames of discord on sensitive topics like this one.

In the U.S., census numbers influence the allocation of public funds, political districting practices, and other processes related to wealth, power and opportunity. Thus, the news about Hispanics outnumbering Blacks was not universally welcome. Some Hispanic leaders downplayed the milestone's significance in the press and public forums, emphasizing shared agendas, interests and values across the two populations (Scherer, 2003). Yet there was a history of competition between the groups (McClain & Karnig, 1990; Ríos & Mohamed, 2003). An established sociological theory helps explain this social dynamic: Blalock's (1967) power-threat theory posits that the larger the minority group, the greater the threat to the majority, which acts to protect its dominant status through legal controls and other measures. Competition over economic resources, and for political power, leads to discrimination against the growing group. Because in pluralistic societies like the United States multiple minority groups seek resources, opportunities and influence, ascendant groups are often perceived as threatening not only to the majority, but to other minority groups as well. Merkert (2010) added a media component to Blalock's original model, asserting media's importance as an intervening variable affecting minorities' visibility and perceived competition among other groups. The presence of a burgeoning Spanish-language media that is alleged to promote Hispanics' interests at the exclusion of others could certainly compound the sense of threat among Blacks and others.

Rodríguez (2007) used critical race theory to conduct a framing analysis of how three types of newspapers—mainstream, Hispanic and African American—reported the 2003 story of Hispanics outnumbering Blacks. The dominant frame for coverage was competition (a "race") among population groups, present in 80% of the mainstream press articles, 64% of Hispanic press reports and 54% of Black press articles analyzed. Key secondary frames included the difficulties implicit in comparing ethnic and racial groups, the announcement's potential to disunify Hispanics and Blacks who share common interests, and Hispanics' need to improve their standing in U.S. society as their numbers grow.[1] Rodríguez concluded that except for the disunity frame, how each press type framed the story complied with that group's position in accordance with power-threat theory.

NBC Purchases Telemundo

Exactly one month after the September 11, 2001, terrorist attacks on the World Trade Center and the Pentagon, NBC announced its intention to purchase the Telemundo network for $1.98 billion and assume Sony/Liberty Media's $700 million in debt.[2] At the time, Telemundo consisted of 19 owned-and-operated stations, 11 of them full-power, two cable networks—Mun2 and Telemundo Internacional—as well as 40 affiliated stations. Telemundo's stations were located in key Hispanic population centers, reaching an estimated 88% of Hispanic television households nationwide (Penteado, 2001). Given the network's troubled financial history, the economic uncertainty that followed the terrorist attacks, and the high purchase price—estimated at 38 times cash flow—NBC's leadership was clearly anticipating steady growth in the market (Grossman & Hiestand, 2001). Several indicators reported in articles about the acquisition identified upsides that likely motivated the purchase:

- Hispanics represented 14% of TV viewers but accounted for less than 3% of ad dollars spent (Grossman & Hiestand, 2001).
- The buying power of U.S. Hispanics increased 118% between 1990 and 2001, accounting for around $452.4 billion at the time of the purchase (Penteado, 2001). It was projected to reach $1 trillion by the end of the decade (James, 2001).
- Advertising market share for Spanish-language stations had grown 16%–17% annually, while the overall TV ad market dropped almost 6% during the first half of 2001 (Grossman & Hiestand, 2001; Penteado, 2001). Telemundo's ad sales increased from around $150 million in 2000 to $200 million in 2001 (James, 2001).

I should emphasize that NBC's acquisition of Telemundo occurred during a high point of media mergers and acquisitions that were stimulated by the Federal Communications Commission's (FCC) deregulatory efforts, most visibly embodied in the Telecommunications Act of 1996, and the digital technology boom that bracketed the turn of the century along with a related emphasis on media convergence. In addition to Telemundo's growth potential within the Spanish-language television sector, NBC also anticipated operational streamlining and strategic opportunities to attract bilingual audiences. With the acquisition, English-Spanish station duopolies resulted in four significant local markets—Chicago, Dallas, Miami and New York—creating potential management efficiencies and cross-promotion opportunities. Because Telemundo had obtained a second station (KWHY, channel 22) in Los Angeles in June 2001, NBC announced it would sell KWHY to comply with FCC station ownership caps for networks. However, NBC requested and received waivers to the two-station-per-market ownership cap, the so-called "duopoly rule," until 2010 when the cable TV giant Comcast acquired NBC and the issue surfaced again.

The ownership caps were intended to counter the negative effects of media ownership concentration on competition in broadcasting, as well as content diversity. The aforementioned spate of large-scale media mergers and acquisitions in the latter 1990s and early 2000s raised concerns in some quarters about stifled competition, greater barriers to entry and increased homogeneity of media content (e.g., Herman & McChesney, 2001, Bagdikian, 2000).[3] Prior chapters have recounted advocates' legal efforts to halt network ownership changes during different periods of Spanish-language television's development, and 2001 was no exception. A group of Hispanic advocacy and community groups[4] petitioned the FCC to deny NBC's request for an extension in divesting of its third station in the Los Angeles market. The petition expressed concerns about the inherent tension between ownership concentration and content diversity, preserving the integrity of ethnic programming, protecting and expanding Hispanic employment in the industry and addressing the linguistic diversity of Hispanics in the Los Angeles area. In sum, the petition "rais[ed] issues that ensure operation in the public interest, not in the interests of the bottom line" (FCC, 2001, p. 2).[5] Although the FCC denied the petition and extended the duopoly rule waiver for another nine years, it bears noting that media advocacy and legal efforts challenging major shifts in the industry have persisted in the 21st century.

The flip side to Telemundo's gaining more stability and resources as part of a major media conglomerate was the expectation to serve corporate efforts toward developing synergies (a strategic buzzword of the time—see Chapter Seven, note 13) that didn't necessarily benefit the network or its Spanish-speaking audience. Potential projects along these lines included producing Spanish-language versions of the NBC shows *The Weakest Link*, *Dateline NBC* and *Access Hollywood* (DiCarlo, 2001; Sorkin, 2001). Such crossover programs—reminiscent of failed attempts by the same network a decade earlier—were intended to keep Spanish-dominant, English-dominant and bilingual audiences tuned in to content within the NBC family (James, 2001). Another approach involved combined promotional events. In 2004, the two companies hosted a joint event in Los Angeles for soap opera fans in both languages; the clear intent was to "underscore the links between the Spanish-language soap operas on Telemundo and their counterparts on NBC" (Weintraub, 2004). A Univision celebrity's defection to Telemundo provides another example. María Celeste Arraras, an Emmy Award-winning anchorwoman of the news magazine program *Primer Impacto,* announced her new affiliation on the same day the NBC-Telemundo merger received regulatory approval. News reports emphasized that Ms. Arraras's English fluency would allow her to contribute to NBC programs such as *Dateline NBC* and *Today*; Andrew Lack, the chief operating officer for NBC stated, "there aren't going to be any walls between NBC and Telemundo" (Calvo, 2002).[6]

The Latin Boom

The ethos behind the so-called Latin Boom of the late 1990s and early 2000s was summed up by *Newsweek* magazine in 1999: "Latinos are changing the way the country looks, feels and thinks, eats, dances and votes" (Larmer, Chambers, Figueroa, Wingert & Weingarten, 1999). While in some respects reminiscent of platitudes that circulated about the Decade of the Hispanic 20 years earlier, the contested discourse about the nature and veracity of this "boom" demonstrated that significant changes had occurred in the interim. Many marketers and advertisers were already familiar with the population and its profit potential—they focused on subsegments, especially the youth market, and best practices to reach them. Media's fracturing into a "multichannel universe" of narrowcasting and niche publications, together with the Internet's mainstreaming and commercialization, lowered barriers of entry for new competitors while expanding opportunities for cross-platform promotion (creating synergies) among the larger, established players. The Internet also facilitated more direct, public discussion of events and social phenomena, although we must recall that this was the period of listserves, electronic bulletin boards and chat, not the blogging and social media later enabled by Web 2.0. Additionally, two decades of growth for ethnic studies, media studies and related academic programs brought more voices to the discussion of Hispanic identity, communication, social influence, and related topics.

Musical Roots of the Boom

A tragic event garnered international news headlines and turned mainstream America's attention to Latin music: the 1995 shooting death of the Tejano music star Selena Quintanilla Pérez. The response to her murder demonstrated that Tejano's international fan base was larger than many had realized, and the 1997 biopic *Selena* immortalized the young singer while launching Jennifer López to stardom. Of course "J-Lo" would become a central contributor to the Latin Boom that followed. After *Selena*, Latin music's focus turned back to Miami where Emilio and Gloria Estefan were cornering the Hispanic music production market while developing a sound that would become synonymous with the Boom (Cepeda, 2010).

Ricky Martin's inspired performance of "Livin' La Vida Loca" on the 1999 Grammy Awards show is widely credited with launching the trend that brought greater attention, and sales, to other Latin artists, like Enrique Iglesias and Shakira, who "crossed over" by performing in English (Garcia, 1999). Other Boom artists like J-Lo and Marc Anthony are bilingual native English speakers. Thus language again became significant in a debate over identity, authenticity and commercialization. Christina Aguilera, who like Selena Quintanilla Pérez was a native speaker of English and learned to sing in Spanish phonetically, swam against the current of some fellow Boom artists by rerecording in Spanish songs from her 1999 self-titled English-language album (Cepeda, 2010). After earning Best New Artist honors at the 2000 Grammy Awards, she performed "Genio Atrapado," the Spanish version of her break-through single "Genie in a Bottle," at the same awards show the following year. Not unlike the libraries of English-language film and television content translated for export via Latin American pay TV, Aguilar's artistry, visual as well as auditory, became a cultural product repackaged to reach a broader audience base in the U.S. and overseas.

Some critics argued that artists who crossed over to English were pandering to mainstream audiences who chased yet another pop culture fad, but were largely indifferent to the culture behind the music (Navarro, 1999; Moon, 2002). Certainly Latin music enjoyed a deep, influential history not only independently, but also influencing the rich variety of U.S. popular music, as illustrated in the Introduction. Ricky Martin claimed to experience a cultural catharsis after two hit albums sung in English, and returned to recording in Spanish in 2003. His comment, "Latin music has always been here, you just have to open your eyes" (Ogunnaike, 2003) added credence to Valentín's "Columbus Effect" concept, which argues that powerful groups' discovery of something "new" (but which already exists) is quickly followed by its appropriation (cited in Cepeda, 2001, p. 71). The salsa star and actor Rubén Blades expressed a related notion saying, "I hate the word 'crossover' with a passion because it is a racist term for people who can't accept the mixture that has already taken place" (cited in Cepeda, 2010, p. 59). Yet we must be careful not to place all of the blame for negative aspects of the Latin Boom on an imagined mainstream consuming public comprised of historical and cultural ignoramuses: someone creates the content that consumers select. As Dávila (2001) has persuasively argued, an influential Hispanic media and marketing elite cultivates and promotes Latin talent and media texts not only for consumption by U.S. and international Hispanic audiences, but non-Hispanic audiences as well. Limited emphasis on media education and cultural literacy in U.S. public education is an important (lack of) influence as well—some members of the consuming public become easy pickings for the media and marketing elite.

Prior chapters have shown that Hispanic performers of U.S. origin often resent being passed over in favor of Latin American and Caribbean performers. The complaint that foreigners convey an attractive sense of otherness and exoticism, aligns with academic arguments regarding Latins' appeal to the American mainstream (Rodríguez, 1997; Ramírez-Berg, 2002). Yet several of the Boom stars such as Cristina Aguilera, J-Lo and Marc Anthony were U.S.-born and raised, even though marketing positioned them as international rather than American. Observers noted an intriguing aspect of this dynamic: these Latin Boom stars are situated as exotic and intriguing, but not so different as to be alien, or disconnected from the lives of potential audience members (Pellegrini, 1999; Goodwin, 1999). A possible interpretation, from a broader sociological perspective, is that such are the processes by which a complex society adjusts to internal change driven by the increasing diversification of its population. Certainly the media play a central role in such adjustment processes, occupying, as they do, a considerable proportion of the public's time and attention. The effects can become frustrating at the individual level, however: Marc Anthony commented, "this whole crossover thing really annoys me … like I'm coming and invading America with my music. I was born and raised in New York, man" (Goodwin, 1999).

Hispanic Influence through Consumption

Mimicking the close connection between popular music and youth marketing that rock and roll established in the 1950s, the Latin Boom attracted the attention of advertisers eager to reach young bicultural consumers. The 2000 census intensified this interest by reporting that 35% of Hispanics were under 18 years of age, compared to 23% of non-Hispanic Whites (Cartagena, 2005, p. 169). The average age for Hispanics, 28 years, was significantly lower than the non-Hispanic population's 37 years. Like their mainstream predecessors in the 1950s, Hispanic youth were spending larger amounts of discretionary income as well, estimated at $26 billion annually (Hoy, 2004).

Market segmentation labels entered the popular lexicon with "baby boomers" in the 1950s–60s and Generations X and Y, which followed in the 1970s and 1980s–90s respectively. The term Generation Ñ often refers to young, technology-savvy Hispanics, but its use has varied. For example, in 2004 the newspaper *Hoy* identified Generation Ñ as 10- to 20-year-olds; an earlier article in *Newsweek* included people up to 35 years old (Leland & Chambers, 1999). Such wide-ranging differences in usage diminish the descriptive as well as analytical power of the category, yet however broadly defined the term reflected a trend toward demographic segmentation within the broader Hispanic category, and was still in use when this book went to print. A web site named Generation Ñ focuses on popular culture in "a space where your [L]atin heritage influences your choices but doesn't define you."[7] Not surprisingly, industry-oriented consumer research highlighted the youth market's long-term consumption potential once brand loyalties were established (Valdéz, 2002).

One-oft repeated consumer milestone that reemerged during the Latin Boom period was salsa's outselling ketchup in the United States. First reported as early as 1992, it was highlighted again a dozen years later by Mike O'Shea, Telemundo's vice president for business development, during a marketing conference at the University of Pennsylvania's Wharton School (O'Neill, 1992; Knowledge@Wharton, 2004). In the intervening years this economic landmark was cited time and again as symbolic evidence of Hispanics' influence in American culture. Yet, as with music, it emphasized Hispanic consumers' profitability with little engagement of the growing population's influence on American society beyond spending habits and corporate profit/loss sheets.

In a speech to the National Association of Latino Arts and Culture titled "What Happens AFTER a Latin Explosion?" the performance scholar Brian Herrera (2012) offered the following perspective:

> I approach the "Latin Explosion" phenomenon as a performance itself —a dance, almost, that the US culture industry does with Latino artists, performers, and audiences from time to time. And in so doing, I approach the Latin explosion as a recurring, repeatable performance scenario that affirms, typically with great flourish and fanfare, that Latinos are about to be really important within US American culture.
>
> Each Latin explosion typically begins with an excited discovery of Latinos (their numbers, their youth, their diversity, their cultural distinctiveness)—a discovery that heralds the transformative challenge Latinos are about to present to mainstream US culture. Next, the Latin explosion moves to a fascination of sorts with Latino individuals, Latino stories and Latino cultural forms, a fascination characterized by heightened visibility in all media. (Whether everyone's doing the mambo in the 1950s or the macarena in the 1990s, you can know for sure that—in a Latin explosion—the rhythm is gonna get you.) Then, just as abruptly as it began, the Latin explosion typically dissolves as the sudden fascination with all things Latino just as suddenly dissipates and mainstream cultural attention discards the Latin fad to something, to anything, else.
>
> It's like fireworks. An attention grabbing pop, followed by a spectacular display that garners excited attention, which then fizzles, leaving the breathless audience to await the next explosion.

There was a two-decade gap between the Latin explosions covered by this book; it will be interesting to assess the state of Spanish-language television when the next one detonates.

Unfortunately, very little research, either academic or industry-oriented, has interrogated the roles of Hispanic-oriented media in promoting or probing the Latin Boom. The driving interest at the turn of the millennium was the Boom's influence over mainstream consumers. (For example, one article emphasized Latin music sales in a historically non-Hispanic state concluding, "When the road to superstardom runs through Utah, that always helps" [Pellegrini, 1999].) Certainly Spanish-language television and other Hispanic-oriented media promoted Latin artists and reported their cross-over successes. Yet how did they situate audiences to interpret the implications for Hispanic influence in U.S. society, Hispanic collective identity, cultural relations with other population groups and similar topics? Reports and analysis from the Boom period emphasize greater consumer spending, advertiser expenditures and growing numbers of media outlets, but say very little about the sociological aspects. Analysis of how ethnic media frame and engage their target audience groups' status offers fertile terrain for future research that could elucidate the nature and consequences of such ethnic booms in an increasingly diverse United States.

Spanish-Language Internet Portals

As the Internet transitioned from a specialized to mass medium in the mid-1990s, concerns about a digital divide surfaced. Prior to the 1990s, the networked computer was generally regarded as an information device, not a platform for commerce or distributing news and entertainment content. Advocates for less advantaged populations became concerned about such groups' political, economic and educational standing and opportunities if they did not catch up and keep up with computer and Internet technology (Mossberger, Tolbert & Stansbury, 2003). A study by Cheskin Research "found that 42 percent of the nation's 9.3 million Hispanic households had a computer … represent[ing] a 68 percent increase over 1998, compared with a 43 percent increase in computer ownership for the general population" (Hafner, 2000). About 39% of U.S. Hispanics were online (Sutter & Wentz, 2001), and a study conducted in late 2002 reported that half of the respondents had entered the Internet for the first time in 2000 or after— double the rate of the national average (cited in Swartz, 2003). These two examples of Hispanic overindexing on new technologies became a trend in the first dozen years of the 2000s, as subsequent discussions will show.

Network Websites

In 1997, Telemundo's New York affiliate, WNJU, claimed it was the first U.S. Spanish-language TV station to release its full newscast on the Internet (Galetto, 1997). Some content originated from *CBS TeleNoticias*, Telemundo's national news provider at the time, and links to news sources from around Latin America appeared alongside local information relevant to immigrants, residents and Spanish-dominant citizens. This format followed a model that ethnic media has used for two centuries in combining news from countries of origin with local information of particular relevance to immigrant communities. Univision became the nation's first Spanish-language television network to launch its website, *univision.com*, in 1999. Within a year it began attracting seven million unique visitors per month, according to ABC Interactive (cited in Sutter & Wentz, 2001). Also in 1999 the company established Univision Online, an affiliated enterprise intended to coordinate audience interaction with various company contact points (Brownlee, 1999). A subsequent study identified *univision.com* as the most visited U.S. Spanish-language website from 2000 to 2006 (Univision.com touts, 2006). Not surprisingly, this distinction, among other factors, caught advertisers' attention; in 2002 *univision.com* added 66 new advertisers,[8] increasing its base by 500%. About three-quarters were stand-alone contracts, and the remainder were cross-platform deals with Univision broadcast and/or cable (Univision web site, 2002). Unlike other services discussed below, *univision.com* focused solely on the U.S.; in 2007 the site added a video portal allowing users to access clips from Univision TV shows, interviews with Hispanic celebrities, music videos and news segments.[9]

For its part, Telemundo partnered with multiple Internet portals prior to 2008. Early in the decade, *espanol.com* and *quepasa.com* hosted the network's site before it established a more consistent presence with *telemundo. yahoo.com* in 2006. The press release announcing the merger of *Yahoo! en español* with *telemundo.com* included much of the familiar hyperbole from the so-called dot-com era including: "win-win," "expand capabilities," "game changer," "unbeatable platform," and "integrative and immersive media experience" (Yahoo!, NBC, 2006). However, in 2008 Telemundo moved again, to MSN Latino. The likely motivations were MSN's ability to offer robust video, ad-serving technology and international channels along with MSN Latino itself (Telemundo breaks, 2008). Like the Univision site, it featured promotional material for Telemundo television shows, with strong emphasis on feminine beauty and sensuality as well as links to other media under its corporate umbrella. Azteca América, a network whose Mexican origins and growth in the U.S. are discussed below, presented a less commercially-saturated website than its competitors in mid-2015. This is somewhat surprising given the parent company's origins in Mexico's retail sector where it developed a synergy between merchandising and its broadcasting interests through *todito.com*, its Internet portal. Azteca América's Mexican base and market position as a distant third network may account for the less prominent advertising.

In addition to generating advertising revenue, the networks encouraged viewer input and interaction via the Internet, of course. In 2003 Univision aired *Rebeca*, a *telenovela* for which plot lines were determined in part by audience feedback through *univision.com*. Viewers' preferences as expressed online influenced the outcome of three male characters' competition for the female protagonist's affections (Sutter, 2003a). Telemundo began offering online access to some of its programs in 2007, but was less focused on users' influence over Internet-based content, at least in this early stage of development. More recent Internet-based initiatives by the Spanish-language networks are discussed in the next chapter.

Other Hispanic-oriented Internet Portals

Spanish-language television networks were not alone in seeking Hispanic Internet surfers for their portals. In addition to Yahoo!, other mainstream portals that spun off Spanish-language channels included America Online, AT&T, Prodigy, Excite at Home, Lycos and Microsoft/MSN; this brief discussion focuses on independent start-ups and those affiliated with offshore companies. We must bear in mind that early in its mass-use phase the Internet had a built-in demographic filter of sorts—only the more educated and affluent population groups were encountering commercial appeals on line and/or engaging in e-commerce. This had important implications in Latin America and the U.S. Spanish-language sector. One company's struggles also revealed structural limitations on portals operating in Latin America as Internet use expanded.

Based in New York, StarMedia was the first major Internet portal to target both Latin America and the U.S. Hispanic sector. The company emerged in 1996 and began trading publicly in May 1999 when its share price increased 74%, but did not turn a profit thereafter (Block, 1999; Barlas, 2001). StarMedia raised capital again in May 2001, partly from BellSouth. In a vivid illustration of how some Internet companies' fortunes changed drastically in this period, the stock price fell from a high of $70 in July 1999 to just 38 cents in November 2001 (Romero, 2001). Among the reasons attributed to StarMedia's failure was insufficient e-commerce growth in Latin America due to limited credit card use, consumer distrust of online shopping and erratic package delivery (Barlas, 2001).

Yupi.com launched in 1997 from Miami Beach, an area that became known as "Silicon Beach,"[10] for its concentration of dot-com startups (Adams, 2000). Its founder was a Dominican investment banker, Carlos Cardona. In 1999, *yupi.com* acquired CiudadFutura (Future City), one of the first online communities for Spanish speakers. Two years later the struggling portal was acquired by *t1msn*, Microsoft Corp.'s Spanish-language joint venture with Telmex (Sutter & Wentz, 2001).

Quepasa.com emerged in mid-1998, and the following year mounted a national promotion campaign via billboards, radio and television with messages featuring one of its minority investors, the singer Gloria Estefan.[11] Telemundo acquired a 15% share of the company in 1999, the same year it began trading on the NASDAQ stock exchange. After being dropped from the exchange and liquidating its assets in December 2000 during the dot-com crash, *quepasa.com* changed ownership and relaunched in 2002 (Tharp, 2000). The portal abandoned its news and information orientation in 2008 in favor of a social networking emphasis. For its part, *Espanol.com* was a short-lived venture, opening in 1999 and closing a year later after failing to raise sufficient funding (Adios to Espanol.com, 2001).

Spain's telecommunications giant Telefónica created *terra.com* in 1998, when fewer than 10% of Spanish citizens were online. However, the company discovered fertile ground in the Americas: by 2000 it was largest Internet service provider in Chile, Guatemala and Peru, and the second largest in two major markets, Brazil and Mexico (Lynch, 2000). In 1999 *terra.com* was the only non-U.S. firm ranked among the world's top 20 Internet companies (Tremlett, 2000). *Terra.com* inaugurated its U.S. service in January 2000 in partnership with IDT, a long-distance phone provider. The partners announced an ambitious marketing plan to spend $65 to $85 million in their first year of operation and in early 2000 announced a content partnership with MTV Latino (Simpson, 2000).

Elsitio.com, based in Argentina, made an initial public offering in December 1999 that generated $131 million. In 2001 the company merged with Ibero-American Media Partners, a joint venture of Venezuela's Cisneros group (minority investors in Univision) and the Houston-based private equity firm Hicks, Muse, Tate & Furst, which became increasingly involved in financing Hispanic-oriented electronic media. The new venture was named Claxson Interactive Group. *Elsitio.com* experienced more trouble in 2002, reducing staff and scaling back its operations to Argentina, Mexico, Chile, Uruguay and Brazil (Ramirez, 2002).

Like many other dot-com ventures of the period, none of these Spanish-language portals generated significant profits. They attracted attention and investment with their potential to produce revenue as more Spanish-speaking consumers began spending online, but operating costs were high and revenue streams limited. The proliferation of Spanish-language Internet sites parallels the Latin Boom as well as reports on Hispanic population growth related to the 2000 U.S. Census (Benitez, 2000; Klein, 2000). Although the dot-com bubble's bursting in spring 2000 reduced the field of competitors in rapid and dramatic fashion, the Hispanic market's digital dimensions gained visibility in the media and popular culture. Commercial Internet development in Mexico merits brief discussion before we turn our attention back to television.

In 2001, the research firm Jupiter Media estimated 2.2 million computer users in Mexico, up from only 300,000 in 1994; Jupiter projected 12.7 million users by 2005, in a country of approximately 100 million (Cevallos, 2000; Jacobs, 2001). Half-a-dozen companies launched portals to tap the burgeoning market, although their growth slowed with the economic downturn in 2001. Prior to television networks' entry, the portal market was largely shared among the aforementioned StarMedia, *terra.com*, and *elsitio. com* services. Another major player, *t1msn*, the joint venture between the telecommunications giant Telmex and Microsoft, launched in March 2000.

Televisión Azteca was the first Mexican network to acquire its portal, *todito.com*, in a partnership with Grupo Dataflux in 1999. In addition to the niche-oriented interactive channels, live chat, e-commerce and classified ads found on many portals, *todito.com* offered digitized streaming video content of TV Azteca's programs and numerous tie-ins to its various shows, celebrities and advertisers. It bears repeating that *todito.com*, which closed in 2007, provided a third (cyber) leg to the synergy between Televisión Azteca and Elektra retail stores—Elektra sold computer equipment, and various goods and services from other Salinas Pliego family enterprises were hawked online (Todito.com launches, 2000). Although Televisa's portal *esmas.com* did not launch until May 2000, the company's stock value received a strong bump in December 1999 amid anticipation that it would join the Telmex/Microsoft venture (Tricks, 2000). At the unveiling of *esmas.com* Televisa's CEO, Emilio Azcárraga Jean called the Internet "the most important project for Televisa today" emphasizing that "all the Group's resources—magazines, records, music, production, radio and television—will support [the] new project" (Crane, 2000). Indeed many of the competitive advantages that Televisa enjoyed over TV Azteca engaged in the online competition.

Azteca América

Azteca América launched its U.S. operations in July 2001 with a single station, KAZA, in Los Angeles. It was originally conceived as a joint venture between a program provider, Televisión Azteca, the network that reintroduced competition to Mexican television in the mid-1990s, and Pappas Telecasting Co., a California-based television station group. Harry Pappas, who along with two brothers developed a national chain of successful independent and affiliated stations beginning in 1971, had been eyeing the Hispanic television market for a decade prior to entering discussions with TV Azteca in 1998 (McClellan, 2000). The original partnership plans followed a familiar model: an 80–20 ownership split between the U.S. and Mexican companies, respectively, in order to conform to foreign ownership restrictions. Not surprisingly, the network would initially rely on content from Mexico, especially prime time *telenovelas* and significant portions of news content. Domestic contributions would principally consist of talk and magazine shows during the day parts (McClellan, 2000). However, Pappas backed away from the original arrangement in October 2001; consequently Azteca held 100% ownership of the network, but had no financial stake in the affiliated and independent stations that broadcast its content and advertising. As Piñon (2011) points out, this led to some unprecedented distribution arrangements, including local marketing agreements whereby commercial time was divided between national and local/regional spots instead of a 50–50 revenue split as originally conceived.

At the turn of the century, Univision held a dominant position in the market, reaching 92% of the U.S. Hispanic audience and claiming 75% of an estimated $1.1 billion in Hispanic advertising (McClellan, 2000). NBC's acquisition of Telemundo promised to place the network on firmer competitive footing. What space, one might reasonably ask, was left for a new entrant to the U.S. Spanish-language television market? Harry Pappas emphasized that because the 15% annual growth rate in Hispanic advertising spending "lifted all boats," the new network could capture new business without having to lure advertisers and audiences from established networks[12] (McClellan, 2000, p. 27). Azteca América prided itself on offering advertising opportunities to Hispanic-owned small businesses that couldn't afford to advertise on Univision (Romano, 2005). Network representatives cited competitive advantages derived from Azteca's identity as a Mexican product, and brand recognition among viewers maintaining close ties with Mexico—recall that around 60% of the Hispanic population counted in the 2000 U.S. Census was of Mexican origin (Piñon, 2011).[13] To the network's disadvantage, most of the signals reached audiences through low-power stations, cable systems transmitting such stations, or satellite, sometimes resulting in poor over-the-air signal quality and/or difficult to locate cable channels (Piñon, 2011).

Azteca América's station rollout was encumbered by an economic downturn related to the dot-com bust, which tightened credit and was exacerbated by economic uncertainty in the wake of the September 11, 2001 terrorist attacks. Univision and Telemundo also hampered the network's growth through their own expansion efforts. Univision's purchase of USA Network, which launched as Telefutura in 2002, is discussed below. For its part, NBC Universal responded within days when Pappas failed to close its acquisition of KXTX in Dallas/Fort Worth, a property which had already been highlighted in the trade press as Azteca's flagship station and technical operations center (e.g., McClellan, 2000).[14]

Despite these challenges, Azteca América steadily expanded. KAZA in LA reached 18% of *national* Hispanic television households, and by December 2002 affiliate stations had been added in San Francisco and Houston as well as the key New York and Miami markets, extending the coverage to 52% (Piñon, 2011; Tegel, 2002). By May 2003, 24 affiliated stations were available to nearly 60% of the Spanish-speaking audience (Wentz, 2003). In 2005 Azteca América was carried in 42 markets, many with low-power stations; these numbers expanded to 52 markets and 89% coverage in 2008 and 66 markets in 2011 (Romano, 2005; Azteca America leads, 2011). These strides in coverage growth were achieved largely through affiliation agreements with station groups, which led to simultaneous conversions of multiple stations, rather than individual changes. Besides Pappas Telecasting's six stations—which withdrew in 2007—other groups included Una Vez Mas, owner of 26 Azteca América affiliates in early 2014, mostly in Texas; and McGraw Hill TVC (acquired by E.W. Scripps in 2011), with properties in three Colorado cities as well as San Diego and Bakersfield, California (Piñon, 2007; Ariens, 2011). Some Azteca affiliates located in markets with an English-language station from the same ownership group have co-produced local news as a cost-saving measure (Romano, 2005).

When Pappas Telecasting reneged on its plan to own and operate an Azteca América station group, it criticized the network's non-competitive programming and poor ratings performance (Bachman, 2007). Station KAZA continued to be operated by Azteca, a situation opposed by NBC Universal, as explained below. Pappas launched its own network called TuVision, but within a year several affiliates sought Chapter 11 bankruptcy protection and the network ceased operations in 2009.

Clearly it has been a challenge for any upstart broadcaster to break Univision's and Telemundo's well-established U.S. network duopoly. Azteca América originally swam against the current of pan-Hispanic appeals by differentiating its content as authentically Mexican, which was particularly problematic in Eastern cities. Thus the network shifted its branding efforts toward the pan-Hispanic in the mid-2000s, as Beck (2010) describes. After the 2006 ownership change at Univision, Azteca América claimed to be the only national level Hispanic-owned network in the U.S. (Piñon, 2011). Also in 2006 Azteca officially reached 70% Hispanic television household coverage, and was listed on the Nielsen Hispanic service, overcoming a significant obstacle with advertisers (Beck, 2010). Azteca América has achieved minor bragging points in its relatively short history, such as the strongest prime time growth for audiences age 18–49 (up 38%) in February 2011—Telemundo increased 8% and neither Univision nor Telefutura posted positive primetime growth—yet we must keep in mind that Azteca's audience base is significantly smaller than its competitors, leaving ample room for growth (Azteca America leads, 2011).

Azteca América is a 21st century example of the close relationship between Mexican and U.S. Hispanic television sectors that has characterized the industry from its start. Televisión Azteca in Mexico provided leadership in expanding the network through affiliation agreements while providing the network's core programming. Yet as a relative newcomer running in third place behind Univision with approximately 70% market share and Telemundo with 20%, the network faces a formidable challenge. A longstanding conflict with NBC Universal has not helped matters.

Azteca–NBC Conflicts

The Televisión Azteca–NBC relationship dates to the early 1990s when Azteca obtained the former Imevisión network from Mexican government and NBC's evening news program anchored by Tom Brokaw was retransmitted on Televisión Azteca stations with a Spanish voiceover. As discussed in the previous chapter, the companies' relationship became adversarial later in the 1990s, leading to a proposed settlement in 2000 whereby NBC would pay $26 million in exchange for a 1% stake in the company (Mandel-Campbell, 2000). However, the deal fell through when TV Azteca backed out, claiming that NBC had not held up its side of the agreement to provide programming and technical assistance (Malkin, 2006). Speculation had surfaced before the aborted settlement that NBC might become the U.S. partner in Azteca América. However, NBC's acquiring Telemundo in 2001 positioned the networks as competitors, rekindling past hostilities. The failed deal led to a series of tit-for-tat actions on both sides of the Rio Grande, some mundane and others dramatic.

In mid-2001, Telemundo, while still under Sony/Media Liberty's leadership, filed a complaint with the FCC claiming that Azteca affiliate KIDN-TV interfered with the signal of their own station, KVEA (Consoli, 2001a). (KIDN-TV switched its call letters to KAZA in June, 2001.) Telemundo continued to challenge Azteca's presence in Los Angeles, claiming that a foreign entity unlawfully controlled a U.S. broadcast property. The FCC was not persuaded and permitted Azteca to operate the station under a local licensing agreement, even after Pappas Telecasting broke ties with the station and network. Telemundo's effort to discredit and otherwise challenge Azteca's U.S. operations intensified after an incident in Mexico City that could easily have appeared on a racy news magazine show at either network.

On September 22, 2006, Televisión Azteca reporters, cameramen and attorneys accompanied an estimated 50 security guards and armed Mexico City police who stormed the studios of Nostromo América (Belman, 2006; Malkin, 2006). The production company was recording an episode of *Quinceañera*, a reality show in which 14-year-old girls and their mothers compete to win an elaborate coming-of-age party for the girl, along with an opportunity to appear in future Telemundo programming. Production was halted and equipment, wardrobes and other assets seized. At issue was the participation of the producer Giorgio Aresu and host Alan Tacher who, Azteca claimed, violated non-compete clauses in their contracts by participating in the show (TV Azteca embarga, 2006). Although the Televisión Azteca lawyers carried a judge's injunction, many interpreted the raid as a poorly masked effort to exclude Telemundo from the Mexican market shortly after it had applied for a national broadcasting license. During the campaign that brought him to power, Mexico's president-elect, Felipe Calderón, advocated increased competition in Mexican industries, citing television specifically (Malkin, 2006). Telemundo, facing competition in the U.S. from Televisa and TV Azteca, sought to compete on their home turf through an alliance with billionaire Isaac Saba Raffoul of Grupo Casa Saba. In addition to the studio raid, this potential alliance also engendered aggressive, negative reporting regarding Mexican pharmaceuticals—Saba Raffoul's principal industry—on TV Azteca and Televisa news programs (Malkin, 2006).

Telemundo and the professionals at issue emphasized Azteca's anti-competitive behavior in their public denunciations of the raid. Giorgio Aresu claimed he had never actually signed a contract with the network, and Alan Tacher said he was being treated like other performers, including Mauricio Ockman, for whom Azteca "made life impossible" after they left for jobs at Telemundo or elsewhere in the U.S. (Embarga TV Azteca, 2006).

Telemundo's president Donald Browne stated, "We're looking for just a reasonable playing field—not even even—just to be able to show our product in Mexico" (Malkin, 2006). After the raid, NBC Universal renewed its (unsuccessful) effort against Azteca's involvement at station KAZA in Los Angeles, reporting in its complaint, "some of the police officers were riding in a TV Azteca van with the logo obscured with white cardboard, while others arrived in police vehicles with their license plates removed," and also emphasizing the Security and Exchange Commission's investigation of Azteca CEO Ricardo Salinas Pliego for fraud (James, 2006). Luis J. Echarte, chairman of Azteca América countered, "we view this as a very simple ploy to damage our reputation. They came to Mexico and they violated our laws, and then they went back up to the States, and now this" (James, 2006).

The deep pockets and information gathering/reporting capacities of large media enterprises such as Televisión Azteca and NBC Universal have the potential to magnify conflicts when they occur, as we will see again at the beginning of the next chapter in a showdown between Televisa and Univision. The Azteca-NBC conflict emphasizes yet again the international dimension of U.S. Spanish-language television, a characteristic has remained constant through changing political, economic, social and technological contexts since the industry's origins.

Telefutura

For its part, Univision responded to competition from Azteca América by acquiring available television stations, making the upstart network's expansion more difficult. Certainly there were other motivations behind Univision's purchase of USA Network's 13-station group in December 2000 for $1.1 billion cash and another $100 million in debt, but taking a large group of stations located in key cities off the market was high among them (Sutter & DiOrio, 2000). As noted above, the Telecommunications Act of 1996 and subsequent deregulatory actions by the FCC stimulated numerous mergers and media buyouts in the years bracketing the new millennium. A policy change that was particularly important for Univision's acquisition of USA Network concerned duopolies, or one entity's ownership of two television stations in a given market. The key provision in the revised rules "permit[ted] common ownership of two television stations within the same DMA if eight full-power independent television stations (commercial and noncommercial) will remain post-merger, and one of the stations is not among the top four-ranked stations in the market based on audience share" (FCC, 1999). Thus Univision and Telefutura stations (the new network name adopted in 2001) could legally operate in the same market.[15]

The USA acquisition, approved by the Federal Trade Commission in May 2001, created duopolies for Univision in seven markets: Chicago, Dallas, Houston, Los Angeles, Miami, New York and Tampa. Economizing on operating expenses in these cities was very attractive, and the acquisition provided Univision a station ownership foothold in five additional markets: Atlanta, Boston, Cleveland, Orlando and Philadelphia (Consoli, 2001b; Sutter & DiOrio 2000). Collectively, these Telefutura stations represented a formidable addition to Univision's existing stable of 44 broadcast stations in 27 markets nationwide, 25 owned and operated and 19 affiliated (Liebeskind, 2002). With such a strong national footprint and significant coverage overlap in key local Hispanic markets, the two networks needed to be clearly differentiated. Pursuing a "counterprogramming" strategy, Telefutura would focus on younger audiences and men by broadcasting music programs, movies and sports, especially during primetime when *telenovelas* dominated Univision's schedule. That's not to say that *novelas* would not appear on Telefutura—they broadcast during the day so the network could attract other demographics during peak viewing hours. Not surprisingly, questions arose whether Univision would cannibalize its own audience with Telefutura; Univision said it expected the new network to draw about 25% of its audience from Univision itself, 25% from Telemundo, and the remaining 50 percent from a combination of increased TV viewing and attracting new viewers (Consoli, 2001b).

Once again the audience for Spanish-language television grew with the appearance of a new option. National viewership of prime time Spanish-language television increased by four share points shortly after Telefutura's first broadcast, available to 72% of Hispanic households, on January 14, 2002. As Morales (2002) explains, "the core of this new audience came mostly from English-language television, which declined during TeleFutura's first two weeks of broadcast by three share points." At the local level, there were 50% to 60% increases in Spanish-language TV viewership recorded in Chicago, Los Angeles and Miami with minimal impact on Univision or Telemundo viewing (Downey, 2002). Telemundo later published its own report that emphasized the fleeting nature of the phenomenon, indicating that Telefutura's audience had declined nearly 40% a month after its premiere (Morales, 2002).

Univision did not expect immediate results from the new network, and Wall Street concurred, with one analyst predicting Telefutura would lose between $15 and $20 million in its first year (Stamler, 2002). In any case, Telefutura fortified Univision's dominant position in U.S. Spanish-language television at a time when new competitors were entering the field and a deep-pocketed corporation was acquiring Telemundo. Revenue from the Univision-Telefutura-Galavisión-Hispanic Broadcasting Corp. nexus helped double Univision's earnings in the third quarter of 2003 compared to a year earlier (Sutter, 2003b). By the first half of 2004, Telefutura's lineup of talk and variety shows made it the second most popular Spanish network in the early morning and daytime slots among adults 18 to 49 years old (Hoag, 2004). This success presented Telemundo with a two-front battle just as the new owner, NBC, took control. During 2002–2004, a key transitional period for Telemundo, the network gained 119,000 prime time adult viewers compared to Telefutura's 216,000 (Hoag, 2004); Univision's competitive strategy bore fruit. Telefutura relaunched as UniMás in January 2013, a topic the next chapter takes up in greater detail (James, 2013).

The Univision–Hispanic Broadcasting Corp. Merger

In the same deregulatory atmosphere that helped inspire the Telefutura launch in June 2002, Univision announced its intention to merge with Hispanic Broadcasting Corp. (HBC), the country's largest Spanish-language radio group, which earned nearly double the revenues of the closest competitor, Entravision.[16] The nearly $3 billion deal would bring 68 Spanish-language radio stations (18 AM and 50 FM) under Univision control. Univision did not own radio stations outright at the time, but was a 30% equity partner in Entravision, which owned and operated 55. HBC's stations were concentrated in states having large Hispanic populations, some in the same cities as Entravision stations. The intended acquisition was consistent with the trend of large-scale media mergers during the dozen years bracketing the new millennium, indicating to some observers the Spanish-language sector's rise in prominence. Yet the sector's status became a sticking point in approving the controversial deal as opposing sides debated whether it should continue being considered a separate market, or lumped in with the general market. A proposed (further) relaxation of broadcast ownership rules during the approval process brought additional public and congressional scrutiny to the FCC and the Univision-HBC deal at a time when Spanish-language media were outperforming many of their English-language counterparts in broadcasting and music.[17]

The Department of Justice (DoJ) approved the merger, with conditions, in February 2003. The department's concerns centered around Entravision owning 49 television stations, most of them Univision affiliates, and as noted above, 55 radio stations in many of the same markets having HBC stations (Sandoval, 2006; Ho, 2003a). The DoJ, as Stoll and Goldfein (2003, p. 3) explained, was concerned about "anticompetitive skewing of Univision/HBC's post-acquisition competitive incentives" if Univision continued to wield significant influence over Entravision's governance. Therefore, the DoJ served an injunction prohibiting the acquisition without limits on Univision's influence (Dept. of Justice, 2003). The concern was that given the high degree of ownership concentration in U.S. Spanish-language radio, advertising buyers would be forced to do business with Univision, which would benefit from advertising sales at either company, but would likely favor advertising contracts with HBC because they yielded higher profits (Serratore, 2004). To diminish potential conflicts of interest, Univision agreed to several conditions: reducing its Entravision stake from 30% to 15% in three years and 10% in six years, converting its shares to non-voting status, relinquishing its veto power over radio station sales, and forfeiting its seat on the Entravision board (Sutter 2003c; FCC approves, 2003;

Sandoval, 2006). The agreement satisfied the DoJ but, predictably, other interests objected for a variety of reasons.

The loudest protestations from within the industry emanated from Telemundo and Spanish Broadcasting Systems (SBS), a Miami-based network of 27 radio stations that had failed in an effort to merge with HBC. Telemundo argued that the union would concentrate too much power in one entity at a time when half of all U.S. Hispanics sought news and entertainment from Spanish-language broadcasting (Ho, 2003a). The network also asserted that the FCC would never approve such a deal in the general market,[18] raising the issue whether the Spanish-language sector should continue to be regulated separately. Univision countered that it competed with both English- and Spanish-language networks because many Hispanics viewed both, and that Spanish should be considered a different format, not a distinct market (Ho, 2003a). For its part, SBS echoed Telemundo's concerns about competition, arguing that Univision's control over Hispanic broadcasting would increase from 50% to 69% after the merger; power that would be wielded by Univision's non-Hispanic ownership (Halonen, 2003). In a common refrain, those opposing the merger argued that so much control concentrated in a single player would reinforce barriers to entry for potential competitors while reducing the diversity of content available for audiences (Serratore, 2004).

Some brief background indicates how the Univision-HBC merger became a political football in Washington D.C. in mid-2003. Media regulation had long been a contentious issue, due in part to a highly politicized environment and sometimes-cozy relationships with industry at the FCC (Crowley, 2011). During the latter 1990s and early 2000s a number of mergers and acquisitions of large media players created huge conglomerates whose holdings and interests spanned the globe (Bagdikian, 2000; McChesney, 2004). In June 2003, only months after the invasion of Iraq that further polarized U.S. public opinion, the FCC announced ownership rule changes that would raise limits on the number of media enterprises a company could own in a specific market. Interestingly, although the FCC commissioners split along party lines—Republicans Michael K. Powell (Chairman), Kathleen Q. Abernathy and Kevin J. Martin favoring and Democrats Jonathan S. Adelstien and Michael J. Copps opposing—many Republicans in congress and elsewhere resisted the changes, responding to their constituents and/or anticipating a consequent narrowing range of news and opinion. The rule change's basic provisions were to relax limits on cross-ownership of radio and television stations as well as newspaper/broadcast station ownership in medium and large markets; raise the cap on television ownership in large markets from three to four; and raise the percentage of the national audience that TV networks could reach through owned-and-operated stations from 35% to 45% (Labaton, 2003). A flood of responses followed as an array of individual citizens and organizations, both for-profit and not, expressed their opinions to the FCC and congress.[19] The timing of the Univision-HBC case, its potential impact on the Hispanic vote—recall that earlier in 2003 the Census Bureau announced that Hispanics had become the largest U.S. minority—and the ethnic ownership issue combined to garner substantial press attention.

The National Hispanic Policy Institute (NHPI) was among the groups encouraging that attention, helping Spanish Broadcasting System to spread its message (Mulkern & Farrell, 2003).[20] Besides the aforementioned domination of Spanish-language broadcasting, the NHPI warned of Hispanic media control by non-Hispanics, and Univision becoming a mouthpiece of conservatism. The first issue echoed the battle for control of Univision in 1986 in which Anglo-owned Hallmark Cards and First Capital of Chicago prevailed over a Hispanic investment group, TVL. In 2003, although the majority of Univision's upper management was Hispanic, its chief executive officer and principal investor, A. Jerrold Perenchio, was not. Opponents of the merger also emphasized that HBC's CEO, McHenry Tichenor was also non-Hispanic, and Republican (Gregor, 2003). However, little attention focused on how Perenchio's ethnicity had affected Univision's performance during the prior decade; the concerns were based on a long-standing assumption that ethnic media best meet the interest, convenience and necessity of their audiences when managed by members of the same ethnic group. Such thinking led to a bill by some high-profile U.S. senators as Crabtree and Sutter (2003) explain:

> Democratic Sens. Hillary Clinton (N.Y.), Edward Kennedy (Mass.) and Mark Pryor (Ark.) introduced a bill that would force the FCC and Congress to analyze the effect of media concentration on Americans who rely on minority-language broadcasts for their news, information and entertainment. While the bill could not prevent the Univision deal from going through, it would address serious concerns about minority media concentration. Specifically, the legislation would require the FCC to submit a report to Congress by Jan. 1 on the "ownership and control" of broadcast television and radio stations serving language minorities.

Senate Bill 1525 was introduced by Senator Kennedy on June 31, 2003 then referred to the Committee on Commerce, Science, and Transportation where, apparently, it languished. Univision's public response to these challenges was, "efforts to tar this merger as a non-Hispanic takeover of Hispanic media is a case of mistaken identity at best and a competitor's smear job at worst" (Halonen, 2003).

The second issue also focused on Jerrold Perenchio, a leading contributor to Republican political candidates. He was especially generous with California Governor Pete Wilson—no friend to most Hispanics for his hard line on immigrants—and both George Bushes, contributing more than $710,000 to Bush election campaigns (Grover, Grow & Smith, 2004). Leading Democratic senators including Clinton, Kennedy and Tom Daschle

(SD) warned of a Spanish-language equivalent of conservative-leaning Fox News on Univision, with no countervailing perspectives available in Spanish due to the network's market control (Mulkern & Farrell, 2003). A network spokeswoman challenged the assertion that Mr. Perenchio influenced Univision news and would do so at HBC: "his political views are as irrelevant as those of [The Walt Disney Co. chief Michael] Eisner or [Viacom CEO Sumner] Redstone" (Halonen, 2003). The statement also underscored Univision's claim that it competed in the general market, not just the Spanish-language sector, a topic discussed in further detail below.

Another ominous scenario projected by opponents of the Univision-HBC merger featured the radio giant Clear Channel Communications whose rapid growth was emblematic of deregulatory largesse to some observers, and which commonly served as the media consolidation boogeyman. Prior to the merger Clear Channel was HBC's largest shareholder, with a 26% stake. Spanish Broadcasting Systems filed suit against both Clear Channel and HBC on June 12, 2002, the day that the Univision-HBC merger was announced, claiming the companies had tried to weaken its market position prior to an acquisition attempt[21] (Spanish broadcaster sues, 2002). Univision stated that following the merger Clear Channel would hold only a 3 percent voting interest in Univision, with no board seats or involvement in the company's operations (Halonen, 2003). As it turned out, Univision bought back Clear Channel's shares in January 2004, and later that year Clear Channel began building its own national stable of Spanish-language radio stations (Leeds, 2004). Clear Channel's involvement in the merger, although minor, likely the raised the political stakes for some participants and observers alike.

To gain more positive ground when it thought approval was imminent (although not occurring for another six weeks), in early August 2003 Univision released a list of 85 national and regional Hispanic organizations that endorsed its merger with HBC. The list included some organizations the reader will recognize as Univision opponents on prior actions: the League of United Latin American Citizens, the National Hispanic Media Coalition, the National Puerto Rican Foundation, and the National Council of La Raza (Crabtree & Sutter, 2003). The last of these expressed some reservations and claimed to have secured a commitment that Univision would air additional, higher quality news and public affairs programs on both television and radio (Kirkpatrick & Shah, 2003). Univision also gained support from the Democratic Congressional Hispanic Caucus and other prominent Hispanic Democrats. FCC Chairman Michael Powell received supportive letters from Democratic congressmen such as Ciro Rodriguez (TX) and José Serrano (NY), citing the merger's benefits to Spanish-language media and the Hispanic audience (Chairman and senior, 2003). New Mexico's Hispanic Democratic governor Bill Richardson also sent a letter of support—it was reported that he had received a $167,667 campaign donation from Chartwell Holding, a real estate company controlled by A. Jerrold Perenchio (Grover, Grow & Smith, 2004; Watzman, 2012).

Such was the political backdrop as the FCC's review of the merger dragged on longer than anticipated, due in significant part to fallout from the agency's proposed ownership rule changes and dissent among the commissioners (FCC delays, 2003). The FCC approved the merger on September 8, 2003, but required the company to sell two HBC stations—one each in Houston and Albuquerque—to comply with ownership caps. The business deal was consummated shortly afterward, on September 22. The commissioners split along party lines, as they had on the ownership rule changes: three Republican commissioners approving and two Democrats opposing. The dissenting commissioners, Adelstein and Copps, were strident in their objections, which were appended to the commission's decision; the following are select quotes that the press culled from the dissent (FCC, 2003).

- "The company is aptly named Univision—'one vision'—because that describes what is likely from Spanish-language media from now on."
- "For millions of Spanish speakers who rely exclusively or predominantly on Spanish-language media, this merger threatens a dramatic loss of diversity, competition and localism."
- "Today's decision takes media consolidation to new and threatening heights for those who receive their news and entertainment in Spanish. One company will be the gatekeeper to the news and entertainment that this population will receive over their airwaves."
- "Latinos are under-represented not only in boardrooms, but in newsrooms as well … it is cause for alarm because additional consolidation can only reduce opportunities for Latinos and other minorities in this country."
- "Rather than allowing further media concentration by Univision, we should have focused instead on ways to promote more minority participation in our media … before the next wave of consolidation makes a complete mockery of that objective."

The FCC's Republican majority of Powell, Abernathy and Martin took a different view, finding that the HBC license transfer was in the public interest and convenience, erected no barriers to market entry, would not undermine diversity, and would not create a shortage of media outlets for Spanish speaking audiences (Serratore, 2004). They argued the merger "will give Hispanic media a better opportunity to compete against big media companies, capturing more advertising revenue to allow it to expand unique language and cultural offerings to its audiences" (Ho, 2003). Furthermore, the Republic commissioners viewed treating Hispanics as "an insular group removed from the general mainstream of news, entertainment and information [as] troubling … that approach could prove a limitless notion by opening up claims that there should be language-specific, or even viewpoint-specific, ownership rules" (FCC approves, 2003). Thus the deep ideological and partisan divides that characterized U.S. politics during the first two decades of the 21st century were represented in the positions taken by FCC commissioners on a central case impacting Spanish-language television's development.

Appeals and Analysis of the Univision–HBC Merger

As one would expect, the National Hispanic Policy Institute and other organizations appealed the FCC's decision in federal court, arguing that it was "arbitrary, capricious and violate[d] well-established FCC rules and policies" (Seiberg, 2003). The complaint centered on the FCC's definition of Univision's product market, which followed the network's own assertion, "Spanish-language media is simply a format and should not be considered a separate market ... Univision competes directly with both English and Spanish-language networks for viewers and advertisers" (Univision spokeswoman Stephanie Pillersdorf cited in Ho, 2003b). This position favored the merger's approval because Univision held a minor presence in the general market, yet enjoyed a commanding presence among Spanish-language media, and would become the dominant player in radio as well as television. In specific regulatory terms, the appeal focused on Univision's investment in Entravision, and whether it was "attributable," that is, whether the investor (Univision) could exert control over the target (HBC). If an investment is declared attributable, the FCC must regulate the two media companies as if they were a single entity (Seiberg, 2003). Thus, the NHPI argued that the FCC confused the market distinctions by determining that Univision's minority investment in Entravision was attributable for television assets but not for radio—recall that Entravision owned Univision-affiliated TV stations as well as radio stations that competed against HBC outlets (Seiberg, 2003). NHPI and others also emphasized the disconnect between the DoJ treating English and Spanish as separate markets in its analysis while the FCC did not. The U.S. Court of Appeals for the District of Columbia dismissed the National Hispanic Policy Institute's challenge in April 2004, ruling that the group did not have standing to intervene in the case.

Because the market definition issue was likely to exert the greatest influence over Hispanic-oriented broadcasting in the future, legal and media scholars focused on this aspect of the Univision-HBC merger. Although they differed on federal agencies' accuracy in defining Univision's market, the scholars generally agreed that the merger processes and outcome carry implications for the future. We begin by reviewing two legal approaches. Sandoval (2006) focuses on the DoJ's review, criticizing its conclusion that Spanish and English media constitute separate markets, and expressing concern about potential "disincentives to broadcast in Spanish or other minority languages" (p. 449). The DoJ's position overlooks competition for advertising time among market players specializing in Spanish and English media, she argues, diminishing the fact that a variety of market players, including companies specializing in English radio such as Clear Channel,

Infinity, and ABC Radio, had acquired Spanish-language stations (Sandoval, 2006, p. 447). She concludes that assessments of market competition should focus on market dynamics within a geographical area rather than language difference.

Another legal scholar, Serratore (2004), takes a contrary view in arguing that both Univision and the FCC contradicted well-established positions in order to get the merger approved. Although Univision protested being treated "separate but equal" vis-à-vis English-language competitors, Serratore stresses that the network adamantly defended retaining its waiver of the advertising spot sale rule (73.658 [i], originally granted in 1978), which was only granted to "fledgling" Spanish-language broadcasters. As Spanish Broadcasting System pointed out in its complaint, the FCC had segregated Spanish-language media not only by extending the spot sales waiver for a quarter century, but also in proffering cable carriage specialty signals and waiving newspaper/broadcast television cross-ownership restrictions (Serratore, 2004). Furthermore, only a year earlier the FCC had granted NBC Universal extended time to divest of one Los Angeles television station in order to comply with ownership caps; the same courtesy was not extended to ABC network when it merged with Disney. Serratore's article concludes: "Spanish speakers deserve equal treatment and consideration from a Commission that congratulates itself on its noble goals of competition, localism and diversity. These goals should apply equally to all" (2005, p. 271).

Coffey and Sanders (2010), media scholars who research policy issues, take a demand side product market approach in analyzing the FCC's treatment of the merger. They argue that rather than conducting micro-level analysis focused exclusively on the industry, the agency should have examined macro-level impacts on the Hispanic audience. Like Serratore, they contend that English and Spanish constitute separate markets and highlight the approval's inconsistency with the FCC's past handling of Spanish-language media. In a challenge to Sandoval (2006), Coffey and Sanders (2010) emphasize media products' unique character, which comprises "the ideas and values essential to a functioning democracy," and underscore the FCC's responsibility to act in the public interest (p. 67). The authors criticize the FCC majority's view that language difference constitutes a format, not a market, imploring the agency to "become fluent in its own policy" (p. 89). Perlman and Amaya (2013) take a more critical, less legalistic approach yet, like Serratore (2004) and Coffey and Sanders (2010), express concern for the audience's well-being. Their focus is on the Hispanic population's speech rights which, when violated, contribute to the group's political disenfranchisement. The authors employ participatory democratic theory to demonstrate how U.S. regulators have consistently overlooked Hispanics' rights by mishandling diversity issues, and the narrow pursuit of neoliberal policies that favor commercial interests over communities (Perlman & Amaya, 2013).

Whatever position one takes on regulatory agencies' handling of the Univision-HBC merger or how language market boundaries should be drawn (if at all), it seems clear that the merger will influence U.S. Spanish-language broadcasting's competitive structure at least through the first quarter of the 21st century. Univision is well entrenched as the market leader and, as the next chapter illustrates, endeavors to manage market shifts such as increased attention to English media consumption by Hispanics (e.g., the Fusion network project with ABC) and mobile and online media consumption (e.g., UVideos). Telemundo and Azteca América are pursuing similar projects, of course. Among the strongest indications that Spanish-language media is encroaching on mainstream media business was the press's and political establishment's close following of the Univision–HBC merger fight, which approximated the level of attention devoted to prior English-language media mergers (Gross 2003).

Nielsen and Ratings Issues

Another indicator of Spanish-language television's maturation was its migration from a specialty service, the Nielsen Hispanic Television Index (NHTI), to the National People Meter general market index in 2006. As discussed in prior chapters, the lack of reliable ratings for Spanish-language television viewing hampered network efforts to sell advertising at optimal rates, leading to the NHTI's launch in 1992. As the networks and their audiences grew, and Spanish-language stations began to outperform English-language competitors with increasing frequency, the demand for standard comparisons increased. Yet recruiting households that adequately represented the linguistically diverse Hispanic population remained a challenge. The issue came to a head during the early 2000s as Nielsen began installing Local People Meters (LPMs)[22] in large-market television households, causing shifts in ratings data.

The sensitivity of Hispanic television household sampling surfaced before the LPMs were implemented. In mid-2000, Univision pressured Nielsen to adjust the New York metro market sample to include more Spanish-speaking households; in order to reach parity with the population statistics, the number of meters would have to increase from 21 to 43, out of 500 total (Blair, 2000). When English-language station managers got wind of this possibility they pushed back forcefully, anticipating a dip in their ratings and revenues if the sample were adjusted. Shortly thereafter Nielsen began rolling out its LPMs, first in Boston in 2002, then New York in 2004. In New York the company again faced resistance, not only from Univision but also News Corp. (the owner of UPN stations) as well as a number of civic and political organizations that were concerned about Hispanic and African American viewership being undercounted and shows canceled. The disgruntled groups were represented in their fight against Nielsen's LPMs by the Don't Count Us Out Coalition, which was partially funded by News Corp. (Univision was not a member).

The major showdown between Univision and Nielsen occurred in Los Angeles, however. On June 9, 2004 Univision sought a preliminary injunction in the Superior Court of California to prevent Nielsen from implementing its LPMs a month later. Specifically, Univision sought

> 1) to enjoin Nielsen from engaging in unfair, unlawful and deceptive business practices by launching its LPM service in Los Angeles utilizing flawed sampling and weighting methodologies; 2) to enjoin Nielsen's false and misleading advertising with respect to its LPM data; and 3) damages for trade libel.
>
> (Univision, 2004)

Univision's complaint focused on undercounting young Spanish speakers and large Hispanic families, and overstating the number of U.S. Hispanic households that speak mostly or only English.[23] Nielsen countersued within two weeks arguing that Univision made false statements regarding the LPM sample composition, weighting procedures, and differences in the ratings generated by the then current system and LPM (McClintock, 2004). Nielsen's court filing argued that Univision

> seeks to prevent the L.A. market's use of a modernized, improved and more accurate system that is already in use nationally across the United States and locally in New York and Boston, because it results in lower ratings for some of Univision's programs ... Univision seeks to influence what should be an impartial system of measuring viewers, in order to maintain inflated, less accurate ratings for certain of its programs over those of its competitors whose ratings are rising.
>
> (Hoheb, 2004)

The California court found in favor of Nielsen in early July 2004, permitting the LPM rollout to proceed. Univision vowed to continue pursuing its complaint, but within five months the two companies agreed to drop their lawsuits.

In June 2005 the companies entered a five-year contract by which Nielsen provided LPM data to Univision in 34 markets; in December they announced Univision's inclusion in the National Television Index—Nielsen's general market ratings—while the National Hispanic Television Index would continue functioning until mid-2007 (Sutter, 2005; Mandese, 2005). A similar announcement regarding Telemundo appeared shortly after, and Televisión Azteca joined the service in August 2006 (De la Fuente, 2006). This key development allowed the Spanish-language networks to begin selling advertising based on a single, unified general market sample instead of separate national Hispanic ratings, the National Hispanic Television Index, as they had since 1992. Market growth drove the change: ad spending on Spanish-language television grew from $220 million in 1992 when the NHTI launched, to $3 billion in 2006, its last full year of operation (James, 2007). The industry reached yet another maturation milestone in 2011 when the Nielsen Station Index (NSI), the basis for local ratings "sweeps," incorporated

Hispanic-oriented content. Nielsen announced that its general market panels were sufficiently representative of Hispanic households to measure their viewing behavior accurately (McCabe, 2011). As with the HBC merger only a year prior, Univision positioned itself as a stalwart market player in its contentious dealings with Nielsen. Yet the companies' reaching conciliation also showed that Univision was willing to compromise when prudent. In the next chapter we will see this pattern repeated, only a year after the Nielsen dustup as Univision locked horns with its long-time international ally, Televisa.

Labor Issues in the New Millennium

A Univision station in a relatively small yet growing market, KFTV in Fresno/ Visalia California, garnered national news coverage in spring 2000 as eight union workers staged a hunger strike to protest their low wages. The employees had joined the Communication Workers of America the previous summer and were discouraged by the slow pace of negotiations with station management; they claimed that although the station led local ratings, they were paid far less than counterparts at English-language stations—$35,000 versus $80,000 annually in the news anchor position, for example (Univision workers, 2000). Univision management at the station and headquarters were characteristically tight-lipped regarding the dispute, although the station manager let slip that she considered the protest "a garden-variety labor dispute in connection with a first contract" (Univision workers, 2000). The dispute was resolved on April 1, 2000 after 43 days of fasting; only three of the original eight workers completed the fast due to health concerns. The employees gained 20% to 40% pay increases and five months' back pay among other concessions, such as a master control room operator being permitted a lunch break during his ten-hour shift (Calvo, 2000b). The strike's location held historical significance as a site of the United Farm Workers' efforts to improve working conditions and unionize mostly Hispanic agricultural workers during the 1960s and '70s. Univision (at that time Spanish International) news had covered those important efforts, and most of the strikers had relatives who worked the fields, or had done so themselves. It must have been a vexing experience for strikers and their supporters to travel by bus to the Bel Air neighborhood of Los Angeles to protest outside the elegant home of Henry Cisneros, president of Univision and former Secretary of Housing and Urban Development, who had refused to address the strike, even during an appearance in Fresno (Calvo, 2000a; Calvo, 2000c).

On the heels of the strike in Fresno another labor dispute brewed at KMEX in Los Angeles, the flagship among Univision-owned stations since its construction in 1962. In October 2000 approximately 120 members of the National Association of Broadcast Employees and Technicians-CWA walked off the job stating that management had not adequately addressed their concerns about job parameters, employment security and wages since the union's contract with the station had expired the previous March (DiOrio, 2000). The dispute was settled in mid-November following a 15-hour negotiation session between station management and the union. Signing bonuses and 20% wage increases resulted, but the major point of contention concerned technology: union workers sought exclusive rights to access production equipment while management wanted nonunion employees to have access as well. Ultimately it was agreed that "primary work" would be done by union members, while "incidental work" could be performed by others (Cleeland, 2000). During this peak period in television's digitization process, some technicians with skillsets grounded in analog technology were being swept aside by innovation and more up-to-date workers who they considered interlopers.

Shortly after NBC Universal purchased Telemundo in 2002, the American Federation of Television and Radio Artists (AFTRA) began efforts to union-ize station employees in select markets as well as production personnel at studios in South Florida. The union focused its efforts in NBC Universal duo-poly markets where NBC and Telemundo stations shared management and resources. In some cases the NBC employees were unionized and Telemundo's were not—in all cases the Spanish-language employees were paid lower sal-aries. Chicago's Telemundo affiliate, WSNS, became the target of AFTRA unionization efforts in early 2003 when the union rallied local support and encouraged advertisers to boycott. The union advocated a separate bargain-ing unit for WSNS prior to its integration with WMAQ (NBC) under the duo-poly (Trigoboff, 2003). A collective bargaining agreement between the WSNS and the National Association of Broadcast Employees and Technicians was eventually signed by the station and the union in November 2006.

AFTRA also made a push in Florida, a right-to-work state, where much U.S. Spanish-langauge television production occurs, but met with limited success. In 2002 AFTRA commissioned the Chicano Studies Research Center at the University of California at Los Angeles to conduct a study of compensation and work conditions among personnel at Spanish-language TV and radio stations in the Los Angeles area. The study found conditions similar to those in Fresno discussed above: workers at Spanish-language sta-tions earned an average 70% less than English-language counterparts, only two Spanish stations were unionized compared to all English stations, and health and retirement benefits were significantly better for English-language workers (Valenzuela & Hunt, 2002). While a portion of these disparities can be explained by the smaller revenue stream generated by Spanish-language media, this chapter has shown that Spanish-language television was quickly gaining ground in the early 2000s. Clearly, equity issues exist that require attention—an important first step would be to conduct up-to-date research on salary and other equity-related data across a number of local markets.

Conclusion

Spanish-language television experienced a notable growth spurt during the first six years of the new century. The main contributing factors included rapid population growth, increased visibility of Hispanic culture during the Latin Boom, two new network launches, NBC Universal's investment in Telemundo and the high-profile Univision–HBC merger. Census figures revealed a third consecutive decade of substantial growth in the Hispanic population, a fact that was reaffirmed by reports that Hispanics had surpassed Blacks as the nation's largest minority group in 2003. The Latin Boom in popular culture, especially music, underscored demographic reports of Hispanics' growing presence and influence. New opportunities for commerce, cultural consumption and interactive communication across time and space by distant users were opened through the growth of Spanish-language and Hispanic-oriented Internet portals. The Azteca América initiative demonstrated that the U.S. Spanish-language sector remained attractive territory for expansion by Mexican entrepreneurs four decades after Spanish International Network initiated the industry, and Telefutura reaffirmed the industry's audience growth potential. Univision's power to roil the nation's political and economic waters and its tenacity in resisting Nielsen's rollout of local Peoplemeters depicted a weighty and determined competitor.

As often occurs in the natural world, however, some awkwardness accompanied the industry's growth spurt. The Latin Boom revealed again commercial markets' tendency to overgeneralize cultural characteristics and elide the identity differences among people of Latin American and U.S. Hispanic origin—unfortunately few alternatives to the narrow definitions were presented in mainstream media. NBC's conflicts with Televisión Azteca demonstrated a fierce territoriality and almost juvenile aggression between two substantial players, while the Univision–HBC merger illuminated some petty one-upmanship as well as limitations of the U.S. regulatory and political systems. Labor disputes at both Univision and Telemundo showed that while the Spanish-language sector moved toward direct competition with mainstream television, certain internal conditions were far from reaching parity.

Media convergence had already circulated as a buzzword within media industries and academe for at least a decade prior to the period covered by this chapter. The transition from analog to digital media accelerated in the early 2000s, and the Internet's potential to effectively distribute a wide variety of media became unmistakable. We have seen in this chapter that in addition to the broader technological and structural transformations taking place, substantial change occurred simultaneously or in short succession within the Spanish-language television sector. This initial treatment has identified the general elements that came together, but their wider implications deserve closer scholarly attention.

Notes

1. Only the Hispanic press engaged the frame about improving the group's standing.
2. "This is the most significant day in the history of Spanish-language television," concluded Jim McNamara, chief executive of Telemundo, "this is the day that Spanish-language television came of age" (James, 2001).

3. The FCC's proposal in June 2003 to further relax cross-ownership rules for newspapers and broadcast media engendered a substantial and overwhelmingly negative public response that congress was compelled to respond to, thereby politicizing the ensuing debate (Scott, 2003).

4. The petitioning organizations were the Puerto Rican Legal Defense and Education Fund, National Council of La Raza, League of United Latin American Citizens, National Hispanic Media Coalition, NOSOTROS, Mexican American Grocers Association, National Puerto Rican Coalition, and the National Association of Hispanic Publications (FCC, 2001).

5. Univision's main response to NBC's acquisition was to tighten its ties with Televisa and Venevisión through an exclusive U.S. programming agreement valid through 2017.

6. The short series *Kingpin* about the life of a Mexican narcotrafficker aired on both Telemundo and NBC in 2003, but was cancelled after six episodes (and some negative press about stereotyping).

7. http://generation-ntv.com/about-2/all-bout-n.

8. The new advertisers included some major players like Coca-Cola, Pepsi, Citibank, Bank of America, Verizon and BancoChase (Univision web site, 2002).

9. As concerns another technology, in 2005, Univision formed a home entertainment division to specialize in Spanish-language DVD. Although Hispanics constituted about 14% of U.S. population, only 1% of DVD sales were in Spanish-language (Spanish language DVD, 2005).

10. This moniker is claimed by several other cities as well, including San Diego, Los Angeles, Brighton, England and Melbourne, Australia.

11. Other prominent investors in *quepasa*.com included both George Bushes and the former football star John Elway.

12. Chapter Five recounts how the arrival of what would become a Telemundo station (KVEA) to Los Angeles in 1985 actually *increased* viewership on the 23-year-old Univision affiliate, KMEX.

13. This argument echoed Emilio Azcárraga Milmo's assertions in the latter 1980s about Galavisión stations reaching targeted audiences of Mexican origin while Univision and Telemundo appealed too broadly (see Chapter Five).

14. Ironically, this facility that would play a central role in Telemundo's network operations did business under an English-only policy prior to its acquisition: a local marketing agreement with the prior owner, Christian Broadcasting Network, had stipulated such (McClellan, 2000).

15. Of course creating duopolies was an appealing prospect for other groups as well. Disney, Viacom and News Corp. were other suitors for USA Network (Sutter & DiOrio, 2000).

16. Catherine Sandoval (2006) explains deregulation's impact on the U.S. radio industry: "before the Telecommunications Act [of 1996], the largest radio company in America owned sixty-four stations. By 2004, the largest radio company, Clear Channel, controlled nearly 1200. For smaller broadcasters, the imperative to expand in order to compete is especially intense." (p. 387).

17. Univision Music Group had launched in 2001 with three labels: Univision Records, Fonovisa Records (acquired in 2002 from Televisa) and Disa Records. Universal Music Group acquired the group in 2008 and organized it under the label Universal Music Latin Entertainment.

18. Steve Mandala, Telemundo's executive vice president for sales commented, "we think it would be the equivalent of Viacom buying Clear Channel and maybe throw in NBC, AOL online and Sony Music" (cited in Teinowitz, 2003).
19. Because so many petitions were filed—mostly against, but some in favor of the new rules—the U.S. Court of Appeals for the Third Circuit intervened and in June 2004 overturned most changes to media ownership limits and directed the FCC to conduct a new review.
20. Another ardent supporter of SBS in opposing the merger was Senator Bob Menendez of New Jersey who had purchased stock in the company at its initial public offering in 1999 (Byrd, 2013).
21. SBS claimed that Clear Channel and HBC undermined its 1999 initial public offering, discouraged market analysts from reporting on the company and encouraged SBS investors to divest (Spanish broadcaster sues, 2002).
22. Frank Ahrens (2004) offers of a succinct description of the LPM: "The people meter is designed to record what channels are being watched at any time. It allows individual family members to identify who was watching a particular show by punching a button on a remote control. Nielsen already uses the system to tally national network viewing habits. It wants to extend the system to determine how shows fare in local markets."
23. Univision's suit argued that Nielsen's LPM contained: "21 percent too many Hispanic homes in which only English is spoken and 40 percent too many homes in which mostly English is spoken. At the same time, it contains 37 percent too few homes in which only Spanish is spoken … also undercounted are young Hispanics between the ages of 18 and 34, … by some 27 percent" (Hoheb, 2004).

References

Adams, David. (2000, May 14). La vida loca.com. *St. Petersburg Times*. Retrieved from Lexis-Nexis database.

Adios to Espanol.com: Bid4Assets.com auctions assets of bankrupted Internet portal. (2001, April 14). *Daily Record*, 5.

Ahrens, Frank. (2004, June 11). Nielsen sued over TV ratings method: Univision says 'People Meter' undercounts minorities. *Washington Post*, E05.

Ariens, Chris. (2011, October 3). McGraw-Hill sells TV stations to Scripps for $212 million. *TV Spy*. Retrieved from http://www.mediabistro.com/tvspy/mcgraw-hill-sells-tv-stations-to-scripps-for-212-million_b24080.

Azteca America leads primetime viewer growth among Spanish broadcast television networks, with a 38% increase from last year among viewers age 18–49. (2011, March 3). *PR Newswire*. Retrieved from EBSCOHost database.

Bachman, Katy. (2007, April 3). Pappas terminates affil. pact with Azteca. *Mediaweek. com*. Retrieved from Lexis-Nexis database.

Bagdikian, Ben. (2000). *The media monopoly* (6th ed.). Boston, MA: Beacon.

Barlas, Pete. (2001, June 14). STARMEDIA Latin American web portal struggles to make profit. *Investor's Business Daily*, A6.

Beck, Chad Thomas. (2010). Azteca America's performance of Mexicanness in the pan-Hispanic television market. *International Journal of Cultural Studies, 13*(3), 271–289.

Belman, Benjamín. (2006, October). TV Azteca tras el control televisivo. *Revista Fortuna*. Retrieved from http://revistafortuna.com.mx/opciones/archivo/2006/octubre/htm/TVAzteca_control.htm.

Benitez, Cristina. (2000, January 30). Internet supporting the explosion of Latino culture. *Contra Costa Times*, H4.

Blair, Jayson. (2000, July 17). TV advertising drives fight over size of Spanish audience. *New York Times*. Retrieved from http://www.nytimes.com/2000/07/17/nyregion/tv-advertising-drives-fight-over-size-of-spanish-audience.html.

Blalock, Hubert M., Jr. (1967). *Toward a theory of minority-group relations*. New York, NY: Wiley.

Block, Sandra. (1999, May 27). A star shines among IPOs Net services firm StarMedia's stock soars 74%. *USA Today*, 1B.

Brownlee, Lisa. (1999, November 19). Univision's .com-petition over ads: Rivals get heave-ho. *New York Post*, 37.

Byrd, Mary Lou. (2013, February 13). The Menendez file. *Washington Free Beacon*. Retrieved from http://freebeacon.com/politics/the-menendez-files.

Calvo, Dana. (2000a, March 16). Bilingual dilemma: Big paycheck or little pond? *Los Angeles Times*. Retrieved from http://articles.latimes.com/2000/mar/16/entertainment/ca-9292.

Calvo, Dana. (2000b, April 1). Fresno TV employees approve contract. *Los Angeles Times*. Retrieved from http://articles.latimes.com/2000/apr/01/news/mn-14873.

Calvo, Dana. (2000c, March 4). TV news staff using hunger as weapon in contract fight. *Los Angeles Times*. Retrieved from http://articles.latimes.com/2000/mar/04/news/mn-5157.

Calvo, Dana. (2002, April 11). Telemundo hires talent from rival. *Los Angeles Times*. Retrieved from http://articles.latimes.com/2002/apr/11/business/fi-telemundo11.

Cartagena, Chiqui. (2005). *Latino Boom!: Everything you need to know to grow your business in the U.S. Hispanic market*. New York, NY: Ballantine Books.

Case, Tony, & Freeman, Michael. (2003, February 17). Hearing the Hispanic boom. *Media Week, 13*(7).

Cepeda, Maria Elena. (2001, winter). "Columbus Effect(s)": Chronology and crossover in the Latin(o) music "Boom." *Discourse, 23*(1), 63–81.

Cepeda, Maria Elena. (2010). *Musical imagiNation: U.S.-Colombian identity and the Latin music boom*. New York, NY: New York University Press.

Cevallos, Diego. (2000, January 13). Major competition for piece of internet. *Business and Industry* (Global Information Service Interpress Service).

Chairman and senior member of Democratic Congressional Hispanic Caucus support Univision-Hispanic broadcasting merger. (2003, August 13). *Business Wire*.

Cleeland, Nancy. (2000, November 16). Workers OK deal to end KMEX strike. *Los Angeles Times*. Retrieved from http://articles.latimes.com/2000/nov/16/business/fi-52763.

Clemetson, Lynette. (2003, January 22). Hispanics now largest minority, census shows. *New York Times*. Retrieved from http://www.nytimes.com/2003/01/22/us/hispanics-now-largest-minority-census-shows.html.

Coffey, Amy Jo, & Sanders, Amy Kristin. (2010). Defining a product market for Spanish-language broadcast media: United States v. Univision Communications, Inc. and Hispanic Broadcasting. *Communication Law and Policy, 15*, 55–89.

Consoli, John. (2001a, July 2). Station problems for Azteca: Planned new Hispanic broadcast network encounters distribution setbacks. *Mediaweek*. Retrieved from Lexis-Nexis database.

Consoli, John. (2001b, December 10). Telefutura talks tough: Univision spinoff projects $100 million in advertising revenue in first year; Network TV. *Mediaweek*. Retrieved from Lexis-Nexis database.

Crabtree, Susan, & Sutter, Mary. (2003, August 8). Foes fire broadside at Univision combo. *Daily Variety*, 4.

Crane, Agnes. (2000, March 1). Mexico: Televisa and TV Azteca. *Advertising Age International*, 42.

Dávila, Arlene. (2001). *Latinos, Inc.: The marketing and making of a people*. Berkeley, CA: University of California Press.

De la fuente, Anna Marie. (2006, August 29). Azteca's aboard Nielsen. *Variety*. Retrieved from http://variety.com/2006/scene/news/azteca-s-aboard-nielsen-1200340988.

DiCarlo, Lisa. (2001, October 12). Will NBC-Telemundo deal spur consolidation? *Forbes*. Retrieved from http://www.forbes.com/2001/10/12/1012telemundo.html.

DiOrio, Carl. (2000, October 24). Profitable Univision sees strike. *Daily Variety*, 39.

Downey, Kevin. (2002, February 4). Boffo launch for Telefutura: Young-skewing Univision net pulling new viewers. *Media Life*. Retrieved from http://www. medialifemagazine.com:8080/news2002/feb02/feb04/5_fri/news2friday.html.

El Nasser, Haya. (2003, June 19). 39 million make Hispanics largest U.S. minority group. *USA Today*. Retrieved from http://usatoday30.usatoday.com/news/nation/census/2003-06-18-Census_x.htm.

Embarga TV Azteca estudios de Telemundo en México. (2006, September 26). *El Universal*. Retrieved from http://www.eluniversal.com.mx/notas/377506.html.

Ennis, Sharon R., Ríos-Vargas, Merarys, & Albert, Nora G. (2011, May). *The Hispanic population: 2010* (Census Brief No. C2010BR-04). Retrieved from U.S. Census Bureau website: http://www.census.gov/prod/cen2010/briefs/c2010br-04.pdf.

FCC approves merger of Univision and Hispanic Bcstg. Corp. (2003, September 23). *Communications Daily*. Retrieved from Lexis-Nexis database.

FCC delays approval of Univision deal. (2003, September 15). *Weekly Corporate Growth Report*. Retrieved July 11, 2011 from http://findarticles.com/p/articles/mi_qa3755/is_200309/ai_n9241802.

Federal Communications Commission. (1999, August 5). FCC revises local television ownership rules (FCC News Release 99–2090). Retrieved from http://transition.fcc.gov/Bureaus/Mass_Media/News_Releases/1999/nrmm9019.html.

Federal Communications Commission. (2001, December 3). In re: Telemundo Communications Corp. and TN Acquisition Corp. petition to deny and motion to dismiss (FCC doc. No. BTCCT-20011101ABW).

Federal Communications Commission. (2003, September 22). FCC grants conditioned approval of Univision/HBC merger [Press release]. Retrieved from http://www.fcc.gov/encyclopedia/media-bureau-2003-headline-archives.

Galetto, Mike. (1997, August 28). Telemundo affiliate site: News in Spanish, online. *Electronic Media, 16*(35), 10.

Garcia, Guy. (1999, June 27). Another Latin boom, but different. *New York Times*, 25.

Goodwin, Christopher. (1999, July 28). Hispanic smash hits obscure a cultural iniquity. *The Australian Sunday Times*, 16.

Gregor, Alison. (2003, September/October). What's Spanish for big media? *Columbia Journalism Review*, 62.

Grieco, Elizabeth M., & Cassidy, Rachel C. (2001, March). *Overview of race and Hispanic origin* (Census 2000 brief C2KBR/01–1). Retrieved from www.census.gov/prod/2001pubs/c2kbr01-1.pdf.

Gross, Daniel. (2003, June 27). The Univision division. *Slate.* Retrieved from http://www.slate.com/articles/business/moneybox/2003/06/the_univision_division.single.html.

Grossman, Andrew, & Hiestand, Jesse. (2001, October 16). NBC says si to Telemundo [International ed.]. *Hollywood Reporter, 370*(24), 78.

Grover, Ronald, Grow, Brian, & Smith, Jeri. (2004, August 9). The heavyweight on Latin airwaves: Jerry Perenchio's sprawling Univision network gives him huge Hollywood clout. *Business Week, 3895*, 62.

Hafner, Katie. (2000, April 6). Hispanics are narrowing the digital divide. *New York Times,* G6.

Halonen, Doug. (2003, June 2). Dems object to Univision buy critics fear pro-GOP slant to Spanish-language radio and television. *Television Week, 22*(22), 1.

Heim, Sarah J. (2003, May 19). Crossover cachet. *Adweek, 44*(20), 28.

Herman, Edward S., & McChesney, Robert W. (1997) *The global media: The new missionaries of global capitalism.* Washington, DC: Cassell.

Herrera, Brian Eugenio. (2012, June 12). *What happens AFTER a Latin explosion?* Keynote Address presented at National Association of Latino Arts and Cultures Regional Workshop, Albuquerque, NM. Retrieved from https://performances.wordpress.com/2012/06/16/what-happens-after-a-latin-explosion-keynote/.

Ho, David. (2003a, September 23). Univision, Hispanic merger criticized. *Associated Press Online.* Retrieved from Lexis-Nexis database.

Ho, David. (2003b, July 3). Telemundo opposes merger of rival Univision with Hispanic Broadcasting. *Associated Press Online.* Retrieved from Lexis-Nexis database.

Hoag, Christina. (2004, August 40). TeleFutura's second wind. *The Miami Herald.* Retrieved from http://www.latinamericanstudies.org/latinos/telefutura.htm.

Hoheb, Marisa. (2004, June 24). Nielsen: Univision's all wet in Los Angeles. Court response argues the LPM is far superior. *Media Life Magazine.* Retrieved from http://www.medialifemagazine.com:8080/news2004/june04/jun21/3_wed/news 2wednesday.html.

Hoy. (2004, August). *Understanding the Hispanic market* [PowerPoint presentation]. Retrieved from http://www.umsl.edu/~naumannj/Geography%20PowerPoint%20Slides/extra%20g1002%20powerpoints/North%20America/Understanding%20the%20Hispanic%20Market.ppt.

Jacobs, Stevenson. (2001, February). Cyberw@rs. *Business Mexico,* 42–47.

James, Meg. (2001, October 12). NBC to acquire Telemundo Network for $1.98 billion. *Los Angeles Times.* Retrieved from http://articles.latimes.com/2001/oct/12/business/fi-56173.

James, Meg. (2006, December 1). NBC seeks to bar Spanish rival in L.A. *Los Angeles Times.* Retrieved from http://articles.latimes.com/2006/dec/01/business/fi-nbc1.

James, Meg. (2007, August 27). Nielsen ends separate Latino TV survey. *Los Angeles Times.* Retrieved from http://articles.latimes.com/2007/aug/27/business/fi-nielsen27.

James, Meg. (2013, January 7). Univision to revamp its secondary Spanish language network. *Los Angeles Times.* Retrieved from http://articles.latimes.com/2013/jan/07/entertainment/la-et-ct-unimas-telefutura-spanish-language-network-20130105.

Kirkpatrick, John, & Shah, Angela. (2003, September 23). Merger to create biggest Spanish-language media firm in U.S. *Dallas Morning News.* Retrieved from Lexis-Nexis database.

Klein, Debra A. (2000, September 7). Variety of new Latin music sites seek English-speaking audience. *New York Times,* G11.

Knowledge@Wharton. (2004, November 8). Salsa outselling ketchup? Marketing to Hispanics is hot. *HispanicBusiness.com*. Retrieved from http://www. hispanic business.com/news/newsbyid.asp?idx=19335&page=1&cat=&more=.

Labaton, Stephen. (2003, June 3). Deregulating the media: The overview; Regulators ease rules governing media ownership. *New York Times*, C9.

Larmer, Brook, Chambers, Veronica, Figueroa, Ana, Wingert, Pat, & Weingarten, Julie. (1999, July 12). Latino America. *Newsweek*, 48.

Leeds, Jeff. (2004, September 17). Clear Channel is expanding in Spanish radio. *New York Times*. Retrieved from http://www.nytimes.com/2004/09/17/business/media/17radio.html.

Leland, John, & Chambers, Veronica. (1999, July 12). Generation Ñ. *Newsweek*, 52.

Liebeskind, Ken. (2002, January 14). Hola Telefutura. *Media Post News*. Retrieved from http://www.mediapost.com/publications/article/14022/hola-telefutura.html.

Lynch, David J. (2000, January 20). Net company Terra aims for Hispanic connection. *USA Today*, 1B.

Malkin, Elizabeth. (2006, December 6). Mexico's newest TV drama is a bid to block a third broadcaster. *New York Times*. Retrieved from http://www.nytimes.com/2006/12/06/business/worldbusiness/06tele.html?pagewanted=all&_r=0.

Mandel-Campbell, Andrea. (2000, May 3). NBC takes stake in TV Azteca broadcasting: US TV network to invest Dollars 26m in Mexican company following settlement of dispute. *Financial Times*, 34.

Mandese, Joe. (2005, December 20). Nielsen adds Spanish to TV ratings babel stream. *Media Daily News*. Retrieved from http://www.mediapost.com/publications/article/37692/nielsen-adds-spanish-to-tv-ratings-babel-stream.html.

McCabe, Mary Beth. (2011, May 24). The end of Spanish Nielsen ratings [Web log post]. Retrieved from http://marybethmccabe.wordpress.com/2011/05/24/the-end-of-spanish-nielsen-ratings.

McChesney, Robert W. (2004). *The problem of the media: U.S. communication politics in the 21st century*. New York, NY: Monthly Review Press.

McClain, Paula D., & Karnig, Albert K. (1990). Black and Hispanic socioeconomic and political competition. *American Political Science Review*, 84(2), 535–545.

McClellan, Steve. (2000, December 4). Room for tres? Pappas takes on Univision and Telemundo. *Broadcasting & Cable*, 26–28, 32.

McClintock, Pamela. (2004, June 22). Nielsen counts on court. *Variety*. Retrieved from http://variety.com/2004/biz/news/nielsen-counts-on-court-1117906867.

Merkert, John. (2010). The changing face of racial discrimination: Hispanics as the dominant minority in the USA—a new application of power-threat theory. *Critical Sociology*, 36(2), 307–327.

Moon, Tom. (2002, July 7). Cultural disconnect masks the diversity of Latin music. *Philadelphia Inquirer*, H1.

Morales, Magaly. (2002, February 20). Telefutura claims success with younger viewers. *Ft. Lauderdale Sun Sentinel*. Retrieved from http://articles.sun-sentinel.com/2002-02-20/lifestyle/0202190327_1_telefutura-telemundo-sn.

Mossberger, Karen, Tolbert, Caroline J., & Stansbury, Mary. (2003). *Virtual inequality: Beyond the digital divide*. Washington, DC: Georgetown University Press.

Mulkern, Anne C., & Farrell, John Aloysius. (2003, June 2). Univision deal arouses D.C. ire: Dems fear non-Hispanic, conservative control in Spanish-media merger plan. *Denver Post,* A-10.

National Research Council. (2004). *The 2000 census: Counting under adversity*. Washington, DC: National Academies Press.

Navarro, Mireya. (1999, October 4). After a summer of high-profile coverage of Hispanic culture, some wonder if it will last. *New York Times*, C17.

Ogunnaike, Lola. (2003, May 20). Crossover star tries crossing back; Ricky Martin returns to his Latin roots. *New York Times*, E1.

O'Neill, Molly. (1992, March 11). New mainstream: Hot dogs, apple pie and salsa. *New York Times*. Retrieved from http://www.nytimes.com/1992/03/11/garden/new-mainstream-hot-dogs-apple-pie-and-salsa.html.

Pellegrini, Frank. (1999, May 13). America goes mucho loco for Ricky. *Time*. Retrieved January from http://content.time.com/time/magazine/article/0,9171,24750,00.html.

Penteado, Claudia. (2001, November). Telemundo's price is sign of Hispanic power. *Ad Age Global*, 8.

Perlman, Allison, & Amaya, Hector. (2013). Owning a voice: Broadcasting policy, Spanish language media, and Latina/o speech rights. *Communication, Culture & Critique, 6*, 142–160.

Piñon, Juan. (2007). *The incursion of Azteca America into the U.S. Latino media* (Doctoral dissertation). University of Texas at Austin, Texas.

Piñon, Juan. (2011). The unexplored challenges of television distribution: The case of Azteca America. *Television & New Media, 12*(1), 66–90.

Ramirez, Claudio. (2002, March 1). Claxson dismisses new El Sitio closure rumors. *BNAmericas*. Retrieved from http://www.bnamericas.com/news/technology/Claxson_dismisses_new_El_Sitio_closure_rumors.

Ramírez-Berg, Charles. (2002). *Latino images in film: Stereotypes, subversion, and resistance*. Austin, TX: University of Texas Press.

Ríos Arredondo, Diana Isabel, & Mohamed, Ali N. (Eds.). (2003). *Brown and black communication: Latino and African American conflict and convergence in mass media*. Westport, CT: Greenwood Publishing Group.

Rodríguez, Clara E. (Ed.). (1997). *Latin looks: Images of Latinas and Latinos in the U.S. media*. Boulder, CO: Westview Press.

Rodríguez, Ilia. (2007, October). Telling stories of Latino population growth in the United States: Narratives of inter-ethnic conflict in the mainstream, Latino and African-American press. *Journalism, 8*(5), 573–590.

Romano, Allison. (2005, November 21). Azteca America finds its niche. *Broadcasting & Cable*, 10.

Romero, Simon. (2001, November 20). StarMedia will restate its financial results. *New York Times*, C7.

Sandoval, Catherine J. K. (2006, winter). Antitrust law on the borderland of language and market definition: Is there a separate Spanish-language radio market? A case study of the merger of Univision and Hispanic Broadcasting Corporation. *University of San Francisco Law Review, 40*, 381–449.

Scherer, Michael. (2003, January/February) Census confusion: Have Hispanics surpassed Blacks as the largest minority in America? It depends on who reports the story. *Columbia Journalism Review*. Retrieved from http://mumford.albany.edu/census/2003newspdf/0103CJRwebspecial.pdf.

Seiberg, Jaret. (2003, October 23). Appeal threatens Univision deal. *Daily Deal/The Deal*. Retrieved from Lexis-Nexis database.

Serratore, Nicole. (2004). How do you say "big media" in Spanish? Spanish-language media regulation and the implications of the Univision-Hispanic Broadcasting merger on the public interest. *Fordham Intellectual Property, Media and Entertainment Law Journal, 15*, 203–271.

Scott, Ben. (2003, December). The politics and policy of media ownership. *American University Law Review, 53*(2), 645–677.

Simpson, Ian. (2000, January 20). Terra targets Hispanic market in U.S.: Launches web network. *National Post*, C15.

Sorkin, Andrew Ross. (2001, October 12). NBC is paying $1.98 billion for Telemundo. *New York Times*. Retrieved from http://www.nytimes.com/2001/10/12/business/nbc-is-paying-1.98-billion-for-telemundo.html.

Spanish broadcaster sues Clear Channel (2002, August 1). *New York Times*. Retrieved from http://www.nytimes.com/2002/08/01/business/spanish-broadcaster-sues-clear-channel.html.

Spanish language DVD label launched in U.S. (2005, June 1). *Screen Digest*. Retrieved from http://www.highbeam.com/doc/1G1–133983184.html.

Stamler, Bernard. (2002, January 16). Univision bets on a new Spanish-language network, TeleFutura. *New York Times*. Retrieved from http://www.nytimes.com/2002/01/16/business/media-business-advertising-univision-bets-new-spanish-language-network.html.

Stoll, Neal R., & Goldfein, Shepard. (2003, June 17). Partial ownership interest has Justice Department seeing double. *New York Law Journal, 22*, 3.

Sutter, Mary. (2003a, May 29). Auds writing final act of Univision's 'Rebeca', *Daily Variety*, 23.

Sutter, Mary. (2003b, November 14). Univision unbound: Spanish lingo media group's income doubles. *Variety*. Retrieved from http://variety.com/2003/biz/news/univision-unbound-1117895661/.

Sutter, Mary. (2003c, February 28). Feds OK Univision's deal for Hispanic. *Daily Variety*, 2.

Sutter, Mary. (2005, June 9). Univision rehooks meters. *Daily Variety*, 6.

Sutter, Mary, & DiOrio, Carl. (2000, December 12). Univision nabs Diller's USA stations. *Variety*. Retrieved from http://variety.com/2000/tv/news/univision-nabs-diller-s-usa-stations-1117790303/.

Sutter, Mary, & Wentz, Laurel. (2001, July 16). U.S. conexiones. *Advertising Age, 72*(29), 14.

Swartz, Jon. (2003, January 27). Internet firms woo Hispanics. *USA Today*, 3B.

Tegel, Simeon. (2002, January 8). Azteca adds 2 more U.S. affils. *Daily Variety*, 6.

Teinowitz, Ira. (2003, August 4). Is Hispanic media a market?; FCC to decide as it reviews Univision's pending purchase of Hispanic Broadcasting. *Advertising Age*, 22.

Telemundo breaks with Yahoo!/Inks deal with MSN. (2008, November 19). *Portada Online*. Retrieved from http://www.portada-online.com/2008/11/19/telemundo-breaks-with-yahoo-inks-deal-with-msn-latino/.

Tharp, Paul. (2000, December 28). Quepasa no mas: Hispanic portal folds after Estefan exit. *New York Post*, 30.

Todito.com launches three new interactive channels. (2000, March 27). *PR Newswire*.

Tremlett, Giles. (2000, January 23). Spain's Terra enters US internet race. *Sunday Business*. Retrieved from Lexis-Nexis database.

Tricks, Henry. (2000, February 17). Televisa names portal [USA ed.]. *Financial Times*, 20.

Trigoboff, Dan. (2003, March 10). AFTRA sets election for WSNS(TV). *Broadcasting & Cable, 133*(10), 8.

TV Azteca embarga el plató donde Telemundo graba un concurso de telerrealidad. (2006, September 29). *El País*. Retrieved from http://elpais.com/diario/2006/09/29/radiotv/1159480801_850215.html.

United States v. Univision Communications, Inc. and Hispanic Broadcasting, No. 1:03CV00758. (U.S Dist. Mar. 26, 2003). Retrieved from http://www.usdoj.gov/atr/cases/f200800/200878.htm.

Univision.com touts ranking as no. 1 most visited Spanish-language website. (2006, September 18). *Wireless News*. Retrieved from Lexis-Nexis database.

Univision. (2004, June 10). Univision files lawsuit against Nielsen Media Research to stop Local People Meter implementation in Los Angeles [Press Release]. Retrieved from http://www.businesswire.com/news/home/20040610005227/en/Univision-Files-Lawsuit-Nielsen-Media-Research-Stop#.UtiivBCwZkA.

Univision web site flush with advertisers. (2002, June 10). *Mediaweek, 12*(23), 40.

Univision workers in 4th week of hunger strike over wages. (2000, March 15). *New York Times*, A20.

Valdéz, M. Isabel. (2002). *Marketing to American Latinos: A guide to the in-culture approach*. Ithaca, NY: Paramount Market Publishing.

Valenzuela, Abel Jr., & Hunt, Darnell. (2002, August). Spanish-language broadcasters: Top ratings, second-class status (Latino Policy and Issues Brief No. 3). Retrieved from UCLA Chicano Studies Research Center website: http://www.chicano. ucla.edu/publications/report-brief/spanish-language-broadcasters.

Weintraub, Bernard. (2004, March 22). Love fest for soap opera fans, in two languages. *New York Times*, E1.

Wentz, Laurel. (2003, May 12). Azteca America takes bold step. *Advertising Age*.

Wilkinson, Kenton T., & Merle, Patrick F. (2013). The merits and challenges of using business press and trade journal reports in academic research on media industries. *Communication, Culture & Critique, 6*, 415–431.

Yahoo!, NBC Universal Television Group and Telemundo create leading Internet property for U.S. Hispanic market; Combination of online and on-air assets to redefine U.S. Hispanic media landscape. (2006, May 10). *BusinessWire*. Retrieved from ww.businesswire.com/news/home/20060510005366/en/Yahoo!-NBC-Universal-Television-Group-Telemundo-Create#.UuLsBsznbw4.

9 Fragmentation and Ferment in the Digital Age

This final chapter updates trends the reader is now quite familiar with: the political economy of Spanish-language television, legal disputes, technological change and its impacts, language and demographics, marketing efforts to reach Hispanic consumers more efficiently, and political issues. One element distinguishing the developments discussed here is the rapid pace of change: demographic, market and technological forces continued their momentum from the first six years of the new millennium, even as a global economic downturn precipitated by the U.S. credit/mortgage debacle softened the advertising market and slowed growth in other media market sectors. The chapter concludes by discussing the 2008 and 2012 elections, in which Hispanic voters asserted the political muscle that had been projected, but seldom achieved, for decades prior.

Another Univision Sale

In 2006–2007 Univision changed ownership again. Much had changed in the Hispanic market, the television industry, capital markets and the regulatory environment since 1993 when the Perenchio-Televisa-Venevisión partnership purchased the network and station group. The most significant changes were Univision's return to private ownership after becoming publicly traded in 1996, and the expanded capacity of interactive communication technologies—the Internet and mobile telephones—to handle multimedia content. In this regard, the *Washington Post* identified a particular appeal of Univision within the chaotic climate of media convergence at the time, "the Spanish-language giant delivers a concentrated TV audience with growing consumer clout in an era when viewers are scattering away from television to other media" (Levingston, White, & Williams, 2006, p. D1).

Jerrold Perenchio, who had gained a reputation among his peers for selling media properties at their peak value, decided to sell Univision in early 2006 (Politi & Van Duyn, 2006). In February Univision began courting buyers amid speculation that the company would command more than $40 per share. Univision's value had increased considerably in the wake of its merger with the radio giant Hispanic Broadcasting Corp. in 2003 as well as its expansion in music and digital media. As Coffey and Sanders (2010) explain, "the combined Univision-HBC now controls up to 80% of the Spanish-language broadcast market in some cities, including more than sixty-five radio stations, three television networks, an Internet site and three Latin music labels, in addition to roughly 70% of the Spanish-language advertising market" (p. 58). Those assets, attractive for their potential synergies and revenue flow, reflected the company's success as the dominant U.S. Spanish-language media company. However, other media conglomerates like Disney, CBS and News Corp. had also expanded successfully and, in order to acquire Univision, would have to divest of existing properties in key markets to comply with broadcast station ownership caps (Politi & Van Duyn, 2006). Thus, even in the wake of significant deregulation and elevated ownership caps following the Telecommunications Act of 1996, broadcast station ownership was so heavily concentrated as to render acquisition of Univision a potential liability among several conglomerates that initially expressed interest.

Jerrold Perenchio's minority co-investors, Televisa (11% of stock) and Venevisión (13%), were eager to maintain, even expand, their foothold in the profitable U.S. market and joined a group of private equity bidders including Bain Capital, The Carlyle Group, The Blackstone Group, Cascade Investments (Bill Gates' firm) and Kohlberg Kravis Roberts & Company (Sorkin & Edmonston, 2006). As we saw in Chapter Four, Section 310b of the Communications Act of 1934 restricts foreign ownership and control of U.S. broadcast outlets by companies to 25%, thereby constraining the expansionist aspirations of Televisa and Venevisión. A rival group of private equity firms was headed by the billionaire investor Haim Saban and included Madison Dearborn Partners, Providence Equity Partners, Texas Pacific Group and Thomas H. Lee Partners. Saban, the chairman and CEO of Saban Capital Group, was born in Egypt, spent his adolescence in Israel, then built successful studio recording businesses in Paris and Los Angeles. He rose to Hollywood fame and fortune by launching the Mighty Morphin Power Rangers franchise as well as through a partnership with News Corp. that yielded Fox Family Worldwide, subsequently sold to Disney for $3 billion (plus $2.3 billion in debt) in 2001.

Volatile debt markets affected the bidding process just prior to the June 20, 2006 submission deadline, lowering the per share value of Univision's ultimate selling price as both groups' offers were heavily leveraged—debt in the winning bid represented approximately 12.5 times earnings before interest, tax, depreciation and amortization (Beales, 2007). The debt to earnings ratio caught the attention of business reporters who considered the sale representative of a trend toward leveraged buyouts by private equity firms (Samuelson, 2007; Beales, 2007).[1] The motivation behind such activity was profit, of course: over the prior two decades private equity firms averaged 13.2% annual returns compared to 9.2% for stocks listed on Standard & Poor's 500 Index (Samuelson, 2007). Once again Univision was at the center of a significant trend impacting media industries, yet it became an inopportune time for investors to enter heavily leveraged contracts, even in the relatively recession-resilient Hispanic-oriented media sector. Following the sale, FCC Commissioner Michael Copps expressed his doubts about private equity deals in broadcasting:

> The Commission has never analyzed the consequences of this type of transaction for its ability to ensure that licensees protect, serve and sustain the public interest. I, for one, have some real questions about how the assumption of massive amounts of debt will affect a media company's stewardship of the airwaves.
>
> (Teinowitz, 2007, p. 13)

As with prior network acquisitions, there was last-minute high drama as the Carlyle Group defected from its group, and both bidders missed the auction deadline while they scrambled to shore-up financing (Grover, 2006). On June 27 Univision accepted the Saban-led group's bid of $36.25 per share, or $12.3 billion, an amount well short of the $40+ per share that Perenchio had sought. Among the losing bidders, Televisa complained bitterly, and vocally, that it was not informed of a bid revision by its rival, and had been ignored by Univision executives during the bidding process (Politi, 2006). Not surprisingly, Televisa's representatives on the Univision board voted against selling to the Saban group. Televisa also sold its 11% stake in Univision in 2007 for $1.09 billion—a shrewd move, as we will see (Szalai & Hecht, 2010). At this point, relations between Univision and Televisa—companies with a 45-year history—reached their lowest ebb since the mid-1980s, prior to the forced sale of Spanish International Network. Their concussive legal dispute is discussed in greater detail below.

The Saban group, named Broadcast Media Partners, took control of Univision in March 2007, but only after signing a consent decree and paying a $24 million fine to settle charges that the network had violated children's programming rules by claiming that a teen-oriented *telenovela* was educational. It was the largest fine the FCC had assessed against a television network to date (Bachman, 2007a). Two media advocacy groups, the United Church of Christ and the National Hispanic Media Coalition, had challenged license renewals at Univision stations,[2] claiming failure to comply with the Children's Television Act of 1990 as well as Section 73.671 of the Commission's rules, requiring licensees to air at least three hours of children-oriented programming weekly (FCC, 2007). The Television Act established core guidelines for appropriate educational and informational programming, set criteria for identifying and promoting such shows to parents and children, and imposed limitations on advertising during children's programs (Children's educational television, 2011). In its consent decree with the FCC, Univision agreed to conform to children's programming requirements in the future. This episode demonstrates how advocacy organizations' monitoring activities and legal actions that gained momentum in the 1980s and '90s continues to influence Spanish-language television in the 21st century.

Televisa v. Univision[3]

As noted above, relations between Univision and Televisa reached a low point during the Univision sales process in 2006. Televisa's own *telenovela* scriptwriters could have taken pride in the melodrama that their bosses and lawyers produced on January 22, 2009. Just minutes before Televisa's president and CEO Emilio Azcárraga Jean was scheduled to testify in U.S. federal court, his company reached a settlement with Univision. Televisa sought to sever ties with Univision over $122 million in disputed royalties (James, 2009a). There were two main issues in the suit. First, Televisa claimed Univision had breached the companies' 25-year programming contract by underpaying royalties for Televisa content aired in the U.S. We saw in Chapters Four and Seven that such contracts became key provisions of Univision ownership changes in 1986 and 1992 because they guaranteed access to a steady supply of lucrative programming from Mexico. The second issue concerned rights to Televisa television content accessed via Internet in the U.S. Televisa asserted its right to commercialize such content—many of the same shows that were airing on Univision—because the Internet was a new medium not included in the broadcast program agreement. Univision countered that the companies' programming contract signed in 1992 covered all broadcast media including the Internet (which didn't commercialize until several years later and wouldn't readily handle video content for another decade) (Wentz, 2009).

Tension between Emilio Azcárraga Milmo (Azcárraga Jean's father) and Jerrold Perenchio had followed quickly on the heels of Hallmark's selling Univision to the Perenchio-Televisa-Venevisión group in 1992. The men disagreed over the terms of a program license agreement and how deeply Univision should invest in program production within the U.S. Not surprisingly, Azcárraga favored the status quo of heavy reliance on Mexican (and to a lesser degree Venezuelan) imports while Perenchio wanted to boost domestic production. The tension apparently carried over to Azcárraga Jean after his father's death in 1997, once he had secured his leadership of Televisa. As Perenchio began developing a succession plan, Azcárraga Jean opposed the promotion of chief operating officer Ray Rodríguez, who intended to increase Univision's domestic production. Rodríguez subsequently began withholding royalty payments on select programs, prompting Azcárraga Jean and Televisa's executive vice president Alfonso de Angoitia Noriega to resign from Univision's board of directors in May 2005, citing concerns about the company's leadership as well as the royalty issue (Pettersson, 2009; Szalai & Hecht, 2010).

Televisa filed its lawsuit on May 9, 2005, nine months before the Univision sale process began. The networks' disagreements were not fully resolved until October 5, 2010. A major development during the course of the disagreement was the economic downturn of the late 2000s, a topic we will return to below. The crux of the dispute over underpaid royalties on Televisa content aired in the U.S. focused on unsold advertising time that Univision used for internal promotions (Wentz, 2008). One media journalist observed that the companies had "always squabbled," yet the lawsuit deepened the conflict, engendering "years of dramatic threats and endless sniping" (Wentz, 2008). Such a toxic environment likely prolonged the suit, setting up the dramatic crescendo of a settlement announcement just before Emilio Azcárraga Jean and A. Jerrold Perenchio were scheduled to testify. Although details of the behind-the-doors negotiations have not been released by either company, observers believe that Haim Saban of Univision and Alfonso de Angoitia of Televisa worked out the settlement deal. The revised programming agreement stipulated that Televisa receive rights to $65 million worth of free advertising on Univision stations annually for nine years (James, 2009a). Univision also remunerated Televisa for $46.5 million in unpaid royalties prior to the agreement, and the terms for calculating royalties were simplified and amended in Televisa's favor (Wentz, 2009).

The programming royalty agreement did not address the digital rights issue, however. The same federal judge, Philip S. Gutierrez, presided over negotiations to make Televisa programs available to U.S. audiences via the Internet. Televisa argued that the companies' 1992 program licensing agreement only covered broadcast distribution and the Internet constituted a distinct network. Univision claimed that the programming contract covered all forms of electronic transmission and retransmission, including those not yet developed when the contract began (Keating, 2009). In his ruling on July 17, 2009 Judge Gutierrez sided with Univision declaring that the 1992 agreement "bars Televisa from sending programs to the United States by any means, including the Internet" (James, 2009b).

Settlement of the program royalty and digital rights issues bridged a deep chasm between the companies. The reconciliation was followed by another agreement in October 2010, which expanded their strategic relationship and brought Televisa back into the U.S. Televisa agreed to pay $130 million for a 5 percent stake in Univision. It also negotiated the right to raise its stake to 10 percent within three years, and hold debt that could be converted into 30% ownership (it is not clear how the FCC's 25 percent foreign ownership limit would be averted) (Szalai & Hecht, 2010). Clearly Univision's expanding debt burden was a motivation for welcoming Televisa's reentry, which could yield as much as $1.2 billion for the heavily leveraged company:

> [Univision's] long term debt burden increased sharply from $0.9 billion at the end of 2006 to $10 billion in FY2009 ... As a result of high debt, the company's interest expense increased from $89.2 million in

2006 to $692.4 million in FY2009 ... As a result of high debt burden and fluctuating operating performance, it reported net loss of $314.9 million, $5,127.3 million and $252.1 million, ... in 2007, 2008 and 2009, respectively.

(Datamonitor, 2010, p. 21)

Thus, Broadcast Media Partners' highly-leveraged acquisition of Univision in 2007, combined with the economic downturn's impact on advertising spending, framed the conditions favorable for Televisa's reinvestment in the U.S. network.

The souring of Televisa and Univision's deep, half-century relationship—and the two companies' ability to rectify it so quickly—demonstrates the volatility of contemporary media businesses. In addition to the personal competition identified above, the conflict was fueled by digitization's upsetting of the status quo, economic uncertainties, a new ownership group in the industry eager to prove its chops, and maturation of the U.S. Spanish-language media sector, placing it on more equal footing with its Mexican counterpart. Of course political and economic conditions in Mexico influenced Televisa's hand, as happened during the introduction of free trade discussed in Chapter Seven. Televisa's capacity to exploit Univision's vulnerabilities and forge a deal to the Mexican company's advantage stemmed largely from its ability to sustain a lucrative media dominance in Mexico—a dominance maintained through the company's navigation of that country's risk-laden political riptides (Wilkinson & Saragoza, 2012).

The deal also reaffirmed that the connection with Televisa is vital to Univision; it is an interdependent relationship of mutual benefit whereby the two firms profit from remaining the dominant players in their respective markets. Notwithstanding a difficult business climate and crushing debt, Univision successfully negotiated three important agreements with Televisa in 2009–2010 signaling that its leadership can compromise when necessary. In closing this section it should be noted that the Televisa-Univision dispute had a broad chilling effect on the Spanish-language television industry as some companies and investors preferred to know the conflict's outcome before doing business that the lawsuit's resolution might impact.

Digital Media

Prior chapters have argued the centrality of technological change to U.S. Spanish-language television growth, including the UHF band, satellite distribution, cable television, low-power TV, the Internet and mobile telephony. The latter two have developed at an accelerated pace as key media in the Digital Revolution (Wu & Wang, 2005). During the period covered by this chapter, both the Internet and mobile phones became more practical and commonly used media for audiences to access television content and, not surprisingly, they captured the attention of established and potential participants in Hispanic-oriented media industries. The interactive nature of these technologies also opened new audience feedback channels for the networks, as well as vast amounts of data for networks and their advertising clients to organize and analyze for strategic purposes (Napoli, 2011). Laurel Wentz (2007) of *Advertising Age* describes how the digital boom impacted Hispanic-oriented media:

> The huge change in the Hispanic media world is the digital explosion. Hispanic print media, long digital laggards, finally have online strategies. Social networking is taking off. Online media and the Hispanic TV networks' websites are growing exponentially; Univision.com expects 5 billion page views this year. And mobile marketing is the latest catchphrase. (p. S-1)

In this rapidly shifting environment, a central challenge for U.S. Spanish-language television companies has been establishing a strong Web presence and making sound strategic alliances with new media companies that will point consumers to their television channels, web sites, and other media properties. An initial series of reports on Hispanic consumers' digital media use (2005–2008) was almost universally positive, emphasizing higher-than-average use of some features. However, the subsequent economic downturn restrained many market participants from acting on this information, and later reports (2009–2012) were more reserved, though still confident.

Hispanics' Digital Media Use Reports 2005–2008

Both Univision and Telemundo launched digital media divisions in the early 2000s to reach consumers through interactive technologies such as mobile telephones, digital organizers and mp3 players/iPods. By mid-decade industry research on consumers' use of such technologies was being reported by the business press and trade journals, which had expanded coverage of the fracturing mediascape while employing many of the same tools and strategies they reported about. Thus a relevant point to keep in mind is that digital technologies not only opened new spaces for the creation, distribution, consumption and discussion of media content, but also opened access to industry-related information for many audiences including market analysts, investors, journalists, and, of course, academic researchers.

In July 2005, a partnership between America Online (AOL) and Roper released its third annual U.S. Hispanic "Cyberstudy" (Roper, 2005) focused on demographics, Internet use patterns, and consumption behaviors of Hispanics.[4] The goals and upbeat tone of the report are similar to prior reports on television, yet a major difference is the integrated nature of the Internet and mobile technologies allowing users to seek and post information on a broad array of topics, products and services, as well as consume an array of digital content and interact with other users. Table 9.1 summarizes the study's pertinent findings.

Table 9.1 Select findings from AOL/Roper *U.S. Hispanic cyberstudy* (2005)

44% of respondents had Internet at home; 24% had access at work

52% of respondents had a broadband connection at home compared to 50% of general population respondents

Equal numbers of Hispanic respondents identified as bilingual and English-dominant (40%)

Hispanics reported going on line 9.2 hours weekly compared to 8.5 hours among the general population

56% of online Hispanics were age 18 to 34 compared to 34% of the general population

Hispanics used the Internet more frequently than the general population for listening to music, downloading music and instant messaging

38% of Hispanic respondents regularly or occasionally watched video clips on line (general population = 33%)

42% of Hispanic respondents reported watching TV and being on line simultaneously; 30% reported watching less TV since going on line

---

The AOL/Roper report not only portrays a changing technological environment, industry and audience; it also hints at the new behaviors that engage when audiences may access content on a variety of screens. Subsequent reports addressed these new variables and assessed the industry's response.

As we have seen, reporting on Spanish-language media tends to cluster around major developments, like a network sale or lawsuit, and around regular industry events such as the NATPE programming trade show.[5] Prior to the 2006 "upfronts"—meetings in New York where the networks present their upcoming fall programs for advertisers and the press—*Broadcasting & Cable* reported, "Telemundo, the scrappy underdog of Hispanic TV in the U.S., is taking on top dog Univision by going broadband" (Becker, 2006, p. 12). Telemundo highlighted its ability to repurpose television content on digital platforms, contrasting itself with Univision which was embroiled in a digital rights suit with Televisa. Among Telemundo's efforts to engage viewers online were Internet-only dramas encouraging users to seek clues and chat with characters, blogs written by network celebrities, and an online suggestion box for romantic dilemmas to be incorporated into stories (Becker, 2006). Two questions surrounding the digital shift were whether online advertising could command higher percentages of ad budgets, and whether the cross-platform advantages Telemundo and Azteca América enjoyed could cut into Univision's domain. The prognosis was dim as Univision was projected to attract around $1 billion in ad buys at the 2006 upfronts with Telemundo and Azteca trailing far behind at $400 million and $100 million respectively (Consoli, 2006). 2006 proved to be a profitable year as Spanish-language TV ad revenues grew 14% to $4.3 billion, boosted by election spending and World Cup soccer, to which Univision held the rights (Martinez, 2007a; Wentz, 2007).

Martinez (2007b) reported that about 15.7 million Hispanics owned a mobile phone and Forrester Research indicated that Hispanic mobile-data users were three times more likely to download videos than non-Hispanics. The same year, Telemundo became a founding member of the Open Mobile Video Coalition, which promoted technical standards for mobile digital broadcast TV in the U.S. Two other studies in 2007 offer additional insight into digital media use by Hispanics, and illustrate how differing orientations and conclusions can emerge depending on who conducts the research. A Telemundo report found that online Hispanics consumed more media and adopted more communication technology than the U.S. general population (Yahoo! Telemundo, 2007). The report characterized Hispanics as Internet trend setters because two-thirds had been online for more than five years, 80% had broadband access and 44% had wireless access (51-Hour Day?, 2007). Table 9.2 includes comparative figures from the Yahoo! Telemundo study, *Conexión Cultural/Connected Culture*, which underscored television's continued centrality in Hispanic households and the network's ability to reach these connected consumers.

Table 9.2 Digital Technology Usage by U.S. Hispanics and General Population

Technology or Activity	U.S. Hispanics (%)	U.S. General Population (%)
Have digital camera	79	53
Have cell phone	90	79
Have video game console	66	52
Took photos on mobile phone	61	28
Use text messaging	66	38

Adapted from Yahoo! Telemundo Report, *Conexión Cultural/Connected Culture* (2007).

The Yahoo! Telemundo study employed both qualitative and quantitative research methods, the former consisting of self reports by family members in 24 online Hispanic households in Los Angeles, Dallas and New York, and the latter an online survey of 2,330 respondents plus 306 telephone interviews (Yahoo! Telemundo, 2007). Although still based on self reports, the study demonstrates significant progress in Hispanic audience research since the viewing diary method employed by Strategy Research Co. and others beginning in the 1970s.

A report by the Pew Internet and American Life Project, "Latinos Online" (Fox & Livingston, 2007), included a broader cross section of the Hispanic population, not only those who were already online. The data derived from 6,016 survey interviews conducted by telephone, and the sample was stratified by Hispanic population density as well as country of origin (Fox & Livingston, 2007). The Pew report showed that despite gains heralded by industry sources, significant impediments remained to Hispanics' Internet access and use; key findings are summarized in Table 9.3.

Table 9.3 Select Findings from Pew Center's "Latinos Online" Report (Fox & Livingston, 2007)

56% of Latinos used the Internet, compared to 71% for Whites and 60% for non-Hispanic Blacks.
32% of Latinos who speak only Spanish were on line, compared to 78% of English-dominant Latinos and 76% of bilingual Latinos.
89% of Latinos with college degrees, 10% of the total population, were on line; 70% of Latinos who completed high school, 49% of the total population, were on line; 31% of Latinos who had not finished high school, 41% of the population, were on line.
Latinos (79%) were less likely than Whites (92%) to have an Internet connection at home.
29% of Latino adults had a broadband Internet connection at home compared to 43% of Whites.
Immigrants and those who spoke mostly Spanish were less likely than other groups to use the Internet.
56% of Latino adults were online, 18% of Latino adults had a cell phone but were not online, and 26% of Latino adults had neither a cell phone nor an Internet connection.
67% of U.S.-born Latinos used the Internet compared to 43% of non-U.S.-born Latinos. 80% of second-generation Latinos used the Internet compared to 71% of third-generation Latinos.

The Pew report authors, Fox and Livingston (2007), found that Hispanics with less education and lower English proficiency were largely disconnected from the Internet; they concluded, "as a matter of statistical analysis, if one neutralizes the differences in English proficiency, then the differences in the rate of internet usage between Hispanics and non-Hispanics disappear" (p. 4). Thus language, long the defining characteristic of Hispanic-oriented television in the United States, remained an important partition for digital media early in the 21st century. We return to the language issue below.

In the mid-2000s, Spanish-language television's branded entertainment and product integration were still in early stages of development compared to general market media (de Lafuente, 2008). Thus it follows that reports about Hispanics' digital media use fostered interest in more effective product integration in Hispanic-oriented media narratives, especially across multiple media platforms. Besides countering the ad-zapping capabilities of TiVo and other digital recording technologies, such integration could engage consumers across their various devices. An example was Telemundo's *Gana Mi Casa* (*Win My House*), a six-week online home improvement reality series featuring home makeovers and sweepstakes to win a GMC vehicle and a $10,000 gift card from Lowe's (de Lafuente, 2008). Online and mobile media promoted a Telemundo *telenovela*, *Dame Chocolate* (*Give Me Chocolate*), which interwove Clorox products with the story (Martinez, 2007a). These and other initiatives in the Spanish-language sector ran parallel with general market players' efforts to create synergies across their various holdings under the auspices of convergence (Lawson-Borders, 2006).

Hispanics' Digital Media Use Reports 2009–2012

This second period continued an emphasis on branding and language, with particular attention to social media, mobile technologies, and streaming video. The enthusiasm of earlier reports was tempered by the economic downturn and associated tightening of credit markets that dampened media buying, launching new services and similar activity, although less severely in the Hispanic-oriented segment than the general market (Guskin & Mitchell, 2011). We should bear in mind that economic conditions also impact the business press and trade journals. As was widely reported, many newspapers operating under financial strain reduced staffs, eliminated departments or folded entirely—such cutbacks diminished the volume of reporting on media industries compared to the first six years of the 2000s. Anecdotal evidence also suggests that growth in the number of trade journals devoted to Hispanic-oriented media, whether print, electronic, or both, also slowed following 2007.

Although the Internet's novelty as a distribution medium for video content had worn off by the latter 2000s and early 2010s, its importance grew as an advertising medium and a vital leg in the three-screen[6] strategies of large media companies. In 2010, Hispanics were adopting broadband Internet in the home at a lower rate (45%) than Whites (65%) and Blacks (52%), and used the Internet at about the same rate as Blacks (65%) but less than Whites (77%) (Livingston, 2011). These lower rates did not diminish marketers' enthusiasm, however. The adoption of social media services like Facebook and Twitter routinized Internet use for many consumers, thereby improving the medium's status as a reliable medium for advertising (Dyer, 2010). Of course many users were also accessing social media sites through applications on mobile phones and tablets, not only traditional computers. Hispanic consumers used these devices for e-commerce as well: Hispanics accounted for $2.2 billion in U.S. e-commerce purchases during the first quarter of 2012 (11% of the total) and were substantially more likely than non-Hispanics to purchase certain items like telecommunication and financial services using a mobile phone or tablet (Rodriguez, 2012).

In 2011, the Internet giant Google bolstered the sector's legitimacy by hosting a digital marketing forum concerning online Hispanics. The organizer, Mark López, pointed out that younger users employ digital technology in unique ways, a fact that industry had been slow to recognize and accommodate. This oversight was evident in a report that digital media represented only 3% to 4% of Hispanic media ad spending at a time when 12% of Hispanics used digital media regularly (Cartagena, 2011). López also emphasized that younger Hispanics, like other digital natives, often used digital media for news and entertainment before consulting traditional media like broadcast and print, if at all.

Notwithstanding digital media's rapid development, and the abundant information about many Hispanics' enthusiastic adoption of it, a dearth of compelling Spanish-language Internet content continued (Blackshaw, 2008). This led some bilingual Hispanics to navigate the Web and use social media in English, even though they preferred Spanish (Deploying digital, 2010; Matsaganis, 2011). Thus the need to offer more Spanish-language content on line became a recurrent theme in the trade literature. The television networks were in an advantageous position to provide such content, of course. Univision and Telemundo are likely to remain in fierce competition to attract and retain Hispanic users as new digital platforms and distribution methods emerge.

As described above, Televisa's lawsuit against Univision impeded the U.S. network's ability to offer online access to Televisa content it aired on television, contributing to Univision's becoming the most heavily pirated network on YouTube, the popular video-sharing social network site (Wentz, 2009). Such exposure was good for reinforcing an online fan base, and for cultivating a video-watching routine among Web users, but not for generating revenue from Internet ad sales. Telemundo fared better, because holding the rights to content facilitated integration across the three screens (Wentz, 2011). For its part, in 2007 Azteca América migrated away from its Mexican web site, *todito.com*, to build a U.S.-based presence. While the digital rights to content issue was being adjudicated, Univision began developing online-only content with brand tie-ins. *Vidas Cruzadas (Crossed Lives)* was a 15-episode online-only *telenovela* featuring in-show brand integration with McDonald's, State Farm and L'Oréal (Wentz, 2011). In an effort to build on the success of *Vidas Cruzadas*, the network launched Novelas y Series, an Internet channel featuring short-format content from network programs as well as material from other providers (Univision launches, 2010). In 2012 Univision introduced another online video initiative called UVideos Digital Network to distribute content across multiple devices including smartphones, game consoles and Internet-enabled television receivers.[7] Univision CEO Randy Falco claimed in early 2013 that UVideos was accessible to Spanish-speaking audiences on more than 240 million devices (Szalai, 2013).

Social media gained legitimacy as viable conduits for advertising beginning around 2008, thereby attracting sustained attention from organizations in various media industry sectors. A poll of multicultural marketers found that 36% planned to initiate social networking for the first time in the next year (2009), compared with 19% in the general market. Mobile technology use motivated Hispanic-oriented marketers because, according to a Forrester Research survey of 3,000 adults, Hispanics were more likely than non-Hispanics to use multimedia features on their cellphones: cameras

(65% vs. 48%), video (41% vs. 17%), music (42% vs. 15%) and Internet access (57% vs. 39%) (Wentz, 2008). Furthermore, market research in the late 2000s and early 2010s indicated that Hispanics used social media more frequently than their non-Hispanic peers. A 2009 study by the Center for Hispanic Marketing Communication at Florida State University examined frequency of social media use by multicultural populations (Korzenny & Vann, 2009). English-preferring Hispanics reported more social media use than respondents in four other demographic categories: Spanish-preferring Hispanics, Asian Americans, African Americans, and Non-Hispanic Whites. Spanish-preferring Hispanics ranked either second or third after Asian Americans for most dimensions examined in the study. Not surprisingly, age was also an important factor; respondents under 35 years old used social media more frequently than those 35 and over. Among the older respondents, the two Hispanic groups outranked African Americans and Non-Hispanic Whites (Telenoticias, 2009). Korzenny and Vann (2009) reasoned that the Hispanics' collectivistic values and eagerness to keep in touch with geographically-dispersed friends and family were key factors accounting for their frequent use of social media. This conclusion is corroborated by some marketing experts who see social media as a new *plaza del pueblo* (town square) where Hispanics gather to socialize and stay connected with others (Westlund, 2011).

Subsequent studies confirmed Hispanics' higher than average use of digital technology and social media as well as the benefits to media organizations that utilize them effectively. A study by IAB Research & BIGinsight Data (2012) found that Hispanics are more likely to own a smartphone or tablet—and less likely to own a desktop computer—than the general population. Therefore it comes as little surprise that Hispanics consume more mobile media, download more mobile apps, and watch more mobile video than their general population peers. The Nielsen company, which of necessity began to branch out from its emphasis on television ratings as digital media expanded around the turn of the millennium, reported that Hispanic users' visits to social networks and blogs increased 14% over the twelve months prior to February 2012, and Hispanics were the fastest growing ethnic group on Facebook and WordPress.com, a popular blog site (Hispanics in U.S., 2012). A study by uSamp confirmed Hispanics' heavy social media presence as the group outpaced the general population in its use of Facebook (90% of those polled vs. 81%), YouTube (57% vs. 46%) and Google+ (47% vs. 18%). Yet Hispanics trailed the general population slightly in use of Twitter (31% vs. 33%) and by a large margin on LinkedIn (5% vs. 21%)[8] (Bennett, 2012).

A report on blogging activities found that Hispanics were 37% more likely than the general population to publish a blog, and 12% more likely to read others' blogs (McNaughton, 2012). It also noted the tendency among Hispanic bloggers writing in Spanish to include more promotional content and appeals to interaction compared to bloggers in English who wrote more personal anecdotes and sought connections to their cultural heritage. A key finding from the uSamp study should be emphasized: Hispanic users reported more reticence in sharing personal information on line than did members of other ethnic groups. Among the Hispanics surveyed, 65% were willing to share their names, compared with 87% of non-Hispanics; only 43% of Hispanics would post their relationship status on line, versus 74% of the general population. There were similar distinctions for revealing political affiliations (~32% vs. 53%) and revealing one's date of birth (36% vs. ~50%) (Sass, 2012). This relationship between higher-than-average social media use on the one hand, and restraint in sharing personal information on the other, underscores a complexity in Hispanics' communication technology use that industry participants must take into account.

There several other reasons why such industry research on Hispanics' social media use and other online behavior is relevant to Spanish-language television networks. The principal networks have sought footholds in other digital distribution media to expand their reach among audiences as well as limit competition from alternative sources of information and entertainment. Understanding audiences' interactive media preferences supports network efforts to develop engaging content that will keep users on their channels, web pages, and mobile device apps in the crowded multiscreen environment. Social media and other forms of interactive communication can help networks achieve prosocial outreach goals as well. An example is the Univision program, *¡Edúcate! Es el Momento* (Educate! It's Time) which combined social media (Facebook, Twitter and Google+) with television, live events, and phone banks to promote education and provide Hispanic students and parents with information about educational processes and options. Univision claimed that the event's Twitter hashtag drew over 100 million impressions, and that traffic on its Facebook page increased over 2000% (Schaffhauser, 2012). Clearly there is strong potential for cross-promotional persuasion in the multiscreen environment, whether for profit, prosocial motives, or a combination of both.

The 2010 U.S. Census

Findings from the 2010 U.S. Census confirmed what demographers and the press had been reporting—and many ethnic-oriented media hyping—since before the turn of the century: the country was steadily moving toward majority-minority status. That is, no ethnic or racial group would comprise more than 50% of the population by 2050, a change that had already occurred in four states—California, Hawaii, New Mexico and Texas—as well as the District of Columbia and 9% of the nation's counties (Humes, Nicholas & Ramirez, 2011; Taylor & Cohn, 2012). In 2010, Hispanics and non-Whites comprised 36% of the population, up from 30% in 2000 and 25% in 1990. Whites, the only racial group that lost ground, declined from

69% to 64% of the population in the first decade of the new millennium (Wilson, Gutiérrez, & Chao, 2012).

Hispanic population growth was the most influential demographic force, increasing 43% and accounting for more than half of the nation's population gain of 27.3 million people between 2000 and 2010. Recall the Census Bureau's announcement in 2003 that Hispanics surpassed Blacks as the nation's largest minority population. The 2010 census reported that 50.5 million Hispanic citizens and residents constituted 16.3% of the population (Ennis, Ríos-Vargas, & Albert, 2011). A key change from prior census findings was that more than 60% of the Hispanic population was U.S.-born (Saenz, 2010). This development has important implications for Spanish-language media, of course, because most American children use English as their preferred language. That is not to say that young Hispanics do not use or value Spanish, but the increase in the native-born population poses a significant challenge to U.S. Spanish-language media, which have long benefited from high levels of immigration to the U.S from *Spanish-speaking* countries. This is a key demographic factor informing several sections to follow: marketing to Hispanic youths, language shifts, and the emergence of new networks and services.

Marketing: A Focus on Youth

The term "Hispanic youth" joins two market segments that are particularly attractive to U.S. companies early in the 21st century. Demographic details reveal why marketers, advertisers, media outlets and others take such a keen interest in reaching these consumers. Prior to 2010, the Census Bureau reported that more than a third of all U.S. Hispanics were 18 or younger, and half were under 26 years old (Villa, 2009). Subsequent analysis of 2010 census data by the Pew Hispanic Center demonstrated a strong tendency toward U.S. nativity among Hispanics under 30: 58% of adults aged 20 to 29 were U.S.-born, compared to 81% of 14- to 19-year-olds, and 95% of Hispanics aged 10 to 14 (cited in Hispanic millennials, 2012). This trend was expected to continue, with 24% of U.S. youth age 5 to 19 projected to be Hispanic by 2020 (Perez, 2012). Clearly the statistics are compelling, but how are they projected to translate into audiences, and, ultimately, profits?

The spending habits of Hispanic youth are a key factor, especially among Hispanic teens who comprised 20% of the population age 12 to 19 counted in the 2010 census (Perez, 2012). Interest in the group intensified in the early 2000s with statistics such as, "the average Hispanic teen spends $320 a month, 4% *more* than the average non-Hispanic" (Bergantini Grillo, 2003, p. 20, emphasis in the original). With an average age of 27.7 years, compared to 36.8 for the general population, the average Hispanic consumer has a longer potential future of consumption, an important trait when considered in conjunction with Hispanics' tendency toward brand loyalty that marketers have emphasized since the 1980s (Westlund, 2011; Blackshaw, 2008). These characteristics, among others, motivated the creation of youth-oriented English-language pay TV channels like SíTV, launched in 2004.

Furthermore, in a study by Forrester, Hispanic teens with Internet access reported spending almost $150 more per month than their non-Hispanic counterparts (Barber, 2009). Market research also indicates that young Hispanics wield significant influence over family purchasing patterns, especially of technology products, which comes as little surprise given second-generation Hispanics' higher levels of education, higher household incomes and earlier adoption rates for technology than their parents (Barber 2009; Mun2, 2008). Collectively, in 2007 Hispanics earned the distinction of controlling more disposable personal income than any other minority group, commanding a buying power of $863 billion (Mcfarlane, 2007).

Yet statistics can only tell part of the story. Like prior generations of Hispanic youth, millennials[9] inhabit a world embracing two cultures and languages. They develop and express identities drawn from broader American attributes communicated by their peers, as well as U.S. Hispanic and country-of-origin influences from their families and ethnic communities. As one report put it, Hispanic youth "feel empowered, uniquely advantaged and optimistic because they can pick and choose the aspects of each culture that suit them best" (Understanding today's, n.d.); a different report by the Mun2 network found that young Hispanics identify with youth culture first, Latino culture second and American culture third.[10] There are significant ways in which 21st century youth differ from prior generations, including the demographic and cultural shifts underway in U.S. society (which give youth a deeper pool of cultural influences to draw from), and the greater pervasiveness of material culture and mediated communication in day-to-day life (De Zengotita, 2005). The possibilities are intriguing, and the challenges daunting, for those wishing to reach the Hispanic youth demographic; a common refrain among experts is that to be effective, the appeal must be genuine. There's also a general consensus in the trade journal literature that young Hispanics use English more frequently and fluidly than Spanish, which is valued as a cultural conduit to one's roots and an important element of family life and identity. Taken together, these points signal the importance of considering (and researching) language carefully, especially so for youth-oriented media focusing on popular culture such as music, entertainment, gaming and fashion.

As the Hispanic population skews younger, as well as more English-speaking and digitally savvy, what are the implications for Spanish-language television? Certainly television's domain among American youth in general is weakening as other media options appear, but Hispanic youth appear to be moving away from television more slowly than their White peers. A study by researchers at Northwestern University indicated that Hispanics 8 to 18 years old watched an average 3 hours and 8 minutes of non-time-shifted television daily compared to two 2 and 14 minutes for Whites (Rideout,

Lauricella & Wartella, 2011). Other research found that English-dominant Hispanics consume Spanish-language media—including up to 30% of their television viewing—because family members are present, and to maintain connections to their culture of origin (Sonderup, 2004). The youth-oriented Latin Boom beginning in the late 1990s was closely related to technological shifts and companies' synergistic ambitions as the major Spanish-language networks established their web and mobile media presence. The networks' online and mobile strategies were not oriented to *abuelitas* watching *telenovelas*—they were aimed at a tech savvy youth and young adult population some of whom were driven to Spanish content through retro-acculturation motives (Hinojosa, 2013). Not surprisingly, in light of this discussion, Hispanic youth tend to vary more in their linguistic consumption of media than do older Hispanics.

Language

Spanish-language television networks have long been concerned that diminishing immigration from Latin America could reduce their audience size. Two developments early in the 21st century have fueled such a possibility: U.S. births outpacing immigration as the principal driver of Hispanic population growth, and the economic downturn beginning in 2007, which made the U.S. a less attractive work destination for potential migrants. By April 2012, net migration to the U.S. from Mexico fell to zero, according to a report by the Pew Hispanic Center, and similar dynamics occurred with other Spanish-speaking countries (Passel, Cohn, & Gonzalez-Barrera, 2012). Two key concerns are how many English-dominant Hispanics will consume television and other media in Spanish, and how will their content preferences align with Spanish-dominant audiences. Industry reports about Hispanic youth suggest the situation may be less dire than some have argued: young Hispanics consume Spanish-language media as part of their media mix, and according to Eduardo Perez (2012), who labels them the "Spanglish generation," youth seek "*culturally relevant* messaging delivered in English *and/or* Spanish through a variety of highly targeted but disparate media channels and tactics" (italics in original). Thus, engaging young audiences with Spanish is possible, but there's a premium on content relevance and quality.

Language, a characteristic that has long defined the U.S. Hispanic population in media as well as other societal venues, remains relevant even as its complexities become more salient through increased research and discussion. A study of language use conducted by the Pew Research Hispanic Center in 2011 found that among all Hispanics polled, 45% watched TV mostly in English, 28% mostly in Spanish, and 26% reported watching equally in both languages (Taylor, Lopez, Hamar Martínez & Velasco, 2012). Figure 9.1 illustrates how Spanish viewership decreases while English viewing increases after the first generation.

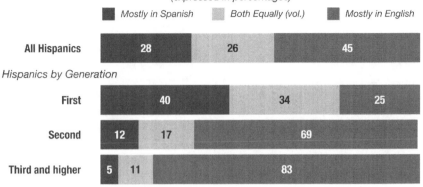

Figure 9.1: Hispanics' Language Preference in TV Viewing
(expressed in percentages)

■ Mostly in Spanish   ░ Both Equally (vol.)   ▒ Mostly in English

	Mostly in Spanish	Both Equally (vol.)	Mostly in English
All Hispanics	28	26	45
First	40	34	25
Second	12	17	69
Third and higher	5	11	83

Hispanics by Generation

Notes: N=1,220. Response of "Don't know" and "Refused" are not shown.
Source: Pew Hispanic Center, 2011 National Survey of Latinos

Adapted from Pew Hispanic Center data: Taylor, Lopez, Hamar Martínez, & Velasco (2012).

These findings clearly present an opportunity to English-language television, but one that the industry has been slow to recognize and act upon, according to some observers (Vega & Carter, 2012). For their part, the major Spanish-language networks have taken note and begun reaching out to English-speaking Hispanics. In 2011 Telemundo initiated English subtitling and started offering "Spanglish" in select programs in order to "focus on a more acculturated, more bilingual" audience according to network president Emilio Romano (Chozick, 2011). Univision announced plans to provide close-captioned English subtitles for its primetime *telenovelas*, citing the genre's "broad appeal that crosses culture and language" (James, 2012). A key strategic challenge of these initiatives was to draw in English-dominant and bilingual viewers without alienating their base of Spanish-dominant audiences. Technology again plays a central role.

Electronic tools that to some observers signal the decline of language differences have underscored the intricacy and intractability of the language challenge in audiovisual media. In the Digital Age language functions as a multiedged sword cutting in several directions (Chambers & Schilling, 2013). Users are able to find and consume information and entertainment in multiple languages more easily and at lower cost than in the past, facilitating the retro-acculturation desires of many younger Hispanics wanting to maintain or improve their Spanish.[11] On the industry side, audience data are gathered more efficiently and in greater volume whether through self-report, media analytics, data mining or other means. This "big data" helps producers tailor content to specific audiences reached through particular media channels more precisely than ever before. The challenge, of course, is that audiences have increasing options to choose among, and the wealthiest producers are best situated to rise above the din. During the early phases of digital transition, Univision and Telemundo have enjoyed such positions of advantage, but how they respond to the language challenge will have strong bearing on their ability to retain an advantage in the future.

The networks' forays into Internet and mobile phones have been quite successful. *Advertising Age* (2012) again cited *univision.com* as the top Spanish Internet portal, and although Hispanics as a whole trailed Whites and Blacks in broadband Internet adoption, Spanish-dominant and bilingual Hispanics were among the fastest-growing adopters (Brenner & Rainie, 2012). Matsaganis's (2011) study of broadband Internet adoption found that Hispanics having regular high-speed Internet access were less likely to consider television their top communication resource (23%) compared to those with irregular access or none at all (77%). Respondents also preferred television in Spanish about 3-to-1 over English. *Advertising Age* (2012) cited a different study indicating that bilingual users were 39% more likely to own an Internet capable smartphone than users in the general population, and Spanish-dominant users were 17% more likely to have a smartphone. These statistics strongly suggest that the Spanish-language television networks will be seeking audiences via Internet and mobile devices well into the future.

New Networks and Services

The initial efforts to reach underserved bilingual and English-dominant Hispanics occurred in the late 1990s and early 2000s, roughly coinciding with Azteca América's emergence. Given the changes and opportunities discussed in this chapter, it comes as little surprise that new initiatives appeared. The V-me network (playing on the Spanish "veme," or "watch me") launched in 2007 as a for-profit, public-private venture between Educational Broadcasting Corp. the corporate parent of WNET New York, and the Baeza Group and Syncom Funds, an investment group and venture capital enterprise, respectively. Although Educational Broadcasting Corp. is a minor partner, V-me's content appears on Public Broadcasting System (PBS) affiliate stations as well as pay television systems, and markets itself as public television in Spanish (Jensen, 2007). V-me emphasizes education and enrichment through programs focused on nature, food, current affairs, hobbies, etc. for adults, and learning for kids including Spanish versions of successful English-language shows such as *Thomas & Friends, Angelina Ballerina, Barney* and *Bob the Builder. Nuestro Barrio (Our Neighborhood)*, a *telenovela*-format program partially underwritten by Freddie Mac, the beleaguered lending institution, integrates information on financial literacy without the steamy romance characteristic of the commercial form. V-me originally launched on 18 PBS-affiliated stations reaching an estimated 60% of Hispanic television households; two years later it claimed to reach 70% of such households through 40 affiliated stations (V-me rides digital, 2009).

In 2011 Sí TV changed its name to NuvoTV. The network continues to broadcast in English and focus on the youth market, calling itself "the first and only English-language television network created for American bicultural Latinos, 18–49" (NuvoTV, 2012). In 2013 program genres included lifestyle, comedy and reruns of syndicated series like *Prison Break* and *Cash Cab*. Original productions favored reality formats including shows on modeling, mixed martial arts, ink (tattooing) and profiles of Hispanics exploring their cultural roots. In September 2012 NuvoTV announced that a minority investor, the actress and singer Jennifer López would contribute her creative, production and marketing talents to the network. Press releases emphasized the rising demand for English-language content among U.S. Hispanics, as well as López's yearning for more Hispanic characters on English television as she was growing up (Steinberg, 2012).

Several partnerships announced in 2012 demonstrated the fluid state of Hispanic-oriented television as well as major media corporations' eagerness to gain footholds among English-speaking and bilingual audiences in the U.S. Pantelion Films, a partnership begun in 2010 between Mexico's Televisa and Lions Gate Entertainment, a Hollywood film and television studio, announced it would move more aggressively to produce Hispanic-oriented English-language television (James, 2012). The partnership's main emphasis remained on film production and distribution as this book went to press. In January 2012 News Corp.'s Fox International Channels Company announced its partnership with RCN network in Colombia to launch MundoFox, a fourth U.S. Spanish-language broadcast television network.[12] MundoFox rolled out nationally in August 2012 with station KWHY in Los Angeles serving as the flagship. RCN has deep experience in telenovela production including the hits *Betty La Fea* (*Ugly Betty*), which became and international sensation, and *El Capo* (*The Drug Boss*), both of which have broadcast on MundoFox and are available online. Initially, most news content originated from RCN's 24-hour news channel, NTN24, with plans to increase contributions from U.S. stations as the network matures.

Another major joint venture announced in 2012 is a 24-hour cable news channel named "Fusion" between ABC and Univision, which launched in October 2013. Fusion's content caters to English-speaking millennials, especially Hispanics; a web site and social media channels supplement the news channel (Carrasquillo, 2012). Clearly this is new terrain for Univision, which, as prior chapters have demonstrated, has long reinforced the Spanish language as a defining characteristic of Hispanics. Cesar Conde, president of Univision Networks, offered a statement that would have been unthinkable before the 1990s: "this joint venture is an extension of our vision to deliver the most relevant news and information, regardless of language, to all Hispanics" (Ford, 2012). The network initiated movements in this direction by offering English subtitles on its primetime *telenovelas* and some other shows including *Sábado Gigante* (James, 2012). However, as Albarran (2012) noted, the ABC-Univision partnership faces challenges in blending the two companies' management styles and corporate cultures.

In addition to the online and mobile content services Novelas y Series and UVideos discussed above, Univision also launched two genre- (and largely gender-) specific networks aimed at niches within the Spanish-speaking audience. The ever-increasing capacity of pay television systems, along with a trend toward combining Hispanic-oriented channels together in premium packages, enables the larger networks to more narrowly target the same general audiences their "broadcast" channels reach (Napoli, 2011). On March 1, 2012 Univision debuted specific channels devoted to *telenovelas* ("tlnovelas") and sports ("Univision Deportes"). Not surprisingly, the channels' content is accessible via Internet and mobile phone; both channels were enabled by settlement of the lawsuit between Televisa and Univision, and Televisa's subsequent acquisition of 5% of Univision in 2010. The network already has a strong sports presence among Hispanics through its Univision brand, but faces considerable competition from rivals Fox Deportes and ESPN Deportes. In its continued effort to reach audiences through non-broadcast channels, Univision also entered contracts to make its content available on the Hulu streaming service and Microsoft's X-Box game consoles (Bercovici, 2012a).

Another ownership change at Telemundo occurred amid this new network and partnership activity. In January 2011 Comcast Corp.'s $13.8 billion purchase of a 51% stake in NBC Universal was approved. Two years later, the cable television giant acquired the remaining 49%, plus other assets, from General Electric for $16.7 billion, citing favorable financing terms. Hispanic advocacy groups were less vocal about ownership concerns than in 2001 when NBC acquired Telemundo from Sony and Liberty Media, although Comcast executives signed a (non-binding) memorandum of understanding with a group comprised of the Hispanic Association on Corporate Responsibility, the National Hispanic Leadership Agenda, and the National Hispanic Media Coalition (Memorandum, 2010). Comcast committed to increasing Hispanics' employment and involvement in corporate governance, programming, procurement and community outreach. Nonetheless, in 2011 concerns were raised about the dearth of local news broadcast on Telemundo stations in comparison with English-language counterparts in the same markets (Torres, 2011). In response, Telemundo promised to increase resources allocated to its owned-and-operated stations.

In closing this section it is important to stress that a variety of online video streaming services such as Hulu Latino and Netflix are competing with Spanish-language television networks and their ever-increasing online offerings. This is but one of multiple fronts on which the networks will face new competition in the decades to come.

Immigration and Political Issues

In the 2012 presidential election Hispanics demonstrated their political influence by voting to reelect Democratic President Barack Obama by a margin of almost 4 to 1 over his Republican opponent Mitt Romney. Throughout the campaign immigration consistently polled as a key issue among Hispanic voters (Lopez & Taylor, 2012). Even though it was widely reported that during his first term Obama's administration had deported more undocumented people than any prior administration, Gov. Romney's strong stand against illegal immigration and undocumented workers in a hotly-contested Republican primary alienated many Hispanic voters. Such voters vary in their political stances and policy preferences toward immigration, but share concerns over narrow, often negative representations of Hispanics by media and politicians, as well as mainstream news reports' tendency to emphasize immigration as the only major Hispanic issue while overlooking others such as education, the economy, jobs and crime (Palacios, 2012; Santa Ana, 2013).

Spanish-Language Television and Election Coverage

Comparative studies of election coverage by English- and Spanish-language television offer insight into the political content that newscasts provide voters. This topic is crucial in light of several dynamics already discussed: language and media use, population growth, and Hispanic voters' power to swing elections at the local, state and national levels. DiSipio (2003) reported that 57% of bilingual speakers prefer watching news in Spanish compared to only 16% who favor English, and 27% who prefer watching both. This finding underscores the importance of Spanish-language news for reaching Hispanic audiences, but we must keep in mind that many of those viewers are not eligible to vote—61% by DiSipio's count.

Oberholzer-Gee and Waldfogel (2006) sought to understand how local Spanish-language television news affects voter turnout by evaluating television newscasts' influence on local civic engagement, a key issue in policy discussions of broadcasting localism. The researchers compared Hispanic voter turnout during the 1994 and 1998 elections in metropolitan areas having, and lacking, regular local Spanish-language TV news broadcasts. They found that local news availability raises Hispanic turnout by more than four percentage points, and that access to news in Spanish led about 20% of viewers to start voting (Oberholzer-Gee & Waldfogel, 2006). This link between Spanish-language news availability and electoral participation deserves more attention by political communication researchers, especially in the content-rich Digital Age when information is available via multiple platforms.

Alexandre and Rehbinder (2008) engaged in "critical and grounded watching" of Univision and Telemundo national newscasts for 14 weeks leading up to the 2000 presidential election. The authors encountered some characteristics of election coverage common to English-language television, such as emphasis on "horse race"[13] aspects and excessive and imprecise reporting on poll results, yet other elements such as Hispanic-oriented reporting on Latin America, education, health care and immigration distinguished the Spanish networks. Although Univision provided more comprehensive campaign coverage, the authors noted that Telemundo offered a number of original, in-depth reports on election-related topics[14] (Alexandre & Rehbinder, 2008).

Hale, Olsen, and Franklin Fowler (2009) compared English- and Spanish-language television coverage of the 2004 presidential elections at the national and local levels, finding that English-language networks devoted substantially more national newscast time (26%) to election coverage than did Spanish-language networks (17%). The same difference appeared at the local level, though with much smaller amounts of newscast time devoted to election coverage: 9% and 7% respectively (Hale, Olsen, & Franklin Fowler 2009). The authors found that Spanish-language stations tailored election coverage more closely to Hispanic interests than did English-language counterparts, yet Spanish stations made little effort to close the gap between low Hispanic political participation and high population growth. They concluded that Spanish-language stations had limited ability to influence their viewers regarding U.S. political campaigns compared to English-language stations (Hale, Olsen, & Franklin Fowler 2009).

Immigration Marches, Legislation and Debate

In the spring of 2006 immigration policy topped news agendas in U.S. media as millions marched in towns and cities nationwide in response to House Resolution 4437, the Border Protection, Anti-Terrorism, and Illegal Immigration Control Act—also known as the Sensenbrenner Bill—which would classify as federal crimes immigration violations, including helping immigrants enter or remain in the country. Spanish-language media, especially radio,[15] played a central role in encouraging turnout to many rallies, including two in Los Angeles and Dallas where crowds were estimated at more than 500,000 (Félix, González, & Ramírez, 2008). A national debate ensued, with opposing positions stridently defended. Spanish-language television news devoted extensive news coverage to the marches, aired special reports, and preempted scheduled programming to report about numerous marches nationwide on May 1, 2006 (Miller & Fernandez, 2006). Spanish-language radio was clearly an important catalyst for mobilizing Hispanics to act, but many turned to Spanish-language television for coverage (Ojito, 2006). Subsequent research by Barreto, Manzano, Ramírez and Rim (2009) confirmed that Spanish-language media consumption was an important mobilizing agent among Hispanics who joined the protests and marches. The authors also reported broad support for the immigration rallies among Hispanics of different national and regional origins; 70% or more of the respondents in all subgroups supported the demonstrations. Although the largest marches took place in the Southwest, opposition to HR 4437 and support for immigrant rights became a national intra-Hispanic movement, facilitated to a large degree by Spanish-language and Hispanic-oriented media, including television. Spanish-language media's ability to foment group consciousness among Hispanics has been documented on other topics besides immigration (Kerevel, 2011).

Four years after the marches, in April 2010, immigration returned to the national spotlight when Arizona's state legislature passed State Bill 1070, a measure requiring non-citizens to carry documents, and mandating that state law enforcement officers attempt to determine a person's immigration status during a traffic stop, detention or arrest, or in other situations presenting the opportunity to inquire about an individual's immigration status. The bill, and public responses to it, received abundant attention from national news media, including the Spanish-language television networks. Vigón, Martínez-Bustos, and González de Bustamante (2012) studied both qualitative and quantitative elements of Telemundo's and Univision's coverage for two months after the bill passed, finding that they devoted twice as much news time to the bill and general immigration issues compared to English-language networks. The Spanish networks also aired a number of special programs regarding the Arizona bill and immigration which incorporated diverse perspectives from a broad range of Hispanics, thereby offering a 'counterframe' to the narrow representations of Hispanics typically offered by English-language television news (Santa Ana, 2013).

On May 14, 2010, Univision aired a special commercial-free program called *Inmigración: Un debate nacional (Immigration: A National Debate)*. Hosted by *Noticiero Univision* anchors María Elena Salinas and Jorge Ramos, the program alternated between network studios in Miami and Univision affiliate KTVW in Phoenix.[16] Panelists at both locations included representatives of national Hispanic organizations, experts in immigration law and public policy, members of congress, Arizona state and local officials, and Hispanic immigrants. Taking advantage of Univision's ample resources, the program streamed live on the Internet, offered closed captioned in English and broadcast on Univision radio stations. On the one hand, the special program signaled Univision's status as an ethnic medium, informing its audience on a key topic for the vast Hispanic community (Wilson, Gutierrez, & Chao, 2012). On the other hand, by framing the complex issue in bipolar terms,[17] the network may have taken the counterframe too far by emphasizing extreme perspectives of those favoring S.B. 1070, thereby reinforcing the 'othering' tendency that is all-too-common in U.S. television news (Vigón, Martínez-Bustos, & González de Bustamante, 2012). The complex challenges facing Spanish-language networks as U.S. news organizations reaching a diverse Hispanic population have been well documented by others (e.g. Rodriguez, 1999; Dávila, 2001; Mora, 2014), yet there's much more to be done.

The 2008 and 2012 Elections

Voting is a crucial arena where Hispanic influence failed to achieve its potential for a quarter-century during and after the 1980s, the "Decade of the Hispanic." That shortfall appears to be changing. In the 2008 presidential race, then Democratic Senator Barack Obama received 67% of

Hispanic votes compared to 31% for Republican Senator John McCain (Lopez, 2008). Estimates of Hispanic representation within the voting public range from 7% to 9%—recall that the 2010 census counted Hispanics at nearly 17% of the U.S. population, and that some Hispanics are not eligible to vote. Obama's support was particularly strong in states with large Hispanic populations:

> Obama carried the Latino vote by sizeable margins in all states with large Latino populations. His biggest breakthrough came in Florida, where he won 57% of the Latino vote in a state where Latinos have historically supported Republican presidential candidates (President Bush carried 56% of the Latino vote in Florida in 2004). Obama's margins were much larger in other states with big Latino populations. He carried 78% of the Latino vote in New Jersey, 76% in Nevada, and 74% in California.
>
> (Lopez, 2008)

During the 2006 midterm elections, Univision gained a $6 million increase in political spending (including its radio operations) over the $16 million it garnered in the 2004 presidential contest (Goetzel, 2008). Nevertheless, political ad spending on Spanish-language television lags in many markets. According to Kantar CMAG, in 2010 Miami area stations captured 31% of all advertising, but only 12% of political ad revenues, and in Denver Spanish-language TV took 14% of general advertising, but barely over 1% of political ads (Sass, 2012). This paltry 1% mirrors the portion of advertising budgets that the McCain and Obama campaigns dedicated to Spanish-language television in the 2008 campaign (De la Fuente, 2012).

Several weeks following the 2012 contest which reelected Democratic President Barack Obama, a news headline claimed, "Hispanics favor Dems but didn't decide election" (York, 2012). One can easily imagine the initial relief of Republican strategists, tempered by the knowledge that Hispanic voters favored Obama over Mitt Romney 71% to 27% (Lopez & Taylor, 2012; Bercovici, 2012b). Hispanics' growing political influence and how to reach and appeal to Hispanic voters more effectively became major talking points among Republicans for several months following the 2012 elections.[18]

Political spending in Spanish-language media was at issue in 2012 as well. By July, the Obama campaign had spent almost 12 times more on Spanish-language advertising than Romney: $6.1 million compared to $521,000 (NBC News cited in Fabian, 2012). These amounts were a pittance compared with total spending, prompting the United States Hispanic Chamber of Commerce (USHCC) to commission a study of the problem. In 10 so-called battleground states for the Hispanic vote, $355 million was spent on political advertising between January 1 and Election Day (November 6); of that sum, $22.8 million, or 6% went to Spanish-language advertising

(Foley, 2012). The president and CEO of USHCC, Javier Palomarez, summarized the organization's concerns:

> Political commentators from both sides of the aisle have said repeatedly that 2012 is the "year of the Hispanic voter." And, in fact, Hispanic voters are poised to play a decisive role in some of the most hotly contested battleground states from Nevada to Florida. But you wouldn't know it from the advertising of our political parties. Thus far in 2012, both parties seem to be spending comparatively little trying to reach Hispanic voters on the media platforms they prefer. The difference between rhetoric and action is striking and, frankly, troubling. (Spending still lags, 2012)

In demographic terms, Hispanic voters comprised about 10% of the 2012 voting population, representing between 10.5 and 12.5 million voters (Taylor, Gonzalez-Barrera, Passel, & Lopez, 2012). Although most registered Hispanic voters are English-dominant, reports indicated that Spanish-language media must be included in any effective political reporting and advertising mix targeting Hispanics (Radalat, 2012). As concerns Hispanic-related election issues, it comes as little surprise that once again the press covered immigration more heavily than other topics such as jobs, the economy and crime.

Given Hispanics' youthful demographic skew and heavy use of social media use discussed above, it follows that voter registration and participation campaigns targeting young Hispanics would employ social media. Organizations such as the National Council of La Raza and VotoLatino executed get-out-the-vote campaigns via YouTube, Twitter and Facebook, using young celebrities like Demi Lovato and Wilmer Valderama for public service announcements (Carrasquillo, 2012). The major Spanish-language television networks got involved as well. Telemundo's campaign "Tu voto, tu futura" (Your vote, your future) pursued a multiplatform approach in encouraging Hispanics' participation in the 2010 midterm elections, and continued that effort in 2012. Univision participated in the *Ya es hora* (It's time) coalition with other Hispanic-oriented media organizations as well as the National Association of Latino Elected Officials and National Council of La Raza, the nation's largest Hispanic advocacy organization. *Ya es hora* has been urging Hispanics to begin the naturalization process toward citizenship, and to register to vote, since the immigration marches of 2006.

Conclusion

The developments covered here demonstrate that the close interactions among business, legal/regulatory, technological, demographic, and political forces that have influenced U.S. Spanish-language television since its inception in the 1960s expanded in the period from 2006 to 2013. Broadcast Media Partners' purchase of Univision for $12.3 billion in 2006 and

Comcast's acquisition of Telemundo as part of NBC Universal in 2011 mark Spanish television's arrival as a profitable sector among commercial media in the world's wealthiest media market. The *Televisa v. Univision* lawsuit's dampening effect on Hispanic-oriented media business illustrates the nexus between commerce and legal disputes when influential players are involved. The fact that digital media rights to television content were hotly contested in the lawsuit reflects the ascendance of Internet and smartphones as distribution media during this period.

Technological advances in communication also played key roles in demographic and political issues. Market research revealed that Hispanics over-index on the use of some smartphone features, but also shows that they are more reticent than other demographic groups to share personal information through social media. Marketing trends link Hispanics' youthful demographic skew with attributes of digital natives, but not without the long-standing challenge of how to employ an effective blend of cultural and linguistic appeals. Similar challenges in designing resonant appeals face politicians and political parties seeking support from the Hispanic vote, now perceived as a less monolithic collective than in decades past, due in significant part to advances in polling, data mining, information shared on social networks and other digital depositories falling under the "big data" moniker.

This trend toward media interactivity allowing Hispanics to directly assert their preferences for content, products and candidates is a key factor distinguishing the period covered in this chapter from prior ones. Digital technology has accelerated audience fragmentation as well as the political and cultural ferment unleashed by hot-button issues, such as immigration, on which Hispanics may disagree in policy terms, but generally resent becoming the defining issue of Hispanic involvement in U.S. society. Providing broader representations of such domestic involvement and U.S. Hispanics' connections with the wider Latin world are the anchors of Spanish-language television's continued relevance in a splintering media universe. *Telenovelas*, variety shows and other staple genres are essential on the entertainment front, and show few signs of diminishing in popularity or impact.

Finally, an increased volume of industry-related information, its greater availability in the public domain, and improved ease of access have simultaneously facilitated and complicated the work of industry professionals and academic researchers. While proprietary information remains a key weapon in the arsenals of industry competitors, more statistics and analyses are becoming publicly available from research companies, organizations like the Pew Hispanic Center, trade journal sources such as the Hispanic Fact Pack published annually by *Advertising Age*, and academic sources like the Selig Center for Economic Growth at the University of Georgia. A growing challenge is keeping up with, and making sense of, the information deluge. Some of the author's industry contacts claim having to dedicate substantial time during nights and weekends to stay current with industry developments through the business press, trade journals and other sources. This theme is taken up in greater detail in the Conclusion, but it bears emphasizing that the information wave propelled by digitization gained considerable momentum during the first dozen years of the 21st century.

Notes

1. Thomson Financial reported that private equity firms purchased 654 U.S. companies in 2006, a quarter of all corporate mergers and acquisitions, representing an 18-fold increase since 2003 (cited in Samuelson, 2007).
2. Stations WQHS-TV in Cleveland, Ohio and KDTV in San Francisco, California.
3. Some information and argumentation in this section is drawn from a study I coauthored with Alex M. Saragoza of the University of California at Berkeley (Wilkinson & Saragoza, 2012).
4. At the time, AOL was still a part of AOL/Time Warner, and Roper was being acquired by the GfK Corporation. It should be noted that the survey methodology employed, random digit dialing, was challenged by the rapid growth of cellular telephones—part of the same transformation the survey sought to elucidate.
5. National Association of Television Program Executives, a large trade convention where program buyers and sellers meet to conduct domestic and international business.
6. These were television, Internet and mobile phones. By the time this book went to press a fourth screen had been added, tablets.
7. UVideos launched with three online "webnovelas" produced in close collaboration between production units at Televisa and Univision (De la Fuente, 2012). Apparently the estranged partners had buried the proverbial hatchet.
8. This finding regarding the professional networking website LinkedIn deserves greater scrutiny among researchers due to its potential impact on Hispanics' career and professional development opportunities.
9. A person born between the latter 1980s and early 2000s who grew up amid digital technology and is attributed with narcissism and/or a sense of entitlement by some older adults.
10. It should be noted that due to its target market Mun2 has a direct interest in promoting youth-oriented appeals.
11. Language translation tools are broadly available, permitting the conversion of text or dialog, as are language learning and reference programs accessible through various digital media platforms, from lesson-oriented programs on DVD or the Internet to function-focused mobile phone applications.
12. In February 2015 the network claimed affiliations with 62 stations in 22 U.S. states, two Mexican states and Puerto Rico (MundoFox. [2015]. Wikipedia. Retrieved from http://en.wikipedia.org/wiki/MundoFox).
13. Campaign coverage that emphasizes who is ahead in the election "race," typically with heavy reporting of opinion poll results.
14. Alexandre & Rehbinder (2008) also observed that whereas the Republican campaign of George W. Bush initiated persistent and consistent outreach out to Spanish-language media beginning in the late-summer convention period, Democrat Al Gore's campaign only began such efforts in the final weeks of the campaign.

15. Eduardo "Piolín" Sotelo who hosts *El Piolín por la Mañana* (Piolín in the Morning), a top-rated morning radio show, is credited with organizing other Spanish radio hosts to encourage listeners to attend rallies and write letters to congressional representatives.
16. Available at https://www.youtube.com/watch?v=_d7IPFWMJ58.
17. A Univision press release announcing the event stated it would "provide a platform for *both sides* to discuss key issues surrounding immigration policy in the U.S." (emphasis added). Univision announces participants in town hall on immigration "Inmigración: Un Debate Nacional." Retrieved March 12, 2013 from http://corporate.univision.com/2010/press/univision-announces-participants-in-town-hall-on-immigration-%E2%80%9Cinmigracion-un-debate-nacional%E2%80%9D/#axzz2NLDsWX00.
18. Some argue that the Republican primaries and the party's general stance toward ethnic difference communicated an "us vs. them" perception that contradicted Hispanics' typical collectivist worldview and deep-seated cultural pride (Palacios, 2012).

References

The 51-hour day? Yahoo! Telemundo research shows online U.S. Hispanics consume and adopt more media and technology than general population. (2007, March 28). *Hispanic PR Wire*. Retrieved from http://www.hispanicprwire.com/News/in/8328/12/the-51-hour-day-yahoo-telemundo-research-shows-online-us-hispanics-consume/.

Advertising Age. (2012, July 23). *Hispanic fact pack: Annual guide to Hispanic marketing and media* [2012 edition]. *Crain Communications*. Retrieved from http://www.adagewhitepapers.com/adage/hispanicfactpack2012/?sub_id=DQtSG96buZUlU#pg1.

Albarran, Alan. (2012, October 18). *The market for Spanish language television news in the United States: A macro analysis.* Paper presented at "Hispanics and the Media: The Emerging Power" conference, Florida International University, Miami, Florida.

Alexandre, Laurien, & Rehbinder, Henrik. (2008). Watching the 2000 presidential campaign on Univisión and Telemundo. In F. A. Subervi-Vélez (Ed.), *The mass media and Latino politics: Studies of U.S. media content, campaign strategies and survey research: 1984–2004* (pp. 154–177). New York, NY: Routledge.

Bachman, Katy. (2007a, March 28). FCC Oks Univision sale. *Adweek*. Retrieved from http://www.adweek.com/news/advertising-branding/fcc-oks-univision-sale-88438.

Barber, Tamara. (2009, August 17). Hispanic youth are influential and empowered spenders [Web log post]. Retrieved from http://blogs.forrester.com/tamara_barber/09–08–17-hispanic_youth_are_influential_and_ empowered_spenders.

Becker, Anne. (2006, May 1). Telemundo's broadband bonanza. *Broadcasting & Cable, 136*(18), 12.

Bercovici, Jeff. (2012a, July 18). The next media jackpot: The fight for the $1 trillion Hispanic market. *Forbes*. Retrieved from http://www.forbes.com/sites/jeffbercovici/2012/07/18/the-next-media-jackpot-the-fight-for-the-1-trillion-hispanic-market/print/.

Bercovici, Jeff. (2012b, July 18). The making of el presidente 2012: Spanish-language TV and the election. *Forbes.* Retrieved from http://www.forbes. com/sites/jeffbercovici/2012/07/18/the-making-of-el-presidente-2012-spanish-language-tv-and-the-campaign.

Bergantini Grillo, Jean. (2003, March 23). What a niche audience! *Broadcasting & Cable, 133*(12), 20.

Barreto, Matt A., Manzano, Sylvia, Ramírez, Ricardo, & Rim, Kathy. (2009). Mobilization, participation, and solidaridad: Latino participation in the 2006 immigration protest rallies, *Urban Affairs Review, 44* (5) 736–764.

Beales, Richard. (2007, March 1). Univision deal put the bling into the LBO trend: A deal struck by the Spanish-language broadcast group last year has proved a case study on leveraged buy-outs. *Financial Times* (London), 43.

Bennett, Shea. (2012, April 13). Hispanics love social media (and they're more careful about online privacy). *Adweek.com SocialTimes.* Retrieved from http://www.adweek.com/socialtimes/hispanics-social-media/462480.

Blackshaw, Pete. (2008, September 22). Spanish-language content surprisingly lacking on Internet. *Advertising Age,* 52. Retrieved from Lexis-Nexis database.

Brenner, Joanna, & Rainie, Lee. (2012, December 9). Pew Internet: Broadband. *Pew Internet and American Life Project.* Retrieved from http://pewinternet.org / Commentary/2012/May/Pew-Internet-Broadband.aspx.

Carrasquillo, Adrian. (2012, August 6). Urgent social media efforts by Latino organizations aim to get Hispanic youth registered to vote. *NBCLatino.com.* Retrieved from http://nbclatino.com/2012/08/06/urgent-social-media-efforts-by-latino-organizations-aim-to-get-hispanic-youth-to-register-to-vote.

Cartagena, Chiqui. (2011, February 3). With Google in the game, will Hispanic digital (finally) grow? *Advertising Age.* Retrieved from http://adage.com/article/the-big-tent/google-hispanic-digital-finally-grow/148641/.

Chambers, John Kenneth, & Schilling-Estes, Natalie (Eds.). (2103). *The handbook of language variation and change.* Hoboken, NJ: John Wiley & Sons.

Children's educational television. (2011, May 19). Federal Communications Commission, Bureau of Consumer & Governmental Affairs. Retrieved from http://www.fcc.gov/guides/childrens-educational-television.

Chozick, Amy. (2011, October 25). Telemundo blends English into a mostly Spanish lineup. *New York Times.* Retrieved from http://www.nytimes.com/2011/10/26/business/media/telemundo-seeks-spanglish-speakers-in-aim-for-new-viewers.html?pagewanted=all.

Coffey, Amy Jo, & Sanders, Amy Kristin. (2010). Defining a product market for Spanish-language broadcast media: United States v. Univision Communications, Inc. and Hispanic Broadcasting. *Communication Law and Policy, 15,* 55–89.

Consoli, John. (2006, May 29). Digital dominance. *MediaWeek,* SR22.

Datamonitor. (2010, November 12). *Univision Communications company profile.* Retrieved from www.datamonitor.com.

Dávila, Arlene. (2001). *Latinos, Inc.: The marketing and making of a people.* Berkeley, CA: University of California Press.

De la Fuente, Anna Marie. (2012, June 15). Latino TV's pol position. *Variety.* Retrieved from EBSCO database.

De Lafuente, Della. (2008, January 21). Vidal goes mobile for Sprint. *AdWeek.* Retrieved from Lexi-Nexis database.

De Zengotita, Thomas. (2005). *Mediated: How the media shapes your world and the way you live in it.* New York, NY: Bloomsbury Publishing.

Deploying digital strategies. (2010, April 12). *MediaWeek*. Retrieved from EBSCO database.

DeSipio, Louis. (2003). *Bilingual television viewers and the language choices they make*. Claremont, CA: Tomas Rivera Policy Institute.

Dyer, Pam. (2010, March 21). We're addicted to social networks: 48% of us check them in bed. *Pamorama.net*. Retrieved from http://www.pamorama.net/2010/03/21/were-addicted-to-social-networks-48-of-us-check-them-in-bed/#ixzz2Q6qLmqc8.

Ennis, Sharon R., Ríos-Vargas, Merarys, & Albert, Nora G. (2011, May). *The Hispanic population: 2010* (Census Brief No. C2010BR-04). Retrieved from U.S. Census Bureau website http://www.census.gov/prod/cen2010/briefs/c2010br-04.pdf.

Fabian, Jordan. (2012, August 2). The air war: Obama has outspent Romney 12–1 in Spanish-language ads. *Univision News Tumblr*. Retrieved from http://thisisfusion.tumblr.com/post/28576613716/obama-outspent-romney-in-spanish-ads.

Federal Communications Commission (FCC). (2007, March 27). FCC approves transfer of Univision Communications Inc., and enters into $24 million consent decree with Univision concerning children's programming requirement [Press release]. Retrieved from http://hraunfoss.fcc.gov/edocs_public/attachmatch/DOC-271810A1.pdf.

Félix, Adrián, González, Carmen, & Ramírez, Ricardo. (2008, December). Political protest, ethnic media, and Latino naturalization. *American Behavioral Scientist*, 52(4), 618–634.

Foley, Elise. (2012, November 16). Spanish-language election ad numbers 'disappointing,' Hispanic Chamber president says. *Huffington Post*. Retrieved from http://www.huffingtonpost.com/2012/11/16/spanish-language-ads-election-2012_n_2145241.html.

Ford, David. (2012, May 7). ABC News and Univision News plan to join forces to create pioneering joint venture: Multiplatform news and information service for U.S. Hispanics. *ABC News*. Retrieved from http://abcnews.go.com/blogs/headlines/2012/05/abc-news-and-univision-news-plan-to-join-forces-to-create-pioneering-joint-venture-multiplatform-news-and-information-service-for-u-s-hispanics/.

Fox, Susannah, & Livingston, Gretchen. (2007, March 14). Latinos online: Hispanics with lower levels of education and English proficiency remain largely disconnected from the Internet. *Pew Internet & American Life Project/Pew Hispanic Center*. Retrieved from http://www.pewinternet.org/files/old-media/Files/Reports/2007/Latinos_Online_March_14_2007.pdf.pdf.

Goetzl, David. (2008, March 1). Latino stations win big in Texas. *Broadcasting & Cable*. Retrieved from http://www.broadcastingcable.com/article/101946-Latino_Stations_Win_Big_in_Texas.php.

Grover, Ronald. (2006, June 21). What price Univision? *Business Week*. Retrieved from http://www.businessweek.com/print/bwdaily/dnflash/jun2006/nf20060621_3015_db016.htm?chan=db.

Guskin, Emily, & Mitchell, Amy. (2011). *Hispanic media: Faring better than the mainstream media* (State of the News Media 2011 Report). Retrieved from Pew Research Center's Project for Excellence in Journalism website http://stateofthemedia.org/2011/hispanic-media-fairing-better-than-the-mainstream-media/.

Hale, Matthew, Tricia Olsen, and Erika Franklin Fowler. (2009). A matter of language or culture: Coverage of the 2004 US elections on Spanish-and English-language television. *Mass Communication and Society*, 12(1), 26–51.

Hinojosa, Maria. (2013, April 28). For some young Latinos: Donkey jaws and Latino roots [Code switch: Frontiers of race, culture and ethnicity]. *National Public Radio.* Retrieved from http://www.npr.org/blogs/codeswitch/2013/04/28/179277601/ for-some-young-latinos-donkey-jaws-and-latino-roots.

Hispanic millennials require new marketing strategies. (2012, May 15). *Hispanic Marketing/Target Latino.* Retrieved from http://hispanic-marketing.com/bl/ demographics/hispanic-youth/hispanic-millennials-require-new-marketing -strategies/.

Hispanics in U.S. highly active on mobile and social. (2012, April 20). *Nielsen Wire.* Retrieved from http://www.nielsen.com/us/en/insights/news/2012/hispanics-in-u- s-highly-active-on-mobile-and-social.html.

Humes, Karen R., Jones, Nicholas A., & Ramirez, Roberto R. (2011, March). *Overview of race and Hispanic origin: 2010* (Census Brief No. C2010BR-02). Retrieved from U.S. Census Bureau website http://www.census.gov/prod/cen2010/ briefs/c2010br-02.pdf.

IAB Research & BIGinsight Data (2012, October 10). *Hispanic consumers and digital media.* Presentation for IAB Multicultural Agency Day. Retrieved from http://www.iab.net/media/file/Hispanic-Digital-Consumer.pdf.

James, Meg. (2009a, January 23). Univision and Televisa settle high-stakes lawsuit. *Los Angeles Times.* Retrieved from http://articles.latimes.com/2009/jan/23/ business/fi-televisa23.

James, Meg (2009b, July 18). Univision prevails against Grupo Televisa in fight over telenovela episodes on the Internet. *Los Angeles Times.* Retrieved from http:// articles.latimes.com/print/2009/jul/18/business/fi-ct-univision18.

James, Meg. (2012, January 24). Lionsgate and Grupo Televisa to expand TV partnership. *Los Angeles Times.* Retrieved from http://latimesblogs.latimes. com/entertainmentnewsbuzz/2012/01/lionsgate-and-televisa-announce-tv- partnership.html.

Jensen, Elizabeth. (2007, February 7). Public television plans a network for Latinos. *New York Times,* E1. Retrieved from Lexis-Nexis database.

Keating, Gina. (2009, June 9). Televisa, Univision spar over Internet rights. *Reuters.com.* Retrieved from http://www.reuters.com/assets/print?aid=USN09 40236720090609.

Kerevel, Yann P. (2011, June). The influence of Spanish-language media on Latino public opinion and group consciousness. *Social Science Quarterly, 92*(2), 509–534.

Korzenny, Felipe, & Vann, Lee. (2009). Tapping into their connections: The multi- cultural world of social media marketing. *Quirk's Marketing Research Review.* Retrieved from http://hmc.comm.fsu.edu/files/2012/02/2009-Multicultural- World-of-Social-Media-Marketing-Article.pdf.

Lawson-Borders, Gracie L. (2006). *Media organizations and convergence: Case studies of media convergence pioneers.* Mahwah, NJ: Lawrence Erlbaum.

Levingston, Steve, White, Ben, & Williams, Krissah. (2006, February 9). Univision offers a prized market segment. *Washington Post,* D1–D7.

Livingston, Gretchen. (2011, February 9). *Latinos and digital technology, 2010* [Pew Hispanic Center 2010 National Survey of Latinos]. Retrieved from Pew Research Hispanic Center website http://pewhispanic.org/files/reports/134.pdf.

Lopez, Mark Hugo. (2008, November 5). *The Hispanic vote in the 2008 election* [Hispanic Trends Report]. Retrieved from Pew Research Hispanic Center website http://www.pewhispanic.org/2008/11/05/the-hispanic-vote-in-the-2008-election/.

Lopez, Mark Hugo, & Taylor, Paul. (2012, November 7). Latino voters in the 2012 election. *Pew Research Center: Hispanic Trends.* Retrieved from http://www.pewhispanic.org/2012/11/07/latino-voters-in-the-2012-election/.

Martinez, Laura. (2007a, May 14). Integration opportunities fuel Hispanic nets' growth. *Advertising Age.* Retrieved from http://adage.com/article/special-report-upfront07/integration-opportunities-fuel-hispanic-nets-growth/116584/.

Martinez, Laura. (2007b, April 23). Mobile video booms among Latinos. *Advertising Age.* Retrieved from http://adage.com/article/hispanic-marketing/mobile-video-booms-latinos/116160/.

Matsaganis, Matthew D. (2011, December). *Broadband adoption and Internet use among Latinos.* Retrieved from Tomás Rivera Policy Institute website http://www.twcresearchprogram.com/pdf/TWC_MatsaganisReport.pdf.

Mcfarlane, Cynthia. (2007, May 9). Get connected with Latinos in Nuevo America—Interacculturation: Blended cultures fuel mainstream. *Ad Age.* Retrieved from http://adage.com/article/cmo-strategy/connec ted-latinos-nuevo-america/116598.

McNaughton, Marissa. (2012, January 26). Social media use by Hispanic Americans grows 38% in one year. *The Realtime Report.* Retrieved from http://therealtimereport.com/2012/01/26/social-media-use-by-hispanic-americans-grows-38-in-one-year/.

Memorandum of understanding between Comcast Corporation, NBC Universal and the Hispanic Leadership Organizations. (2010, May 25). (DMEAST #12321437 v29). Retrieved from Federal Communications Commission's electronic comment filing system website http://apps.fcc.gov/ecfs/document/view?id=7020550506.

Miller, Martin, & Fernandez, Maria Elena. (2006, May 2). The May Day marches: Immigrant story takes precedence on TV, radio: Some stations and networks preempt scheduled programs to expand their coverage of the rallies held around the nation. *Los Angeles Times,* A18.

Mun2. (2008). *Me2: A two part Latino youth study.* Report commissioned by Mun2, Telemundo Network Group.

Napoli, Philip M. (2011). *Audience evolution: New technologies and the transformation of media audiences.* New York, NY: Columbia University Press.

NuvoTV (2012, September 12). Jennifer Lopez and NuvoTV announce exclusive creative, production and marketing partnership. *Rho Ventures Archived News.* Retrieved from http://www.rhoventures.com/1202b11a-a72c-43fe-b26e-8f548bd41ff2/archived-news-2012-details.htm.

Oberholzer-Gee, Felix, & Waldfogel, Joel. (2006). *Media markets and localism: Does local news en Español boost Hispanic voter turnout?* (No. w12317). National Bureau of Economic Research. Retrieved from http://www.researchgate.net/profile/Joel_Waldfogel/publication/227354257_Media_Markets_and_Localism_Does_Local_News_en_Espanol_Boost_Hispanic_Voter_Turnout/links/0deec524ea5a5f0a3c000000.pdf.

Ojito, Mirta. (2006, April 30). Voice of (Hispanic) America. *New York Times.* Retrieved from http://www.nytimes.com/2006/04/30/arts/television/30ojito.html?pagewanted=all&_r=0.

Palacios, Stephen. (2012, November 13). Note to Republican Party: It's not immigration. *Huffington Post Latino Voices.* Retrieved from http://www.huffingtonpost.com /stephen-palacios/note-to-republican-party_b_2118985.html.

Passel, Jeffrey, Cohn, D'Vera, & Gonzalez-Barrera, Ana. (2012, April 23). *Net migration from Mexico falls to zero—and perhaps less* [Hispanic Trends Report].

Retrieved from Pew Research Hispanic Center website http://www.pewhispanic .org/2012/04/23/net-migration-from-mexico-falls-to-zero-and-perhaps-less/.

Pettersson, Edvard. (2009, January 6). Univision may lose top shows in Televisa royalty case (update1). *Bloomberg*. Retrieved from http://www.bloomberg.co.jp/ apps/news?pid=90970900&sid=aXbTHMN4Sx2s.

Perez, Eduardo. (2012, June). *The Spanglish generation: Tapping it to grow and conquer market share* [Sourcebook of Multicultural Experts 2012/13: The Hispanic Market]. Retrieved from http://multicultural.com/multicultural_markets / hispanic_market.

Politi, James. (2008, June, 28). Saban consortium buys Univision for Dollars 12.3bn. *Financial Times* (London), 32.

Politi, James, & Van Duyn, Aline. (2006, June 28). Spanish TV drama's final scene may yet need further rewrite Aline van Duyn on the twists and turns of the saga surrounding Univision's sale—Is the latest episode the end or a cliffhanger? *Financial Times* (London), 32.

Radalat, Ana. (2012, May 7). In race for White House, push for Latino voters is on. *Advertising Age, 83*(19), 104. Retrieved from EBSCO database.

Rideout, Victoria, Lauricella, Alexis, & Wartella, Ellen. (2011, June). *Children, media and race: Media use among White, Black, Hispanic and African American children*. Retrieved from Northwestern University's School of Communication Center on Media and Human Development website web5.soc.northwestern.edu / cmhd/wpcontent/uploads/2011/06/SOCconfReportSingleFinal-1.pdf.

Rodriguez, América. (1999). *Making Latino news: Race, language, class*. Thousand Oaks, CA: Sage.

Rodriguez, Fernando. (2012, July 26). Six things advertisers need to know about the growing Hispanic market. *Advertising Age*. Retrieved from http://adage.com / article/the-big-tent/advertisers-reach-growing-u-s-hispanic-market/236336/.

Roper Public Affairs. (2005). AOL & Roper Hispanic Cyberstudy 2005 [Third annual]. Retrieved from http://michaelsaray.com/%20News%20Articles/AOL% 20Latino.htm.

Saenz, Rogelio. (2010, December). Population bulletin update: Latinos in the United States 2010. Retrieved from *Population Reference Bureau* website www.prb.org/ pdf10/latinos-update2010.pdf.

Samuelson, Robert J. (2007, March 19). The enigma of private equity. *Newsweek*. Retrieved from http://www.newsweek.com/2007/03/18/the-enigma-of-private-equity.print.htm.

Santa Ana, Otto. (2013). *Juan in a hundred: The representation of Latinos on network news*. Austin, TX: University of Texas Press.

Sass, Erik. (2012, August 14). Political ad spend on Hispanics trails political clout. *Media Daily News*. Retrieved from http://www.mediapost.com/publications/ article/180836/political-ad-spend-on-hispanics-trails-political-c.html#axzz 2NOCvzkhY.

Schaffhauser, Dian. (2012, October 31). Univision taps social media to promote Hispanic education. *TheJournal.com*. Retrieved from http://thejournal.com/ articles/2012/10/31/univision-taps-social-media-to-promote-hispanic-education. aspx.

Sonderup, Laura. (2004, April). Hispanic marketing: A critical market segment. *Advertising and Market Review*. Retrieved from www.ad-mkt-review.com/ public_html/docs/fs075.html.

Sorkin, Andrew Ross, & Edmonston, Peter. (2006, September 12). Televisa still covets Univision. *New York Times*. Retrieved July 13, 2011 from http://www. nytimes.com/2006/09/12/business/media/12place.html?.

Spending still lags on Spanish-language election ads. (2012, October 1). *Hispanic Business*. Retrieved from http://www.hispanicbusiness.com/2012/10/1/spending_still_lags_on_spanishlanguage_election.htm.

Steinberg, Brian. (2012, September 12). Jennifer Lopez to take minority stake in cable's Nuvo TV. *Advertising Age*. Retrieved from http://adage.com/article/media / jennifer-lopez-minority-stake-cable-s-nuvo-tv/237139/.

Szalai, Georg. (2013, February 21). Univision Communications fourth-quarter financials improve. *Hollywood Reporter*. Retrieved from Lexis-Nexis database.

Szalai, Georg, & Hecht, John. (2010, October 6). Televisa, Univision deal ushers in new era. *The Hollywood Reporter*. Retrieved from http://www.adweek.com/news/television/televisa-univision-deal-ushers-new-era-116270.

Taylor, Paul, & Cohn, DeVera. (2012, November 7). *A milestone en route to a majority minority nation* [Social and Demographic Trends Report]. Retrieved from Pew Research Center websitehttp://www.pewsocialtrends. org/2012/11/07/a-milestone-en-route-to-a-majority-minority-nation/.

Taylor, Paul, Gonzalez-Barrera, Ana, Passel, Jeffrey, & Lopez, Mark Hugo. (2012, November 14). *An awakened giant: The Hispanic electorate is likely to double by 2030* [Hispanic Trends Report]. Retrieved from Pew Research Hispanic Center website http://www.pewhispanic.org/2012/11/14/an-awakened-giant-the-hispanic-electorate-is-likely-to-double-by-2030/#fn-16896–1.

Taylor, Paul, Lopez, Mark Hugo, Hamar Martinez, Jessica & Velasco, Gabriel. (2012, April 4). *When labels don't fit: Hispanics and their views of identity – Part IV Language use among Latinos* [Hispanic Trends Report]. Retrieved from Pew Research Hispanic Center website http://www.pewhispanic.org/2012/04/04/ iv-language-use-among-latinos/.

Teinowitz, Ira. (2007, April 2). Univision ties up deal to go private: Broadcast Media Partners now controls media giant. *Television Week*, p. 13.

Telenoticias Hispanic Public Relations. (2009, September 25). Hispanics top the charts in use of social media [Web log post]. Retrieved from http://telenoticiasusa. com/ blog/archives/hispanics-top-the-charts-in-use-of-social-media.

Torres, Joseph. (2011, May 19). Comcast's meager promises to Telemundo. *Free Press*. Retrieved from http://www.freepress.net/blog/11/05/19/comcasts-meager-promises-telemundo.

Understanding today's Hispanic youth identity in the U.S. (n.d.). In *Hispanic marketer's guide to cable* (pp. 124–125). Retrieved from http://www.thecab.tv /main/ bm~doc/understanding-hispanic-youth-identity-in-the-u-s.pdf.

Univision launches mobile and web novelas channel. (2010, February 22). *TV Technology*. Retrieved from http://www.tvtechnology.com/exhibitions-&-events/0109/univision-launches-mobile-and-web-novelas-channel/204985.

Vigón, Mercedes, Martínez-Bustos, Lilliam, & González de Bustamante, Celeste. (2012). Not business as usual: Spanish-language television coverage of Arizona's immigration law April-May 2010. In O. Santa Ana & C. González de Bustamante (Eds.), *Arizona firestorm: Global immigration realities, national media, and provincial politics* (pp. 203–225). Lanham, MD: Rowman & Littlefield Publishers.

Villa, Jose. (2009, July 16). The Hispanic youth market—Too big to ignore. *MediaPost.* Retrieved from http://www.mediapost.com/publications/article/109929/the-hispanic-youth-market-too-big-to-ignore.html.

V-me rides digital transition to rank as 4th largest U.S. Hispanic broadcaster. (2009, June 12). *PR Newswire.* Retrieved from http://www.prnewswire.com/news-releases/v-me-rides-digital-transition-to-rank-as-4th-largest-us-hispanic-broadcaster-62105612.html.

Vega, Tanzina, & Carter, Bill. (2012, August 5). Networks struggle to appeal to Hispanics. *New York Times.* Retrieved from http://www.nytimes.com/2012/08/06/business/media/networks-struggle-to-appeal-to-hispanics-without-using-stereotypes.html.

Wentz, Laurel. (2007, April 23). Expect more growth in '07. *Advertising Age,* S-1.

Wentz, Laurel. (2008, January 7). Multicultural players make social networks, mobile their priorities. *Advertising Age,* 18.

Wentz, Laurel. (2009, January 22). Univision, Televisa Settle TV-programming dispute. *Advertising Age.* Retrieved from http://adage.com/article/hispanic-marketing/univision-televisa-settle-tv-programming-dispute/134031/.

Wentz, Laurel. (2011, May 16). More than TV: Univision sells Hispanic expertise. *Advertising Age.* Retrieved from http://adage.com/article/hispanic-marketing/tv-univision-sells-hispanic-expertise/227558/.

Westlund, Richard. (2011, April 27). Finding the gold in Hispanic marketing. *Adweek.* Retrieved from http://www.adweek.com/sa-article/finding-gold-hispanic-marketing-130612.

Wilkinson, Kenton T., & Saragoza, Alex M. (2012, Fall). Cuando potencias hegemónicas riñen: "Televisa vs. Univision" Communications vista a través de una lente de gestión de medios. (When hegemons quarrel: Televisa vs. Univision Communications viewed through a media management lens.) *Global Media Journal Mexico 9,* 16–34.

Wilson, Clint C. II, Gutiérrez, Félix, & Chao, Lena M. (2012). *Racism, sexism, and the media: Multicultural issues into the new communications age* (4th ed.). Thousand Oaks, CA: Sage.

Wu, J. H., and Wang, S. C. (2005). What drives mobile commerce? An empirical evaluation of the revised technology acceptance model. *Information and Management, 42,* 719–729.

Yahoo! Telemundo. (2007). *Conexión cultural/Cultural connection: Research results based on U.S. Hispanic use of media and technology.* Miami, FL.

York, Byron. (2012, November 22). York: Hispanics favor Dems, but didn't decide election. *Washington Examiner.* Retrieved from http://www.washingtonexaminer.com/hispanics-favor-dems-but-didnt-decide-election/article/2514164.

Conclusion

This book's objective has been to examine the first 50 years of Spanish-language television development in the United States through an integrated approach enveloping the business, legal/regulatory, technological, demographic and political forces that have influenced the industry and which, in turn, it has impacted. Observing the industry's growth in this comprehensive way reveals the complexity of related factors that have increased Hispanics' impact on U.S. society during the early decades of the 21st century. These last few pages pull together salient themes from the chapters.

The principal, although not exclusive, sources informing this book are business press and trade journals reports and academic research. I have tried to demonstrate how they may complement one another in illustrating a media industry's development within a broader context of change. As discussed in the Introduction, such materials offer benefits as well as shortcomings, requiring researchers to apply clear-eyed consideration and corroboration through other sources. The tools that researchers employ to identify, access and analyze secondary sources transformed drastically over the period this book covers, implying that how we apply those tools must change as well. As information technology advances and media industries continue to expand, so will the availability of industry-related reports and academic research. We must bear in mind, however, that greater accessibility to information is not analogous to its increased credibility (Wilkinson & Merle, 2013). Threats to validity will persist, in varying ways, far into the future. I hope that others will take up this important methodological issue, especially as it applies to the study and understanding of ethnic-oriented media.

A recurring theme from the first chapter to the last is U.S. Spanish-language television's connections with industries and audiences in Latin America. From its origins as an initiative to increase offshore demand for Mexican programs, to becoming a multibillion dollar industry in which Telemundo emerged as the second largest program distributor behind Televisa (Mendoza, 2014), international connections have remained constant. (Another related constant worth noting has been the presence and influence of an Emilio Azcárraga, across three generations.) Yet surprisingly, in light of the deep transformations chronicled in this book, programming patterns have changed very little. Notwithstanding increases in domestic production levels, programs produced and/or distributed by Televisa continue to dominate U.S. prime time, and its programming contract with the Mexican company remains a major competitive advantage for Univision. Whether attributed to willful market domination, as from a critical orientation, or the normal outcome of market forces, from a neoliberal perspective, U.S. Spanish-language television continues to rely on imported content. This programming dynamic remains entrenched even as advances in digital technology open new sources of competition that broadcast networks must respond to, and which open new spaces for content creation and consumption as well as interaction among Spanish-speaking audiences worldwide.

The persistence of international influences in Spanish-language television is attributable to a number of factors, including regulation—or, more accurately, lack thereof—by the Federal Communications Commission and other agencies. The FCC has taken a largely *laissez faire* attitude toward the sector, except when compelled to act, as when it received complaints of foreign ownership and control in the 1980s and charges of monopoly control in the early 2000s. Some early observers like López and Enos (1974) and Gutiérrez and Schement (1981) advocated expanding the prosocial functions of Spanish-language television, which would have involved some level of government support and/or intervention—but to no avail. The federal government acted more as arbiter of disputes than promoter of a valuable resource reaching a disadvantaged population. A growing commercialism ensued, and U.S. Hispanic media professionals and advocates alike have complained of Mexican and non-Hispanic corporate dominance of the medium. In this regard, it bears mentioning that while advocates and others engage in fervent struggles, audiences are determining outcomes with their remote controls, computer cursors and mobile devices. The federal government's deregulatory orientation toward media and communication has been clear since the 1980s, and showed no signs of abating as this book went to print.

The central demographic theme during the period covered by this book is Hispanic population growth as measured by the decennial U.S. Census (see Appendix A). Immigration was especially impactful from 1960 to 2000, and clearly has been a central factor in the steady growth of U.S. Spanish-language media. Unfortunately, our understanding of the Hispanic population's longitudinal development is hampered by constant changes in ethnic, racial and nation-of-origin categories as well as data-gathering techniques by the U.S. Bureau of the Census. Especially significant for Spanish-language television in the 2010s was domestic births driving the population increase, which indicates that U.S.-born Hispanics' preferences and experiences will exert increasing influence over media industries. Spanish-language television will continue to serve as an important medium for Spanish-dominant immigrants as well as bilinguals and some English-dominant Hispanics seeking specific content, but the industry will need to adapt more thoughtfully to the tastes of U.S.-born audience members who are digital natives, sensitive to identity representations and select (as well as create) content from a broad array of media choices.

Over the half-century covered by this book, language has diminished somewhat as the defining parameter for the industry. From the 1960s through 1980s the use of Spanish determined what constituted Hispanic media; since then a broadening recognition that Hispanics are also bilingual and English-dominant has diversified the sector and challenged the Spanish-language networks (Johnson, 2010). This trend is likely to continue, with labels such as "Hispanic-oriented" and "Latino/a-oriented" supplanting "Spanish-language" as accurate industry descriptors. The population's language loyalty is another significant variable. Paxman (2004) raised an important question: have Spanish-language media *benefited* from a higher degree of language loyalty among their audiences, or have they primarily *contributed* to it? The direction of influence may clarify in coming decades, along with generational differences in language use and loyalty. These are key issues for the future of Hispanic-oriented media, as evident in the heavy emphasis on reaching so-called millennials[1] in the mid-2010s.

The technological advances were driven by entrepreneurial energy and acumen in the industry's early years, as demonstrated by astute management of the UHF band, satellite distribution, repeaters and low-power television. In the 1980s and '90s management successfully adapted to technological advances, and the arrival of digital television and the Internet demanded unprecedented levels of investment and human capital to keep pace with accelerated technological change. Fortunately for the industry, the size and spending power of the U.S. Hispanic population grew rapidly during the digitization process, providing essential capital and exposure. The steady growth of Spanish-language television's core business—traditional television broadcasting and cable—continued in the new century, a time when other industry sectors saw their audiences decline as competitive new technologies appeared. In this sense, the Spanish-language networks were in an enviable position during the first dozen years of the new millennium.

Audience members' increasing technology options was another important shift. In the 1960s through 1980s, viewers' decisions centered on whether to adopt a major technology such as UHF (purchasing the set and/ or converter) or subscribing to cable television. In the 21st century consumers choose among an array of options for accessing pay television (cable, satellite, on-demand), Internet (subscription, streaming, social media) and mobile devices (computers, phones, tablets, watches). Thus, power over technology has literally shifted to the hands of consumers, leaving the industry to cover multiple bases simultaneously and endeavor to push consumers toward their content—and their clients' advertising—on multiple platforms. Hispanics' tendency to overindex on certain technologies like computer purchases, time spent on the Internet and viewing videos on mobile devices offer advantages to competitors, like Spanish-language television networks, who know such consumers best. The 21st century trend toward big data influencing media management decision making will likely become a fiercely competitive front not only among Hispanic-oriented media, but also with mainstream media organizations vying for the attention and loyalty of Hispanic consumers.

This book's final two sections illustrate a mainstreaming process whereby the profile and functions of Spanish-language television came to more closely resemble those of large English-language players. Telemundo joined a major mainstream conglomerate, NBC Universal, and a group of private equity companies acquired Univision for $13.7 billion. These developments show the value of Spanish-language television stations and networks as key assets in contemporary U.S. media—they no longer reside on the margins as in earlier decades.

Periods of heightened attention to the Hispanic population and market have stimulated mainstream companies' investment in the sector. A report during the Decade of the Hispanic, the 1980s, brought Hispanic media to the attention of Henry Silverstein of Reliance Capital Group who subsequently became president of Telemundo, and Latin Boom coverage in the early 2000s brought renewed attention to the Hispanic sector when Internet technology and its adoption by consumers was also expanding. The industry's intense interest in the Hispanic youth demographic in the 2000s and 2010s manifests these concurrent developments in popular culture and communication technology. A related trend involved Hispanic celebrities assuming prominent leadership positions at new networks as Jennifer López took on ownership, spokesperson and creative director roles in NuvoTV, and the film director/producer Robert Rodriguez launched Rey TV. Importantly, both are well known in the Hispanic-oriented and mainstream sectors, where they can attract credibility and investment alike. This may indicate a future trend of more celebrities becoming entrepreneurs in Hispanic-oriented media. Clearly the character and implications of boom periods merits greater attention from researchers.

The principal market value of investors/spokespersons/artists like López and Rodriguez is their ability to generate profits, of course. In this sense they reinforce the deeply commercial trajectory of Spanish-language, and Hispanic-oriented, television. As noted above, in the 1960s and '70s some observers saw television as a potential development tool for the Hispanic population. For example, López et al. (1973, p. 77) called for more programs in Spanish to focus on individual and community development, such as kids-oriented educational programs during the morning hours (when stations were dark), and, more generally, informational programs on health, housing, employment, education and the arts. Obledo and Joselow (1972) made a similar appeal. Although improvements have occurred, a significant lack persists at a time when most channels broadcast full time, and alternative distribution platforms are available. U.S. Spanish-language television has become a commercially dominant big business that, like many of its mainstream counterparts, does not appear to take closely to heart its mandate to serve the public interest, convenience and necessity.[2] The general lack of oversight in the wake of deregulation, along with the language barrier that diminishes regulatory scrutiny of Spanish-language television, have contributed to heavy commercialization and some advocates' and audience members' concerns about representation.

Furthermore, the ethnic tensions revealed in the "Cubanization" protests of the late 1980s and the Montaner issue in 1990 persist and could erupt at any time. Employment as well as editorial and creative influence over the industry among professionals of different national origins remain sensitive issues. The creation and national dissemination of locally-produced programs has not developed to the degree promised by executives and predicted by some observers (De Uriarte, 1980), thereby perpetuating the tendency toward network and other professionals imagining and projecting a national, pan-Hispanic television audience (Wilkinson, 2002; Dávila, 2001). This orientation reflects a long-standing tension between the recognition of intragroup diversity among Hispanics themselves, and the desire to simplify characteristics and categorization of the group to outsiders, especially advertisers and others who might invest in the market. We may reasonably expect this dynamic to shift over time as non-Hispanics learn more about the group's nuances, and as more details become available through increased research and big data analysis trends.

In 2011, Univision repeatedly invited viewers to help it celebrate 50 years of broadcasting in the United States. The flashing images and peppy voiceovers did not—and indeed could not—reflect the thought, money, toil, successes and failures packed into those 50 years by the pioneering Spanish International companies and determined competitors like Telemundo and others. Energetic, persistent and at times visionary individuals led those efforts, and people with such attributes are sure to carry the industry forward in future decades. As Spanish-language television moves closer to the mainstream it is important to recall the rich history of development that brought it there. My main objective in research and writing this book has been to chronicle just that.

Notes

1. See note 9 in Chapter Nine.
2. Examples include the $24 million fine that the FCC levied against Univision for violating children's programming rules, and continuing concerns about the sexual objectification of many women who appear on screen (Glascock & Ruggiero, 2004; Nitz, Reichert, Aune, & Vander Velde, 2007; Sarabia, 2014).

References

Dávila, Arlene. (2001). *Latinos, Inc.: The marketing and making of a people*. Berkeley, CA: University of California Press.

Glascock, Jack, & Ruggiero, Thomas E. (2004, fall). Representations of class and gender on primetime Spanish-language television in the United States. *Communication Quarterly, 52*(4), 390–402.

Gutiérrez, Félix, & Schement, Jorge R. (1981). Problems of ownership and control of Spanish-language media in the United States: National and international policy concerns. In E. G. McAnany, J. Schnitman, & N. Janus (Eds), *Communication and social structure: Critical studies in mass media research* (pp. 181–203). New York: Praeger.

Johnson, Melissa A. (2010). Incorporating self-categorization concepts into ethnic media research. *Communication Theory, 20*, 106–125.

López, Ronald W., & Enos, Darryl D. (1974). Spanish-language-only television in Los Angeles County. *Aztlán, 4*(2), 283–313.

López, Ronald W., Enos, Darryl D., Nichols, Lee, LaRosa, Frank, Mellema, Joel, & McGrew, Don. (1973). *The role and functions of Spanish-language-only television in Los Angeles*. Claremont, CA: Center for Urban and Regional Studies, Claremont Graduate School.

Mendoza, Jorge. (2014, August 31). Telemundo attracts a growing number of Mexican actors. *El Universal in English*. Retrieved from: http://www.eluniversal.com.mx/in-english/2014/telemundo-mexican-actors-93723.html.

Nitz, Michael, Reichert, Tom, Aune, Adonica Schultz, & Vander Velde, André (2007). The sexualization of television news journalists as a promotional strategy. *Journal of Promotion Management, 13*(1–2), 13–33.

Obledo, Mario, & Joselow, Robert B. (1972). Broadcasting: Mexican-Americans and the media. *Chicano Law Review, 1*(1), 85–98.

Paxman, Andrew. (2004, December). *An ethnic media success story: The early years of Spanish-language radio, 1924–1970*. Unpublished manuscript, Department of History, University of Texas at Austin, Austin, Texas.

Sarabia, Martha. (2014, June 10). La televisión en español … ¿Es grosera? ¿Qué piensas? *La Opinión* (Los Angeles, CA). Retrieved from http://www.laopinion.com/television-en-espanol-es-grosera-vulgar&sref=mn.

Wilkinson, Kenton T. (2002, summer/fall). Collective situational ethnicity and Latino sub-groups' struggle for influence in U.S. Spanish-language television. *Communication Quarterly, 50* (3/4), 422–443.

Wilkinson, Kenton T., & Merle, Patrick F. (2013). The merits and challenges of using business press and trade journal reports in academic research on media industries. *Communication, Culture & Critique, 6*, 415–431.

Appendix A

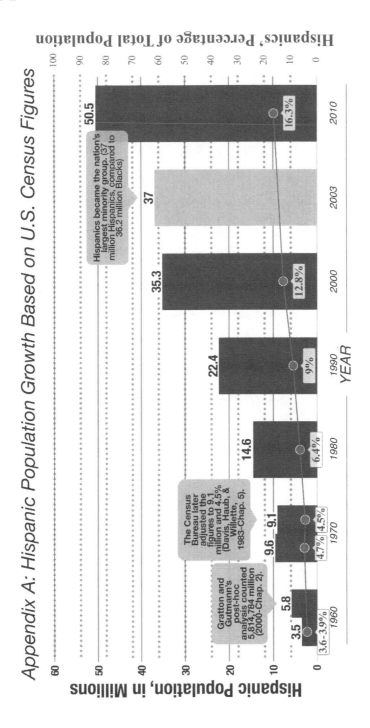

Appendix A: Hispanic Population Growth Based on U.S. Census Figures

Appendix B

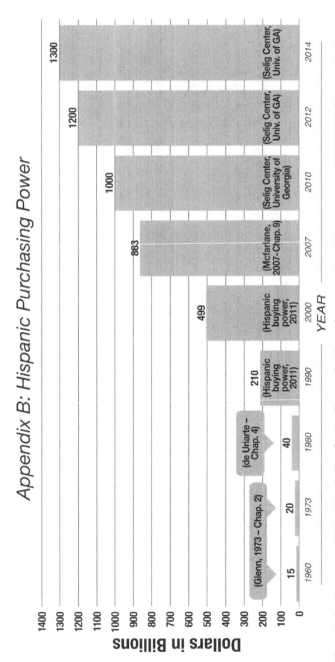

Hispanic buying power. (2011, July 1). The Shelby Report. Retrieved from: www.theshelbyreport.com/2011/07/01/hispanic-buying-power/

Appendix C
U.S. Spanish-Language Television Timeline

1950s

1954 – Rene Anselmo hired to work at Teleprogramas de México
1955 – Telesistema Mexicana formed by three competing channels in Mexico
 - Raoul Cortez initiates Spanish-language TV broadcasts on KCOR-TV in San Antonio, Texas

1960s

1961 – KCOR-TV purchased by Emilio Azcárraga Vidaurreta and fellow investors, call letters changed to KWEX. (Spanish International)
 - Spanish International Network (SIN) created to distribute programs and sell advertising
1962 – KMEX launches in Los Angeles (Spanish International)
1965 – WNJU launches in New York metro area (Independent)
1967 – KLXA launches in Los Angeles (Independent)
1968 – WXTV launches in New York metro area (Spanish International)

1970s

1971 – Spanish International acquires WAJA in Miami, changes call letters to WLTV
1972 – Spanish International Communications Corp. (SICC) station group founded
 - KFTV launches in Fresco, CA (Spanish International)
1974 – Magnaverde Corp., a premium sports/special events promoter created by Rene Anselmo
1975 – KDTV in San Francisco acquired (Spanish International affiliate)
1976 – Frank Fouce Jr. and Bruce Corwin file stockholder derivative lawsuit against SIN
 - SIN becomes first U.S. commercial TV network to distribute programs by satellite
1978 – FCC grants SIN waiver of national spot sale rule
 - "Carrier-of-the-week" satellite procedure abolished

1979 – KTVW launches in Phoenix (Spanish International affiliate)
   - SIN is first U.S. television network to receive low-power TV licenses
   - GalaVision cable TV network launched by Rene Anselmo

1980s

1980 – Spanish Radio Broadcasters Association files complaint that SICC stations are under illegal foreign control
1983 – FCC designates SICC stations for review
   - PanAmSat satellite initiative begins
1985 – Estrella Communications (Reliance Capital Group) buys KBSC in Los Angeles, converts format to Spanish, changes call letters to KVEA
1986 – Federal administrative law judge rules finds SICC violated foreign ownership rules
   - court-ordered sale of SICC stations – Hallmark Cards and First Capital of Chicago win bidding competition ($301.5 million)
   - Spanish International Network name changed to Univision
   - Reliance Capital Group acquires John Blair & Co. as basis for Telemundo Network, includes stations in Miami and San Juan, P.R.
   - Controversy surrounds arrival in Miami of Televisa (Mexico) news anchor Jacobo Zabludovsky to lead SIN newscast.
1987 – Hallmark and First Chicago take control of Univision stations
   - Telemundo becomes a publicly held company with initial public offering
1988 – Hallmark and First Chicago purchase Univision network ($275 million)
   - Telemundo enters co-production agreements with CNN and MTV
   - Telemundo station groups expands
1989 – Both Univision and Telemundo increase domestic program production in Miami
   - Nielsen Hispanic Television Index launched
   - Numerous pay television services in Spanish target U.S. and Latin American viewers

1990s

1992 – Univision announces sale to partnership of Jerold Perenchio, Televisa (Mexico) and Venevisión (Venezuela)
   - Nielsen Hispanic Television Index releases data
   - Telemundo undergoes debt restructuring
   - Joaquin Blaya leaves Univision to become president and CEO of Telemundo
1993 – Mexican government privatizes Imevisión network–becomes Televisión Azteca

1994 – Mexico joins Canada and U.S. in North American Free Trade
      Agreement
      - Televisión Azteca enters partnership with NBC
1996 – Telecommunications Act codifies deregulation trend in U.S. media
      - Spanish-language Internet portals begin launching
1997 – Telemundo announces sale to Sony & Liberty Media
      - Telemundo's WNJU posts full newscasts on Internet
1999 – Univision launches website, Univision.com
      - Ricky Martin's Grammy performance launches the Latin Boom

2000s

2001 – Telemundo announces sale to NBC
      - Azteca América network launches with KAZA in Los Angeles
2002 – Univision launchesTelefutura Network (formerly USA Network),
      creates station duopolies in seven cities
2003 – Univision's plan to purchase 68 radio stations from Hispanic
      Broadcasting Corp. approved
      - Plot of Univision's telenovela *Rebeca* influenced by audience
      feedback on website
2004 – NBC merges with Vivendi Universal to become NBC Universal
      - SíTV launches as first English-language channel directed to
      Hispanics
2005 – Televisa (Mexico) files suit against Univision over program royal-
      ties and Internet distribution rights
2006 – Univision announces sale to several private equity firms, Broadcast
      Media Partners led by Haim Saban
      - Spanish-language media cover large pro-immigration marches
2007 – Univision buyers pay largest fine to date for violating children's
      programming rules ($24 million)
2009 – Televisa v. Univision lawsuit resolved

2010s

2011 – Comcast Corp.'s purchase of 51% stake in NBC Universal is
      approved ($13.8 billion)
2012 – MundoFox partnership between Fox International and RCN net-
      work (Colombia) announced
      - Univision launches *tlnovelas* and *Univision Deportes* channels
2013 – Fusion, a joint project of Univision and ABC launches
      - Comcast purchases remaining 49% of NBC Universal ($16.7
      billion)
      - Univision receives top audience ratings July sweeps

Index